# British Foreign Policy, National Identity, and Neoclassical Realism

# British Foreign Policy, National Identity, and Neoclassical Realism

Amelia Hadfield-Amkhan

ROWMAN & LITTLEFIELD PUBLISHERS, INC.
Lanham • Boulder • New York • Toronto • Plymouth, UK

Published by Rowman & Littlefield Publishers, Inc.
A wholly owned subsidiary of The Rowman & Littlefield Publishing Group, Inc.
4501 Forbes Boulevard, Suite 200, Lanham, Maryland 20706
http://www.rowmanlittlefield.com

Estover Road, Plymouth PL6 7PY, United Kingdom

British Library Cataloguing in Publication Information Available

**Library of Congress Cataloging-in-Publication Data**

Hadfield, Amelia.
   British foreign policy, national identity, and neoclassical realism / Amelia
Hadfield-Amkhan.
      p. cm.
   Includes bibliographical references and index.
   ISBN 978-0-7425-5567-9 (cloth : alk. paper) — ISBN 978-1-4422-0546-8
(electronic)
   1. Great Britain—Foreign relations—19th century. 2. Great Britain—Foreign
relations—20th century. 3. National characteristics, British. 4. Great Britain—
Politics and government—19th century. 5. Great Britain—Politics and
government—20th century. I. Title.
   JZ631.H33 2010
   327.41—dc22

                                                          2010016342

⊗™ The paper used in this publication meets the minimum requirements of
American National Standard for Information Sciences—Permanence of Paper for
Printed Library Materials, ANSI/NISO Z39.48-1992.

Printed in the United States of America

DEC 1 7 2013

To Adnan and Alexander

# Contents

# Preface

Considerate la vostra semenza:
fatti non foste a viver come bruti,
ma per seguir virtute e canoscenza.

—Dante Alighieri[1]

This book is the fruit of a long and abiding interest in national identity and a more recent interest in the cultural underpinnings of foreign policy. Its contents represent a rather colorful family, blending British history, International Relations theory (IR), and cultural studies. This cross-disciplinary foundation has required some fairly muscular bridge building over the years, but it is an exercise not without its rewards.

The first reward is the enjoyment gained in blending disciplines and subfields, allowing me to incorporate history, English literature, theories of nationalism and identity, comparative politics, and finally IR theory in coming to grips with state behavior. This conglomeration transformed an undergraduate interest in Englishness into a long-standing commitment to exploring the role of national identity in the mythology and behavior of states. I was, for instance, struck early on by T. S. Eliot's *Notes towards the Definition of Culture* and its ability to decode postwar British society and the motivations behind British foreign policy. Eliot argues that "we become more and more aware of the extent to which the baffling problem of 'culture' underlies the problems of the relation of every part of the world to every other."[2] Eliot is correct, but there is still work to be done in linking national culture to foreign policy, and in understanding how national identity and nation building have emerged, in the words of

Henry Kissinger, as new concepts "not previously found in the diplomatic vocabulary."[3]

The second reward has allowed me to remain passionate about history. I first caught "naval fever" years ago from reading Robert K. Massie's *Dreadnought*.[4] I then contracted a bad case of "tunnel fever" from reading the satisfyingly histrionic invasion literature of 1882. I nearly succumbed to jingoistic fervor by surveying the media discourses of the Falkland Islands crisis. And I am still tussling with the schizophrenia of various British attempts to define its role in Europe. Suffice to say, a very real interest in seeing history as a living national narrative led to later analyses to discern how national stories act as resources, justifications, and sometimes excuses for a state's foreign policy behavior.

The case studies were a delight to write. Chosen to represent points of crisis from the past two centuries, they draw on a series of rather unusual connections. They demonstrate how, for example, in 1882, the role of landscape and invasion literature played a central role in quashing the construction of a tunnel to France, why particular London plays touched a nerve about navy fever, accelerating the construction of eight dreadnoughts in 1909, how media-sponsored jingoism and vicarious imperialism operated in a postwar climate to explain the robust defense of far-flung islands, and finally how attributes of sovereignty, economic nationalism, and multiculturalism continue to underwrite British attitudes toward Europe and the euro.

Drawing on a wide range of historical, political, and cultural materials, the case studies all explore how nineteenth-, twentieth-, and twenty-first-century English and British national identities are catalytic for British foreign policy decisions. They allow the reader to examine these episodes from the dual vantage point of cultural input and foreign policy outcome. They also individually and collectively highlight the role of decline. There is something rather compelling about the diminishment of a great power over time, the erosion of cultural certainty, the slippage of material leverage. All states must admit to some form of change in the span of their existence. Hovering between ambition and delusion for more than two centuries, Britain, and its English "core," has undergone a most radical transition. The changes that have forced its society and government into periods of deep self-reflection are carved into its culture and etched into its policy stances on key issues of sovereignty, territoriality, security, and monetary policy. These same issues act as meta-themes of the case studies, showing the reader the infinitely complex task by which successive periods of British government elites, and the wider populace, relied upon the "ancient lights" of an unspoken but implicit code of Englishness to direct their course in the world.

Lastly, after having explored the role of national identity from a cultural, comparative, literary, and historic perspective, IR theory set me on the path to considering how it also obtains as a political force and a foreign policy variable. The students and teachers of IR theory who read this text will be aware that structural realism continues to dominate most schools and subfields within IR, including foreign policy analysis (FPA). Realism's steadfast focus upon the dynamics of power, aggregation, and balance has maintained the elegant but conceptually abbreviated framework of structural equilibrium but underplayed a host of other factors better suited to explaining both national policy choices and international distributions of power. As a result, the discipline in both its American and European incarnations lacks the tools to study the ethnic, cultural, and national nuances affecting the foreign policy of the modern nation-state.[5] I would suggest that the best remedy to date is neoclassical realism, which acknowledges the major principles of realism regarding state behavior, but does not regard them as a priori to, or exclusively exogenous of, other forces. I have found that neoclassical realism operates neatly and persuasively to explain a range of foreign policy issues. Its canon is readable and interesting, its advocates progressive and alive to new perspectives. States are understood to be competitive, even warlike, but also innately social vessels containing unique collective perceptions, varying institutional setups and myriad histories, all of which produce a political culture that is *purposive*, not *purposeless* in the final analysis. National identity, as a key driver of political culture, functions in the four case studies as an *intervening variable* that connects the external challenges of the Victorian, Edwardian, and postwar eras with the particularist domestic responses of the British state and its underlying English nationhood to visibly influence its foreign policy behavior.

## ACKNOWLEDGMENTS

Over the past few years, the following people have read, commented on, or informed my work, and I would be remiss in not thanking them: Chris Brown, Valerie Hudson, James Rosenau, Andrew Williams, Thierry Balzacq, and Richard Whitman. Within the School of Politics and International Relations at the University of Kent, where much of the text was completed, I should like to acknowledge Ruth Blakeley, Jonathan Joseph, Michael Burgess, and my Brussels supervisor, Jarrod Wiener. All these individuals have directly and indirectly helped me to ponder and refine many of the concepts and approaches found within the following pages. The University of Kent also granted study leave to complete the research during its initial preparation at the University of Kent Brussels, and its final stages in Canterbury. I particularly wish to thank Zeynep Arkan and Joseph Dutton, two postgraduate students in our department, for their invaluable and cheerful help in formatting and finalizing the text under considerable time pressure, while James Worley Soeren Keil provided last-minute formatting assistance.

The British Academy, the International Studies Association (ISA), and the University Association for Contemporary European Studies (UACES) have all granted funds to enable me to travel from Istanbul to San Francisco, from Zagreb to Cambridge, for conference attendance, the presentation of research, and archival explorations. I would also like to thank Ronald Linden from the University of Pittsburgh and series editor at Rowman & Littlefield. Our chance meeting at a conference in The Hague in 2006 turned a quick drink into an uproarious dinner, during which I expounded on the merits of national identity and he proposed a suitable harbor for my research. His advice on the preparation of the proposal and the approach to manuscript has been invaluable. I also wish to thank Jessica Gribble, former associate editor at Rowman & Littlefield, for her enthusiastic advocacy of the original project, as well as senior editor Susan McEachern for their professional support and friendly assistance.

I take greatest pleasure in thanking those family members who have put up with endless yarns about dreadnoughts, rantings about realism, pontifications on Parliamentary bills, sermons on security, orations on the euro, lectures on the Falklands, and of course enthusiastic outpourings about national identity. I would like to acknowledge the loving support of my parents, Ann and Alec Hadfield, who have always encouraged my academic efforts and have taken great pride in the various outcomes that have resulted over the past few years. My sisters, Mary and Elizabeth, have been constantly supportive, providing both sisterly encouragement and friendship.

While he himself would be happier if I omitted this final acknowledgment, this book would simply not have been possible without the loving encouragement of my husband, Adnan Amkhan. For a lawyer, Adnan has a suspiciously large number of social science texts and a highly refined understanding of international relations. His dedication to logical thinking and intolerance of obfuscation have acted as a tonic to the heavy verbiage that can accrue in multidiscipline approaches. His boundless patience with my research and his personal pride in the outcomes have genuinely helped steer me toward any illuminations that may appear in the following pages. Finally, I have had the privilege of mothering my son during his first year while the manuscript took shape. This book is therefore dedicated both to Adnan and the princely Alexander Caspian.

## NOTES

1. Dante Alighieri, *La divina commedia, Inferno,* canto 26, lines 118–120. Translates as "Consider your origin; you were not born to live like brutes, but to follow virtue and knowledge."

2. T. S. Eliot, *Notes towards the Definition of Culture* (London: Faber and Faber, 1962), 27.

3. Henry Kissinger, *Diplomacy* (London: Simon & Schuster, 1994), 648.

4. Robert K. Massie, *Dreadnought: Britain, Germany, and the Coming of the Great War* (New York: Random House, 1991).

5. Yale H. Ferguson and Richard W. Mansbach, "The Past as Prelude to the Future? Identity and Loyalties in Global Politics," in *The Return of Culture and Identity in IR Theory,* ed. Yosef Lapid and Friedrich Kratochwil (Boulder, CO: Lynne Rienner, 1996), 21.

# 1

# Introduction

> Every border excludes as much as it includes, and these successive redefinitions of nation act like circles in the set theory of numbers, overlapping and intersecting one another. . . . How does interaction with others define us and define our neighbors?
>
> —Alberto Manguel[1]

Identity matters. The need to express who we are as individuals and groups is one of the strongest societal forces in existence. Expressions of identity at the national level feature as characteristics by which nations identify themselves, usually against a series of "others." These national characteristics are no mere menu of attributes, they portray the character of a given people, one in which their history, traditions, values, and state institutions fuse into a form of collective self-reference. Identities are largely culturally derived. They may be primordial, constructed, or enforced but all are derived from the national narrative that informs a given society and its surrounding state unit, of its character, its values and traditions, its territory, people, and institutions.

The roots of identity are also political. Political expressions of national identity therefore affect the contours of a state's history, dictate its national interest, and underwrite its foreign policy. As such, identity demands attention as a key factor influencing the makeup of state units, the choice and ranking of their national interest, and the motivation and execution of their domestic and foreign policy. Identities are central in helping the modern nation-state to define and defend itself, both existentially and practically. Within the social sciences, identities have slowly emerged as a category of analysis, revealing the various cultural and political forces that drive national groups and influence the policies of the state unit.

The primary goal of this book is simply to shed more light on the links between the "input" and "output" of foreign policy. Specifically, it illustrates how national identity operates visibly to inform the national interest, and viably to constitute and motivate the foreign policy choices of states. This goal is then further refined to explore how aspects of contemporary English and British national identity have influenced understandings of the English nation, the British state, the content of British national interest, and the rationale of British foreign policy. This is accomplished in four separate case studies: the attempt in 1882 to construct a subterranean tunnel to France, the 1909 naval race to build eight Dreadnoughts before Germany, the 1982 Falklands War with Argentina, and the 2003 decision to retain the pound instead of adopting the euro, the currency of much of the European Union. As will be seen, all four episodes provide rich historical examples by which to observe forms of contemporary national identity operating as foreign policy "inputs" derived from cultural and political discourses, catalytic to the "outputs" of British foreign policy.

The second goal is to draw attention to the burgeoning school of thought known as neoclassical realism and its utility as a conceptual framework. Emerging over the past decade from a predominantly American perspective, neoclassical realism fuses classical realist understandings of states and state behavior with sophisticated treatments of domestic forces. As explored in chapter 2, neoclassical realism has proven to be a robust method by which to explore national identity as an "intermediary variable," helping analysts to connect the external forces of international society with the particularist forces of domestic decision making.

The focus on foreign policy constitutes the third component. The book demonstrates the tremendous range that national identity possesses both as a theory of state (entailing unit-level construction and composition) *and* as a theory of foreign policy (entailing unit-level policy choice). With the practical assistance lent by neoclassical realism, identity operates as an intermediary variable that helps us to deconstruct the cultural and political history of a unit, examine the ambiguous interplay between "state" and "national" structures, explore the formation of national interests, and ultimately appreciate the constitutive and even causal influences of national culture upon the formulation of foreign policy.

From the perspective of working with cultural forces, national identity remains for many an unapproachable and thus unusable factor. For those keen on avoiding the deluge of definitions and methodological demands that accompany the treatment of culture in analysis, identity can feasibly be treated as a rather thin feature. For instance, functioning merely as a generic, instrumental category describing state behavior in terms of roles—

balancer, peacekeeper, regional leader, hegemon, and so on—identity can operate as a category or label expediently adopted by states, and easily changed. Understood merely as a form of national *attire* rather than a deployable *attribute*, national identity has languished as an ambiguous series of characteristics by which to identify a state, or through which a population identifies *with* a state. Within IR theory, constructivism has certainly raised the status of identity as a workable variable. Identity operates as part of the endogenous machinery of state formation and plays a key role in the socializing processes of states. This has allowed a healthy new focus on identity as a catalytic factor affecting state behavior; however, mainstream constructivism provides only an abbreviated introduction into the full potential of identity to determine national interests and orient foreign policy. For many, identity remains a corporate state label, an all-purpose aggregate that bundles all manner of intangible forces in an unpalatable lump. While some categories of state identity do indeed function in this way, a deeper understanding of national identity generated by cultural studies, sociology, social psychology, anthropology, and history still hovers on the sidelines. For those keen to plumb such interdisciplinary depths, the challenges are certainly tougher, but the analytical rewards are likewise greater.

This book advocates a richer perspective, one where national identity is not only a generic state attribute common to the form of all national societies and modern state units, but also an utterly unique nexus of symbols and strategies that provides the state with the unique content of political culture, from which it can construct its national interests and orient its foreign policies. As one of the most potent and pervasive social forces, national identity is a form of "self-ordering, calling forth particular social structures and functions and values."[2] Identities help to define and to defend the ordered self at the individual, societal, and state level, in cultural, economic, and political ways. As Philip Allott suggests, from identity derives three central structures of statehood: national security, as "the primary interest of the nation"; national culture, in order to educate, enliven, and commemorate the nation's unique characteristics; and government, as the "axiomatic basis for the derivation of legislation and executive action."[3] Together, the structures of national security, culture, and government are bound up in a layered process of self-ordering that allows all people to feel connected in some sense to their wider—if imagined—national community, while simultaneously placing this same power of intangible association in the service of a unified government with defined policy aims.[4] As history shows, this has frequently been done powerfully enough for individuals to live by and to die for their identity. Both the governing elite and national publics are particularly affected by the portrayal of national identity as symbolic of their worth and uniqueness; contextualized by interactions with a series of external others, the national community gradually constructs a series of self-referential *narratives* that over time constitute a national political culture.

Containing both strategic and symbolic elements, national political cultures operate in three ways. First, they function as a repository for both sophisticated and abbreviated forms of national self-identification; second, they are indicative of the material resources and normative principles required to secure and prosper the state unit, usually by informing the content and sequencing of the national interest; third, national political cultures underwrite the motivations for a spectrum of foreign policy stances drawn upon by the state for its continued existence in international society. Thus, the generic issues of security, strategy, cooperation, conflict, alliances, isolationism, and regionalism that all states face can only be fully understood as foreign policy responses wholly derived from a genetic national political culture that is as imagined as it is tangible, as symbolic as it is strategic, and as mythic as it is material.

To understand how foreign policy can be simultaneously generic and genetic, how, in Kissinger's words, it must be both "based on some fixed principle in order to prevent tactical skill from dissipating into a random thrashing about" and capable of constant redefinition "upon each occasion as it arises," one must take a step back and understand the central role that national identity plays in constructing foreign policy. This in turn requires one to appreciate the enduring paradox by which national identity itself is characterized.[5] Simply put, the process by which a national society chooses to identify itself, its interests, and its actions is both *identical to* and *utterly different from* those of its neighbors. This generic/genetic dyad comprises all national identities (and frequently compromises analyses that fail to account for it). All identities—individual, collective, national, regional, multilateral—are perennially torn between their originating ideals seen as fixed and ageless and the need to constantly adjust to internal and external change via ongoing redefinition. As will be seen, this paradox is duplicated precisely in the composition and orientation of foreign policy.

## WHY NATIONAL IDENTITY AND FOREIGN POLICY?

Is an approach linking national identity and foreign policy particularly novel? Arguing that national identity plays an important—even causal—role in both public and foreign policy, as well as affecting state behavior and international patterns, may strike many as obvious. For those outside mainstream IR, ideas, ideologies, histories, and institutions have always been a natural source for the substance of public and foreign policy. National identity if anything may appear to be overdone in many fields, seized upon as an easy, even trendy, method of explaining the apparent oppositions of social fluidity and permanence. Equally, foreign policy studies is a natural arena in which to examine the cultural imperatives that drive the domestic and discursive dynamics of each nation-state in its international interactions. Surprisingly however, neither the role of national identity nor its catalytic connections to foreign policy have been the focus of any sustained investigation within mainstream IR or indeed within foreign policy analysis (FPA). Indeed, the limited treatment of both still implies that theorists are culpable of a "continu[ing] neglect [of] domestic politics and transnational relations, the very factors that had much to do with the unexpected end of the Cold War," as well as various post–Cold War transformations and post-9-11 security issues.[6] Further, the failure of theorists to envisage the nature of Cold War policy fallout plays a key role in the rise of domestic factors favored by neoclassical realists, which forms the main conceptual foundation for this book.

Using a conceptual foundation based on neoclassical realism, the central aim is, therefore, to suggest that national identity determines a critical mass of cultural self-reference and self-preference, which when politicized, gives substantive content to the national interest and justificatory form to its foreign policy. Neoclassical realism has developed into an especially intriguing school of thought to pursue such a question because it enhances the explanatory power of classical realist principles with the inclusion of domestic, "second image" dynamics. The new tripartite methodology thus incorporates the pursuit of power as the independent variable, a specific foreign policy outcome as the dependent variable, and domestic contextual influences (such as the perception of the nation or national power) as the intervening variable. For this text, national identity functions as the chosen *intervening variable* that constitutively—and on occasion causally—connects the pursuit of power at the behest of external forces with the particularist domestic construction of foreign policy. When deconstructed, national identity reveals itself as a composite of majoritarian and marginal discourses revolving around "core values," ideas, histories, and traditions that over time crystallize into forms of collective self-reference and preference. Policy makers then draw upon symbolic and/or strategic aspects of this national narrative to assist them in ranking a series of national interests and/or to provide the justificatory content for a particular policy. Foreign policy is therefore the vehicle by which a national state defines and defends itself in the context of international "others." Simply put, we can understand the translation of historically derived national values into state policy as the transformation of the *discourse* of national identity into the *discursive practice* of foreign policy.

Within the four case studies, national identity operates as a repository with the capacity to explain the strategic aspects of British foreign policy on military, territorial, and financial issues, as well as the symbolic aspects of the national self. The fluctuating national identity at work in British foreign policy is familiar to most. Certainly much British foreign policy from the eighteenth century onward possesses a unique, but not necessarily uniform, bias toward pragmatism, isolationism, and exceptionalism, while twentieth-century policy contains increasing levels of defensive anxiety and existential angst. In deconstructing Palmerston's famous assertion of 1856 that British "interests are eternal, and those interests it is our duty to follow," Kissinger suggested that British foreign policy "required no formal strategy because its leaders understood the British interest so well and so viscerally that they could act spontaneously on each situation as it arose, confident that their public would follow."[7] Many have accepted this at face value. However, the current approach can take neither the absolutist quality of British interests, nor the intuitive informing of these interests for granted. Instead, it examines how external forces driving Britain's pursuit of state power and security were pursued according to, and mediated by, the internal dynamics of English exceptionalism. Frequently, this national self is sourced from understandings of Englishness, subsumed beneath, but not wholly negated by, an overarching British national identity. As a result, the forms of Englishness encountered in the four case studies largely informs the strategic content of British foreign policy, rather than its tactical implementation.

To be clear, the attributes of Englishness and Britishness explored in the case studies are not taken as given. Both Englishness and Britishness operate as historical discourses whose core attributes retain vestiges of changelessness while undergoing enormous transformations; the former can be traced to medieval forms of self-reference, and the latter are associated with attempts to construct the unit of Great Britain from the early eighteenth century onward. As a discursive but functionally unproblematic intervening variable by which to test foreign policy outcomes, national identity has been chosen simply because it represents the most accessible portion of national culture by which to analyze British foreign policy choice. Specifically, national identity functions as the most concentrated core of self-conceptions inherited by a society. The majority of identities operate by crystallizing salient domestic forces that inform the nation-state of its modes of self-reference at any given time. These modes of self-reference subsequently provide a cognitive filter by which both public and elite decision makers understand the plethora of external challenges, the forms of self-preference and policy stances required to successfully reposition the state relative to others.

Under the aegis of neoclassical realism, national identity operates as an active intervening variable that, first, rejects realism's traditional foreclosure on domestic explanations and, second, provides a linchpin between domestic ideas of Englishness and the foreign policy practices of the British state. This may provide something of a remedy to Rosecrance and Stein's la-ment that there is presently "no realist strategy to deal with domestic social forces in other countries," as well as demonstrating to IR mainstreamers how national identity effectively underwrites both the contours of national power and the substance of foreign policy decision making.[8] From the perspective of FPA, the text puts into practice Valerie Hudson's assertion that foreign policy is no less than"the exploration of culture's consequences."[9]

This does not mean that engaging with national cultures is easy. Isolating key components of a nation's political culture, and separating the threads of national identity from that culture, will always be a challenging endeavor. However, as Clifford Geertz suggested more than thirty years ago, national culture is exceptionally useful precisely because it provides analysts with a "historically transmitted pattern of meanings embodied in symbols, a system of inherited conceptions expressed in symbolic form by means of which men communicate, perpetuate, and develop their knowledge about and attitudes towards life."[10] Rather than a troublesome variable, national cultures are a profoundly accessible source of information for analysts regarding societal formation and its behavior in the form of the nation-state. As Linda Colley recently observed, analyzing any national state "*only* as a state—as a purely official and administrative construct—is to neglect the complex and multifarious impact this invention had at different times on the daily texture of its peoples' experiences, and increasingly on their ideas and identities."[11]

For theorists keen on explaining both individual policies and aggregate behavior, culture should therefore be the first port of call, not "the explanation of last resort."[12] As Finnemore and Sikkink have argued, "researchers who make their arguments about norms, culture, and ideas . . . need to specify ideational causal claims and mechanisms clearly, think seriously about the micro-foundations upon which theoretical claims about norms rest, and evaluate those claims in the context of carefully designed historical and empirical research."[13] Correspondingly, within the micro-foundations of British national culture, the ideational mechanism of choice is that of national identity. Englishness and Britishness are shown to operate as value-based forms of collective representation, with a discernable impact upon key foreign policy decisions.

## OVERVIEW OF THE CHAPTERS

This study is divided into two parts. Grounded in the precepts of neoclassical realism, chapters 2 and 3 represent respectively the procedural and substantive qualities of national identity. Chapter 2 introduces the conceptual developments within IR that have led to the rise of neoclassical realism as a most potent methodology by which to treat national identity. As the intervening variable, national identity is thus situated between external influences upon the British pursuit of power and security and the domestic contextual influence upon four specific foreign policy outcomes. On the basis that self-referential modes work to "defend or promote a [particular] political order," chapter 3 examines the generic/genetic dyad by which national identities, interests, and foreign policies are constituted, as well as the particular sequencing of these three features in the transformation from statehood to statecraft.[14] Chapters 4 through 7 comprise the case studies that subject a variety of historical data to the concepts and analyses of chapters 2 and 3.

The case studies provide evidence that a national identity informs foreign policy during times of high crisis *and* less fractious periods, and that it does so in ways that allow both consensus and division to arise over the particular forms of identity selected to underwrite foreign policy. The case studies are not snapshots of Britain in crisis or at war. Cases including the First or Second World War would be methodologically unwieldy and would not necessarily reveal the unquiet relationship between assumptions of Englishness and their impact on British foreign policy orientation. The case studies instead present the British state during four periods of high or intermediate challenge in which four key aspects of national power undergo critical domestic appraisal as a result of external forces, including national security, ontological security, territorial integrity, and economic sovereignty.

The aim of the case studies is not to present the reader with a fourfold show of British mythology or to treat identity as a categorical given. Rather, the aim is to show that at key points in history, both English and British national identity has reliably informed the strategic content of British foreign policy in terms of an exceptional sense of the national self. Naturally, British foreign policy has on occasion been at odds with either public consensus or with majoritarian forms of self-reference in defining national power and determining its use. No foreign policy rests immovably within its generic contours; indeed the point is to examine the varying ways in which the genetic content of foreign policy is influenced relative to other internal forces, as well as external dynamics. Choosing four other cases may naturally have produced a somewhat different vision of British foreign policy, but—it is argued—probably not vastly different from the four core value-based policies found here. As Kissinger argued, due to the historically "representative nature of its political institutions" and the nature of its "open debates" in constructing policy, "the British people displayed extraordinary unity in times of war."[15] Substantively however, this suggests that there are key cultural discourses underwriting such a bipartisan foreign policy practice.

The Naval Scare of 1909 can, for example, represent a security dilemma, a maximizing of egoist agent power qua Kenneth Waltz, a military buildup as per Paul Kennedy, or the logical end of Edwardian retrenchment according to E. H. Carr and other historians.[16] However, with the addition of a cultural perspective, far more variables are added to this analysis, allowing one to examine statecraft in both instrumental terms and in detailed socio-cultural, historical ways. As the case studies make clear, national identities possess a surprisingly robust core that is easily accessible as a script for national action on the international stage.

In Chapter 4, Englishness is seen to influence the context of the national interest regarding English territory, the enormous public outcry at attempts to build a tunnel to France in 1882 and the political decision to prevent it. Chapter 5 focuses on the 1909 Naval Scare and the hugely emotive policy decisions regarding the construction of the first Dreadnought battleship and the future role of the British fleet. In this case study, national values regarding its waning naval supremacy are challenged both internally through a sense of domestic decay and externally by the threat from Germany. Chapter 6 picks up these same themes, investigating how Englishness influenced the decision to invade the Falklands, the range of domestic and international justifications behind the policy, and the impact on the nation, regarding forms of renewed Britishness. Chapter 7 concludes with an analysis of the highly public and emotive fracas generated in 2003 over the possible adoption of the euro. Here, as in the previous three studies, Englishness actively constitutes the discourse of national self-representation, producing a specific nexus of interests and forms of national "selfness," which in turn affect policy making.

Within the school of neoclassical realism, case studies are intrinsic components of the two-level analysis of external and internal forces influencing the inputs and outputs of foreign policy. The following studies embody a methodology that examines a portion of national identity and the policies of the time for potential constitutive and causal links according to four elements. Each case is first lodged firmly within its *historical* background and resulting political discourse, namely, the modes of self-referential meaning arising from top-down forces. Second, discursive emanations in the form of public and press output are examined in connection with this historical background and in relation to the political discourse for its ability to function as a locus of collective meaning. Third, the synthesizing nexus of *political* interests and *cultural* identities are examined for their ability to produce broad themes and distinct images of selfness and meaning that sharpen the sense of collective identity, lending discrete unitary form to the resulting discourse of identity. As will be seen, each case study has generated a body of both political and public discourse focused upon discrete themes of national selfness from which analysis can reasonably follow. In theory, "the corporate identity of the state generates several basic interests or 'appetites'"—herein understood as discursive modes of collective self-reference and *policy preference*.[17] In practice, the four cases have been judged to demonstrate a broad national theme that predominated in the realm of identity in both political and public discourses *and* that functions as a determining variable within the environment of policy formulation.

Finally, the *transference* of this discourse into forms of preference and policy is examined in detail. What the case studies reveal is that self-reference and policy preference are dialectically connected. Changes in the national identity can trigger deep change in state interest and policy; equally, shifts in the material and ideological structure of the nation-state can hasten alterations in the body of collective values and symbols. The majority of identities are unsurprisingly riven between themes of continuity and change, and subsequent national policies are likewise divided. Given these dyadic complications, the real challenge is the study of which path is taken and why, for example, a given foreign policy reasserts aspects of statehood based on themes of constancy inherent in the national narrative or why policies display substantive shifts in order to consciously break with the national past. It is broadly correct to argue, as does Peter Katzenstein, that social theorists must "insist [first] that the national identities of states are crucial for understanding politics and [second] that they cannot be stipulated deductively," but rather must be "investigated empirically in concrete historical settings."[18] Indeed, the following case studies are designed to uphold this salient methodological point, reinforcing Alexander Wendt's original claim that foreign policy functions as "a direct enactment or reflection of [its] identity politics."[19]

The use of British foreign policy decisions as case studies is a practice well honed by innumerable luminaries. As David Deudney explains, modern British foreign policy—and its inherent theme of decline—provides "particularly rich case stud[ies] in the relationship between grand strategic choice and international theory [as] the downward trajectory of British power was accompanied by debate over alternatives often supported with sophisticated theoretical claims about world politics."[20] The objective, therefore, is not a roll call of well-known historical episodes, but a neoclassical realist analysis of the foreign policy decisions taken in 1882, 1909, 1982, and 2003 using the intervening variable of national identity. Further, within the neoclassic realist school of thought, case studies are increasingly the litmus test by which to determine the flexibility and overall innovation held out by this new approach. As Ariel Ilan Roth explains, "pairing variables that are reductive and idiosyncratic with well-constructed and empirically testable hypotheses" will ultimately change neoclassical realism's role from "pure critique to an independent paradigmatic alternative."[21] In other words, a combination of imagination and methodological precision is the ideal tool for a more robust approach to foreign policy analysis.

## TERMINOLOGY

A brief word is necessary to explain the mechanics at work in the process of transference between the narrative forms that identities frequently take within political culture and ensuing foreign policy practices. Neither wholly theoretical nor entirely historical, the present methodology combines constitutive analysis and "interpretive understanding with causal explanation" by blending IR's epistemological categories of Understanding and Explaining.[22] The argument advanced is that the ideational content at work in national identity speaks to both strategic and symbolic aspects of national interest and can impact constitutively and causally upon foreign policy choice. Ideas obtain constitutively in the creation of social norms; they then work causally to inform, affect, or alter modes of practice at the national level. The epistemology of Understanding focuses upon constitutively understood shared meanings and makes use of the tools of classification and unification. These two function by "subsuming observations under a [single] concept."[23] "Explanations by concept" revolve around the explanatory power found in unification, allowing one to "classify and unify a diverse and complex set of phenomena under a single concept."[24] In this way, the vast panoply of nation-state forces may be subsumed within the overarching concept of national identity. Applied to the case studies, the social and discursive phenomena comprising the English national unit revolve around the single concept of Englishness and emanate within the singular concept of policy preference. Further, the nexus of national identity may be likewise distilled in influencing aspects of policy formation. The methodology at work in the case studies is, thus, first, to *classify* aspects of the English national identity, and second, to establish how national identity works as a *unifying* form (i.e., Englishness) in affecting the content of certain foreign policies.

The second epistemological approach is that of Explaining, which draws upon positivist approaches to social mechanisms.[25] While the Explaining perspective has an established core within mainstream realism, IR is described by a history of positivist interpretations that are arguably highly constitutive in nature—a result no doubt of IR's attempt to straddle both the scientific and hermeneutic traditions. This study attempts to create something of an epistemological equilibrium in balancing the ideational content of identity with empirical assessments of interest, which together make up the substance of foreign policy. With its emphasis on the dual aspect of foreign policy choice (e.g., power and perspective, identity and interests, material and context), the neoclassical realist foundation adopted here helps to reinforce this equilibrium.

Lastly, a brief clarification should be made regarding the use of constitutive and causal mechanisms. As elaborated above, constitution is a relatively simple concept entailing the subsuming, influence, or transference of one mode of meanings wholly into the mode of another, generally in tacit fashion. Causal mechanisms entail more directly agential forms and clearer attribution. Causal theories in general make use of dependent and independent variables in analyzing how factor A causes factor B through the variables of independence, precedence, and association.[26] As various theorists have argued, no social theorist can ever "hope to know a causal effect for certain," and as such, dependent and independent variables cannot be used with any great efficacy, or proven with any degree of reliability.[27]

Causal mechanisms and constitutive forces together and separately show how a broad change, alteration, influence, or form of agency on the part of one party has occurred due to the causal forces of another party. This assessment is based on the argument of King, Keohane, and Verba that the central objective of causal theories is "to explain changes in the state of some variable or system," rather than to attempt to locate or prove them definitively or empirically.[28] This study suggests that national identity can be treated as an innately independent, causal variable of national interest choice and foreign policy behavior, because causal links and constitutive forces *can* and *do* exist between the two, with the result that the discourse of national identity as an input is catalytic in the output of foreign policy as a discursive practice.

## ENGLISHNESS AND BRITISHNESS: CORE OR CRUCIBLE?

National identity is alive and well. It is also maddeningly elusive. The ambiguity of English national identity has not prevented a league of historians, analysts, and politicians from commenting upon its rather mysterious, even mongrel, contents.[29] This in turn has promoted terminological ambiguity that accompanies investigations into the realm of English and British identity. Opinion is heavily divided as to whether, and how, these two national constructs operate as separate, dual, or integrated units. Krishan Kumar, for instance, argues that England has enjoyed a political ascendancy within the British Isles that has allowed its "inner empire" to include its immediate neighborhood: Scotland, Wales, and Ireland. England's outer empire is far more extensive, that of the far-flung territories from Canada to India, which at one point comprised one fifth of the world's surface and one fourth of its population.[30] Both the inner "local" empire of the Isles and the outer imperial empire denote raw English power operating as the irreducible cultural core of the British political unit, making it easy "to see all the major events and achievements of national life as English."[31] However, this can be historically problematic. As Linda Colley suggests, Britain and the Britons represent an "amalgam and amalgamations of peoples" that together "possessed distinct connotations of fusion and union between English, Scottish, Welsh and Irish" and which saw individual Scots and Irishmen playing major roles in shaping both Britain and its empire.[32] Colley is persuasive in arguing that from the 1707 Treaty of Union onward, the forging of a British identity occurred "in reaction to an "Other" that was partly real and partly imagined," including France, Catholics, and Jews, Europe in general, and colonized peoples within the Empire.[33] Colley however is less persuasive in discerning the uneasy relationship between English and British identities. Her approach suggests that Englishness exists within the crucible that is Britain, that is, as one of a number of local identities that since 1707 have been substantially subsumed within the container of the British nation-state. As the British state is a political construct superimposed over a series of internal nations, including England, British identity becomes a cultural construct "superimposed on much older allegiances."[34] Britishness is thus an overarching identity that "co-existed with, and sometimes appeared more important than the particularities of being English, Welsh or Scottish."[35] Certainly the possession of multiple identities is possible. More likely, however, a given society is animated and motivated by the interpretation that best fits its own internal composition and works well in response to external challenges at given periods. Both English identity and British identity are social interpretations regarding the formation of a community; cultural interpretations regarding the particularist qualities of collective expression; and political interpretations in relation to formal institutions by which that community's expressions are codified in law, administered in institutions, reflected in interests, and represented in policy.

The idea of an overarching British identity is persuasive. However, its two key features are its civic, cosmopolitan composition and its impermanence in the face of crisis and stress, a condition in which earnest demands on English core values, or the mediating filter of Englishness, arise. Britain may thus be regarded as a procedural rather than a substantive crucible, meaning that the British state imparts a clear sense of Britishness regarding the *method* of policy, but is at times deeply reliant on the substantive content of Englishness to underwrite the *motivation* of its policies. Incorporated within contemporary Britishness is a separate sense of Englishness that acts as a cultural compass, that informs Britishness and underwrites a credible majority of British foreign policy. This is particularly the case when there is a perceived rift or vacuum in the British national self, which triggers this underlying English spirit. Colley herself suggests that a "broad, assertive and aggressive sense of Protestant distinctiveness often co-existed with a marked perception of vulnerability and of external threats."[36] I would argue that the contemporary replacement of Protestant distinctiveness with "secular exceptionalism" has undermined neither the ability of British foreign policy to display qualities of assertiveness and anxiety nor the emotive ability of Englishness to inform that same policy on points of cultural uniqueness and political slippage.

The present case studies examine this English/British duality further, exploring how particular external threats that strike at the *identifying* qualities of a nation-state are generally responded to via *identity*. In the case studies, this reassertion takes the form of a strengthened cultural affiliation with Englishness via augmented political support for Britain. It is not therefore a question of whether some or all of British foreign policy "was pre-eminently and throughout an English enterprise."[37] It was assuredly not. Rather, the suggestion is that at times of strain and crisis, the animating, justifying, and orienting force of British policy is implicitly drawn from its national identity, which in general contains key elements of Englishness. While the Falkland case study (and to a lesser extent the euro example) demonstrates that this identity can also incorporate components of contemporary Britishness, the other three examples are congruent with the bulk of contemporary British foreign policy, which generally exhibits the enduring "emotional, intellectual and political dominance of the concept of England over that of Britain."[38] Indeed, Englishness has been so thoroughly absorbed into forms of Britishness precisely *because* Britishness is such a successful overarching, but not all-consuming identity, and because Britishness is ultimately inconsistent in its generalist ability to inform the whole of its national society of their particularist forms of self-reference. While Britishness retains a critical mass of political identifiers and exists as a political culture, Englishness can perhaps be more strongly argued to act as a cultural identity. In Bernard Crick's pithy observance, "to identify with 'British' is not the same as identifying with the warmth and width of English, Scottish, Welsh or Irish. 'British' is a limited utilitarian allegiance simply to those political and legal institutions which still hold this multi-national state together."[39] The key cultural drivers informing British political culture, however, are generally English, allowing England to exist as "a synecdochical expression not just for the island of Britain but for the whole archipelago" of its inner empire.[40] It is thus Englishness that enjoys a comprehensiveness generally attributed to Britishness, because it is the English cultural remit that has expanded to absorb other groups from early on.

What follows is an examination of how aspects of English identity were drawn upon periodically to constitute the cultural interior of external British action, at times when British identity itself faltered. This corresponds with historical evidence indicating that during periods of English cultural ascendancy, English national identity is generally at its most reticent, with Britishness the main identity.[41] In other words, English national identity is restrained precisely during periods when it enjoys greatest sway over its various "British endeavors." Kumar refers to this as missionary nationalism, a form of nationalism that shifts the emphasis "from the creators to their creations."[42] In his view, the English "did not so much celebrate themselves as identify with the projects—the "mission"—they were, as it were providentially, called upon to carry out in the world."[43] During times of political, economic, and cultural ascendancy, the outcome is not boisterous nationalism but "English inhibition in the matter of national self-assertiveness" carried out by the British state simply because it was "impolitic to beat the nationalist drum, in the face of rule over different peoples and different lands."[44] One cannot deny episodes when national fervor got the better of tacit patriotism, but generally, one can separate out pre-nineteenth-century *English national identity* as a tacit echo of the vigorous *political culture of Britishness* that the English created in their inner and outer empires.

The tipping point of perceived threat begins in the early nineteenth century and continues as a phenomenon of contemporary Britain. The majority of dominant civilizational and economic missionary projects envisaged within the purview of Englishness and executed by British agency have passed away. Such changes are bound to have a very real effect on this society, because it represents a significant break in "the diachronic link of connecting the past through the present to the future via our individual and common projects."[45] The English have spent the past two centuries confronted with the very real need to contemplate their national existence and past history in the face of historical change that has thrown their particular national attributes into sharp relief against a series of "others" and has rapidly rewritten their national destiny. Thus, while ascendancy ensures the cultural assuredness and political clout to make that history, character, and destiny self-evident, decline prompts an existential need to redefine core aspects of the national self and to defend them through national interest and ultimately through foreign policy.

The case studies indicate the "strongly Anglo-centric" nature of political motivations and cultural perceptions that constitute policy decisions; British foreign policy itself is thus vividly marked by an inherently exclusivist but "socially expanded concept of Englishness" that continues to undermine ongoing attempts at more inclusive visions of Britishness.[46] Stapleton, for instance, argues that

> For all its selectivity and increasing remoteness, [the] roots in the national psyche of England . . . have proved difficult to shift. The churches, landscapes, writers, beliefs and people . . .celebrated as quintessentially "English" . . . continue to find a response against the attempts of recent politicians and planners to bury the familiar contours of the national past in favour of a modern, youthful and "creative Britain."[47]

The core English unit, its ascendant history of social, political, and cultural forms of self-expression arises because England, as a political unit *and* a cultural reference point, is the first serious signifier in the longer and broader history of the British state unit. By 1066, "England was by then a nation state" in the broadest sense of the term.[48]

The British state arose later, established on English assets and ambition, though as suggested, its collective sense of self-identification was, until the nineteenth century, embedded in grand civilizational projects rather than a set of structures that could be said to constitute a national identity. Prior to that era, English political culture was based on a combination of political institutions established within the public and royal courts of the early Middle Ages and reinforced through "the foundations of eighteenth-century rationalism," as well as a more esoteric sense of mythological uniqueness based on geographic, historical, religious, and linguistic ancestry.[49] There was, therefore, an early English state, and a blossoming English political culture attractive and powerful enough to become the governing and conceptual foundations for the "inner empire" that grew up around it.

As Colls argues, the national English self was both "whole" and sovereign, first through its "political constitution" and again "through the agencies of mass communication"; this in turn *formed* the British state and ultimately *informed* the wider identity of Britishness.[50] However, this uneasy overlap of English national self at the heart of the British political unit has produced very real ambiguities regarding the inside and outside of the state. As Gamble points out, profound insularity has "developed by defining first England and then Britain in opposition to Europe, while the sense of openness was achieved by conceiving England as the centre of a global empire and a global hegemony."[51]

Historians have traditionally done the heavy lifting in sorting out such confusions, but political scientists and commentators have recently made inroads in exploring how Englishness and Britishness obtain culturally and/or politically. Of the former, Ilya Prizel and Krishan Kumar regard Englishness an instrumental and modern form of national identity associated primarily with rational and civilizational projects prompting a foreign policy invested with a sense of mission. Of the latter, Robert Colls and Philip Dodd, Richard Rose, Bernard Crick, Tom Nairn, and Raphael Samuel have all argued for the common culture represented by Englishness to be regarded as catalytic to the formal political identity of Britishness.[52] To this camp may now be added the conceptual fruits yielded by neoclassical realism, which allows us to investigate how Englishness obtains within the hallmarks of British foreign policy depending on the perception of external threat and disturbances in the overarching British identity. All three perspectives, however, appear to converge around a common—if enigmatic—counterpoint; the juxtaposition of the "thick" quality of Englishness as a broad cultural identity against the "thin" quality of Britishness and British political culture. Englishness denotes timelessness and mystery; it conjures up "chronicles of ancient sunlight," a charming and rusticated identity that bespeaks a sense of self rather than method of statecraft. As described by Raphael Samuel, Britishness appears tougher, more temporally grounded in key historic episodes, a "political identity which derives its legitimacy from the expansion of the nation-state . . . [whose] associations are diplomatic and military rather than literary, imperial rather than—or as well as—domestic. Compared with 'English' it is formal, abstract and remote . . . [denoting] a citizenry rather than a folk."[53]

This perspective is endorsed above, but it comes with a caution not to separate England entirely—as an exclusively cultural form of national identity—from Britain, as a solely political category. As illustrated in the next chapter, the divisions between nation and state, and between political and cultural forms of self-reference are both ambiguous and arbitrary. Tackling this ambiguity and getting to the root of national identity requires us not only to engage with studies of nationalism but also to appreciate the very real political dynamic at the heart of Englishness and the ability of Britishness to generate its own political culture.

For now, this chapter concludes with a few observances. First, the hallmark of English uniqueness is the historic, linguistic, and markedly cultural separateness that has no less force than other, overtly ethnic, forms of distinctiveness. Other European countries have produced vivid forms of ethno-nationalism based on "common ancestry, kinship of blood, shared language, and linkage to native soil" that denote the very heart of historic and modern senses of Englishness.[54] Indeed, even where such characteristics are absent from a given national identity—as with Britishness—it is perhaps the very longing for such salient forms of kinship that fashions identity into the forms of collective-wide imagining pervasive enough to affect its behavior relative to others. Second, English national identity is here examined from the perspective of the decline and slippage prompted by the circumstances of the late nineteenth century and the changes this decline has prompted in both the national discourse and its foreign policy. During this period, we see the English "need for nationhood" as an exercise in defining and asserting the collective self, rather than the "projecting" of that self in civilizational and imperial projects. For a teleological identity like Englishness (premised upon projects and projection), challenges to those same projects constitute a double blow, undermining the project itself and subsequently fostering a broader sense of insecurity in the motives and character of the national architects themselves. Thus the greatest demonstrations of grandeur, power, and swagger take place precisely because "real power was already on the wane."[55]

The case studies each exemplify moments of national self-reflection prompted by the appearance of European rivals and increased tension within the inner empire of the isles.[56] The challenges to territorial integrity, naval supremacy, national security, and financial viability collectively symbolize a new world of confrontation in which the English self is forced to tackle the loss of former areas of British political influence and confront the sense of cultural entitlement that had accompanied its grand projects. From the mid-nineteenth century onward, the central policy challenge was to reconcile a formerly docile national identity strongly attached to "a preference for political stability and institutional continuity" with the vast political changes and cultural challenges posed by neighbors near and far.[57] Such attempts reached a breaking point on several occasions between frustrated political ambitions borne out of radical upheavals and deep-seated cultural predispositions for continuity, permanence, even timelessness. It should be borne in mind that while the British political state suffered various political, economic and cultural losses, "it never experienced the abrupt and comprehensive modernization of institutions and replacement of its political class which many other countries have had to undergo."[58] This required its political elite to defend the value of continuity and stability in the face of flux. Englishness thus constitutes something of a double reaction to *fin-de-siècle* upheavals, a collective attempt to confront the tension between insularity and openness and between continuity and change.[59]

The pluralist mix of identities thrown up with the stirring of English national identity alongside older senses of Britishness—and the reciprocal historiography that has subsequently emerged as an area of study—is beyond the scope of this book. What is central is the "English political and cultural domination" that has left its mark on the political constitution and foreign policy behavior of the larger British state unit, within which the English political unit has been subsumed.[60] The impact of Scots, Welsh, and Irish upon English society has undoubtedly created tremendous diversity within the identity of Britishness, but under examination is the particular interaction between the national identity of the English component of the British Isles—as a result of various aspects of nineteenth-century decline—and its political "sponsor" of the British state.[61] The key point, therefore, is that Englishness obtains in British foreign policy. Englishness—as a cultural template—gives form to British political culture, *defines* the content of British national interests, and *determines* the orientation of British foreign policy. As a national narrative, Englishness operates as a template for British foreign policy from the beginning of the nineteenth century, arguably in response to the decline of key projects, as well as the rise of nationalism in its inner and outer empires. The following case studies prioritize the particularist discourse of reactive English exceptionalism that constitutes the heart of nineteenth-century English national identity and subsequently can be identified to drive the interests and affect the foreign policy of the broader British state unit during that and the following centuries.

## NOTES

1. Alberto Manguel, *The City of Words* (Toronto: Anansi Press, 2007), 2.

2. Philip Allott, *The Health of Nations: Society and Law beyond the State* (Cambridge: Cambridge University Press, 2002), 110.

3. Allott, *The Health of Nations*, 110.

4. Benedict Anderson, *Imagined Communities: Reflections on the Origin and Spread of Nationalism* (London: Verso, 1991).

5. Henry Kissinger, *Diplomacy* (London: Simon & Schuster, 1994), 95, 98.

6. Peter J. Katzenstein, ed., *The Culture of National Security: Norms and Identity in World Politics* (New York: Columbia University Press, 1996), xii. Risse-Kappen, too, notes how, in the words of Stephanson, "[The Cold War] was launched in fiercely ideological terms as an invasion or delegitimation of the Other's social order, a demonology combined of course with a mythology of the everlasting virtues of one's own domain." Thomas Risse-Kappen, "Collective Identity in a Democratic Community: The Case of NATO," in Katzenstein, *The Culture of National Security*, 374. Mueller concurs, arguing that "the key element in the demise of the Cold War derived from changes in ideas." John Mueller, "The Impact of Ideas on Grand Strategy," in *The Domestic Bases of Grand Strategy*, ed. Richard Rosecrance and Arthur A. Stein (Ithaca, NY: Cornell University Press, 1993), 55.

7. Kissinger, *Diplomacy*, 96.

8. Richard Rosecrance and Arthur A. Stein, "Beyond Realism: The Study of Grand Strategy," in Rosecrance and Stein, *The Domestic Bases of Grand Strategy*, 18.

9. Valerie M. Hudson, "'Culture and Foreign Policy: Developing a Research Agenda," in *Culture and Foreign Policy*, ed. Hudson (Boulder, CO: Lynne Rienner, 1997), 5.

10. Clifford Geertz, *The Interpretation of Cultures* (New York: Basic Books, 1973), as quoted in Hudson, *Culture and Foreign Policy*, 3.

11. Linda Colley, *Britons: Forging the Nation, 1707–1837* (New Haven, CT: Yale University Press, 2009), xiv.

12. Lucian Pye, "Political Culture Revisited," *Political Psychology* 12, no. 3 (September 1991): 504, as quoted in Hudson, *Culture and Foreign Policy*, 2.

13. Martha Finnemore and Kathryn Sikkink, "International Norm Dynamics and Political Change," *International Organization* 52, no. 4 (Autumn 1998): 890.

14. Michael N. Barnett, "Regional Security after the Gulf War," *Political Science Quarterly* 111, no. 4 (Winter 1996–1997): 598.

15. Kissinger, *Diplomacy*, 100–101.

16. See Kenneth N. Waltz, *Man, the State and War* (New York: Columbia University Press, 1959); Paul Kennedy, *The Rise and Fall of the Great Powers*, London: Fontana Press, 1989); E. H. Carr, *What Is History?* (London: Penguin, 1961).

17. Alexander Wendt, "Identity and Structural Change in International Politics," in *The Return of Culture and Identity in IR Theory*, ed. Yosef Lapid and Friedrich Kratochwil (Boulder, CO: Lynne Rienner, 1996), 51.

18. Peter J. Katzenstein, "Introduction: Alternative Perspectives on National Security," in Katzenstein, *The Culture of National Security*, 24. The "empirical" investigation of broad historical and cultural concepts at work in constituting the environment of identity and policy is precisely the goal of the following four case

studies. See also Yale H. Ferguson and Richard W. Mansbach, "The Past as Prelude to the Future? Identity and Loyalties in Global Politics," in Lapid and Kratochwil, *The Return of Culture and Identity*.

19. Wendt, "Identity and Structural Change in International Politics," 51.

20. Daniel Deudney, "Greater Britain or Greater Synthesis? Seeley, McKinder, and Wells on Britain in the Global Industrial Era," *Review of International Studies* 27 (2001): 187.

21. Ariel Ilan Roth, "A Bold Move Forward for Neoclassical Realism," *International Studies Review* 8, no. 3 (September 2006): 488.

22. Yosef Lapid, "Culture's Ship: Returns and Departures in International Relations Theory," in Lapid and Kratochwil, *The Return of Culture and Identity*, 13.

23. Alexander Wendt, "On Constitution and Causation in International Relations," *Review of International Studies* 24, special issue (1998): 110.

24. Wendt, "On Constitution and Causation," 111.

25. Wendt, "On Constitution and Causation," 111. See also John J. Mearsheimer, "The False Promise of International Institutions," *International Security* 19, no. 3 (Winter 1994–1995): 41.

26. In stricter terms, causality can be determined by adhering to the following three rules: A and B must exist independently, A must precede B in time, and that B depends upon A in order to have occurred.

27. Gary King, Robert O. Keohane, and Sidney Verba, *Designing Social Inquiry: Scientific Inference in Qualitative Research* (Princeton, NJ: Princeton University Press, 1994), 79.

28. King, Keohane, and Verba, *Designing Social Inquiry*, 79.

29. See, for instance, Peter Ackroyd, *Albion: The Origins of the English Imagination* (London: Chatto and Windus, 2002); Robert Colls, *Identity of England* (Oxford: Oxford University Press, 2002); Raphael Samuel, *Theatres of Memory: Past and Present in Contemporary Culture*, vol. 1 (London: Verso, 1994), also *Island Stories: Unravelling Britain, Theatres of Memory*, vol. 2 (London: Verso, 1998); Jeremy Paxman, *The English: A Portrait of a People* (London: Penguin, 1998); David Cannadine, *Class in Britain* (London: Penguin, 1998); Judy Giles and Tim Middleton, eds., *Writing Englishness, 1900–1950: An Introductory Sourcebook on National Identity* (London: Routledge, 1995); Roger Scruton, *England: An Elegy* (London: Pimlico, 2001); Stefan Collini, *English Pasts: Essays in History and Culture* (Oxford: Oxford University Press, 1999); Julia Stapleton, *Political Intellectuals and Public Identities in Britain since 1850*, (Manchester, UK: Manchester University Press, 2001); David Matless, *Landscape and Englishness* (London: Reaktion, 1998); Michelle Weinroth, *Reclaiming William Morris: Englishness, Sublimity, and the Rhetoric of Dissent* (Montreal: McGill-Queen's University Press, 1996); and less recently, Martin J. Wiener, *English Culture and the Decline of the Industrial Spirit, 1850–1980* (Cambridge: Cambridge University Press, 1981).

30. Scores of texts exist on British imperialism and empire. Most helpful for this book has been the work of P. J. Cain and A. G. Hopkins, *British Imperialism 1688–2000* (London: Pearson Education, 2002), as well as the four-volume *Oxford History of the British Empire*, variously edited.

31. Krishan Kumar, *The Making of English National Identity* (Cambridge: Cambridge University Press, 2003), 2.

32. Colley, *Britons*, xvii.

33. Colley, *Britons*, xix.

34. Colley, *Britons*, xv.

35. Colley, *Britons*, xxvi.

36. Colley, *Britons*, xxiii.

37. Colley, *Britons*, xxiv.

38. Adrian Hastings, *The Construction of Nationhood: Ethnicity, Religion and Nationalism* (Cambridge: Cambridge University Press, 1997), 63.

39. Bernard Crick, *The Independent*, 22 May 1993.

40. Kumar, *The Making of English National Identity*, 7.

41. The argument made by Kumar is instructive and indeed persuasive on this point, as is the concept of missionary national identity that explains this reticence.

42. Kumar, *The Making of English National Identity*, x.

43. Kumar, *The Making of English National Identity*, x.

44. Kumar, *The Making of English National Identity*, x.

45. Friedrich Kratochwil, "History, Action and Identity: Revisiting the 'Second' Great Debate and Assessing its Importance for Social Theory," *European Journal of International Relations* 12, no. 1 (2006): 16.

46. Stapleton, *Political Intellectuals and Public Identities*, 148.

47. Stapleton, *Political Intellectuals and Public Identities*, 160.

48. James Campbell, "The United Kingdom of England: The Anglo-Saxon Achievement," in *Uniting the Kingdom? The Making of British History*, eds. Alexander Grant and Keith J. Stringer (London: Routledge, 1995), 31, as quoted in Colls, *Identity of England*, 35.

49. Ilya Prizel, *National Identity and Foreign Policy: Nationalism and Leadership in Poland, Russia and Ukraine* (Cambridge: Cambridge University Press, 1998), 21.

50. Colls, *Identity of England*, 50.

51. Andrew Gamble, *Between Europe and America: The Future of British Politics* (Hampshire, UK: Palgrave Macmillan, 2003), 35.

52. Robert Colls and Philip Dodd, eds., *Englishness: Politics and Culture 1880–1920* (London: Croom Helm, 1986); Richard Rose, "The United Kingdom as a Multi-National State," in *Studies in British Politics: A Reader in Political Sociology*, ed. Richard Rose (New York: St. Martin's Press, 1976), 115–50; Bernard Crick, *National Identities: The Constitution of the United Kingdom* (Oxford: Blackwell, 1991); Tom Nairn, *The Enchanted Glass: Britain and its Monarchy* (New York: Vintage, 1994); and Raphael Samuel, *Patriotism: The Making and Unmaking of British National Identity*, vols. 1, 2, and 3 (London: Routledge, 1989).

53. Raphael Samuel "Preface" in Samuel, *Patriotism: The Making and Unmaking of British National Identity*, vol. 1, xii–xiii, cited in Kumar, *The Making of English National Identity*, 16.

54. Prizel, *National Identity and Foreign Policy*, 24.

55. David Cannadine, "The Context, Performance and Meaning of Ritual: The British Monarchy and the 'Invention of Tradition,' c. 1820–1977," in *The Invention of Tradition*, ed. Eric Hobsbawm and Terence Ranger (Cambridge: Cambridge University Press, 1984), 126.

56. Kumar, *The Making of English National Identity*, 196.

57. Gamble, *Between Europe and America*, 36.

58. Gamble, *Between Europe and America*, 37.

59. Gamble, *Between Europe and America,* 37.

60. A. J. P. Taylor's comment on J. G. A. Pocock's "British History: A Plea for a New Subject," *Journal of Modern History* 47, no. 4 (December 1975): 622.

61. J. G. A. Pocock, "The Limits and Divisions of British History: In Search of the Unknown Subject," *American Historical Review* 87, no. 2 (1982): 311–36, as quoted in Kumar, *The Making of English National Identity,* 13.

# 2

# Conceptual Foundations

## Neoclassical Realism, Foreign Policy Analysis, and National Identity

As a category of analysis, national identity has enjoyed decades of treatment in the social, psychological, and cultural areas of the social sciences. Until recently, however, it has lain dormant in political studies.[1] Theorists interested in using national identity in IR theory are frequently stymied at the outset, centrally because, in its postwar development, "international relations . . . lost its constitutive, 'national' component by becoming overwhelmingly state centric" and predominantly materialist.[2] The lack of a strong and consistent treatment of national identity as a key variable is indicative of an anticulturalist and antihistoricist attitude that until recently characterized mainstream IR. These two central problems have produced two ironic outcomes. The first outcome is a generally accepted sidestepping by contemporary realists of state and substate motivations to inform power-seeking behavior as an explicit feature of realist theory. Realists in general fail to adequately acknowledge the social processes that both construct the state and give rise to state behavior.

The second outcome is the inclusion of precisely these same variables as a tacit feature of realism and other variants, including neorealism, neoliberalism, and constructivism, all of which are guilty of "smuggling in unacknowledged cultural factors that do most of the explanatory work within ostensibly materialist theories."[3] This has produced a situation in which, having failed in "purging their theory of social content," the majority of IR theorists resort to incorporating ad hoc social and cultural content to gloss over gaps in otherwise unexplainable theories of material causality.[4]

The textual interpretation of post-1945 realism is a central offender in this dual issue, perpetrating ongoing misreadings of the works of Thomas

Hobbes, Hans Morgenthau, and E. H. Carr inter alia, generally by failing to acknowledge the endogenous origins and ideational applications of power. While the more recent neorealist-neoliberalist debate encompasses ideational aspects in its institutional theory, they—like mainstream constructivism—continue to regard unit-level attributes of interest and identity as static, non-causal, nonlinear qualities whose aggregate impact matters at the exogenous level to foster socializing patterns. Despite some recent attempts to plug this gap from a variety of directions, there currently exists "no canonical treatment of identity in political science" as a sustained part of state theory or as an analysis of foreign policy.[5]

Realism has traditionally foreclosed on possibilities that rank ideational forces on equal footing with materialist, structuralist ones in determining the pursuit of power. Following mainstream perspectives, the realist state is a generic, ahistorical, and abstract unit, deployed unrepresentatively precisely to reinforce the naturalness of IR's statist discourse. Systemic and structuralist forces remain the privileged paradigm; contingent, ideational and historical dynamics remain the loser. Yet as Gilpin and others have long suggested, realism's conflictual view of international affairs is due to "the primacy in all political life of power and security in human motivation."[6] While there are more sustained analyses of the specific role that power plays in the construction of the state, and the motivational role of security in societal and state behavior, these are generally not done in a way that connects to foreign policy analysis (FPA), or that makes use of the extensive endogenous and ideational suppositions underwriting current realist theory. The outcome is mainstream interpretations that continue to privilege systemic effects by avoiding the causal motivations that inform policy and orient state behavior.

Exploring such constitutive causes does not require a wholesale transplant of culturalist perspectives into realism (although the results would be vastly enriching), merely clearer recognition "that what makes actors effective in world politics derives not from the sovereignty they possess or the legal privileges thereby accorded them, but rather lies in relational phenomena, in the authority they can command and the compliance they can thereby elicit" in pursuing and maximizing their power.[7] Such relational phenomena include the nexus of culture, norms, values, and rules that provide modes of self-reference for the national unit and frameworks of purposive action for the state. Identity, as the ultimate mode of political and cultural self-reference, operates in realism not merely as a positive and accessible connection between statehood and statecraft, but also as an ancillary cultural output directly connected to the externalized preference orientations of the realist state unit.

Before the redeeming features of neoclassical realism are examined, realism itself requires a brief examination. As Wendt has argued persuasively, realism's present weakness is its "growing reliance on social factors to do their explanatory work [tacitly]"; as such, it increasingly "lends itself to any number of possible consequences," which in turn places it in danger of becoming "a candidate for a degenerating research program in IR theory."[8] Three possible solutions suggest themselves. First, the works of classical realism should be reread to grasp their original emphasis upon the fundamental role of endogenous attributes, the behavioral consequences of unit preferences, and the link between statehood and statecraft.

Second, the causal ambiguity and terminological inaccuracy in IR caused by these misreadings must be redressed. Causally, as Wendt states, "to get from anarchy and material forces to power politics and war neorealists have been forced to make additional, *ad hoc* assumptions about the social structure of the international system" and its actors.[9] As such, these ad hoc assumptions may be partly successful in producing greater explanatory power, but only because "the crucial causal work is done by social, not material, factors," a mechanism that, in reality, undoes much of the systemic reliance of neorealist arguments.[10] In addition, realism contains an element of calculated removal regarding the power of explanation in its terminology. Indeed, there is a tacit implication that by simply advocating the toughest, most evidential line of argument, realism is somehow exempt from explaining structural or unit processes in any greater detail. The result is a clear and unworkable dichotomy between self-evident phenomena that fall easily within the broad remit of realist explanations and a plethora of under-analyzed social and cultural variables radically at odds with overall realist theory. Neglecting cultural variables, realism moves uncomfortably close to a self-contained tautology by tacitly admitting their existence while assuming that with the passage of time they will inevitably succumb to the irrepressibly materialist pull of realist-manufactured gravity. Relocating the original social factors in realist themes reorganizes the quality of causality that obtains in both system and actor and widens its extant terminology.

Third, more attention should be given to those who have indeed reread realist texts, including John Herz, Arnold Wolfers, Joseph Nye Jr., George Kennan, Thomas Schelling, and Inis Claude, all of whom charted the early development of twentieth-century realism along a path of synthesis between endogenous structures and exogenous forces.[11] These theorists stand as exceptions to the realist fondness for stark, under-analyzed explanations.

The final point, therefore, is the need to revive realism in a way that permits rereadings that capture more precisely the inputs and outputs of foreign policy as the building blocks of state behavior. As observed by John Vasquez, "The great virtue of realism is that it can explain almost any foreign policy event. Its great defect is that it tends to do this after the fact, rather than before."[12] Including national identity as a key variable affecting both the internal construction and external orientation of state units is an excellent start, and may successfully shake up the overall realist research program. For the purposes of identity theory and foreign policy analysis, there is far greater explanatory power to be found within the social, constitutive possibilities of Hobbes, the ideational content and national attributes of Morgenthau, the agency of Carr, and the promise of Waltz's second image. The use of national identity in a theory of state recognizes the objective existence of the state as the senior political unit and its policy-based behavior stimulated largely as a result of external challenges, but it also emphasizes the lack of any determinism regarding the ontological status of such categories. In this way, we can transform ontological stasis into epistemological possibilities, retaining classical realist factors by including them "as aspects of the social construction of human agency in a culturally full international society."[13] This means appreciating both the traditional strengths of classical realism in explaining state behavior as a foreign policy outcome as well as acknowledging its shortcomings in charting its motivational "inputs."[14] Via identity, states emerge from vacuum-packed realism into a mode far more representative of the political reality of the twenty-first century.

Liberal theory too has failed to live up to the sophistication inherent in its domestic-level approach in telling us anything innovative about foreign policy making. The state is generally treated as a unitary actor, reified into democratic or nondemocratic categories.[15] Liberal IR theory uses a bottom-up approach to reveal merely a static state architecture of unresponsive institutions. The only dynamism is intragroup bargaining over the content and "capture" of policy. Neoliberal institutional theory, while a driver of much innovative theorizing on the European Union, in many cases merely replaces a reified state unit with an equally truncated and deterministic institution (or set of institutions). Rational choice theory underwrites the unitary behavior of both nonstate structure and individual decision maker in terms of efficient interests and immutable identities. As with realism, there exists in liberal thought no actual theory of state, only another underpowered unit absent explanations on construction and motivation.

Within IR theory, constructivism is still largely underwritten by realism's state-centric ontology while using an epistemology adopted from sociology and social psychology. The outcome is an approach in which "prior to the exercise of instrumental rationality," social practices produce forms of knowledge and patterns of behavior, taking the shape of social processes. The innately social processes of self-reference and -preference rest "on an irreducibly intersubjective dimension of human action" in which social and ideational processes generate both cohesion and contestation within and between units.[16] Taken together, this produces a broad pattern of interactions (both ideational and material) within the social framework of the unit and international system. Disassociating itself from the immutable realist categories of structural determinism, the international political system from the constructivist perspective is constitutively different and conceptually more flexible than its realist and neorealist counterparts.

The work of Alexander Wendt has dominated much recent constructivist theory. Basing his approach within the fissures of the neorealist-neoliberal debate, Wendt has—according to some—forged a tentative *"via media"* between explanatory and constitutive theory by blending rational and reflexive concepts.[17] Wendt's own position however remains unclear. Committed to the anarchy *problématique* through his acknowledged continuity with neo-realism, Wendt simultaneously promotes a deeply reflexivist approach. He favors causal explanations on one hand but retains space for the constitutive forces on the other. The structural idealism that results is therefore split between systemic imperatives on one side and the necessary inclusion of intersubjective, ideational factors on the other. But is identity, as a social attribute, truly capable of being uploaded to the system level, with outcomes that can be seen and understood? One wins points by arguing that realism's "putative causal powers must be challenged if process and institutions are not to be subordinated to structure."[18] But there is less clarity about the subtler forces constitutive of the state itself, how it builds its social structure, politicizes its historical and cultural interests, and fashions its foreign policy. Wendt correctly observes that "foreign policy behavior is often determined primarily by domestic politics, the analogue to individual personality, rather than by the international system," which has deep effects on the intersubjective meanings shared between states within the wider system.[19] But this is undermined by the argument that the autonomy of national units makes the constructed nature of their identity less important, relying heavily upon unarticulated forms of causality driving the "distribution of ideas" at work within units themselves, in order to make the system intrinsically social.[20] Worse, despite maintaining that states behave routinely in terms of national interests and identities, Wendt only examines these clearly endogenous categories at the systemic, rather than unit level.[21] The type of identity Wendt thus prioritizes is the "corporate identity," denoting interests, responsibilities, and rationality at work within the broader international society and its corresponding practices of "corporate agency."[22]

From this perspective, constructivism falters because it fails to provide insight into the foundational socializing forces that give rise to national culture, collective identities, and political interests as well as their ensuing forms of behavior in small and large groups. This makes it difficult to acknowledge the role of the domestic as a viable explanatory space, capable of generating dialectics constitutive and causal of individual foreign policies, and speaking to unit motivation as a system attribute. As Pasic argues, despite "an abundance of theorizing on nationalism and other societal factors . . . Wendt's justifications for their general dismissal propagates the mainstream understanding that these levels of analysis are systemically exogenous, empirical/historical, or simply unnecessary for theory."[23] Presenting IR with a revisionist form of neorealism, Wendt (and others) has admitted that "showing how state identities may be endogenous to the system . . . is ultimately an empirical question that depends on the depth of structures at each level of analysis."[24] However, this admission is virtually useless if he and others believe that "a theory of the states system need no more explain the existence of states than one of society need explain that of people."[25] No state interacts within the various "others" constituted by the international system without some preexisting identity of its own, however rudimentary, and by which to determine its own needs and preference.

It would be inaccurate to suggest that IR has wholly neglected the role of identity—or that it has failed to make amends. Rereadings of classical realism, as well as the critical school of constructivism, and the burgeoning work of poststructuralists have provided positive ground upon which to build, and are helping the "ship of culture," as described by Yosef Lapid, to pass more effectively into "IR's theoretical line of vision."[26] Yet mainstream IR remains both supported and hampered by the "profound durability" of neorealist and neoliberalist theory that still operates on the basis of identities and interests as disassociated from state behavior, and a continued neglect of the "historical bombardment of influences from social and cultural institutions [in] constitut[ing] what we call identities and interests."[27] This alone highlights the need for progressive perspectives, and a transformative rather than static IR lexicon. What is needed at this stage is a unit-based theory of preferences in which the domestic forces of ideas and identities acts as a counterpart to the ongoing variety of external stimuli. This requires a greater emphasis upon the realm of *domestic politics* and upon the mediating forces at work in the constructing of national power as the unit of analysis.

The newest terrain upon which to undertake this challenge appears to be neoclassical realism, which, since the mid-1990s, has emerged as a singularly engaging theory capable of accepting a pleasingly wide range of cultural and material variables comprising foreign policy. This development is a viable new addition to both FPA and IR research agendas, not only for its full-bodied explanatory power but also for its ability to suggest a framework for a discrete theory of foreign policy.

## NEOCLASSICAL REALISM: BUILDING
## A COMPREHENSIVE THEORY OF FOREIGN POLICY

Gideon Rose's 1998 survey article entitled "Neoclassical Realism and Theories of Foreign Policy" was the first comprehensive evaluation of neoclassical realism, suggesting that a canon had emerged that effectively comprised new theory-set foreign policies.[28] A brief reminder of Rose's original observations, followed by a brief explanation of the main thrust of neoclassical realism and a review of the latest contributions to its fast-emerging research agenda, is therefore necessary in order to effectively situate the present analysis of national identity and British foreign policy.

While IR theory tacitly operates as an explanatory framework for the further analysis of foreign policy, it is rarely approached in such a fashion. Despite the obvious implications of individual and aggregate state behavior to be drawn from its mainstream, only a few of its theories are explicitly connected with the attempt to theorize foreign policy.[29] Most familiar are offensive and defensive realism, both of which accept the underlying neorealist axiom that foreign policies comprise an "output" of power-seeking state action, and that in aggregate state behavior is the core feature of the international structure. The two realisms differ radically, however, in prioritizing a unitary, rational viewpoint of the state, and privileging systemic variables in explaining state behavior. The role of security is particularly critical. Security is a rare commodity for offensive realists, so foreign policies that maximize a state's relative advantage are seen to best explain individual state behavior and subsequent systemic patterns. Less edgy, the defensive realists view security as rather more abundant and threats to security are managed by sensible foreign policies of balancing via expedient allying; only rogue states or misperceptions throw such behavior off course.

In contrast, *Innenpolitik* theories, which include the broad church of liberal theories and variants such as democratic peace theory, prioritize domestic factors like political, national, and economic ideology; the role of the national character; partisan policy entrepreneurship; or the composition of institutions and subnational groups. From this perspective, the internal dynamics of a state alone explain its foreign policy decisions, with very little room for systemic influences.[30] As Rose points out, the drawback of these three approaches is generally one of emphasis. Each focuses too much upon one dominant factor—be it domestic or systemic—in explaining foreign policy at the expense of the other. The two realist approaches take little account of internal, cultural factors, while *Innenpolitik* theories fail to appreciate that foreign policy "cannot transcend the limits and opportunities thrown up by the international environment."[31] More broadly, all three draw upon a simplistic division between security-seeking power, defined narrowly by realists as material capabilities and resources, and interests as purely subjectively perceived and culturally defined by *Innenpolitikers.*

Theorists of IR and foreign policy alike require an escape from this conceptual cul-de-sac, but how? First, they must replace realism's pathological focus on security as an exclusively material/military issue with broader explanations for the forms of authority, influence, and even discourses utilized by states over others. Second, greater appreciation is needed for the increasingly integrated, or "inter-mestic," quality of international and domestic policy realms that states now daily negotiate.[32] As Rose explains, this is the particular virtue of neoclassical realism, which

> explicitly incorporates both external and internal variables, updating and systematizing certain insights drawn from classical realist thought. Its adherents argue that the scope and ambition of a country's foreign policy is driven first and foremost by its place in the international system and specifically by its relative material power capabilities. This is why they are realist. They argue further, however, that the impact of such power capabilities on foreign policy is *indirect* and complex, because systemic pressures must be translated through intervening variables at unit level. This is why they are neoclassical.[33]

Although neoclassical realism is a serious contender for entry into the contemporary IR canon, its present orientation is toward building theories of foreign policy, a research agenda that also informs the present study. The key question is therefore "what foreign policy dynamic does neoclassical realism examine?" The answer is a clearer understanding of both the *continuities and the variations* arising in the foreign policy decisions of a given state. One combination of external opportunities and domestic constraints may induce some tactical alterations but a basic adherence to key strategy (e.g., U.S. Cold War grand strategy, 2003 euro case study); while a combination of external threats and mobilized domestic consensus may result in major strategic initiatives that may or may not run against a deeper sense of self-reference (e.g., 1882, 1909, and 1982 case studies).

Foreign policy within neoclassical realism is determined by a twofold use of systemic and domestic-level variables, locating causal dynamics at both these levels, but focusing expressly on domestic dynamics to explain the external behavior of a state. Externally, anarchy remains the dominant, characteristic of the system in which a multitude of states exist. Anarchy as the primary and "permissive cause of international conflict," along with unequal power distribution among states constitutes the makeup of the international system.[34] Internally, these structural forces are heavily affected by the structure of a given state; the ability of its policy makers to understand these forces in terms of threats and opportunities; and the capacity to construct foreign policies that are effectively obtained from, justified by, and require the mobilization of national cultural and societal resources. Between the two levels lies the intermediary of the state, presenting analysts with a huge variety of factors that might promote or prevent national foreign policies successfully responding to external forces. The next step, according to Lobell, Ripsman, and Taliaferro, is simply to ask "why, how, and under what conditions the internal characteristics of states . . . intervene between the leaders' assessment of international threats and opportunities and the actual diplomatic, military, and foreign economic policies those leaders pursue."[35] The preferred methodology is a tripartite one, in which (1) relative power is categorized as the independent variable, (2) the filtering influences of structures and perceptions constitute the intervening variable, and (3) foreign policy choice itself is categorized as the dependent variable. In this way, neoclassical realism "uses the internal characteristics of states as a guide only to national responses to international constraints."[36]

Straddling structuralism and constructivism, neoclassical realism possesses a wider conceptual foundation by which to define relative power, a more sophisticated understanding of the myriad responses of states in interpreting their external environment, and a clearer appreciation of the mediating influences of state-level forces and structures on the perception of, and response to, systemic pressures. As Ariel Ilan Roth has argued, neoclassical realism incorporates realist axioms of power seeking but is most innovative in rejecting the perennial "privileging of systemic structural variables over second-image factors—those at the level of individual human beings."[37] As an experiment in cross-fertilizing realist parsimony with culturalist detail, neoclassical realism has much in common with the central generalist vs. case-study approach that has long dominated FPA. The ultimate goal is not necessarily predictions but a successful use of a greater number of variables at work in foreign policy choice, by a greater inclusion of both history and culture to produce a clearer overall understanding of why, how, and what states use culturally to operate politically. The true test of this research agenda as progressive will be not the elegance of its form, but the coherence of its contents—in other words, how effectively studies like the present one "integrate systemic and unit-level variables in a deductively consistent manner."[38]

As illustrated in table 2.1, the present study has opted for a twofold approach. As a theory of foreign policy, its top-down methodology is guided by the burgeoning research agenda of neoclassical realism and illustrates the role played by national identity as an intervening variable between domestic foreign policy making and the opportunities and threats of the external environment against which foreign policy ambitions are drawn. As a theory of state, its bottom-up approach unpacks the forces that national identity wields in shaping unique cultural and political senses of self-reference and "nationhood" internal to the state and its national interests. This framework transforms national identity from a misaligned category of last resort to a sound theory of both state and foreign policy analysis.

**Table 2.1    The Twofold Theory Approach**

| Theory | Methodology | Canon | Causal Primacy | Variable Set |
|---|---|---|---|---|
| Theory of foreign policy | Deductive; qualitative | Neoclassical Realism (chapter 2) | Anarchy and relative power distribution | Independent: External forces<br><br>Intervening: national identity<br><br>Dependent: foreign policy choice |
| Theory of state | Inductive; qualitative | Theories of nationalism and cultural studies (chapter 3) | Tribalism and domestic specialization | Independent: National identity → national interest<br><br>Dependent: foreign policy content and orientation |

For the purposes of this study, a neoclassical realist approach holds out a number of offerings. First, it provides a more sophisticated appreciation of causality by "linking clearly specified independent, intervening, and dependent variables in a direct causal chain," allowing the introduction of both domestic and international dynamics in explaining a given foreign policy choice.[39] The concept of an intervening variable is especially helpful because it widens the scope of factors at work in this chain of causality, thus redressing the gap in the "transmission belt linking material capabilities to foreign policy behavior."[40]

The heavy emphasis on using international history to test neoclassical realism's hypothesis is a further benefit, and is particularly salient for the present study. As Paul Schroeder has demonstrated, while the *form* of a realist environment applies to all states, its assumed *content* is built on under-analyzed, ahistorical examples. Further, states cannot categorically be classified as functionally non-differentiated, because their endogenous makeup frequently outweighs external imperatives. The anarchy present in the international system is absent domestically, frequently replaced by a fiercely hierarchical and heterogeneous system that "enforces upon its units the mandate of specialization in order to survive."[41] As Schroeder suggests, "domestic specialization" is not the easy reverse of international anarchy.

Rather, it represents the nexus of core beliefs, symbols, and strategies by which states have historically defined themselves relative to other states. The apex of this specialization is found passively in the national identity, and actively in foreign policy, whose function is to make plain both the generic mandate and particularist uniqueness of a given nation-state relative to others. Substantively, specialization denotes the particularist contours that generate a sense of internal self-reference and external self-representation (including national role conceptions). Procedurally, specialization refers to the protocols and norms by which those beliefs may be enacted internationally. The following case studies magnify Schroeder's understanding, demonstrating that much British foreign policy was informed by core beliefs "to be the special holder of the European balance, protecting small states, promoting constitutional liberty, encouraging commerce, and preserving peace."[42]

Neoclassical realists are therefore keen to demonstrate the role that intervening variables play in widening the scope of forces at work in the analysis of foreign policy, and the broader impact this has on international patterns. Thomas Christiansen, for example, classifies as an intervening variable "the concept of national political power," determined by the varying ability of state leaders to garner human and material resources for their security policy initiatives, in his analysis of the Sino-American conflict of 1947–1958.[43] D'Lugo and Rogowski choose as their intervening variable the role of constitutional fitness in affecting the grand strategy of Britain and Germany. Based on the Anglo-German naval race that preceded World War I, the authors use a second-image focus in assessing "the degree to which a state's political and social constitution supports an optimal projection of military power." Their findings are intriguing, namely, that Germany "proved unable to compete effectively with the United Kingdom in two crucial respects—the formulation of sound strategy and (more surprising) the extraction of social resources for military purposes."[44] Thus, the "antiquated political and social structures" of World War I rather than a traditional analysis of economic or military organization are crucial in understanding precisely how Germany "unleashed the Great War . . . [but] had armed too poorly to win it."[45]

Further contributions to the neoclassical canon are provided by Aaron Friedberg, whose study of British military and economic decline between 1895–1905 uses "assessment" as the intervening variable "between objectives changes in the structure of the international system and the behavior of individual states."[46] Congruent with the overall thrust of the present study, Friedberg includes the role national self-image, perceptions of policy makers, expectations by the public, and the impact of a series of national narratives to augment his ultimate analysis of British foreign policy. Finally, work by Ted Hopf illustrates the use of domestic and international forces for a more refined view of the dependent variable. Russian identity, Hopf suggests, "is simultaneously the product of both domestic identity construction, the interaction between the Russian state and society, and international identity construction."[47]

The third benefit of neoclassical realism is the choice of selecting an intervening variable. There are a number of reasons to choose national identity. Most obvious—but also most under-analyzed—is the realist precept of groupism. Drawing on its sociological, psychological, and anthropological backgrounds, identity provides explanations as to why groups form in the first place, and how groupism takes root as a cultural, and then political, method of collective self-identification. Identity tells us what processes and tools groups use in commanding internal allegiance controlling external threats. Groupism may therefore be "an immutable fact of political and social life," but it still needs to be analyzed as a key realist precept. It is clear that the irreducible "essence of social reality is the group," and that human collectives, not states, are "the building blocks and ultimate units of social and political life."[48] What remains unclear within IR theory is how, and under what conditions, human communities group together into cultural and political units for reasons of physical and existential security, and how—based on an intrinsic sense of who they are—groups come to understand what is in their material and cultural interest vis-à-vis themselves, and relative to others. As suggested, the enduring paradox of identity is that all human communities simultaneously associate themselves with forms that are "like" and familiar (e.g., national culture, nation-state) and against that which is "unlike" and unfamiliar (e.g., others, foreign states). This reveals two subsequent paradoxes in which the interests and the actions of these communities respectively are similarly divided between being both genetically different from and generically similar to others. It is the sheer durability of identity differentiation used by national communities to explain foreign policy that is at the heart of the present study.

To function as a viable intervening category, national identity must on a substantive level fulfill the following three tasks. First, national identity must operate simultaneously as a generic condition of state building and a genetic quality of self-reference to both England and, where appropriate, England-within-Britain. It must secondly act as a repository of core values from which a clear and ranked set of national preferences emerges, allowing the national Self to reliably inform itself of what it wants relative to sustaining that same Self. Third, in responding to challenges to national and ontological security, territorial integrity, and sovereign economic power, national identity must demonstrably inform and orient the foreign policy parameters of Britain with distinct references to the exceptionalist qualities of both England and Britain. Procedurally, national identity needs to operate as a discernable political narrative at the level of elite decision making and a popular cultural narrative at the public level. From here we can explain both continuities in Britain's reactions to a series of Others, alongside visible shifts in its ability to perceive and respond to threats.

In light of the complexities associated with the inductive approach needed to understand national identity, the fourth benefit of neoclassical realism is a comparatively unproblematic view of the state unit. The state is understood to be driven by external forces; as such, its two main features are its national security executive, comprising the political elite, and its national public society, from whom policy content and resources are extracted. In defining the national interest, the elite draws upon and is constrained by the views of the national public and the national culture. The four case studies contain snapshots of the public and elite discourses that arose around each decision, not only to demonstrate the variegated origins of policy content, but in keeping with neoclassical realism's symbiotic view of state and society, "view[ing] policy responses as a product of state-society coordination and, at times, struggle."[49]

As table 2.2 demonstrates, the four historic case studies are divided along the aforementioned tripartite spectrum in which Britain's varying ability to respond to the challenge of external stimuli is widened to include an intervening variable that absorbs both material and nonmaterial elements. In this way, both strategic and symbolic features of national power are accounted for in the 1882, 1909, 1982, and 2003 outcomes. While due account is taken of the material (territorial/military/economic) forces influencing these policy outcomes, priority is given to explaining the role and impact of national identity at work as the chosen intervening variable.

## CONCLUSION

As suggested above, the study of foreign policy has been treated as separate from the analysis of international outcomes and international politics. Yet "existing international relations literature has within it several alternative theories of foreign policy, of which the two most useful starting points are classical realism and defensive realism."[50] Fareed Zakaria suggests that while theories of international politics (including theories of state) currently concentrate on explaining outcomes and results *at* the systemic level, theories of foreign policy must move forward *from* systemic stimuli to account for a far broader range of inputs. A theory of foreign policy—such as neoclassical realism—must therefore explain "why different states, or the same state at different historical moments, have different intentions, goals, and preferences toward the outside world." Such a theory must illuminate

**Table 2.2  Case Studies: The Neoclassical Realist Fremework**

| Independent Variable | Intervening Variable | Dependent Variable |
|---|---|---|
| International Stimulus | Material and Ideational National Forces | British Foreign Policy Outcome |
| 1882: French tunnel plans and external threat implicit in Watkin's plan | Territorial size, integrity and proximity to France; role of island mentality and domestic declinism in Victorian Englishness, role of invasion literature. Two-Power Standard and role of Royal Navy in Edwardian Englishness, role of invasion literature. | Rejection of Tunnel Bill, resurgent focus on standing army, prioritization of English territory in national security and foreign policy, unsteady relationship with France. |
| 1909: German Dreadnought Acceleration | | "Four-plus-four" Dreadnought policy in 1909, increase in 1910 Naval Estimates, prioritization of quantity and strategic quality of capital ships to defend Britain, Two-Power Standard reconsidered relative to German, Russian, and French navies, centrality of naval security in British foreign policy, worsening relations with Germany. |
| 1982: Argentine invasion of Falklands | Strategic and symbolic value of Falkland territory; Argentine vs. Royal Navy capabilities; postimperial agency vs. ontological security as late twentieth-century Britishness, role of media. | Deployment and recapture of Falkland Islands by Royal Navy Task Force of 10,000 during April–May 1982. Changeable relations with various European states, the U.S., and the UN based on support/opposition of Britain. |
| 2003: EU monetary policy: euro adoption | Strategic and symbolic value of the British pound; historic role and material robustness of British economic power, role of media. | Blair's "wait and see policy"; Brown's marginalization of any decision; changeable relations with various European states. |

"the reasons for a nation's efforts" in pursuing a particular goal "but it cannot account for the results of those efforts" in aggregate form, which is instead the domain of international politics.[51]

This is certainly breaking new ground. Until the advent of neoclassical realism, the majority of theories of foreign policy, including those from the U.S.-oriented subfield of FPA, generally concentrated purely on the causal imperatives between a feature of domestic politics and type of state behavior. But a wholly case-specific methodology—despite their virtue of appreciably more detail—has prevented inductivist approaches to foreign policy from engaging with the irreducible international reality in which states operate. As Zakaria suggests, a more workable theory should be able to strike a balance between independent and dependent variables:

> A theory of foreign policy must not ignore domestic politics, national culture, and individual decision-makers. But from the standpoint of social science, a first-cut theory that generalizes across regimes, cultures, and peoples is more useful than a country-specific explanation, since it can be applied to a larger number of cases.[52]

More useful still is the offering of neoclassical realism, which operates in a top-down fashion precisely to explain bottom-up influences with greater accuracy: "a first-cut theory [that] can be narrowed in scope and layered successively with additional [intervening variables] from different levels of analysis—regime types, bureaucratic politics, the psychological tendencies and personalities of statesmen."[53]

The benefits of neoclassical realism are therefore obvious; any decent theory of foreign policy is by necessity situated at the midpoint between international and domestic worlds, and must perforce explain the dual dynamics by which one world influences the other. Thanks to the operating core of neoclassical realism, the fabled "mid-range theory" long-pursued within FPA and FP theory building now seems less of an ideal-type methodology because of the strategic inclusion of the intervening variable, which, as Rose suggests, "makes it a useful framework for carrying out the kind of midrange theorizing that so often is the best social science can hope to achieve."[54]

This chapter has identified key areas of IR theory where national identity may be conceptually useful in analyzing the construction of the national interest, the ensuing promulgation of state preference, and subsequent foreign policy choice. The recent development of neoclassical realism with its ability to "include both the general systemic impulses and the more specific domestic, cultural, and personal ones" arguably presents the most fertile ground by which to analyze the role of national identity in four instances of British foreign policy.[55] As the next chapter illustrates, identity springs from a wide bedrock of culture and the politicization of culture to produce a series of genetic and generic touchstones of self-reference and preferences. Foreign policy instances of Britain's foreign relations with France, Germany, Argentina, and the European Union tell us a good deal about the nation's self-perception relative to "others" on four separate occasions. However, the origins of these policies, which alone can explain their motivation, justification, and implementation, is sourced from a deeper analysis of how both the British state and the English state within the British unit can paradoxically see themselves in terms that are both wholly incommensurate and yet interdependent with others.

## NOTES

1. Peter J. Katzenstein, "Introduction: Alternative Perspectives on National Security," in *The Culture of National Security: Norms and Identity in World Politics*, ed. Katzenstein (New York: Columbia University Press: 1996), 1.

2. Yosef Lapid and Friedrich Kratochwil, "Revisiting the 'National'": Toward an Identity Agenda in Neorealism?" in *The Return of Culture and Identity in IR Theory*, ed. Yosef Lapid and Friedrich Kratochwil (Boulder, CO: Lynne Rienner Publishers, 1996), 105.

3. Ronald Jepperson, Alexander Wendt, and Peter Katzenstein, "Norms, Identity, and Culture in National Security," in Katzenstein, *The Culture of National Security*, 39.

4. Alexander Wendt, "Anarchy Is What States Make of It: The Social Construction of Power Politics," *International Organization* 46, no. 2 (Spring 1992): 397.

5. Ted Hopf, *Social Construction of International Politics: Identities and Foreign Policies, Moscow, 1955 and 1999* (Ithaca, NY: Cornell University Press, 2002), x.

6. Robert G. Gilpin, "The Richness of the Tradition of Political Realism," in *Neorealism and its Critics*, ed. Robert O. Keohane (New York: Columbia University Press, 1986), 304–5.

7. James N. Rosenau, "Nascent Norms: Legitimacy, Patriotism, and Sovereignty," in *Turbulence in World Politics: A Theory of Change and Continuity*, ed. Rosenau (Princeton, NJ: Princeton University Press, 1990), 40.

8. Alexander Wendt, "Constructing International Politics," *International Security* 20 (1995): 79.

9. Wendt, "Constructing International Politics," 80.

10. Wendt, "Constructing International Politics," 80.

11. John H. Herz, "The Rise and Demise of the Territorial State," *World Politics* 9, no. 4 (July 1957): 473–93 and his 1959 text, *International Politics in the Atomic Age* (New York: Columbia University Press, 1959). Also Arnold Wolfers, *Discord and Collaboration: Essays on International Politics* (Baltimore: Johns Hopkins University Press, 1962); Joseph S. Nye, Jr., *Bound to Lead: The Changing Nature of American Power* (New York: Basic Books, 1990); George F. Kennan, "The G.O.P. Won the Cold War? Ridiculous," *New York Times*, 28 October 1992; Thomas C. Schelling, *The Strategy of Conflict* (New York: Oxford University Press, 1960); Inis L. Claude, Jr., *National Minorities: An International Problem* (Cambridge, MA: Harvard University Press, 1955).

12. John A. Vasquez, *The Power of Power Politics: From Classical Realism to Neotraditionalism* (Cambridge: Cambridge University Press, 1998), 324.

13. Naeem Inayatullah and David L. Blaney, "Knowing Encounters: Beyond Parochialism in International Relations Theory," in Lapid and Kratochwil, *The Return of Culture and Identity*, 74.

14. There are numerous realist texts. Extending from Thucydides is Niccolò Machiavelli, *The Prince*, eds. Quentin Skinner and Russell Price (Cambridge: Cambridge University Press, 1988); E. H. Carr, *The Twenty Years' Crisis 1919-1939: An Introduction to the Study of International Relations* (London: Macmillan, 1946); Hans J. Morgenthau, *Politics Among Nations: The Struggle for Power and Peace* (New York: A. A. Knopf, 1948); Kenneth N. Waltz, *Theory of International Politics* (Reading, Ma.: Addison-Wesley, 1979) along with an articulate defense of realism in R. Keohane (ed.), *Neorealism and its Critics*, New York, Columbia University Press, 1986.

15. See, for example, Bruce M. Russett, *Grasping the Democratic Peace* (Princeton NJ: Princeton University Press, 1993) and Michael Doyle, "Kant, Liberal Legacies, and Foreign Affairs," parts 1 and 2, *Philosophy and Public Affairs* 12, no. 3 (1983): 205-35, and no. 4: 323-53 .

16. John Gerard Ruggie, "What Makes the World Hang Together? Neo-utilitarianism and the Social Constructivist Challenge," *International Organization* 52, no. 4 (Autumn 1998): 856.

17. See Wendt, "Anarchy Is What States Make of It" and "On the Via Media: A Response to the Critiques," *Review of International Studies* 26, no. 1 (January 2000): 165-80.

18. Wendt, "Anarchy Is what States Make of it:" 394.

19. Alexander Wendt, *Social Theory of International Politics* (Cambridge: Cambridge University Press, 1999), 2.

20. Wendt, *Social Theory of International Politics*, 5.

21. Wendt, *Social Theory of International Politics*, 9.

22. Alexander Wendt, "The State as Person in International Theory," *Review of International Studies* 30 (2004): 289.

23. Sujata Chakrabarti Pasic, "Culturing International Relations Theory: A Call for Extension," in Lapid and Kratochwil, *The Return of Culture and Identity*, 89.

24. Wendt, "Collective Identity Formation and the International State," *American Political Science Review* 88, no. 2 (June 1994): 385-86.

25. Wendt, "Collective Identity Formation:" 385-86.

26. Yosef Lapid, "Culture's Ship: Returns and Departures in International Relations Theory," in Lapid and Kratochwil, *The Return of Culture and Identity*, 5.

27. Yosef Lapid, "Introduction. Identities, Borders, Orders: Nudging International Relations Theory in a New Direction," in *Identities, Borders, Orders: Rethinking International Relations Theory*, ed. M. Albert, D. Jacobson, and Y. Lapid (Minneapolis: University of Minnesota Press), 1; and Pasic, "Culturing International Relations Theory," 90.

28. Gideon Rose, "Neoclassical Realism and Theories of Foreign Policy," *World Politics* 51, no. 1 (October 1998): 144-72. Rose first coined the term, suggesting that neoclassical realist writing may be divided into three eras. First-wave writing occurred during the 1980s, and includes a historically rich assessment of the great powers' pursuit of relative power by Robert Gilpin, Paul Kennedy, Michael Mandelbaum, and

others. Second-wave writing examines shifts to relative power (including ascendancy and decline) as found in the works of Aaron Friedberg *The Weary Titan: Britain and the Experience of Relative Decline,1895–1905* (Princeton, NJ: Princeton University Press, 1988) and Melvyn Leffler, *A Preponderance of Power: National Security, the Truman Administration and the Cold War* (Stanford: Stanford University Press, 1993). The third wave is by far the most developed, and focuses on the connection between changing capabilities and alterations in policy makers' perceptions of opportunities and threats. Its canon includes, inter alia, Thomas J. Christensen, *Useful Adversaries: Grand Strategy, Domestic Mobilization, and Sino-American Conflict, 1947–1958* (Princeton, NJ: Princeton University Press, 1996); Fareed Zakaria, *From Wealth to Power: The Unusual Origins of America's World Role* (Princeton, NJ: Princeton University Press, 1998); William Curti Wohlforth, *The Elusive Balance: Power and Perceptions during the Cold War* (Ithaca, NY: Cornell University Press, 1993); Randall L. Schweller, *Deadly Imbalances: Tripolarity and Hitler's Strategy of World Conquest* (New York: Columbia University Press, 1998), and *Unanswered Threats: Political Constraints on the Balance of Power* (Princeton, NJ: Princeton University Press, 2006), plus Schweller's 2003 chapter "New Realist Research on Alliances: Refining, Not Refuting, Waltz's Balancing Proposition," in *Realism and the Balancing of Power: A New Debate*, ed. John A. Vasquez and Colin Elman (Englewood Cliffs, NJ: Prentice Hall, 2003); Stelios Stavridis and Christopher Hill, eds., *Domestic Sources of Foreign Policy: Western European Reactions to the Falklands Conflict* (Oxford: Berg, 1996); as well as the multiauthored text edited by Richard Rosecrance and Arthur A. Stein entitled *The Domestic Bases of Grand Strategy* (Ithaca, NY: Cornell University Press, 1993).

29. Indeed, Kenneth Waltz emphatically argued that neorealism provided insights only into the systemic composition of power-seeking outcomes rather than an explicit theory of foreign policy.

30. Rose, "Neoclassical Realism," 147.

31. Rose, "Neoclassical Realism," 151.

32. Christopher Hill, *The Changing Politics of Foreign Policy* (London: Palgrave, 2003).

33. Rose, "Neoclassical Realism," 146 (emphasis added).

34. Steven E. Lobell, Norrin M. Ripsman, and Jeffrey W. Taliaferro, eds., *Neoclassical Realism, the State and Foreign Policy* (Cambridge: Cambridge University Press, 2009), 4.

35. Lobell, Ripsman, and Taliaferro, *Neoclassical Realism*, 4.

36. Lobell, Ripsman, and Taliaferro, *Neoclassical Realism*, 22.

37. Ariel Ilan Roth, "A Bold Move Forward for Neoclassical Realism," *International Studies Review* 8, no. 3 (September 2006): 487.

38. Lobell, Ripsman, and Taliaferro, *Neoclassical Realism*, 11.

39. Rose, "Neoclassical Realism," 166

40. Rose, "Neoclassical Realism," 147.

41. Paul Schroeder, "Historical Reality vs. Neo-realist Theory," in *The Perils of Anarchy: Contemporary Realism and International Security*, ed. Michael E. Brown, Sean M. Lynn-Jones, and Steven E. Miller (Cambridge, MA: MIT Press, 1995), 427.

42. Schroeder, "Historical Reality vs. Neo-realist Theory," 439.

43. Christensen, *Useful Adversaries*, 11.

44. David D'Lugo and Ronald Rogowski, "The Anglo-German Naval Race and Comparative Constitutional 'Fitness,'" in *The Domestic Bases of Grand Strategy*, ed. Rosecrance and Stein, 65.

45. D'Lugo and Rogowski, "The Anglo-German Naval Race," 65

46. Friedberg, *The Weary Titan*, 290.

47. Ted Hopf, "'Identity, Legitimacy, and the Use of Military Force: Russia's Great Power Identities and Military Intervention in Abkhazia," *Review of International Studies* 31 (2005): 225.

48. Lobell, Ripsman, and Taliaferro, *Neoclassical Realism*, 14.

49. Lobell, Ripsman, and Taliaferro, *Neoclassical Realism*, 27.

50. Zakaria, *From Wealth to Power*, 13.

51. Zakaria, *From Wealth to Power*, 14.

52. Zakaria, *From Wealth to Power*, 16.

53. Zakaria, *From Wealth to Power*, 16–17.

54. Rose, "Neoclassical Realism," 168.

55. Zakaria, *From Wealth to Power*, 18.

# 3

## Analyzing National Identity, National Interests, and Foreign Policy

As outlined in chapter 2, neoclassical realism provides the conceptual foundation for the subsequent analysis and case studies, with national identity as the intervening variable. As will be seen, the methodological sophistication of neoclassical realism allows us to include both ends of the equation in stripping down the nuances of national identity. Externally, Britain's relative power position operates in the context of the shifting power of Germany, France, Argentina, and the European Union. Internally, British foreign policy arises from an enduringly politicized national culture that contains a series of in-built expectations of Englishness and Britishness; these expectations in turn serve as both a cultural tripwire and a political template when "identifiers" of the British state are externally challenged. Before looking at features of Englishness and Britishness, this chapter examines how national identity operates as a nexus in which power and perception as well as strategy and symbolism produce a series of national expectations that inform its policy responses. In doing so, the chapter concludes that national identity is not therefore mere window dressing or the external attire of a state, it is the aggregation of politicized cultural attributes, as well as an enduring filter through which all political assessments of national power and external threats are ultimately made.

### FEATURES OF COLLECTIVE IDENTITY

Collective identity can be understood in a variety of ways. First, as a category of analysis, collective identity has in the past half century become the variable par excellence of psychoanalysis and social psychology, as well as cultural, ethnic, national, and gender studies, generating "widespread vernacular and social-analytical use." Its proliferation of meanings and overuse has generated for some "a crisis of overproduction and consequent devaluation of meaning."[1] Ironically, it is precisely its sporadic and instrumental treatment in the political sciences that has allowed collective identity to emerge as a viable, if not altogether new, variable.[2]

Second, as a general category of practice, identity has had a similar form of treatment. The majority of national citizens will recognize the key categories of citizenship, community, nation, and state (along with gender, class, and race) as indicative of their daily lived experience. Such lay categories are generally implicitly understood, gaining prominence only when they are altered in some fashion.[3] As a category of practice by policy makers, collective identity is a wide-ranging justificatory and motivational resource, used to encourage a given community to identify with an issue or set of interests in a specific way by drawing upon what is commonly held between them. As will be seen, groups have a keen interest in both their survival and representation. In pursuance of these goals, a key feature of all societies is the struggle to gain control of the political structures of the state, as the ultimate group. As a result, collective identity features as the enduring "input" for the threefold exercise of group formation, interest construction, and policy practice.

Third, as an external structure, collective identity is a group attribute. More precisely, it is the animating attribute of groupness, the internal dynamic by which humans become and remain a collective unit based on their perceived sameness and their objectively identified commonality. As a group attribute (e.g., of the contemporary state) identity operates according to three types of identification: oppositional (self/other), relational (parent/child), and categorical (gender, race, language, citizenship, etc.). Individual identities are developed in all three types, while the nation or state holds the monopoly on formalizing categorical identities into forms of citizen, immigrant, or refugee, via "identifiers" like passports, photographs, and biometric data. Identifiers grant actors (in this case, state institutions) the power of classifying individuals and codifying identities. Less explicit identifiers also exist within the broad contours of national culture, including discourses and images.

Fourth, as a substantive force, identity is an input of social and political action. Identity is indicative of the interactive and intersubjective processes that create groups and make possible their collective action. This occurs in a number of ways. As a cultural shorthand, identity is indicative of a deeper repository of self-reference, where it functions as a political template for state power and policy. As a cultural factor, identity is not a constant. It waxes and wanes, reaching a pinnacle during exceptional moments of crisis or celebration. As a political template, national identity is consciously drawn upon as an extractive resource by the policy-making elite to justify, lend historical substance, motivate, and orient given foreign policies. Less directly, identity underwrites the long-term sources of collective self-reference and self-preference that define the contours of the state and ultimately fashion its relations with others. Substantively, therefore, collective identity is the basis of social action for cultural and/or political purposes. Identity is also a product of its social and political action. From a systemic perspective, identities and actors exist in something of a feedback loop in which the projection of their collective self inevitably impacts on other actors, prompting action that has a further impact on the origination group, possibly transforming or reinforcing their initial identity.

## Tensions and Paradoxes

Equally implicit in the category of identity are some uncomfortable internal tensions; there may be no getting away from this panoply of dyads but it is necessary to note them. First, as Rogers Brubaker makes clear, identity is "divided between 'hard' and 'soft' meanings, between groupist assumptions and constructivist qualifiers, between connotations of unity and multiplicity, sameness and difference, permanence and change."[4] Brubaker perhaps goes too far in suggesting that such conceptual muddiness "leaves us without a rationale for talking about 'identities' at all and ill equipped to examine the 'hard' dynamics and essentialist claims of contemporary identity politics."[5] So long as national societies and contemporary states use identity (in all its multivalent forms) as a principal motivation for and justification of their behavior, we have an enduring rationale to retain it as a category of analysis. Further, realism and the advent of neoclassical realism are especially well equipped to deal with identity. In prioritizing the state as the core unit, there is in both approaches an implicit sense of groupness at work in the inherently conflictual relations that such groups beget. While we make take issue with the "immutability of tribalism" inherent in groupism, it is clear that "group (or national) identity differential plays an enduring role in the domestic politics and foreign policies of nation-states."[6]

The second paradox is the generic versus genetic issue, which is broken down in two further divisions. First, from an attitudinal perspective, identity (and subsequent interests and behavior) is understood to arise from two opposing sources: they are either prehistoric/biological or contingent/constructed. Yet these sources are not immutable; foundational forms are arguably used constructively to explain one national culture, while the constructed identities of another society may contain cultural or even ethnic roots. In addition to the further tension as to whether identities are static, unchanging, and singular or dynamic, flexible, and fragmented, the foundational/modernist tension has for more than a century divided the analysis of nationalisms and nations into primordial and constructed categories, a dyad explored in the following section.

Second, from an attributional perspective, identity is an apparently generic characteristic, common to individuals and groups alike. The paradox of the group is therefore to identify what unites them in common fashion by what sets them distinctively apart. Groups also differ greatly in their ability to endow themselves with a framework for self-reference; as such, their method of identifying their own group, and subsequently of identifying themselves *with* the group, inevitably contain differences unique only to them. Rather than fruitless searching to establish which came first, group or identity, or the quality or quantity of generic qualities vs. genetic qualities in a given category, more assistance may come from looking at the method of affiliation between a society and its unit. Of real interest, then, is the role of identifiers. As explored above, identifiers are distinguishing factors that grant actors the power of classifying and naming. States have long acted as key agents of such processes of identification. However, it is here suggested that states provide tangible and distinguishing identifiers in the form of territory, security, currency, population, language, institutions, and symbols, all of which assist the general population in first *identifying* their state (as a national citizen), as a key step to subsequently identifying *with* their state (as a citizen *of* the nation). State identifiers like national security, sovereignty, territory, political institutions, and economic power comprise the familiar tenets of *statehood* in IR. However, identifiers also play a vital role in *statecraft* because they operate as the bearers of a politicized culture, operating at the interface between the external demands of the system and the internal structural requirements of the state that guarantees the survival of the group as a national society within an overarching political structure.

State identifiers are common to the majority of contemporary states; however, the method by which states balance their response to external challenges with the differing composition of their internal societal-structural demands ranges widely. This not only confirms the appropriateness of the neoclassical realist methodology in tackling this deductive-inductive tension, but suggests that collective identity formation, as the origin of both generic state signifiers and particularist "genetic" responses is an equally suitable variable to discern both causal and constitutive connections between foreign policy inputs and outputs. More importantly, it suggests that we need not be flummoxed by the generic/genetic dyad that seemingly applies to all identities, interests, and foreign policies. It is simply a matter of discerning how "particularist self-understandings" differ from "putatively universal self-interest."[7] The suggestion is that all identities, interests, and policies share common attributes in their generic form; but the actual content of these three categories will clearly differ from state to state. Or, to put it another way, *procedurally*, identity, interests, and foreign policy operate according to generally universal methods of inductive group formation, preference construction, and policy inform-ing. *Substantively*, the particularist nuances of *forming* a nation and then a nation-state; *fashioning* interests to promote material, cultural, and po-litical survival; and *framing* short- and long-term foreign policy responses congruent to the internal needs and external threats of a given state will be a result of its unique genetic makeup—including its material, historical, cultural, and dispositional attributes.

## CULTURAL VS. POLITICAL ROOTS

Deconstructing the generic/genetic dyad at the heart of groupism means engaging with the oppositions and hybrid outcome of "cultural" and "political" (or ethnic and civic) nationalism. This dyad explains the societal forces begetting both nationalism and their associated types of nationhood. It also flags up the intractable ideological tensions con-nected to nationalism, which since the late sixteenth century have ranged variously from militarism, fascism, and ethnocentrism to self-determi-nation, democracy, and citizenship. Nationalism has a disconcertingly wide range of normative options, depending on the ultimate ends of a given community, and a historically protean quality that prevents even the widest of its categories from being effectively rendered as typologies. Nevertheless, this has not prevented a number of rather magisterial clas-sification projects including those by Friedrich Meinecke, Hans Kohn, and Anthony Smith,[8] who have produced a political, constructed, mod-ernist, Western variant drawn against its cultural, primordial, historicist, Eastern counterpart.

In these and other studies, political nationalism is principally identified as an instrumental and rational approach to the nation-state derived from the ideals of "a civic polity of educated citizens united by common laws and mores . . . a cosmopolitan rationalist conception of the nation . . . within a specific territorial homeland."[9] For political nationalists, the objec-tives of a civic polity "are essentially modernist: to secure a representative state for their community so that it might participate as an equal in the developing cosmopolitan rationalist civilization."[10] Accordingly, political nationalism is informed by the various mechanisms of governance that assist in imposing a constructed political uniformity within the state as a whole. Cultural nationalism differs by regarding nations as "primordial expressions" of the spirit of individuality, founded "not on 'mere' consent or law but on passions implanted by nature and history."[11] Cultural na-tionalism relies instead upon the contextualizing element of history and the roots of ethnicity in pinpointing key forms of domestic self-expression. The culturalist view of nation-state formation relies on preexisting social and cultural forces in the construction and execution of certain political goals, thereby transforming an a priori cultural body into a subsequently politicized entity. The instrumentalist view argues that cultural elements are in no way predetermined, but operate as a repository of values by which to legitimate a largely artificial process in which institutional mechanics predate and produce a nation. The more familiar contemporary variant is civic vs. ethnic nationhood. The end of civic states is a cosmopolitan form of civic nationalism based on broad citizenship and achieved via liberal, democratic, and inclusive means. The nationalism of ethnic states is based instead on a common ethnicity, and its exclusivist membership focuses more on preserving the "natural" divisions between groups and its means are particularist, essentialist, even excessive.

The central problem here is the highly subjective quality of every one of these definitions. While Smith attempted to draw the sting from definitions of ethnicity by suggesting that "commonly accepted 'nations' . . . do not invoke a common ancestor" but rather a common culture, Eric Hobsbawm responded with the reverse argument by arguing that the majority of European separatist movements have defined themselves ethnically for so long that ethnic identity is now coterminous with even civic categories of peoplehood.[12]

There are a number of responses to this dyad. One is to argue that what is common to both types is a *social base*, which allows the construction of either civic *or* cultural processes by which to distinguish the unit against others. Thus, whether a social unit that identifies itself (usually as a nation) in terms of its emergent ethnic, cultural attributes or in terms of its political goals (usually as a state), it draws upon the same underlying social core from which both its civic and cultural elements emanate.[13] Thus, as Mueller suggests, "Societies are not ideal communities; they are not necessarily united by a common aim, interest, or moral ideal [but rather] by a unity forged from an overlapping network of *social* relationships, including instrumental interaction governed by salient standards."[14]

A second response is to think of the nation-state as a hybrid unit that conflates cultural and civic identities, a unit in which the process of lodging essentialist national qualities within a recognizably universal state structure is balanced by the politicization of its intersubjective social components. Collective identity is therefore expressed through sovereignty, guaranteed by security, and underwritten by political structures that instantiate a wide variety of cultural forms of selfness.[15] As Smith suggested, the majority of nations are defined *in relation* to their state through cultural, psychological, territorial, historical, and ultimately political categories, fusing both instrumental and symbolic factors.

A third response is to focus upon the nation and the state as two separate units that can viably exist in congruence according to different sets of identifiers, but whose overlapping impact inevitably produces discernable but uneven patterns of influence depending on internal cohesion and external challenge. As suggested above, the "thicker" cultural quality arising from historically national communities tends to obtain in terms of substantive *content*, while the "thinner" political quality promoted by historically political communities generally obtains as the procedural *form* of a state unit. In this way, the state remains the key structure by which the majority of internal national groups are effectively framed.

Rather than a conceptual endgame, a more practical solution may simply be to find historic and contemporary examples that support these types. Brubaker's contemporary updating of Meinecke's *Staatsnation* and *Kulturnation* is both conceptually instructive and empirically helpful. Here, civic vs. ethnic forms are replaced with a "state-framed" form in which the nation "is congruent with the state, and is institutionally and territorially framed by it," and a "counter-state" form in which the nation "is imagined as distinct from, and often in opposition to, the territorial and institutional frame of an existing state or states."[16] A state-framed *Staatsnation* makes the state the central factor, rather than the quality of its membership. This implies that the nation remains a self-contained unit existing within an overarching state structure. However, neither the national nor the state unit need contain solely cultural or political characteristics, respectively; as Brubaker suggests, "state-framed nationhood or nationalism enables us to talk about the way in which linguistic, cultural, and even (narrowly) ethnic aspects of nationhood and nationalism may be framed, mediated and shaped by the state."[17]

A "state-framed" unit is particularly helpful for locating England within Britain. First, England has operated as a self-contained political unit within a wider British structure even before the chronicler the Venerable Bede wrote his *Ecclesiastical History of the English People* around AD 730.[18] Second, English culture has never been ethnic in nature but deeply political, territorial, and institutional from the outset: English "political culture" is therefore equally constitutive of both its particularist cultural origins and its existence as an English state rather than merely a nation. Third, subsequent forms of Britishness contain ideational and cultural (rather than merely statist) qualities, proving that "state-framed nationalisms are often imbued with a strong cultural content."[19]

However, England within the "state-frame" of Britain only works in the absence of internal problems and external pressures, eliminating the need for England to imagine itself in reference to British or international others. When internal strife breaks out regarding the constituent unit of England itself, or when external crises affect the British unit and the role of England within it, then the "counter-state" mode is more applicable. As the case studies indicate, under conditions of strain, the English populace and elite together actively imagine England as distinct from Britain in terms of its perceived political seniority and in opposition to Britain in terms of cultural and even institutional particularism. As a counter-state to Britain, English national identity reveals the height of its reflexivity: operating first as a vehicle to reinforce highly particularist modes of the national Self "as English," and second, as a platform to disseminate English modes as both normative and justificatory for the British national self, and the subsequent formation of British foreign policy. The state signifiers of English land, British sea, and British overseas territories, as well as the principles of political and economic sovereignty are potent enough for external threats to them to provoke serious counter-state dynamics in which an English self attempts to reassert itself as historically acquisitive and governmentally privileged in relation to the overarching British unit. This also allows a crucial understanding to be reached, namely, that despite constructivist allegations about the fluctuating, fragmented, and deeply contested nature of identities, national political identities—with a few prominent exceptions—do not historically exhibit signs of immediate change or transformation. What does shift, what is contingent, and what renders such change apparent are the societal, political, and structural conditions against which identities are drawn. Identities are not inherently contingent, but they are dependent upon a variable context. This is precisely why collectives forge narratives, not to reinforce their identity per se, but to provide greater traction between it and its relational, potentially destabilizing, settings.

The following definition of a nation-state can therefore be advanced using the following criteria. First, the nation-state is defined as an innately social object. Second, the nation-state is demarcated physically by its territory, by which the social collective defines its subsequent sense of exclusivity. Third, a nation-state's sense of its identity-based exclusivity and policy-dependent destiny arises from a particular combination of social norms and values at work in both its cultural and civic realms. Fourth, national social norms and values acquire legitimacy via a received and unique history, which help to define and refine the national identity, national interests, and policy practices of the unit. The nation-state is thus an inherently value-based and historicized unit. Fifth, the nation-state's civic-cultural foundation permits both generic and particularist forms of self-identification to flourish—seen in the adoption of general roles and specific attributes respectively. In other words, within the pervasive category of identity, each nation-state unit possesses a distinct sense of its own identity, which may be "deployed" in service of both national interests and foreign policy in a top-down fashion and generated to give definition to those interests and meaning to that policy in a bottom-up manner.

## PUTTING IDENTITY TO WORK

As a working category, national identity operates in two distinct ways. First, it provides a framework by which to explore the uneasy correspondence between the politicized borders of the state and the cultural boundaries of the nation. Second, it provides an interesting method of exploring the sense of the national self, in reference to the formation of its own preferences and relative to the preferences of others. In this way, national identity provides a conceptual tool by which to analyze both the reflexive and instrumental elements of preference at work in policy preference by treating them as a series of narratives or "discourses" regarding unit preferences, interests, and policy practices. As will be seen, identity discourse is an effective method by which to investigate the constitutive and causal forces that create the behavioral outcomes found within the environment of policy construction. Moving from its civic-cultural and normative-social bedrock, identity is here examined as a form of nation-state discourse that informs and enacts the discursive practices of the unit as a form of "performed" behavior.

The process whereby national units become embedded within a series of intersubjectively held understandings is a gradual one.[20] Formed from the substratum of culture, ideology, norms, and institutions, identities work over time to construct a discrete but inherently relational environment. The world in which identities are constructed is a multilayered one, a bounded intersubjective structure that over time becomes a community of meanings, actors, and ultimately agency. Identities help to make sense of the external world by conventionalizing and categorizing a range of external, unfamiliar actors and forces. After establishing a method of individual and collective identification, actors then incorporate these reference points into a "particular set of associated discursive practices."[21] A ubiquitous psychological phenomenon, identity is a quintessential element of every social actor and their manner of interacting with others. From the methodological perspective, identity theory functions as a heuristic device to explain how national societies form a series of intuitive judgments about their chosen manner of association, the desired method of governing that association, and the pursuit of order and predictability by which that governing unit operates among others, fashioning yet another international society, with its own superstructures. In this way, "culture and identity are summary labels for phenomena that have an objective existence" but a deeply subjective content.[22] National identities present theorists with epochs' worth of national history in which these very processes and phenomena have become etched into the contours of a historic or contemporary state, and whose cultural *outputs* obtain as visible political *outcomes*. As Robert Cooper observed, "The fundamentals of a country's policy go deeper than its national interests" because "the real question is how those interests are defined," and how they came to be "connected to the identity of the country and its people."[23]

National identity is therefore an *associative attribute* that helps to define, and ultimately defend, the political and cultural components of a state-based national society. Identity defines the interests that are defended in foreign policy. This is both a hugely subjective, symbolic process involving the mechanics of discourse—by which meaning, thought, and language are used to bind the unit as a social, political, and cultural whole—and a visibly instrumental process involving brute, material resources and calculations of strategy and power. Just as the nation simultaneously encompasses both civic and ethnic components, territorial and genealogical qualities, national identity itself denotes a riot of dualities: tangible and intangible, symbolic and strategic, internal and external, stable and fluid, political and cultural, generic and genetic, and so on. Identity is merely the vehicle by which these dualities are fused—unevenly, challengingly, persuasively—together. And the nation-state is the carrier of the identity and its two chief offspring: the national interest and ensuing national policy. More formally, national identity works to incorporate the national ideologies of particularist purpose with the instrumental mechanics of territory, legitimacy, and sovereignty, which, taken together, form statehood.

The best known duality of identity is the "self-other" dichotomy. Many rich and varied arguments can be drawn from the self/other dyad, including structurationist arguments regarding unit and system or postmodern arguments about inside/outside, center/periphery, and so forth. Numerous aspects of this study examine the English unit "self" in its interactions with both real and perceived "others." Within the aegis of identity theory, the terms *other* and *otherness* refer to a modality of self-knowledge by which "to organize political reality through a demarcation of inside from outside, of Same from Other."[24] The history of nationalism, from which identity theory gains its focus, is similarly marked by the radically uneven nature of this process. Outlined by Tom Nairn, the irregular uses of self and other

> [have] invariably generated an imperialism of the centre over the periphery; one after another, these peripheric areas have been forced into a profoundly ambivalent reaction against this dominance, seeking at once to resist it and to somehow take over its vital forces for their own use. This could only be done by a kind of highly "idealist" political and ideological mobilization, a painful forced march based on their own resources: that is, employing their "nationality" as a basis.[25]

The issues of boundaries, borders, and all manner of oppositional constructs highlight an ambiguity of meaning and illustrate the hybrid nature of identity. However, like all social ideas and constructs, this is not always adequately analyzed merely by adhering to the sharply demarcated unit modalities of "inside" and "outside" premised on the self/other dyad.

Clearly, the content of identity regarding the location, sense, and discourse of the national self and its conceptual other is difficult to isolate. While appreciating the measures of flux at work in the construction of meanings and the use of discourse, this study does not deconstruct ideas of "national self" and "otherness" past the point of meaning or utility. Separated so starkly from the continent during its formative millennia, the Victorian, Edwardian, and postmodern British identities have traditionally been understood to consolidate their respective "selves" from within their own, endogenous cultural terrain in parallel with a series of rival "others." Englishness versus European otherness, Britishness versus post-European others are a series of self-other dichotomies, each side richly confident of their own individual uniqueness vis-à-vis the commonality of others. Neoclassical realism is a particularly appropriate conceptual foundation for the self-other dichotomy because it retains the traditional view of external influences as the key instigator of state behavior—in which rival identities are a part—and yet incorporates the novel variable of domestic perceptions that are molded in response to the attributes of others.

There may, however, be some unexplored potential in this traditional view. Can we perhaps take issue with the assertion made by David Campbell that "strategies of otherness made foreign policy possible"?[26] This view may actually reify the division between internal and external realms in terms that are solidly oppositional, with the result that the categories of "self" and "other," when applied to the nation unit are rendered unproblematic. Perhaps the concept of Otherness need not solely represent outright opposition in the form of an actor, but an alternative concept of equal dynamism to that embedded in the Self which may be readily incorporated simply as a relational, rather than oppositional ideology, history, or Self. Such a process represents a far greater challenge than warfare or externalized threats to power. Deniz Kandiyoti remarked with clarity that "the question of what and who constitutes the West, or any Other, often has less to do with the outside world than with the class, religious, or ethnic cleavages *within the nation itself.*"[27] Thus multiple strategies of national selfness perceived as definitive can arise before any concept of "otherness" comes into play.[28] In other words, the English or British "other" is not necessarily located beyond the English or British unit, but instead "emerges forcefully, within cultural discourse, when we *think* we speak most intimately and indigenously "between ourselves."[29]

Identity thus proves itself to be an accessible and fascinating conduit into the collective mind-set that lies behind foreign policy decisions taken in peace and in war. Foreign policy analysts in general, and neoclassical realists in particular, who approach the content of national policy will find that it comprises, deploys, and enacts particular aspects of the national identity in defense of a cultural image and a set of political interests. It is thus vital to regard national identity both as a foreign policy input and an outcome of social processes that shape groupness and all subsequent forms of material and existential power seeking. Identity also transforms the static signifiers of statehood (including security, sovereignty, territory, and economic power) into dynamic forms of statecraft, simply by activating them as identity-based policy.

## IDENTITY, INTERESTS, AND POLICY

Ideas matter.[30] And ideas are matter. Ideas constitute the beliefs and values that are the foundation for political culture. Ideas within political culture take on agency by translating values, norms, and principles into causal beliefs that in turn produce outcomes in the form of national decision making. In this manner, ideas both constitute material interests and state power and possess discernable, even causal, effects.[31] The ideational base underlying policy decisions is a "complex model of connections between culture and state behavior, mediated by cultural 'strategies of action,'" in which the broad subset of national culture represents and generates "symbolic [causal] vehicles of meaning, including beliefs, ritual practices" from art forms to interest choice to policy composition.[32] Peter Katzenstein outlines that "state interests do not exist to be "discovered" by self-interested, rational actors"; rather, interests, as a form of predefined cultural preference, "are constructed through a process of social interaction."[33]

By including domestic politics alongside external stimuli, it is possible to see how precisely a state's particular *statehood* informs the practice of its *statecraft*. This is because the two are linked through the formation of specific interests and informed by ideational patterns of self-reference that articulate both idea-based and material issues. The discourse of the national state regarding its statehood produces, through an articulation of its interests, the mechanics of policy construction.[34] This can occur in a bottom-up fashion whereby underlying trends of history and social culture yield a nexus of understandings and practices drawn upon by the state to define itself.[35] It can also occur indirectly through national institutions, particularly in the forums of education and media, filtering toward the national community in the form of an overarching discourse, or "chief narrator," from the top down.

The mechanism linking identity to both preference-based interests and policy are the "culturing" effects of underlying norms. Norms are understood to symbolize the cultural and institutional components of states' international and domestic environments. More precisely, because norms function as collective expectations regarding the behavior of a specific identity, they generate a consistent context for identity that produces interests consistent with that identity and policies supportive of those interests.[36] Indeed, the salience of norms connects identity with its discursive forms and policy enactments. As Theo Farrell argues, "how much a norm is evident in discourse, encoded in institutions, and implemented in polities, as well as the degree of conditionality attached to it, will determine its strength."[37] Norms thus provide the supporting framework for the tripartite dialectic of identity-interests-policy.

First, actors embody their culture and associated institutional structures, which constitute the basic national community and sense of national identity. Through the panoply of history, social development, cultural definition, mercantile forces, education, centralization, and politicization, each national unit is seen to create and project a range of identities, which, as a quorum, permits it to function as a singular actor. Second, state identity moves forward from normative structures to coalesce around a range of specific interests, previously articulated as ideational preferences. This occurs because national interests (particularly those touching on security and territory) rely upon a previous and specific construction of the national self-image to define the ideational scope of its preferences, which, in turn, define the broadly material-based conception of its specifically "national" interests. Preference-based interests arise when identities unify in a workable image or narrative with sharply articulated, defensible goals. The central point in this process is that over time states develop an interest in enacting and sustaining a given identity, particularly if it gains them the strategic value of prestige in the international realm. In this manner, identity provides a crucial link between the genealogical structures promoting forms of civic and cultural-unit selfness and the manner in which those values become politicized as national interests.

Third, preference-based interests themselves represent a form of constitution by informing the content and range of policy decisions. They also represent a measure of causality by instantiating a process that culminates in a discrete decision and consequential behavioral outcomes. Through interests, the discourse of national self-reference is put into active and constitutive practice when a decision is made that transforms it into policy. Norms follow the same identity-interest dialectic as above; as such, "constancy in underlying identity helps to explain underlying regularities in national . . . interests and policy," rather than the regularizing forces of the system writ large.[38] Equally, shifts in identity will likely prompt alterations in state policies.

Simply put, who an actor perceives itself to be determines the choice of goals and the manner of enactment. As Ted Hopf puts it, "In telling you who you are, identities strongly imply a particular set of interests or preferences with respect to choices of action in particular domains, and with respect to particular actors."[39] Identities generate and subsequently give shape to interests; interests in turn depend upon a particular type of identity in relation to its Self and perceived Others. The concept of "identity-based interest" operates when decisions are taken as a direct result of such ideas, themselves implying a range of interests. Identity is not a rival causal mechanism in relation to interests, but serves as an adjacent force by which to refine the choice and ranking of preference and from there, the definition of national interests.[40] Like their identity, actors construct their subsequent interests contextually. The contextual meaning of social processes and the identification of a series of goals provides an actor with a constitutive coherence that instantiates a form of *identity*, along with regulative patterns that promote a type of *behavior*. Judging their external reality based on the type of meaning it holds for their identity and preference-based interests at both the state and system level, actors "perform" a given identity by basing behavioral decisions according to whether the ideational scope of their *preference* and the material scope of their *interests* is in conjunction with the context of the surrounding environment, and whether it supports or challenges their identity. Forms of causality are derived from actions effected in the pursuit of interests, and for the purposes of this study are understood to be discernable as distinct policy decisions that reflect the scope of defined interests and nature of constituted identity of a given nation-state unit.

Understanding foreign policy as the outcome of identity-based interests is revealing, and indeed persuasive when examining the viewpoints of active diplomats such as Robert Cooper. Following Allott's original division, Cooper suggests simply that interests may be both generic and genetic, and that both grow out of the national identity. Generic national interests shared by all countries—survival, basic security, baseline prosperity, necessary regional stability—are classified by Cooper as a "second-order matter" in that they are generally absent in a particular ideational background and generally "do not touch the core of a country's values or identity."[41] Routine foreign policy can be managed in a discourse that consciously avoids references to values and is tactically negotiated, rather than strategically imperative. For most states, a canon of well-defined national interest accompanies standard foreign policy stances on both short- and long-term issues. However, occasional foreign policy decisions that are wholly strategic in nature require the reexamination of interests relative to the more unique background of identity from which they first emerged. Here, interests are defined as unique to or "genetically" derived from the attitude and resources of the country itself, prompting "decisions about ends as well as means; decisions that define interests rather than decisions that are governed by them."[42] As such, moments of crisis involving war, allies, threats, and opportunities cannot be decided solely by referring to a generic national interest or material balance sheet, but are more likely to be informed by the national narrative, in which national selfness is determined neither by strategy nor tactics but draws on culturally derived, existential themes in which the very definition of the state and its ultimate purpose is constituted. As Cooper presciently argues, "What is being defined is national identity. At such times a country may be acting out its national myth or even creating a new one. Out of this new identity flows the national interest."[43]

## The Role of Discourse in Identity and Policy Formation

Discourse has already been highlighted as a multigenre vehicle by which cultural and political modes of self-reference are made widely available to the public. Encompassing both cultural genres and political messages, discourses are the primary mechanism by which key ideas are transmitted into the public and policy arena. Politicians know this. As R. B. Hall argues,

> If actors did not expect discursive practices to generate these constitutive effects, it is difficult to explain why they labor so diligently on the construction of representations and narratives . . . [and] to construct and reconstruct the social meanings of the policy preferences of [self and] other actors, thereby reconstituting the normatively legitimate parameters of state policy.[44]

National discourses are simply a series of social ideas derived from particular contexts that encourage people "to think and frame their aspirations in terms of the idea of nation and national identity."[45] Emanating from official, unofficial, political, cultural, conservative, risqué, rhetorical, and media-based sources of the corpus of national discourse, discursive approaches generally entail textual analysis of deconstruction and decoding. Whether textually, orally, or archive-based, discourse operates as a tool of interpretation, as well as a hermeneutical method of penetrating identities as a causal factor of policy production. For the purposes of the present study, discourse functions by revealing the constitutiveness and causality of the "performative frameworks and networks which can semiotically encompass the narrative production of national identity."[46] As evidenced in the case studies, national discourses reveal how tangible and intangible forces alike are rendered politically meaningful by policy makers who consciously locate these forces within an overarching national narrative in order to legitimate policy decisions. Discourse produces a bounded, thematic narrative of the national self based on broad themes and recognizable images. Establishing both central and peripheric themes within the unitary form of a discourse represents a "summoning" and stabilizing of a central portion of the national self that accompanies the national unit in consolidating its modes of self-reference.

The discourse of English and British identity reveals itself to be any "managed space in which some statements and depictions come to have a greater value than others" and come to function as a "constitutive literality."[47] Thus, individuals, groups, sociohistorical developments, cultural forms, and political objectives are all participants in the "discursive economy" of the national unit simply because discourse represents a form of social practice in which beliefs and expectations become reconstituted at the national level. Discourse, in other words, functions as a narrative process revealing the primary terrain of the national state and its abiding themes of self and interest as well as a range of secondary, figurative semblances of self. Both literal and figurative, political and mythic forms of the national self are drawn upon by policy makers for a series of justificatory and motivational reasons that together produce a politicized narrative in the service of the state. This narrative is not uncontroversial. At no point in history is any national identity so wholly stable that it obtains as an unproblematic, uncontentious, universally representative monolith of nation-state unity. The national state contains within it the potential to continually rewrite, reinscribe, reconstitute, and reconstruct itself. As a result, the core of identity that entails the broadest, most common themes generally obtains a measure of stability, while peripheral elements remain in constant flux, reconstituting themselves in relation to the center. If this process cannot be effected in a secure fashion, a rival discourse may successfully challenge the dominant themes of nation.

In sum, national discourse is the forum by which "cultural context shapes strategic actions" by way of policy; this may be undertaken broadly by "engag[ing] in practices that attempt to rewrite the cultural landscape," or more specifically, by methods in which "actors deliberately package and frame policy ideas to convince each other as well as the general public that certain policy proposals constitute plausible and acceptable solutions."[48] National identity is therefore a critical and enduring factor in the expression of foreign policy. Equally, policy itself may be understood as a transformative and performative political practice central to the maintenance of the national identity. The case studies put these suggestions to the test, viewing Englishness as a discursive identifying attribute of the English nation-state. For England, deeply associated with spatiotemporal concepts, the roots and practices of its origins translate from discourse to policy in their conversion from a culture of remembrance to a "politics of memory."[49]

Within the four case studies, discourse is divided into two central areas of national meaning: the political discourse, distilled in a broadly top-down manner, and the public discourse (comprising elements of media and culture) emanating from within the unit itself and extending outward in equivalent bottom-up fashion. Both political and public discourses resonate demonstrably with the core identities of the English nation-state, constituting in narrative fashion the *"literality* of social relations" and political preference during four distinct periods.[50] The case studies are examined from a perspective that takes into account the high historic, cultural, and political congruence found within the discourse of identity, with the expectation that these forms of collective selfness will transfer discernably both constitutively and causally into the discursive practice of policy. The discourse of the English national identity provides a body of meanings from which to isolate themes and analyze adroitly four distinct historical events. The discourse of Englishness may effectively be "read" and analyzed as a form of symbolic representation, because the idea of "external reality" at work in these four instances reveals a set of meanings "that is *internal* to [the] discourse" and thereby linked to both elements of English self-reference and policy preference.[51] Discourse is thereby an excellent mechanism by which to illustrate the thematic resonances that occur in the lived reality of the national state, and that emanate in causal and constitutive fashion to affect policy formulation.

## Identity and Policy

The process by which identity affects policy takes place when national identity is transformed from a thematic discourse into a discursive practice within the explicit formulation of policy stances or decisions. To clarify, the national identity transforms from a passive entity as a broad narrative of images and themes into specific discursive policy practices. The cyclical quality is implicit: identity is constantly cast and recast through the foreign policies operating in its name, while foreign policies themselves produce and reproduce the identity of the policy maker. The identity of the state is discernably and performatively enacted in two ways. First, identity may be constituted tacitly through a discourse, which provides a discursive framework of core national meanings that passively affects the cognitive processes associated with decision making. Much national culture serves precisely this role, existing as a broad, historical frame of self-reference by which meanings are promoted and disseminated in gradual fashion. Within this body however, as the definition of national identity demonstrates, there exists a second, more focused civic-cultural locus, a more contextually specific "frame" that consolidates particular themes and images within a dominant discourse.

Each of the following case studies possesses broad discursive narratives, the broadest being that of self-referential Englishness and Britishness as a form of patriotic, nationalistic, or even jingoistic association with ascendant England in relation to broader aspects of the British Isles. There are a number of dominant discourses that mediate precisely how this patriotism plays out in defining the English and British unit, its interests, and its identity vis-à-vis others; these include the discourses associated with territorial integrity arising from island geography, naval greatness, differentiated senses of national security, and economic sovereignty. Each of these discourses is examined in relation to a specific event in which both public and policy makers "strategically deploy frames to situate [broader] events and to interpret problems . . . to galvanize sentiments as a way to mobilize and guide social action, and to suggest possible [policy] solutions."[52] As will be seen, narratives of the English and British self-reference have, for decades, been deployed by state officials and the wider public to interpret their national world relative to a host of international others. The most powerful forms of national self-reference arise from key themes of territory, security, sovereignty, and prosperity in which a uniquely English response is drawn upon to contextualize, underwrite, and even perform an act of policy. For present purposes, policy making is an actionable reflection of the purposive nature inherent in national discourse based on strategic efforts by key groups to forge shared understandings of their world and their self-image that subsequently legitimate collective action.

The "moment" when discursive identity informs the practice of policy can be refined in a number of ways. It can occur semantically, symbolically, even visually by way of images. Images are, for instance, the key explanatory feature in Cottam's work. She emphasizes "the importance of cognitive images in political decision making" in which national images

> act as organising devices permitting policy makers to simplify and comprehend. . . . Images filter information . . . [and provide] summary perceptions of the power, sophistication, threat, or opportunity posed. . . . Once an individual state [self or other] is perceived through an image, these summary perceptions influence the perceiver's expectations about the behavior of that state. . . . Finally, images influence the selection of tactics and instruments used in the pursuit of policy goals.[53]

Here the psychological images by which the nation defines itself produce a series of policy preferences in the form of national interests, along with the procedural methods by which to implement them, either as tactic or strategy.

If images offer too specific a transition from cause to effect, Valerie Hudson's 1997 study on culture and foreign policy offers a tripartite explanation in which national culture operates first as a broad system of shared meaning, second as a more specific framework of values and preferences, and third as an explicit template for policy action. In its first incarnation, statesmen deal only with the broad contours of their political culture as a broad system of "shared meaning"; these systems, however, provide analysts with a critical mass of "discourses, values, and implicit rules that express and shape political action and intentions, determine the claims groups may and may not make upon one another, and ultimately provide a logic of political action."[54] Identity here serves as a broad behavioral link to distinguish in-groups from out-groups, and indicates "that the relationship between a culture and the acts it performs in the international arena must be fairly strong."[55]

The nuts and bolts of this relationship are examined at the second level via strategic cultural and national role conceptions. Both these approaches examine cultural effects to explain how given nations arrive at value preferences that may either promote cooperation or provoke serious misunderstandings. Still at the fringes of IR and even FPA, strategic culture affords analysts a surprisingly thorough set of approaches involving process-tracing of the specific "cultural and historical differences predisposing each nation to the choice it actually made."[56] National role conceptions provide an alternative approach to the concept of the national self that is cultivated in culture and activated in policy, where states perform chosen roles because they are congruent with deeply held national beliefs. Cracking the cultural code is the third and most in-depth step of Hudson's role of culture in foreign policy: national culture providing not merely a set of cultural understandings but a ready blueprint for international action: a set of preformed templates for foreign policy making. This step also moves us into the realm of decision-making analysis; here national culture provides an active context for the choice of interests, but the state is actually activated in its behavior by individual decision makers. The catalytic link between culture and policy thus occurs in "defining an operational code [which] involves identifying core beliefs of a leader or group, as well as preferred means and style of pursuing goals. It is this last half of the operational code definition that helps us determine what templates of action may exist within a nation with respect to foreign policy."[57]

All three perspectives are reflected to some extent in the case studies. Englishness is the cultural bedrock providing a shared system of meaning that helps construct the English cultural unit within (though not limited to) the British political unit. The challenge at this level is to identify discernably English discourses, values, and rules that shape British political culture and affect the intentions of its decision makers and the action of the state. More deeply, English norms and values attached to key ideas of difference, superiority, morality, and historical exclusivity vs. political cosmopolitanism, and so on are examined for their role in molding and driving British strategic culture and role playing in the four chosen studies, as well as generating particular cultural predispositions and pathologies. Articulated visions of British role-playing at home and abroad are investigated, but generic role playing is generally assumed to derive from more particularist features of Englishness cultivated a priori. Lastly, and most pertinently, the aim of the next section is to investigate the operational code linking English political culture to the British operational foreign policy code. English discourses highlight both the shared system of intersubjective identities and the value preferences that constitute the maxims for action underlying particular political actions. The challenge therefore is to draw upon English perspectives as a means to explain British policy predispositions. These perspectives are available in the form of discourses, which provide constitutive strata underwriting long-term stances as well as specific "scripts of action" that provide snapshot, episodic moments that may act more causally to precipitate behavior.

To conclude, the national state and its policy-making instruments contain "no ontological status apart from the various acts which constitute its reality."[58] Incorporated into policy through the unitary form of discourse, identity constitutes the only form of reality available to the national state: its innately self-referential nature. National policy is a direct enactment of national identity. And discourse is the bridge. Discourse provides the link between identity as a cultural phenomenon with "bundled political objectives" and policy as the discursive enactment of that phenomenon. Identity is the content, discourse the form, and foreign policy the vehicle. Thus, "it is through these very public pronouncements that the discursive strategies [of identity] deployed within them have their constitutive effects" within policy.[59] What such a perspective suggests, and indeed what the case studies prove, is that in the discursive transference from identity meanings to policy practices, neither historical changes nor systemic alterations regarding a perceived threat lessens the instinct to use foreign policy as the chief vehicle to make plain national values and mandates. As will be seen, English concepts regarding its national attributes of order, authority, exactitude, fairness, and civility comprise both the content of its domestic identity and that of the national policy emerging from the Cabinet, the Foreign Office, and Parliament itself. Indeed, policy content is demonstrably proven to establish both an interpretive and an active framework for forms of national self-reference.

## NOTES

1. Rogers Brubaker, *Ethnicity without Groups* (Cambridge, MA: Harvard University Press, 2004), 29.
2. A possible exception to this is the generally constant acceptance of culture and collective identity as key variables by FPA as it emerged in the United States from the

1960s onward. Stemming from symbolic interactionist sociology, the work of Peter Berger and Thomas Luckmann qualifies as a starting point for the use of identity in the social sciences: *The Social Construction of Reality: A Treatise in the Sociology of Knowledge* (New York: Doubleday Anchor, 1967).

3. Pierre Bordieu, "Identity and Representation: Elements for a Critical Reflection on the Idea of Region," in *Language and Symbolic Power* (Cambridge, MA: Harvard University Press, 1991), 220–28.

4. Brubaker, *Ethnicity without Groups*, 4.

5. Brubaker, *Ethnicity without Groups*, 28.

6. Steven E. Lobell, Norrin M. Ripsman, and Jeffrey W. Taliaferro (eds.) *Neoclassical Realism, the State and Foreign Policy* (Cambridge: Cambridge University Press, 2009), 35.

7. Margaret Somers, "The Narrative Constitution of Identity: A Relational and Network Approach," *Theory and Society* 23 (1992): 605–49.

8. Friedrich Meinecke, *Weltbürgertum und Nationalstaat: Studien zur Genesis des Deutschen Nationalstaates* (Munich: R. Oldenbourg [1907] 1919), Hans Kohn, *The Ideal of Nationalism: A Study in Its Origins and Background* (New York: Collier Books, 1944), and Anthony D. Smith, *Theories of Nationalism* (London: Duckworth, 1971) and *The Ethnic Origins of Nations* (Oxford: Basil Blackwell, 1986).

9. J. Hutchinson, in *Nationalism*, eds. John Hutchinson and Anthony D. Smith (Oxford: Oxford University Press, 1994), 127.

10. J. Hutchinson, *Nationalism*, 127.

11. Isaiah Berlin, *Vico and Herder: Two Studies in the History of Ideas* (London: Hogarth Press, 1976), 158.

12. Smith, *Theories of Nationalism* and Eric J. Hobsbawm, "Ethnicity and Nationalism and Europe Today," in *Mapping the Nation*, ed. Gopal Balakrishnan (London: Verso, 1996); and Eric J. Hobsbawm and Terence Ranger, eds. *The Invention of Tradition* (Cambridge: Cambridge University Press, 1983).

13. As Wiebe observes pithily, "Ethnicity turned into nationalism when cultural consciousness acquired a political objective." Robert H. Wiebe, *Who We Are: A History of Popular Nationalism* (Princeton, NJ: Princeton University Press, 2002), 15.

14. C. McClurg Mueller, "Building Social Movement Theory," in *Frontiers in Social Movement Theory*, eds. Aldon D. Morris and Carol McClurg Mueller (New Haven, CT: Yale University Press, 1992), 23.

15. Smith, *Theories of Nationalism*.

16. R. Brubaker, *Ethnicity without Groups*, 144.

17. R. Brubaker, *Ethnicity without Groups*, 144–45.

18. Bede lists a number of conditions by which English political autonomy was gained, including bounded territoriality; ecclesiastical unity; a unified "gens Anglorum," comprised not by indigenous peoples (Britons, Scots, or Picts) but by former invaders (Angles, Saxons, and Jutes), all of whom speak the same vernacular English language; a unified legal system and vernacular literature, thanks to the efforts of King Alfer; an elementary parliament (the Witan) along with unified economic, bureaucratic, and religious structures; as well as common administrative units and sub-units in the shires and boroughs. Adrian Hastings, *The Construction of Nationhood: Ethnicity, Religion and Nationalism* (Cambridge: Cambridge University Press, 1997), 36–41.

19. R. Brubaker, *Ethnicity without Groups*, 144.

20. A. Wendt, "Anarchy is What States Make of It: The Social Construction of Power Politics," *International Organization* 46 (Spring 1992): 397.

21. T. Hopf, *Social Construction of International Politics: Identities and Foreign Policies, Moscow, 1955 and 1999* (Ithaca, NY: Cornell University Press, 2002), 5–6.

22. Peter J. Katzenstein, "Conclusion: National Security in a Changing World," in *The Culture of National Security: Norms and Identity in World Politics*, ed. P. Katzenstein (New York: Columbia University Press, 1996), 505.

23. Robert Cooper, *The Breaking of Nations: Order and Chaos in the Twenty-First Century* (London: Atlantic Books, 2003), 87.

24. Jens Bartelson, *A Genealogy of Sovereignty* (Cambridge: Cambridge University Press, 1995), 83.

25. Tom Nairn, *The Break-up of Britain: Crisis and Neo-Nationalism* (London: New Left Books, 1977), 341.

26. D. Campbell, *Writing Security: United States Foreign Policy and the Politics of Identity* (Minneapolis: University of Minnesota Press, 1992), 68.

27. D. Kandiyoti, "Identity and Its Discontents: Women and the Nation," *Millennium: Journal of International Studies* 20, no. 3 (1991): 439 (emphasis added).

28. Campbell, *Writing Security*, 68.

29. Homi K. Bhabha, "Introduction: Narrating the Nation," in *Nation and Narration*, ed. Homi K. Bhabha (London: Routledge, 1999), 4.

30. Judith Goldstein and Robert O. Keohane, *Ideas and Foreign Policy: Beliefs, Institutions, and Political Change* (Ithaca, NY: Cornell University Press, 1993).

31. See Emanuel Adler, "Seizing the Middle Ground: Constructivism in World Politics," *European Journal of International Relations* 3, no. 3 (1997): 319–63.

32. Ann Swidler, "Culture in Action: Symbols and Strategies," *American Sociological Review* 51, no. 2 (1986): 273, as quoted in Jeffrey S. Lantis, "Strategic Culture and National Security Policy," *International Studies Review* 4, no. 3 (Fall 2002): 92.

33. Peter J. Katzenstein, "Introduction: Alternative Perspectives on National Security," in Katzenstein, *The Culture of National Security*, 2.

34. Martha Finnemore, *National Interests in International Society* (Ithaca, NY: Cornell University Press, 1996).

35. John G. Ikenberry and Charles A. Kupchan, "Socialization and Hegemonic Power," *International Organization* 44, no. 3 (Summer 1990).

36. Ronald Jepperson, Alexander Wendt, and Peter Katzenstein, "Norms, Identity, and Culture in National Security," in Katzenstein, *The Culture of National Security*, 54.

37. T. Farrell, Constructivist Security Studies: Portrait of a Research Program," *International Studies Review* 4, no. 1 (Spring 2002): 61.

38. Jepperson, Wendt, and Katzenstein, "Norms, Identity, and Culture in National Security," 61.

39. T. Hopf, "The Promise of Constructivism in International Relations Theory," *International Security* 23, no. 1 (Summer 1998): 175.

40. A. Wendt, "Collective Identity Formation and the International State," *The American Political Science Review* 88, no. 2, (June 1994): 385.

41. Cooper, *The Breaking of Nations*, 130.

42. Cooper, *The Breaking of Nations*, 131.

43. Cooper, *The Breaking of Nations*, 132.

44. R. B. Hall, "The Discursive Demolition of the Asian Development Model," *International Studies Quarterly* 47, no.1 (March 2003): 95.

45. Craig Calhoun, *Nationalism* (Minneapolis: University of Minnesota Press, 1997), 6.

46. X. Guillaume, "Foreign Policy and Politics of Alterity: A Dialogical Understanding of International Relations," *Millennium: Journal of International Studies* 31, no. 1 (2002): 11–12.

47. E. Laclau and C. Mouffe, *Hegemony and Socialist Strategy: Towards a Radical Democratic Politics*, trans. Winston Moore and Paul Cammack (London: Verso, 1985), 110.

48. John L. Campbell, "Institutional Analysis and the Role of Ideas in Political Economy," *Theory and Society* 27, no. 3 (June 1998): 381, as quoted in Barnett, "Culture, Strategy and Foreign Policy Change: Israel's Road to Oslo," *European Journal of International Relations* 5, no. 1 (1999): 7–8.

49. J. G. Hajdu, "Japanese Capital on Australia's Gold Coast as a Catalyst of a Localist-Globalist Conflict on National Identity," *Global Society: Journal of Interdisciplinary International Relations* 13, no. 3 (July 1999): 335.

50. Laclau and Mouffe, *Hegemony and Socialist Strategy*, 110 (emphasis added).

51. Campbell, *Writing Security*, 6.

52. Barnett, "Culture, Strategy and Foreign Policy Change," 15.

53. M. Cottam, "The Carter Administration's Policy toward Nicaragua: Images, Goals and Tactics," *Political Science Quarterly* 107, no. 1 (Spring 1992): 126.

54. Valerie M. Hudson, "Culture and Foreign Policy: Developing a Research Agenda," in *Culture and Foreign Policy*, ed. Hudson (Boulder, CO: Lynne Rienner, 1997), 10.

55. Hudson, "Culture and Foreign Policy," 11.

56. Hudson, "Culture and Foreign Policy," 13.

57. Hudson, "Culture and Foreign Policy," 14

58. J. Butler, *Gender Trouble: Feminism and the Subversion of Identity* (New York: Routledge, 1990), 141.

59. Hall, "The Discursive Demolition of the Asian Development Model," 74.

# 4

## The 1882 Channel Tunnel Crisis

### Englishness and Territoriality

> For I dipped into the future, far as human eye could see
> Saw the vision of the world, and all the wonder that would be
> . . .
> Yet I doubt not through the ages one increasing purpose runs,
> And the thoughts of men are widened with process of the suns.
> . . .
> Not in vain the distance beacons. Forward, forward let us range,
> Let the great world spin for ever down the ringing grooves of change
>
> —Tennyson, "Locksley Hall"[1]

Within IR, both culture and identity have suffered a tendency to be seen as merely derivatives of states, with no real independent explanatory power of their own. These case studies suggest a rather different perspective, namely that a "reflexive consideration of the past" aptly highlights both historical and cultural forces that fashion the national identity, and are ultimately catalytic to the substance and indeed process of foreign policy making.[2]

This first case examines the "identity theme" of territoriality at work in the political and cultural discourses arising from the 1882 project to construct a subterranean tunnel between England and France. As will be seen, the physicality of territory "becomes part of the national identity, with places and spaces taking on historical and even mythical significance in the creation of the nation's historical narrative."[3] In 1882, the possibility of a tunnel was perceived as a threat both to the continuity of the English historical narrative, and to British strategies and interests. The tunnel crisis deals largely with the context of an English national identity shifting from a tacit but assured sense of cultural privilege to a reactive, defensive stance toward perceived rivals.

The attempt to link England and France for commercial and diplomatic reasons unleashed an uproar so enormous that it clearly denoted a host of less formally articulated uncertainties regarding English identity and British interests. As a commercial venture to improve communication, trade, and Anglo-French reciprocity, the tunnel was opposed primarily on military grounds and, to a lesser extent, economic grounds. However, beneath both responses lay the fear of losing forever the implicit geographical, cultural, and political separateness by which the island had first identified its English self and its subsequent perception of European others. From this perspective, the tunnel represented a physical and cultural breach that damaged the matchlessness of English native soil and diminished the unique characteristics of its people. The political and cultural reactions to the tunnel proposal are now examined for this catalytic role in the subsequent decision to abstain from the tunnel and the wider foreign relations with France and Europe.

## CHANNEL TUNNEL HISTORY

By 1882, the idea of a link across the English Channel was well-established. The first Channel proposal was conceived in 1751 by the Frenchman Desmaret who submitted his plan to King Louis XV. A more formal plan was presented to Napoleon in 1802 following the Peace of Amiens, suggested by the mining engineer Albert Mathieu and involving a tunnel for horse-drawn traffic. Thirty years later, Thomé de Gamond undertook the first "systematic geological and hydrographic survey of the Channel" in 1833, and in 1866 produced eight designs for a tube, bridge, and tunnel across the Channel.[4] The first English engineers were William Low and John Hawkshaw, who proposed a single-track tunnel. Hawkshaw then formed the English Channel Company in 1872 and conducted subterranean studies around Dover Beach. Low collaborated with de Gamond in 1867, but despite producing a cross-channel proposal that was referred to a Parliamentary committee chaired by Lord Richard Grosvenor with the participation of French engineers, no tangible results emerged.[5]

Three years later, the idea appeared to be picking up steam when an Anglo-French committee of promoters applied to the French government for a perpetual and sole concession to construct a subterranean railway to Dover. The French ambassador immediately wrote to the British foreign secretary, Lord Clarendon, for permission to approve and regulate the tunnel construction "by a diplomatic agreement."[6] Disrupted by the 1870 war with Germany, French initiatives were forcibly shelved until 1872 when the Channel Tunnel Company was registered as an incorporated company in London. Having renewed its petition with the French government to begin experimental construction, the English Board of Trade was appointed in 1873 as an intermediary between the two governments. The board appeared interested in the commercial prospects of an "improvement in the communication between this country and the Continent" and made four suggestions, including an overland bridge, a steam ferry, the extension of French and English harbors midway into the Channel, and lastly a "Submarine Tunnel between Dover and Calais."[7] In line with the liberal attitudes of the Gladstone government, the board recommended to the foreign secretary, Lord Granville, that the project be undertaken with the sole condition that it not be turned into a "perpetual private monopoly."[8] Gladstone himself backed the plan, making clear his "friendly and lively interest [in] all schemes with this object and open to no just objection."[9]

In 1874, the Conservatives swept to power under Disraeli, whose foreign secretary, Lord Derby communicated the government's continuing support for the project. Derby assured the French ambassador in London, the Count de Jarnac, that there appeared "no reason for any doubt [regarding the project] and Her Majesty's Government would, therefore, offer no opposition to it."[10] On 20 January 1875, the "English Channel Tunnel Bill" was set before the French National Assembly; two days later, a similar bill was recommended to Parliament in England by both the Board of Trade and the Foreign Office, who instructed the House to "secure the public interests involved in the construction of the Tunnel."[11] On 2 August 1875, the bill, entitled the "The British Channel Tunnel Company (limited) Act" passed in both countries.[12] The following year, a protocol on the Channel Tunnel was established, and the Anglo-French Joint Commission was assigned to oversee the project.[13] From the debates of this commission emerges the first hint of future problems. The agreement reached was that in the event of any form of national danger, "each Government should have the right to suspend the working of the railway by damaging, destroying, or flooding the Tunnel, whenever such Government should in the interest of its own country, think necessary to do so."[14] This appeared to be a predominantly British suggestion, as the French government required merely "the right of stopping the traffic" rather than anything more serious with regard to national safety.[15] The War Office then registered a complaint at its exclusion from the commission reinforced by ominous warnings that the Tunnel "will put an end to the insularity upon which Great Britain so relies for defence. . . . [This] raises the scheme from a mere commercial undertaking, and invests it with a *political character*."[16]

It soon became apparent that the French promoters had been granted far more extensive concession rights than their English counterparts. The

English promoters were subsequently unable to raise their own capital, the French promoters were then delayed, and ultimately the tunnel project sputtered to a halt. The Anglo-French Joint Commission was itself terminated through lack of interest and the project languished. The commission, however, had been successful in focusing the issue of national security implicit in the tunnel project firmly upon the English psyche; as the War Office Solicitor observed, "The subject is one so novel that no ordinary experience will guide us. The committee [commission] has been formed without any element of that which in an *English* point of view is the essence of the scheme, viz. its effect on the insular position of *Great Britain* in relation to national defence."[17] This response typifies the role of Englishness, which at the end of the nineteenth century functioned as a core set of cultural virtues increasingly drawn on to underwrite the consolidated political identity of Britishness, informing British national interest and ultimately its foreign policy vis-à-vis its security and territoriality.

## Mid-Victorian Attitudes: Railways, Progress, and Englishness

The body of Victorian national attitudes contextualizes the public and political elements that generated the tunnel's oppositional discourse in 1882. This discourse, while couched in the language of national security, defense, fortifications, and conscription reflected broader perceptions of national self-diminishment that featured an utter unwillingness to countenance change, and "recalled the violent opposition, fifty years earlier, to the construction of the early railways."[18] Colonel Clarke of the War Office Scientific Committee suggested that the same progress from superstition to acceptance of the railways would ultimately transform intransigent military perspectives regarding the tunnel:

> It was said by military authorities that the establishment of such improved means of communication and locomotion would tend to weaken and destroy the obstacles nature had given our island home to check the advance of an invader. . . . There were then objectors [to the Southampton to London railway] who asserted that the existence of such a line would offer a tempting invitation to an enemy's fleet for the occupation of the Solent and Southampton water.[19]

These objections had been overcome as the sheer innovation of rail began to transform the island. Engineered by George Stephenson, the Stockton-Darlington Railway opened in 1825 as a coach pulled by horses. The London-Manchester and Manchester-Liverpool lines were operating by the 1830s. By the 1880s, the rail system had increased to thirteen thousand miles. Expanding at an unprecedented rate, the English public "had also become almost besotted with the sensation of speed."[20] Industry prospered, employment rose substantially, iron and coal output increased, all of which resulted in confident home markets and overseas profits for those who exported the technology. The zenith was marked at the Crystal Palace Great Exhibition of 1851 when English and Scottish engineering ingenuity was displayed to international audiences. As William Johnston observed that same year in his survey *England As It Is*, the railroads had produced significant changes "in the habit of society, [in] the affairs of government—the new feeling of power they have engendered . . . above all, the new and excessive activities to which they have given rise . . . can scarcely be exaggerated."[21] The historian Macaulay argued likewise that "locomotion benefits mankind morally as well as materially. . . . [It] not only facilitates the interchange of the various productions, of nature and art, but tends to remove national and provincial antipathies and to bind together all the branches of the great human family."[22] Rail transformed the postal system and the telegraph and broadened the extent of newspapers; indeed "for society in general, the railways brought an escape from enforced parochialism."[23] However, the removal of Macaulay's "national and provincial antipathies" had, in the eyes of his contemporaries, begun to erode the ancient cultural association of the English social unit.

Despite the tremendous upturn in industry and commerce afforded by the railways, there was also a growing sense of cultural decay attached to an invention that had so transformed the physical nature of the English countryside. Two varieties of decay had appeared. In the first, the industrial age, symbolized by the railways, was culpable in undermining broad structures of civilization. In effect, "society's whole scale of values was being inverted by the contemporary mania for railways and industrialization, with the result that materialism was blighting true culture."[24] Echoing the earlier calls of the poets Wordsworth and Coleridge, English social philosophers Matthew Arnold, John Ruskin, and Thomas Carlyle appeared, prophesying in an industrialized wilderness against the speed and pervasiveness of change. "Civilisation," Ruskin declared, "is the economy of power, and English power is coal. If it be so then 'ashes to ashes' be our epitaph! And the sooner the better."[25]

The second variety of decay entailed the modernization and destabilization of individual English sensibilities of home and hearth, which could prompt further national declinism. English society—a paradigm of civility at home and an imperial mandate abroad—still appeared firmly connected to a rural, class-based, customary, and rather solitary ethos ordered along quasi-medieval values.

This society now appeared in danger of disintegrating in the face of material change embodied in a series of metropolitan, egalitarian, collective, and contemporary changes. Industry and the railroads appeared necessary to the political structure and goals of the British state and its new incarnation as the "workshop of the world," but still appeared incommensurate with England's cultural heritage. With each strip of rail, each new factory came a growing sense of "the ugliness, waste, and vital impoverishment that underlay . . . the pomp and commercial prosperity of Victorian civilization," itself divided between British progress (propelled by Scottish as much as English engineering ingenuity) and English nostalgia.[26]

The paradox is clear. English opinion was cognizant of the external imperatives, and the various domestic shifts that had together prompted Britain's staggering industrial development; the *methods* of transformation themselves were altogether too materialist, physically disruptive, and possibly too removed for a crucial segment of the general populace and much of the governing elite to sit easily alongside perceptions of an ancient nation untouched by modernity.

Although a controversial figure for his conflicting views on culture and development, Matthew Arnold imprinted upon the Victorian psyche the idea that "wealth and industry were *necessarily* the enemies of culture," and that "coal, railroads and machinery are . . . automatically pejorative."[27] The true England appeared to languish in the collective psyche as some reassuringly parochial, untouched nation, rather than the industrial powerhouse of Victorian Britain. The division between England and Britain is perhaps at its sharpest during this dislocating, schizophrenic era, which time and again manifests a "yearning for stability, some safe and sure anchorage within a frighteningly fast-changing world."[28] Only in a disconnected, associative material sense was this period reflective of the zenith of English cultural power and British imperial might.[29]

However, while "the railways were built after the more extravagant fears [regarding their construction] had been shown to be groundless," the outcry in 1882 over the tunnel was based on rather different perceptions.[30] The tunnel itself symbolized not the inevitability of expanding if unglamorous progress, but an initiative heralding an array of very real threats including violability, invasion, and defeat, and which were distinctly territorial in ilk and national in symbolism. While the public hysteria provoked by the tunnel "was of hordes of armed Frenchmen pouring through the tunnel and driving on to London," the wider unease revolved around the violation of the sacral nature of English territoriality and, more subtly, the degree to which territorial sovereignty instituted both the English national identity and the political interests of the British state.[31] Such themes were readily taken up by various actors and disseminated in both Parliament and daily newspapers, journals, and "invasion literature," translating themes of English domestic decline into a specific British policy on territorial integrity.

# THE CHANNEL TUNNEL CRISIS: THE POLITICAL DISCOURSE

In 1881, a second proposal made by William Low was put forward by the South Eastern Railway Company, under the chairmanship of Sir Edwin Watkin, M.P.[32] Making use of the South Eastern Railway Act of 1881, Watkin had carried out experimental drilling on the beach and foreshore of Dover, carving out a tunnel of two thousand and twenty yards beneath the sea in the direction of Dover harbor.[33] Announcing his intention to establish a partnership with a French promoter regarding the original 1876 concession, Watkin drew public attention to his venture by placing a Private Member's Bill before Parliament. The Board of Trade intervened, recommending that the War Office establish a departmental committee to examine his project.[34] Chaired by Mr. Farrer of the Board of Trade, the departmental committee was appointed on 22 August 1881 with the mandate of examining the project's feasibility. It soon became apparent, however, that the remit of the Board of Trade was being steadily eroded, with the War Office increasingly called upon to provide expert evidence from senior military and naval personages.

The tunnel project gradually gained national notoriety, as evidenced by the unwillingness of the Board of Trade Committee to make a final decision on "a question of such magnitude," preferring that it "be settled on the responsibility of the Government as a whole."[35] Childers, as the secretary of state for war decided that "before the Government considered the Channel Tunnel question on the wider grounds of national interests, the War Office should appoint a committee of engineers and scientists" to consider the merits of the tunnel.[36] Joseph Chamberlain, as president of the Board of Trade agreed. Under the presidency of Major-General Sir Archibald Alison, the "War Office Scientific Committee" was appointed on 23 February 1882, along with five senior members of the military. Much of the evidence heard by the Scientific Committee was disseminated to both Parliament and the public through the press. The Scientific Committee called upon notable personages from the military and navy to give evidence as to the benefits and disadvantages of allowing a contractor to build a subterranean tunnel between England and France. However, even before the committee completed its inquiries on 12 May, both the House and the national press were demanding fuller explanations of its findings. Despite support for the tunnel that emerged from the committee, the English nation was rapidly becoming convulsed in a discourse of steadfast opposition to it, with the result that "controversy raged while the works were suspended."[37]

## Supportive Discourse

The majority of evidence given to the Scientific Committee was support-ive in its judgment of the tunnel. The committee began with the views of Sir Edwin Watkin, as chairman of the South Eastern Railway. Outlining ways in which "to improve the means of communication between England and the Continent," Watkin elaborated on the speed that a tunnel would af-ford connecting travelers, and the general "untold advantage as a matter of health, and a great economy of time."[38] However, the committee appeared uninterested in the nature of these advantages from the outset, preferring instead to focus upon the themes of invasion and deterrence. Asked to out-line the numerous ways in which the tunnel, once built, could be instantly destroyed, Watkin replied that "there is not a man in a million, I believe, who entertains those ideas about the danger of having a Tunnel; but if you want to destroy it, I can show you many ways."[39]

As an engineer of the Channel Tunnel Railway Company, Sir John Hawk-shaw followed Watkin by arguing that the tunnel would "be of great advan-tage that we, who are now isolated, should, as regards intercommunication for traveling purposes, at all events, be connected with the European system of railways.[40] Rather than expounding on issues of interoperability, Hawk-shaw was instead asked to give evidence regarding the possible fortifica-tions and armaments erected at Dover Castle to protect the tunnel entrance. Attempting to shift the committee's focus by remarking on the sudden interest in security issues, Hawkshaw noted that "I have never heard . . . the military question raised as an objection: it had not frightened anybody in my recollection until quite lately."[41] A new discourse, based on the defense of the national interest by military means, as a result of the threat posed by the tunnel was clearly being formed.

Colonel Sir Andrew Clarke supported Hawkshaw's view and concluded that the "objections" being raised "are almost solely of a military character. . . . We could reduce to a minimum, if not obliterate, all possible risk of danger or even of panic. . . . On all grounds . . . the objections against the Tunnel being made are not capable of being sustained."[42] The surveyor-general of ordnance, Sir John Adye, proved the committee's most unco-operative expert witness, refusing to entertain suggestions regarding the destruction of the tunnel or its security liability.[43] Adye concluded that "as to its dangers in a military sense, and with the most ordinary precautions, I am unable to perceive them."[44] Despite the strong opposition to the themes of invasion and deterrence put by various respondents, the committee concluded it "presumptuous to place absolute reliance upon even the most comprehensive and complete arrangements which can be devised, with a view of rendering the Tunnel absolutely useless to an enemy in every imag-inable contingency."[45]

While the expert views given to the Scientific Committee that regarded the tunnel as practical and beneficial had been the consensus of the majority, attempts to dismiss it on grounds of military insecurity continued to grow. Adye himself unwittingly suggested that as a method of invasion, a determined enemy would need to have "previously secured possession of our end of it . . . and this can only be obtained either by force or by treachery."[46] The implicit suggestion was that via general domestic decline, specific forms of diminishment or "internal invasion" could easily take place; indeed that the enemy—either as a physical "Other" or an oppositional ideational self—was already present, with the result that England "that was wont to conquer others" had through internal decline (and external challenges) "made a shameful conquest of itself."[47] The interest of the committee in the violent methods by which the tunnel might be destroyed echoes the violence inherent in the perceptions of invasion and the abrogation of territorial sovereignty; more subtly, they echo the forms of decay that had over the past century eroded an array of English modes of self-reference. One factor alone lay between issues of national security and the explosion of a full-blown invasion alarm focused on English territorial integrity: the contribution, by both fact and fiction, of a discourse that supported these anxieties. The "facts" were implicit in the evidence given to the Scientific and Parliamentary committees. The "fiction" was provided by the genre of invasion literature rapidly gaining currency as a form of popular culture premised on the potential collapse of national security and the suitably gory consequences.

## Oppositional Discourse

A fortnight before the Scientific Committee had concluded, the government had already announced that, regardless of the subsequent findings of the committee, "the experimental boring of the Channel Tunnel should be stopped . . . until Parliament has come to a decision whether the Tunnel is to be made or not."[48] On 12 May 1882, the Scientific Committee completed its inquiries and submitted to Parliament the finding that "the tunnel was a potential danger to national security."[49] By then the storm had broken and public outrage was pouring down upon Parliament to reject the Private Member's Bill. Gladstone disagreed, believing that if the issue were presented "in the form of a plebiscite or referendum," the English public "would have approved the scheme," but his perspective represented the minority.[50] Two views in particular form the nucleus of the oppositional discourse: those of the adjutant-general, Lord Wolseley, and the field-marshal commander-in-chief of the army: H.R.H. Prince George, the Duke of Cambridge.

The views of Lord Wolseley were particularly severe. They dominated Parliament, flooded the press, and added considerable momentum to the constitutive content of the oppositional discourse and the causal agency implicit in the policy decision to block it.[51] Wolseley's criticisms were threefold. First was the unreliability of the methods proposed to destroy the tunnel, generally by flood or mines. Second was the breach of territorial integrity entailed in eliminating the natural advantage of the Channel and the additional consequence of having to establish a standing army:

> The proposal to make a Tunnel . . . [will] annihilate all the advantages we have hitherto enjoyed from the existence of the "silver streak," for to join England to the Continent by a permanent highway, will be to place her under the unfortunate condition of having neighbours possessing great standing armies. . . . The construction of the tunnel would place us under those same conditions that have forced the Powers of Europe to submit to universal service. . . . The people of England have no intention of imposing such a fearful burden upon themselves.[52]

Third, like the unwitting remarks of Surveyor-General Adye, Wolseley suggested that threats to England took root from internal treachery or external deception, and that precaution was justified:

> But the greatest of all dangers to which the construction of this Tunnel will lay us open, is that one end of it may be seized by surprise or treachery, without any warning. . . . It must be remembered that the works at our end of the Tunnel may be surprised by men sent through the Tunnel itself, without landing a man upon ou[r] shores. A couple of thousand armed men might easily come through the Tunnel in a train at night, avoiding all suspicion by being dressed as ordinary passengers.[53]

Insisting that the proposed measures by the Channel Tunnel Railway and the South Eastern Railway companies were not to "be treated simply as "private bills but . . . as one of great *national* importance," Wolseley's memorandum successfully transformed the tunnel from a private commercial venture into an issue of national security concerning territoriality and foreign relations with France.[54] Where "Adye saw [the tunnel] as a way of cementing Anglo-French relations . . . Wolseley saw the tunnel as a bait tempting France to invade."[55]

The views of Lord Wolseley were lent additional credence by the opinions of Prince George, the Duke of Cambridge, first presented in a memorandum to the cabinet and subsequently widely publicized.[56] The duke based his opinions first on the findings of the Scientific Committee, which he argued "amounted to an absolute condemnation of every existing proposal for a Channel Tunnel"; second, as a field marshal, and as commander–in-chief, whose "plain duty, on military grounds, was to protest most emphatically against the construction of the Tunnel."[57] The duke suggested that fortifying the entire tunnel structure, particularly the Dover Castle entrance, provided no real guarantee of enhanced security. He further argued that in the 1870 German attack on France, "the Vosges tunnels [in France] were left intact from an unwillingness to destroy such splendid engineering works. . . . In consequence, the invading armies, despite all arrangements that had been made for destroying those tunnels, were able freely to employ them."[58] The French had clearly failed to uphold the principle of duty that mandated the preservation of national security interests above all others.

From the duke's viewpoint, it was his "solemn duty to warn Her Majesty's Government of the great risk and danger which will be entailed upon the country by permitting . . . any tunnel to be constructed." In making reference to the subsequent alterations to national status effected by the tunnel, the duke alluded to a core feature of Englishness and a historic feature of the British state, namely, the traditional absence in the islands of a large territorial army. Such a requirement had historically lain beyond the remit of the English national character. England had always relied upon the Royal Navy for its defense, and upon its island status for its security and subsequent perceptions of inviolability. Constructing a new standing army would disengage with the unique island qualities of England that had contributed to its national preeminence:

> We alone, of all European nations, have hitherto escaped the necessity of arming and organising the entire population, but if this tunnel be constructed . . . our only positive security can be found in following the example of our neighbours by creating a vast army like theirs, an army which would probably entail the necessity of a compulsory system of universal military service.[59]

For both English and "Britons . . . conscription smacked of militarist and government interference."[60] Further, the country appeared to be laboring under a great and fatal delusion "that an army of unorganised and very partially trained Volunteers and Militia could, by anything short of a miracle, stand up successfully against a regularly trained and well-organised army."[61] It was not the role of England or the wider British political unit to adhere to such methods of defending its national interest, for "if once the question of military superiority were brought to an issue between us, and any one of these great powers upon English *soil*, the end could only be our destruction as a free *nation*."[62] The Duke had identified the very theme around which both English national identity was defined and British interests defended: namely, its island status, which guaranteed the continuance of England as a realm of separateness, and thus uniqueness. Concluding that the violation of English soil could be effected by the forces of "surprise or . . . treachery," the Duke implored "Her Majesty's Ministers to pause ere they accepted for the nation, whose destinies are in their hands, a new element of danger that would threaten our very national existence."[63]

As a discourse of national security, the Tunnel now possessed the power to shatter the inviolable quality of England, to rupture British geopolitical preeminence and to diminish the uniqueness of its inhabitants. As a

discourse of opposition the tunnel also possessed significant causal qualities in producing a focused policy reaction of some magnitude. Within the
Scientific Committee, the emphasis had shifted from questions of commercial to national interest. Under the influence of Wolseley and the Duke of
Cambridge, it shifted again from a breach of British national *interest* to the
outright imperiling of English national *existence*. Because the tunnel itself
constituted not "the messenger of peace and good-will, but the harbinger
of increased military expenditure, of panics and apprehensions, of possible
invasions, strife and bloodshed," the discourse of 1882 was likewise constituted upon an active defense of English national identity and its characteristics of separateness.[64]

The tangible element representing this deep separateness was the channel
itself, which effectively inculcated territorial integrity as the principal coun-
terargument to the tunnel and ensured that territory continued to underwrite
the core themes of English cultural particularism and British geopolitical
strength. The historic "narrow strait, the 'silver streak" dividing the isles from
the continent, an "insular" natural advantage, which if dismissed would in
the same stroke "render [its] navy, the natural creation and necessity springing from this position, the glory and boast of England, of much less value to
us in case of invasion."[65] Indeed, an additional and formidable rival to the
1882 tunnel project was the Admiralty itself. Behind alarmist scenarios of
foreign armies marching on London via the tunnel was a far more dangerous
possibility, "that of a redundant but expensive Navy, looking on as a helpless
spectator."[66] Like the Duke of Cambridge, Admiral Key considered it his chief
duty to ensure the command of the Channel by an efficient fleet."[67]

A final form of opposition within the political discourse emerged from
the Foreign Office, who agreed with the Board of Trade over the dubious
claims of increased commercial access and with the Admiralty regarding
the challenge to naval policy. Guided by the need to preserve the centrality
of British foreign policy, both Permanent Under-Secretary Lord Tenterden of the Foreign Office and Parliamentary Under-Secretary Sir Charles
Dilke maintained that the tunnel "would materially alter the relations
in which this country stands towards the Continent of Europe, and especially France."[68] Combining the powers of Whitehall and Westminster, the
memoranda employed the same strident tones as Wolseley and the Duke of
Cambridge, describing "the possibility of a European coalition against England, resulting in a successful invasion," the "contingencies in which the
possession of the Tunnel might be the object of secret arrangements among
other Powers," and the benefits arising from the "immunity of isolation."[69]
The two contribute to the historiography, or discourse formation, of the
period, which in the first instance take the form of "fear-mongering over
invasion and full-throated calls for patriotism," but as Hendley reminds us,
"social arguments . . . also played a surprisingly prominent role."[70] The fol-

lowing section examines the sociocultural contribution affecting the final policy decision to scrap the entire tunnel project.

## THE CHANNEL TUNNEL CRISIS:
## THE PUBLIC AND CULTURAL DISCOURSE

The vivacious and irascible Victorian prime minister, Lord Palmerston, had influenced public views on the subject of the tunnel twenty-five years earlier in a comment to H.R.H. Albert, the Prince Consort. The German-born prince had outlined his eagerness regarding a tunnel to the prime minister, to which Palmerston replied tartly, "You would think very differently if you had been born in this island."[71] Wolseley's views echoed these same themes in arguing that "the interest taken in the subject in France is greater than in England" and appeared "natural in a nation with an army of three quarters of a million disciplined men."[72] The vast outpourings of printed public opinion cut a similar swath buoyed by a national consciousness preoccupied with concepts of national uniqueness drawn from a thousand years of geographic separateness. A distinct narrative was generated by the "coverage in newspapers and journals," and contributed fully to constituting a pervasive *national* discourse when printed reactions subsequently emerged from "Parliament, [which] greatly exceeded that given in the previous year."[73] Indeed the majority of published correspondence actively attempted to incite the nation "to a sense of its helpless condition and its powerlessness to resist a formidable invasion," and to indict national projects that contributed to these fears.[74]

### The *Nineteenth Century* Petition

The press reacted typically to the evidence given to the Scientific Committee. *The Times* "rejoiced" to see Parliament fail "to secure for [Watkin] those measures of legislative and judicial sanction necessary to enable him to continue his ridiculous route."[75] *The Railway News* asked stingingly whether "E. Watkin imagine[s] that the British public, having accepted with the most thoroughgoing accord the opinion of the military authorities . . . would [now] be more reconciled to the scheme, because the ruffianism of Paris and Lyons look forward hopefully to the time when they will be enabled to extend their benevolent schemes of rapine, plunder and bloodshed to this country?"[76]

Alongside the media maelstrom, a singular event then took place. The *Nineteenth Century*, a journal of educated middle- and upper-class perspectives on political and cultural themes, became the forum for a mass public petition. As a unified narrative, the petition was far more effective than the barrage of articles, editorials, and pamphlets, and was able to dismiss with

singularly effective—even venomous—candor the advantages of the tunnel. Because of the nature of its signatories, the petition also constituted a
clear social index of the pervasive turbulence of public feeling against the
tunnel. Circulated under the title "Protest against this mad project of turning England into a promontory of France," the petition published articles
and signatories in the April and May issues of 1882, and was effective in
a number of ways.[77] First, it drew together the network of English newspapers, thus providing a powerful discursive nexus of media that anchored
"the registering of a sustained protest."[78] Second, the petition incorporated
the perspectives of notable intellectuals, thus widening the sphere of the
debate from a narrow military preoccupation to wider sections of the well-
informed public. The Poet Laureate, Lord Tennyson, along with Robert
Browning, Herbert Spencer, and Thomas Huxley, signed. The petition then
expanded into the moral realm, further complicating the matter as one of
both national duty and normative obligation to the Christian precepts inherent in Victorian Englishness. In a display of stunning ecumenism, both
Cardinal Manning and the Archbishop of Canterbury signed the petition,
along with two hundred clergymen from various denominations. Morality
then widened to class; members of the aristocracy duly signed, along with
influential members of the professional and working classes, notably the
governor of the Bank of England[79] and the president of the Royal Academy,
who helpfully "confirmed the tunnel would be in bad taste."[80] A final sense
of national urgency was added by the signatures of some seventeen admi-
rals and fifty-nine generals, lending the issue a distinctly military image
endorsed by Wolseley and the Duke of Cambridge.

Comprehensive and representative, the petition symbolizes a genuinely
national discourse that saw "the literary, scientific and artistic world joined
in opposition."[81] Ranging widely in their social spheres, the participants
were united publicly in their "emphatic protest" around a single theme
that "joining England to the Continent of Europe by a Railroad under the
Channel . . . would involve this country in military dangers and liabilities
from which, as an island, it has hitherto been happily free."[82] More importantly, the petition also functioned as a *constitutive* element of the broader
overall discourse by isolating and refining a given theme, popularizing and
politicizing it until it operated as a singular mode of collective self-reference
conveying a theme of specifically "national" content. The ideas at work in
the petition thus arguably possess a measure of causal agency, as they im-
pelled the signatories to declare their position publicly, which in turn was
catalytic to the final resolution of Parliament.

## British Geopolitics and English National Characteristics

Both the petition and the abundant media publications opposing the
tunnel illustrate how deeply the tunnel project had become steeped "in the

domain of psychology more than of business techniques" or even military arguments.[83] Indeed, comments made by the French philosopher Albert Sartiaux in 1914, shortly after the tunnel project had once again been revived and then suppressed, bear out the modal features behind the oppositional discourse generated by the public, the press, and indeed within Parliament:

> When one looks at the objections in Britain for the past forty years to the tunnel, one can see that it is the "imponderables" that are important. Their military and economic fears can be reasonably countered, but not the moral argument. Britain imagines that its splendid isolation is one of the fundamental qualities that determined the progress of the British Empire and it will take a long time for opinion to change.[84]

As illustrated, in addition to reinforcing themes of domestic declinism, the tunnel was also perceived to undermine qualities of the English territoriality that had fashioned the national character. These themes are linked through the understanding that late-Victorian Englishness incorporated the geopolitical ambitions of both Britain and England. Thus, breaching the "silver streak" would reduce the singular uniqueness that the English attached to their insularity as a geographic peculiarity, and the strategic benefits that these afforded the British unit. This explains the argument of the Duke of Cambridge to regard the tunnel not merely as an issue of national security (inherent in the island) but one of national existence (innate in its ambitions and attributes). England, in the words of Clarke,

> was not yet mentally prepared to accept the brutal engineering that would terminate for ever the convenient isolation of "this fortress built by Nature for herself." The emotional inheritance, loaded with the magnificent literary tradition inaugurated by Shakespeare's well-remembered lines about "this scepter'd isle," was far too strong for the less romantic facts of commercial and technological advantage.[85]

The marriage of English territory with English particularism is an ancient one. Familiar to Victorians in 1882, and acclaimed as evidence by its numerous reproductions in defense of English territory, were the words of Shakespeare from *Richard II*, where the island of England is described in magnificent language as:

> [a] royal throne of kings, this scepter'd isle,
> This earth of majesty, this seat of Mars.
> This other Eden, demi-paradise
> . . .
> This nurse, this teeming womb of royal kings[86]

Connotations of Englishness are situated upon the cornerstone of English royal heritage and aristocratic pedigree. The development of this lineage in carving out the political features of the national landscape fashions too the attributes of English gentlemen and women, who, in England or abroad are

> Fear'd by their breed and famous by their birth,
> Renowned for their deeds as far from home,
> For Christian service and true chivalry[87]

Implicit here is the understanding that English (and eventually British) geopolitical strength springs organically from its natural, national advantages. In some sense, English territory begets English attributes and its subsequent political glories in a most natural fashion; they spring innately from the land, effortlessly from the people. From the land to its foreign policy, Shakespeare argued that England must be regarded as

> [a] fortress built by Nature for herself
> Against infection and the hand of war
>
> . . .
>
> This precious stone set in the silver sea,
> Which serves it in the office of a wall,
> Or as a moat defensive to a house,
> Against the envy of less happier lands[88]

Territorial inviolability equals political autonomy, girded by insularity. From Elizabeth I to Victoria, English and later British foreign policy was dedicated to maximizing its imperial capacity abroad, but also to creating a deliberate policy of avoidance involving nearer neighbors. Wolseley, too, acknowledged the "envy of less happier lands" in his memorandum, arguing that a tunnel was "a constant inducement to the unscrupulous foreigner to make war upon us," with England acting as "a bait at the end of the tunnel."[89] Emanating from the sense of physical separateness were concepts of cultural uniqueness, political individuality, and an array of singular qualities by which the nation identified itself and was distinguished from "others."

Initiatives undermining the sufficiency, stability, and distinctiveness of this territory and the wider "fortress" of England were understood in 1882 not only to erode its geopolitical position but to rupture the wider forms of material and ideological selfness peculiar to the cohesion of the English sociopolitical unit. How do these features fit together? As argued by Colin Gray, national culture and subsequent policy choices are linked by perceiving national culture as "modes of thought and action with respect to force, which derives from the perception of the national historical experience, from aspirations for responsible behaviour in national [and international] terms [including] the civic culture and way of life."[90] In this way, national culture provides a constitutive "milieu within which strategy is debated" and which provides a causal tipping point for action.[91] The cultural sense of self at work in broader forms of political identity explains why in 1882, the tunnel was regarded as a breach of the "moat defensive" to the English "house," as a physical representation of the "envy of less happier lands," and the possibilities of "envious siege[s]."[92]

Siege fears were internal as much as external. As Adye had hinted and Wolseley pontificated, far worse than defeat abroad was treachery at home. To provide inducements for treachery was the height of folly. Shakespeare completes his illustration in a manner prophetic of future developments. Should England indeed "lease out" her island reputation:

> England, bound in with the triumphant sea,
> Whose rocky shore beats back the envious siege
> Of watery Neptune, is now bound in with shame,
> With inky blots, and rotten parchments bonds:
> That England, that was wont to conquer others,
> *Hath made a shameful conquest of itself.*[93]

The worst form of conquest is perhaps not foreign invasion invited through "rotten parchment bonds," but rather the conquest of the national self entailed in the ongoing and perceptible slippage of an identity of preeminence and superiority into one "bound in with shame."[94] Both the *Nineteenth Century* petition and Shakespearian versions of nationhood were drawn upon by press and policy makers alike and constituted the combined cultural and political imperatives at work in the oppositional discourse to the tunnel.

## Invasion Literature and the Tunnel

National policies are generated by and frequently representative of the political and cultural elements of the contemporary domestic environment. From the printed dailies to the use of Shakespeare in defense of national interests, English national culture reveals a coincidence of identity-based themes at work in the ethos of policy, informing the English nation of its cultural interests and the British state of its political objectives. The fears inherent in the construction of a tunnel are thus a mixture of national and foreign policy, based on a domestic political culture already steeped in the dichotomy of change vs. changelessness, and the genre of literature that sharpened such fears by adding a new, dangerous, foreign "other." Here, invasion literature works as a "purposive" discourse by consolidating in a given narrative themes of national identity and national interest that ultimately provide the substance for any subsequent policy decisions taken on these same issues. As examined more fully in chapter 5, invasion literature had become a well-established genre of Victorian England, one which merged public and political interests more potently than is generally acknowledged.[95] As an example, the 1871 publication of *The Battle of Dorking* by Sir George Chesney provoked a public crisis regarding military unpreparedness far greater than the usual deluge of public pamphlets. Popular culture and high politics became so thoroughly entwined that Prime Minister Gladstone publicly cautioned the House against the errors of alarmism generated by the popularity of *The Battle of Dorking*, thereby elevating invasion literature from madcap publishing venture to a cultural compass.[96] Invasion literature then transformed again into full-blown foreign policy guide when in September 1871, Parliament passed the first bill allowing the assembly of a large number of troops for training regimes, precisely as advocated by Chesney. In unquestionably clear fashion, a discourse had been generated, constituted by the nature of alarmist anxieties that gripped the country, in which the publication of *The Battle of Dorking* was causally linked to the specific policy decision to modernize the army.

The aim of this type of "purposive fiction" was twofold. First, "to terrify the reader by a clear and merciless demonstration of the consequences to be expected from a country's shortcomings"; second, "*to prove the rightness of national policy* by describing the course of a victorious war in the near future," either a policy taken or in the pipeline.[97] At the time of the tunnel crisis (1882–1883), a wave of invasion narratives was produced.[98] In these narratives, the nation became the dramatized protagonist, while the tunnel lay in antagonist opposition. Dramatic tension was produced in both press and committee evidence, and the English public succeeded admirably in suspending their disbelief regarding invasion. Two of the most popular invasion fictions are briefly examined below, and demonstrate how this culture of anxiety generated a pervasive discourse of alarm that was to have a distinct, long-term effect on British national security.

## How John Bull Lost London

*How John Bull Lost London: The Capture of the Channel Tunnel* is a straightforward narrative in which the tunnel allows a breach of national security permitting French invaders to decimate the English army, raze London to the ground, and then sue for peace. There are a number of interesting clues to the domestic fears promoting the oppositional discourse to the tunnel in 1882.[99] John Smith, the main character "had in a dull sort of way believed his country was quite invincible, till the rough awakening."[100] The tunnel divides national opinion, in which only a "minority of intelligent Englishmen . . . feared that a huge, irreparable blunder was being made . . . but they were laughed to scorn."[101] The English cabinet permits the tunnel. However, due to its obsolete vessels the British navy (always comprising "English ships") is heavily defeated by "the French ironclad navy [which] had equalled . . . that of England."[102]

Sir Wolseley commands the valiant but undermanned troops, who, despite their "firm shooting" and "steady" fighting are grossly outgunned by the French, suggesting quantity may ultimately trump quality in warfare. As the country approaches utter ruin, "the English fleet . . . [which] had never quite lost," returns from Egypt to blockade the Thames, provide reinforcements, and "persuade" the French to retire.[103] The author argues that "England was at length waking up"; his arguments form a cogent political platform regarding the realities of a weak navy, an archaic Admiralty, a nonexistent army, an unfortified coastline, and centrally, the significant national threat entailed in constructing the tunnel.[104] To reassert national greatness, the tunnel is destroyed, with the implication that alarmist discourses must necessarily prevail over policies such as the tunnel that could result in "a terrible blow to English pride."[105]

### Submarina

The second invasion narrative, entitled *Submarina: Green Eyes and Blue Glasses: An Amusing Spectacle of Short Sight*, is a fictional Commons debate on the tunnel between shareholders and legislators.[106] Sir Edwin Watkin is the thinly disguised villain, and England the heroic but incautious protagonist. Watkin is dubbed a traitor for proposing such a scheme, his company members "conspirators" and those opposed full of "firm purpose to shed every drop of their blood in defence of the Silver Streak."[107] The House argues over "impulsive Frenchmen" and "perfidious foreigners" who could use the tunnel to gain access to the south coast. The Tory opposition is depicted not only as the true national party for their patriotic and spirited heckling of Watkin, but the arbiters of a quintessential English value previously outlined by Wolseley and the Duke of Cambridge—*duty*. Tories to a man vow to "never for an instant forget the call of *duty* . . . but shall withstand this atrocious attempt on the safety of [the] country" with fervor and dedication.[108] The Liberals, by contrast, are "men who had . . . wilfully betrayed the trust reposed in them by throwing their country's interests to the winds whenever 'party exigencies' demanded such treachery."[109] The MPs then form a committee whose chairman exhorts "that they would not be true Englishmen . . . if they neglected their obvious duty at that solemn time. . . . That obvious duty . . . [was] the preservation of British interests."[110] The committee fails to reach a verdict, national agitation dies away, and the tunnel is built. The reader is criticized for having participated in the dramatic vehemence of a realistic Commons debate and then assured in the most unconvincing manner possible that "there has never been a single threat directed against Britain which could raise any definite fears . . . of invading through that tunnel."[111]

Both of these narratives convey the vivid anxieties of 1882. *John Bull* illustrates the nation's ability to embrace such polities unwittingly while *Submarina* outlines the implications of a more reasoned rejecting or constructing of the tunnel, both with disastrous results. Using the specific political issue of the tunnel, the "strong or weak points . . . moral, or political, or naval, or military" of these two narratives are "presented in a triumphant or in a catastrophic manner" to effect the cultural context from which policy was fashioned.[112] Such narratives provided additional ballast to the oppositional discourse generated in the press. Discourse in this way functions as a demonstrably broad spectrum of oral and written issue-based opinion providing a ready index of the cultural context constituting and causally affecting policy decisions.

## Case Study Premise: Political and Cultural Discourse and Policy-Making

The original tunnel proposal had been "primarily a business venture, designed to attract financial and commercial groups on both sides of the Channel," with those participating in Anglo-French trade hoping to initiate "the prospect of long-term economic gain."[113] However, neither "material gains" nor the prospect of political amity to "cement the friendship" between England and France could prevail.[114] Denying passage to France, Wolseley tapped into national opinion by stating that the tunnel would "destroy the great defence of the country upon which we have hitherto depended, namely . . . the value of the channel."[115] The Channel, as the guarantor of territorial integrity and physical marker of the nation-navy dyad, could not be tampered with: "We have in the past depended chiefly for our defence upon the Channel, and upon our fleet, and the proposed scheme annuls the use of both."[116]

While the Board of Trade and Scientific Committee of 1882 had both sparked a public maelstrom, their evidence was ultimately inconclusive.[117] A further examination was demanded by Gladstone, who appointed a Joint Select Committee of both houses of Parliament, chaired by Lord Lansdowne, announced on 26 February 1883.[118] The Committee was more comprehensive in scope than its predecessor and interviewed forty individuals, including Watkin, Grosvenor, Hawkshaw, and H.R.H. George, the Duke of Cambridge. Due to the decisive impact of his contributions to the Scientific Committee (subsequently publicized in numerous dailies), it was the evidence of Wolseley that impressed upon the committee what had already been imprinted upon the national consciousness: namely, the combined public and political discourse of territory-based opposition to the tunnel. Bonavia argues that Wolseley's memorandum to the parliamentary committee "is a surprising document, since the adjutant-general did not deal with the *military aspects* as a matter of logistics but *indulged in rhetoric*."[119]

While uncharacteristic as a measure of professional judgment, the Wolseley memorandum is, however, wholly representative of the discursive, emotive, and intrinsically rhetorical responses used by policy makers in determining and defending elements of national identity.

First, Bonavia purports that "Wolseley had forgotten or purposely omitted the requirements of artillery, stores, equipment, road transport, victualling and the support services."[120] In light of Wolseley's military background, this appears a somewhat flawed argument; indeed, Wolseley could have made an excellent case against the tunnel in precisely such military terms. That he failed to mention such issues suggests that his entire perception was grounded in the question of national survival rather than the minutiae of defense and transport. Like the Duke of Cambridge, Wolseley's memorandum (and indeed the plethora of evidence in the daily papers of 1882 and 1883) suggests that not only was the tunnel incompatible with contemporary military logistics, but the entire concept was incommensurate, first, with English geopolitical status, second, with its identity as a naval rather than military nation, and third, with its communitarian ethos as a territory of relatively primordial qualities sacred in its unique separateness and those of its inhabitants.

Military, transport, and security logistics denoted merely material, quantifiable interests; the precept of national survival, however, symbolized the entire spectrum of English identity, including its political and cultural offshoots. As Georges Valbert wrote of the 1882 tunnel panic:

> Those who reduce everything to mathematics and who wish to reckon only with facts forget that the popular imagination is a fact in its own right, and one that has to be taken into consideration. . . . The frightened [English] imagination believes it sees pass through this tunnel many things which they do not like, institutions which displease them . . . every kind of political epidemic and subversive paradox, revolutions, calamities. Pure dreams, one might say! Dreams or the truth, nerves are anathema to reason, and nerves once stimulated often determine the events of the world.[121]

A disturbed national imagination clearly determined the priority of national policy for Wolseley. However, as Cohen argues, "the attention of decision makers [was] drawn to the events in question because they concerned or involved areas strategically or emotionally of high priority."[122] The Tunnel symbolized an abrogation of territorial sovereignty, which, from the English vantage point, was of "immense strategic, historic, and sentimental importance," and an excellent example of combined instrumental and symbolic aspects.[123]

Second, Bonavia criticizes Wolseley for arguing in a rhetorical style. Wolseley's comments, however, echo the blend of historic, literary, and social images found within the Victorian modes of culture, which likewise comprised the framework of identity from which ancillary issues such as defense and security were generated. While oratorical and allegorical in places, Wolseley's demand that "John Bull . . . not endanger his birth-right, his liberty, his property . . . whether he be a patriot or merely a selfish cosmopolitan" is entirely in keeping with Victorian ideals of the preeminent English national self and the characteristic style regularly made use of by politicians of the day.[124]

Insisting on military details regarding the tunnel, Bonavia, like Wendt, remains preoccupied with exogenous and material details, neglecting their endogenous foundations. Both overlook the process whereby the rhetoric of identity fashions the nexus of "selfness" which only subsequently informs external aspects (such as threat) conducted according to the instrumentality of logistics. If these external aspects come under threat, the nexus of self is immediately made use of in reestablishing a workable, coherent sense of self upon which to extend issues of national interest. Wolseley concentrated mainly upon the *figurative* understandings of the English nation, precisely because in his view, the tunnel functioned as a *metaphor* for national threat, rather than simply a military challenge.

It is unsurprising, then, that the tunnel, perceived as an issue of national survival, should be defended in such sweeping tones by individuals who perceived themselves to be defending the very core of corporate English identity. During the 1882 tunnel episode, neither Wolseley nor the Duke of Cambridge, as the highest military personages in England, had conducted themselves as purely military counselors. They are transformed, like the tunnel itself, into national symbols, resorting to history, to Shakespeare, to "poetry, pathos" in a broad "appeal to national passion and national fear."[125]

Two significant elements appeared threatened: the security of Britain as a political unit and the sense of cultural inviolability by which late nineteenth-century Englishness was chiefly defined. Constituting a discourse that stipulated a defense of ontological identity via a retention of territorial inviolability, Wolseley's memorandum had a "decisive effect in influencing the joint select committee," and a causal effect upon the 1883 policy decision by the Liberal government to block any further attempts at tunnel construction.[126] This discourse constituted an ethos of national opposition that characterized the perceptions and motivations of the Board of Trade Committee, the Scientific Committee, and the Joint Parliamentary Committee by *constituting* the content and tone of their various reports. The discourse, then, worked *causally* to produce a policy environment wholly opposed to tunnel construction, which contributed overwhelmingly to the ultimate decision in 1883 to veto the Private Member Bill regarding future tunnel construction.[127] This discourse, springing from public and political roots, also provoked an additional outcome in an unusual display of violence. At the height of the anti-tunnel mêlée in the spring of 1882, after the stimulating effects of the *Nineteenth Century* petition, a mob congregated outside the offices of the Channel Tunnel Company in Westminster and resorted to smashing its windows.

While Lansdowne, as chairman of the Joint Select Committee, was well disposed to the tunnel scheme, only three other members were prepared to sign his final report. Six remained opposed, all of whom submitted individual reports "and none of these secured the entire approval of a majority of the committee."[128] Chamberlain then announced to the House "that the Government had accepted the 6–4 verdict of the Joint Select Committee."[129] With this announcement, "authority to proceed with both tunnels was denied. . . . The defence argument was to remain the British government's reason for refusing authorisation of a Channel fixed link" until 1955.[130] "[D] ismayed by the British Government's decision," French tunneling ceased at Sangette on 18 March 1883 and on 1 July Watkin was compelled to close his tunneling works at Shakespeare Cliff.[131]

Based on a neoclassical realist foundation, the role of discourse in the above analysis is based on the implicit understanding that the political issue of tunnel construction "ceas[ed] to be a private matter for the higher levels of the nation" but concerned the entire population, as members of a social unit with cultural ideas of belonging, and policy-based methods to secure such objectives.[132] Admittedly, "political advantages [or themes], being intangible and in the realm of public attitudes, are . . . difficult to evaluate."[133] However, the force and implications of many political issues regarding security mirrored the vivid persuasiveness used in purposive fiction; it is relatively easy to identify the process whereby politics itself became a national narrative, and equally, how popular culture reflects current political issues. The site of overlap between the two is the realm of discourse, which as a unified body of national reference is able to culturally influence the broad national environment of policy decisions. Again, the direction of thematic conveyance is relatively unimportant. A top-down or bottom-up dialectic illustrates equally well how a narrative focused upon a given theme (such as territoriality) generates a wide-ranging causal impetus for a specific policy change.

In 1883, "Gladstone had maintained that there was no better place in which to establish the *opinion* of the English people than the House of Commons . . . rather than that of the Joint Select Committee."[134] A decade later, Sir Edward Grey maintained that parliamentary decisions regarding the national interest (particularly during periods of crisis) would be dictated on a case-by-case basis, and centrally, "based on the mood of *public opinion.*"[135] There can be no greater demonstration of the constitutive and causal links between discourse and policy than this conscious and articulated awareness by both a prime minister and a foreign secretary of the power of public narrative in affecting parliamentary and policy-based outcomes. In sum, politics provided a narrative spectrum wherein cultural genres provided clear purposive elements. The preface to the anonymous 1884 work entitled *The Siege of London* details the purposive agency of culture, particularly during a time of heightened nationalism or perceived crisis: "The purpose of these stories is either to criticise the action of the party in power, or *to exert enough influence on public opinion to oblige the government to take precautions* against possible troubles or probable conflagrations, and by these means secure the increase and improvement of the means of defending the country."[136]

## CONCLUSION

The uneasy history of the tunnel project reflects the ongoing tension between national modes of historic self-reference and the influence of modernity in a specific government initiative. The objections to the completion of the tunnel in 1994, while absorbing new political realities, still echoed the strain of those of 1882. As chapter 7 will demonstrate, the attitude of England to contemporary Europe continues to be one of cautious self-recognition and wary engagement, gravely marked by "simple xenophobia, the dislike of strengthening links with Europe," a trend which "distinguish[ed] much of the debate over Britain's entry into the Common Market" and characterized the 1994 construction of the tunnel.[137] Indeed, press coverage of the two eras hardly differed at all, and "[o]ver-simplification and mis-statements abounded."[138] The result in both 1882 and 1994 was that "the great British public retained its original [discursive] prejudices and these were reflected in the often irrational attitudes [and policies] of members of parliament."[139]

After the 1882–1883 outcry, the project was given up, and national resources for the following three decades were directed at rebuilding the increasingly obsolete navy. In 1890, the Commons attempted to vote on the tunnel project, but "still in the grip of panic [Wolseley and others] had helped to engender," failed in its attempt.[140] By 1906, a new Anglo-French scheme had been proposed for an electric-rail tunnel. It too met with little success. The project was revived immediately before World War I, but the joint efforts of the Board of Trade and the Committee of Imperial Defence (CID) dismissed it as unfeasible. With the cessation of hostilities, the defense argument was attacked in both military and literary discourse. Marshal Foch "maintained that a Channel Tunnel would have halved the war's length by allowing efficient despatch of the British Expeditionary Force," while A. C. Doyle expounded its merits in the *Fortnightly Review*, a theme subsequently echoed for years by Churchill.[141] By 1929, significant government interest established a royal commission to study the contending schemes of the Channel Tunnel Company and its rival, the London and Paris Railway Company. The findings, while vaguely positive, were quashed in 1930 when the CID again ruled against its suitability. Only after World War II did the perennial argument of national defense finally yield; in 1955 Harold Macmillan was asked "to what extent strategical objections still prevent[ed] the construction of a road-rail tunnel under the Channel; his reply was "[s]carcely at all."[142] However, surveys and the 1963 White Paper failed to ignite interest, and despite some government support, the project was again officially cancelled in 1975.

Under Prime Minister Thatcher, supportive agreements were announced with President Francois Mitterrand in 1984, and royal assent was given in 1987.[143] In 1990, the English and French tunneling machines of the Eurotunnel Company broke through the two Running Tunnels. Work began on the railway itself; its ending commemorated by a eulogy in the *Financial Times* entitled "RIP Little England, buried at sea today."[144] In May 1994, the Channel Tunnel opened for passenger traffic. These developments appear somewhat contradictory to the themes of territorial sovereignty and national inclusiveness examined above. However, it is clear from reviewing the notes by Thatcher and her adviser, Geoffrey Howe, that the tunnel was to represent a number of specifically British, if not English, characteristics (insofar as they were designated as British by Thatcher herself). First, Britain as an innovative, creative, and industrial nation would now *extend* its mechanical genius to creating a unique subterranean link. Despite the historical magnitude of French agency, it was understood to be a British-designed project. Further, the tunnel itself would be British, symbolizing an *extension* rather than an abrogation of sovereignty. Emanating *from* the territory of England the tunnel would extend beneath the English Channel (itself another form of territorial integrity) until it reached its French midpoint, and continue to Calais. This differs from the perspective of 1882 in which the tunnel as a physical feature represented overtly European power extending from France toward the isles, ultimately "invading" the coast of England, an issue that underwrote much of the concern by Wolseley to fortify Dover Castle. Third, the tunnel linked Britain to the Continent as a part of a free-trade zone that upheld Thatcherist principles of free-market capitalism; it was thus an entrepreneurial project inculcating recent ideals of British national sufficiency and regional growth (rather than earlier ideas of English survival) and not a trial project regarding aspects of federalism. Indeed, by the early nineties, the British economy regained strength, an advance that "rested less on Britain's traditional strength in manufacturing, which continued to lag far below pre-1970 levels of production, than on financial services, credit, investment, and a consumer boom."[145]

Engaging in European competition by way of the "Chunnel" was viewed as a way to increase this new strength and add greater focus to the status of London as a global financial center, newly connected to Europe. Lastly, quite apart from any overtly national attribute, and in the high Victorian style of pomp and ceremony, the tunnel was to be a legacy to the nation of renewed Conservative values bestowed by Thatcher herself. As Howe wrote, it became "a grand project. Subsequently she defended it by reference to having done something that will stand in memory of this administration."[146] The impact of the tunnel on English and British identity remains ambiguous. Within a year of its completion, Conservative party anti-Europe policies had become even more vehement, starkly contrasting the physical representation of Anglo-French cooperation operating beneath the Channel. However, cross-channel traffic rose significantly in the first few years of its use; "there were signs that a sympathetic awareness of the Continent was starting to develop which cannot be ignored . . . [in] reach[ing] an accurate conclusion about British attitudes to Europe" in the 1990s.[147]

Stalked by "distrust, bigotry and political indecision," the tunnel possesses obvious implications for English national identity.[148] The opposition to a physical link between English and continental territory is a discourse that cannot be registered in material theories alone. If realists were to judge the event, the English unit should indeed have secured its ability to protect its autonomy while maximizing its interests. Much of the military responses of Wolseley and the Duke of Cambridge would be familiar; however, the vast panoply of domestic motivations at work in 1882 would be unavailable for use in a theory that regards actor states as constrained emanations of the international structure. Further, as the majority of realist theories are innately material in ilk, they are less well disposed to explain how a policy decision was taken based on discourses running counter to the promise of economic gain, political retrenchment, and regional stability.

The 1882 tunnel episode must therefore be analyzed from a domestic perspective, driven by domestic nuances of national self-perception and the need to maintain the role of an autonomous, viable cultural and political entity. Churchill himself realized this: "There are few projects against which there exists a deeper and more enduring prejudice than the construction of a railway tunnel between Dover and Calais."[149] The existence of such prejudice at the heart of the oppositional discourse must therefore be examined from an endogenous perspective that is capable of analyzing the congruence between cultural perceptions and political motivations. As a hallmark of the "obsessive mutual edginess" between English ethos and the continent, this case study establishes the framework in which chapter 8 will explore the most encounters between the English heart of Britain and the European continent.[150] While Barker contends that "the Channel Tunnel will do more to tie Britain in to the rest of Europe than anything dreamed up by the European Union," the current domestic perception regarding the euro appears every bit as intransigent as the attitudes of 1882 toward the tunnel.[151]

# NOTES

1. M. H. Abrams, ed., *Norton Anthology of English Literature*, 5th ed. (New York: W.W. Norton and Co., 1987), 1961.

2. D. Campbell, *Writing Security: United States Foreign Policy and the Politics of Identity* (Minneapolis: University of Minnesota Press, 1992), 18.

3. D. Newman, "Boundaries, Borders, and Barriers: Changing Geographic Perspectives on Territorial Lines," in *Identities, Borders, Orders: Rethinking International Relations Theory*, ed. M. Albert, D. Jacobson, and Y. Lapid (Minneapolis: University of Minnesota Press, 2001), 146.

4. C. S. Harris, "Channel Tunnel Facts," *Geology Shop*, www.geologyshop.co.uk/chtunfacts.htm (11 Feb. 2003), 4.

5. M. R. Bonavia, *The Channel Tunnel Story* (Newton Abbot, UK: David and Charles, 1987), 26.

6. *Channel Tunnel Parliamentary Blue Book*, War Office, 1882, London, Her Majesty's Stationery Office (hererafter HMSO), 2. In 1882, a publication entitled *Correspondence with Reference to the Proposed Construction of a Channel Tunnel, Presented to Both Houses of Parliament by Command of Her Majesty* became available. The text contains original and extensive correspondence, evidence, committee reports, and a range of recorded military and political opinions dating from 1867 to 1882, all of which allowed Parliament to make an informed decision in 1883 regarding the viability of the tunnel project. The Blue Book is an invaluable primary source of the views disseminated in 1882 and has been extensively used as an evidential and agential frame of reference in this case study in examining the discourses of tunnel support and opposition. Other primary sources used for this case study include Cabinet documents from HMSO, assorted documents from the Public Record Office (PRO), the British Railways Board, and War Office (WO) 33/39, *Précis of Papers Relating to Proposed Channel Tunnel*, 1882, London.

7. "Board of Trade Memorandum," *Channel Tunnel Parliamentary Blue Book, War Office*, 12.

8. "Board of Trade Memorandum," 18.

9. "Gladstone to Granville," 21 June 1883, quoted in A. Ramm, ed., *The Political Correspondence of Mr Gladstone and Lord Granville, 1868–1876* (London: Camden, 1952), 845.

10. "Lord Derby Memorandum," *Channel Tunnel Parliamentary Blue Book*, 39.

11. "Board of Trade Memorandum," 40.

12. Bonavia, *The Channel Tunnel Story*, 27.

13. H. Slater and C. Barnett, *The Channel Tunnel* (London: Oxford University Press, 1957), 35.

14. Anglo-French Joint Commission, *Channel Tunnel Parliamentary Blue Book*, 166.

15. Anglo-French Joint Commission, 166.

16. WO (War Office) 32/6269, *War Office Memorandum to the Treasury*, mid-April 1875 (London: PRO) (emphasis added).

17. WO, *War Office Memorandum to the Treasury* (emphasis added).

18. Bonavia, *The Channel Tunnel Story*, 32.

19. WO (War Office) 33/39, *Memorandum*, 12 May 1882 (London: PRO).

20. D. Newsome, *The Victorian World Picture* (London: John Murray, 1997), 30.

21. W. Johnston, *England as It Is: Political, Social and Industrial in the Middle of the Nineteenth Century*, vol. 1 (Dublin: Irish University Press, 1971), 260.

22. W. E. Houghton, *The Victorian Frame of Mind, 1830–1870* (New Haven, CT: Yale: 1957), 41.

23. Newsome, *The Victorian World Picture*, 35. See also G. Best, *Mid-Victorian Britain, 1851–1875* (London: Macmillan, 1979).

24. Newsome, *The Victorian World Picture*, 37.

25. J. Ruskin, *The Crown of Wild Olive. Four Lectures on Industry and War* (London, 1859), 158. Matthew Arnold expounded on a society turned pagan in its worship of railroads and coal, attacking the middle classes not merely for their immoral materialism but their ignorance and dullness, a class dulled by the forces of change and "inadequately equipped for leadership and . . . civilized living." *Culture and Anarchy: An Essay in Political and Social Criticism* ([1869], 1961, London), in Norton, *The Crown of Wild Olive*, 2113.

26. Matthew Arnold quoted in R. Jenkyns, *The Victorians and Ancient Greece* (Oxford: Oxford University Press, 1981), 267

27. Matthew Arnold quoted in R. Jenkyns, *The Victorians and Ancient Greece* (Oxford: Oxford University Press, 1981), 267.

28. Newsome, *The Victorian World Picture*, 38.

29. S. Collini, *English Pasts: Essays in History and Culture* (Oxford: Oxford University Press, 1999).

30. Bonavia, *The Channel Tunnel Story*, 32.

31. Corelli and Barnett, cited in Bonavia, *The Channel Tunnel Story*, 32–33.

32. Sir Edwin Watkin presided as chairman over three companies: the South Eastern Railway (SER), the Anglo-French Submarine Railway Company (1875), and the Submarine Continental Railway Company (1881). However, only the SER rivaled Grosvenor and Hawkshaw's Channel Tunnel Company in the 1882 tunnel crisis. R. Garrett, *Cross Channel* (London: Methuen, 1972).

33. J. Harris, *Private Lives, Public Spirit: Britain, 1870–1914* (London: Oxford University Press, 1993), 4.

34. "Board of Trade Memorandum," 182. See also WO (War Office) 33/39, *Board of Trade Correspondence Relative to Experimental Works in Connection with the Channel Tunnel* (London: PRO, 1882).

35. "Board of Trade Memorandum," 192.

36. Childers, cited in K. Wilson, *Channel Tunnel Visions, 1850–1945: Dreams and Nightmares* (London: The Hambledon Press, 1994), 33.

37. Bonavia, *The Channel Tunnel Story*, 35.

38. "Scientific Committee Findings," *Channel Tunnel Parliamentary Blue Book*, 194–202.

39. "Scientific Committee Findings," 200. Watkin also demonstrated how one could "drown [the tunnel] in five minutes or five seconds . . . [how] by hydraulic arrangements you could close it up, and if you unship the machinery, nobody on earth could open it again for months." "Scientific Committee Findings," 200.

40. "Scientific Committee Findings," 209.

41. "Scientific Committee Findings," 209.

42. "Scientific Committee Findings," 236–38.

43. With some precision, Sir John Adye illustrated the drawbacks to using the tunnel as a method of invasion: "No general, I presume, would dream of bringing his troops . . . for the invasion of England by rail . . . from France to England, through a Tunnel over 20 miles long, and with only a hole to emerge from at the exit. Considering the extreme facility of destroying the invading troops as they successfully arrived, by means of a small force, with a gun or two, at the mouth of the Tunnel, that idea may be dismissed." "Scientific Committee Findings," 218.

44. "Scientific Committee Findings," 219.

45. "Scientific Committee Findings," 258.

46. Scientific Committee Findings," 219.

47. William Shakespeare, *The Tragedy of Richard II*, Act 2, Scene 1, in *The Histories and Poems of William Shakespeare*, ed. E. Dowden (London: Oxford University Press, 1912), p. 121.

48. "Report From the Joint Committee of the House of Lords and the House of Commons on The Channel Tunnel," (*Papers By Command*: 1883) "Précis," iii.

49. "Scientific Committee Findings," 218.

50. A. Muir Wood, J. Bird, J. Thompson, K. Wickenden, H. Grimon, M. Bonavia, "The Channel Tunnel," *The Geographical Journal* 139, Part II (June, 1973): 270.

51. H. C. G. Forbes, *Shall We Have a Tunnel?* (London: Simpkin, Marshall, & Co., 1883), 22.

52. "Memorandum 10 December 1881," *Channel Tunnel Parliamentary Blue Book*, 210.

53. "Memorandum 10 December 1881," 215–16.

54. "Memorandum 10 December 1881."

55. Wilson, *Channel Tunnel Visions*, 27.

56. "Observations by H.R.H. Duke of Cambridge," *Channel Tunnel Parliamentary Blue Book*, 299–305. See also WO (War Office) 32/6269 *Works and Buildings: Channel Tunnel*: Appointment of Joint Commission of English and French Governments on code of regulations for promoters of Tunnel Scheme. Reports of Commissioners and Channel Tunnel Defence Committee. Memorandum by Prince George (Duke of Cambridge) (London: PRO, 1881–1882).

57. Forbes, *Shall We Have a Channel Tunnel?* 35.

58. "Observations by H.R.H. Duke of Cambridge," 299–305.

59. "Observations by H.R.H. Duke of Cambridge," 300.

60. M. Hendley, "Help Us to Secure a Strong, Healthy, Prosperous and Peaceful Britain": The Social Arguments of the Campaign for Compulsory Military Service in Britain, 1899–1914," *Canadian Journal of History* 30, no. 2 (August, 1995): 274.

61. "Observations by H.R.H. Duke of Cambridge," 301.

62. "Observations by H.R.H. Duke of Cambridge," 302 (emphasis added).

63. "Observations by H.R.H. Duke of Cambridge."

64. Forbes, *Shall We Have a Channel Tunnel?* 38

65. Forbes, *Shall We Have a Channel Tunnel?* 6. Lord Forbes's remarks at a public lecture echoed the alarmist tones spread by the press and multiplied across the nation: "we could at any time be taken unawares, and either by treachery or stratagem, the Tunnel which we have ourselves made, should point the way to accomplish this and prove our own destruction." Forbes, *Shall We Have a Channel Tunnel?* 6.

66. Forbes, *Shall We Have a Channel Tunnel?* 45–46.

67. Admiral P. H. Colomb, *Memoirs of Sir Astley Cooper Key* (London: Methuen, 1898), 228.

68. FO (Foreign Office) 881/4652, *Tenterden Memorandum*, 17 March 1882, quoted in *British Documents on Foreign Affairs: Reports and Papers from the Foreign Office*, Confidential Print, Part I, Series F, Vol. 10, Doc. 47, ed. K. Bourne and D. C. Watt (Washington, DC: University Publications of America, 1989).

69. FO (Foreign Office) 881/4652, *Tenterden Memorandum*, 17 March 1882. Tenterden argued that "[a]t present, England is secure because she is out of reach; but once let there be a possibility that by a successful war the conquest of England and the command of her vast resources could be secured, a prospect would be opened to French statesmen which it might be very difficult for a man of genius and ambition to resist. If the Tunnel is once constructed the *immunity of isolation* which England has hitherto enjoyed in regard to continental disputes will be at an end" (emphasis added).

70. Hendley, "Help us to secure a strong, healthy, prosperous and peaceful Britain," 261.

71. I. Holliday, G. Marcou, and R. Vickerman, *The Channel Tunnel: Public Policy, Regional Development and European Integration* (London: Belhaven Press, 1991), 8. Lord Palmerston further vilified the 1857 French commission, making clear his lack of support: "What! You pretend to ask us to contribute to a work the object of which is to shorten a distance we find already too short?"

72. "Memorandum 10 December 1881," *Channel Tunnel Parliamentary Blue Book, War Office*, 210. See also Field Marshal Viscount Wolseley, *The Story of a Soldier's Life* (London: A. Constable and Co., 1903). See CAB (Cabinet) 38/25, No. 36, *Memorandum*, 16 June (London: HMSO, 1882).

73. Wilson, *Channel Tunnel Visions*, 39.

74. "Memorandum, 10 December 1881," 214.

75. *The Times*, 1 December 1882.

76. *The Railway News*, 2 December 1882, 550–51. *The Railway News* appeared aggrieved that the public furor surrounding the tunnel prevented a *rational appreciation* of its possibilities, arguing that "it must indeed be most trying for those who are really interested in this great work to see it continually kept before the public . . . [which has] effectually destroyed any remaining desire for the making of the Channel Tunnel on the part of the respectable British public."

77. J. Knowles, "Protest against This Mad Project of Turning England into a Promontory of France," *Nineteenth Century*, April and May, 1882.

78. Wilson, *Channel Tunnel Visions*, 39. The *Nineteenth Century* petition included the signatures of the editors of the *Morning Post, St. James's Gazette*, the *Spectator*, and *Lloyd's Weekly News*.

79. As Wilson observes, "The House of Lords, the Church of England and the magistracy were especially well represented: the columns of Reverends and JPs very nearly equalled those composed of Lieutenant-Generals, Major-Generals, Lieutenant-Colonels, Majors and Captains." Wilson, *Channel Tunnel Visions*, 39.

80. T. Zeldin, "Europe: The Bulldog Barrier," *Guardian*, 2 November 1990.

81. Bonavia, *The Channel Tunnel Story*, 32.

82. "The Channel Tunnel and Public Opinion," *Nineteenth Century*, April 1882.

83. P. E. Prestwich, "French Businessmen and the Channel Tunnel Project of 1913," *French Historical Studies* 9, no. 4 (Autumn 1976): 706.

84. Fédération des industriels et commerçants français, *Bulletin*, Paris, February 1914.

85. I. F. Clarke, "Forecasts of Warfare in Fiction, 1803–1914," *Comparative Studies in Society and History* 10, no. 1 (October 1967): 97.

86. Shakespeare, *The Tragedy of Richard II*, Act 2, Scene 1, 121.

87. Shakespeare, *The Tragedy of Richard II*, 121.

88. Shakespeare, *The Tragedy of Richard II*, 121.

89. "Memorandum, 10 December 1881," 216.

90. C. Gray, *Nuclear Strategy and National Style* (Lanham, MD: Hamilton Press, 1986), 36–37.

91. Gray, *Nuclear Strategy and National Style*, 36–37.

92. Shakespeare, *The Tragedy of Richard II*, Act 2, Scene 1, 122.

93. Shakespeare, *The Tragedy of Richard II*, 122 (emphasis added).

94. Shakespeare, *The Tragedy of Richard II*, 122.

95. The first singularly potent piece of invasion literature was published in 1871, entitled *The Battle of Dorking*, written by Sir George Chesney, in order to draw attention to the issue of national defense. Wildly popular, it successfully convulsed the nation in the throes of invasion hysteria by relying upon previously inculcated understandings of loss, fragmentation, and unease. Invasion literature also relied upon easily recognized portions of the national identity such that its discursive reversal proved all the more effective in infusing a given narrative with a sharply moral as well as agentially purposive aim.

96. *Annual Register, A View of the History, Politicks and Literature of the Year 1882*, available from ProQuest LLC, Ann Arbor, Michigan (accessed 5 January 2006): 108.

97. Clarke, "Forecasts of Warfare in Fiction," 33.

98. Containing predictive and purposive elements, the majority of invasion literature augmented the oppositional discourse regarding the tunnel, as evident in their titles: A. F., *The Seizure of the Channel Tunnel*; Anon., *The Story of the Channel Tunnel*; Sir William Butler, *The Invasion of England*; Anon., *The Battle of Boulogne; or, How Calais Became English Again*; T. A. Guthrie, *The Seizure of the Channel Tunnel*; all published in London in 1882. There were a number of similar publications in 1883, which as their titles revealed, imply that the tunnel was not an altogether English concern, but a British concern with global implications: Anon., *The Battle of Moy; or, How Ireland Gained Her Independence in 1892–1894*; Anon., *The Battle of Port Said*; Anon., *How Glasgow Ceased to Flourish*; Anon., *India in 1983*; Ulidia Calcutta (pseud.), *The Battle of Newry*.

99. "Grip," *How John Bull Lost London: The Capture of the Channel Tunnel* (London, Sampson Low, Marston, Searle and Rivington, 1882).

100. *How John Bull Lost London,* 13–14.

101. *How John Bull Lost London,* 16.

102. *How John Bull Lost London,* 53.

103. *How John Bull Lost London,* 84.

104. *How John Bull Lost London,* 117.

105. *How John Bull Lost London,* 123.

106. Anon., *Submarina: Green Eyes and Blue Glasses: An Amusing Spectacle of Short Sight* (London: Yates Alexander and Shepheard, 1882).

107. *Submarina,* 7. Indeed, MPs involved in the debate are "deafened by cries of 'Down with France,' 'Down with Watkin,' 'England for Ever,' and other sentiments as brim-full . . . of the most touching and sensible patriotism." *Submarina,* 10. When Watkin attempts to persuade the prime minister of the tunnel's merits, a Radical MP asks the Speaker "whether the Government intended to have [Watkin] incarcerated as a dangerous lunatic, or impeached for high treason." *Submarina,* 12.

108. *Submarina,* 19 (emphasis added).

109. *Submarina,* 22.

110. *Submarina,* 29.

111. *Submarina,* 45.

112. I. F. Clarke, *Voices Prophesying War, 1763–1849* (Oxford: Oxford University Press, 1992), 33.

113. Prestwich, "French Businessmen and the Channel Tunnel," 691.

114. Prestwich, "French Businessmen and the Channel Tunnel," 701.

115. "Farrer Departmental Committee Evidence," *Channel Tunnel Parliamentary Blue Book,* 220.

116. "Farrer Departmental Committee Evidence," 221.

117. See CAB (Cabinet) 41/16/45, *Adjournment of Parliament; The Channel Tunnel; Zululand,* Aug. 12 (London: PRO, 1882). In July 1882, Chamberlain had taken Watkin to the High Court in a final effort to prevent any further digging, accusing him of "a flagrant breach of faith." In August 1882, Watkin's South Eastern Railway Company and the Submarine Continental Company were forbidden by the High Court to continue any work until the outcome of the Joint Select Committee. Wilson, *Channel Tunnel Visions,* 40–41.

118. "Précis of the Report from the Joint Committee of the House of Lords and the House of Commons on The Channel Tunnel," *Papers by Command* (London: HMSO, 1883). The Committee was announced in the House of Lords by Foreign Secretary Granville, which was a clear indication of the level of national security now attached to the tunnel project. Five members of each house were charged "to inquire whether it is expedient that Parliamentary sanction should be given to a submarine communication between England and France; and to consider whether any or what conditions should be imposed by Parliament in the event of such communication being sanctioned." C. Bradlaugh, MP, *The Channel Tunnel: Ought the Democracy to Oppose or Support It?* (London: A. Bonner, 1887), 13.

119. Bonavia, *Channel Tunnel Visions,* 35 (emphasis added).

120. Bonavia, *Channel Tunnel Visions,* 35.

121. G. Valbert, "L'agitation Anglaise contre le tunnel de la Manche," *Revue des Deux Mondes* 51 (1882): 680.

122. R. Cohen, "Threat Perception in International Crisis," *Political Science Quarterly* 93, no. 1 (Spring 1978): 96.

123. Cohen, "Threat Perception in International Crisis," 96

124. "Memorandum 10 December 1881," *Channel Tunnel Parliamentary Blue Book*, 210.

125. Bradlaugh, *The Channel Tunnel*, 17.

126. Bradlaugh, *The Channel Tunnel*, 17; MT (Ministry of Transport) 10/392, *Channel Tunnel Railway Company Bill and the South Eastern and Channel Railway Company Bill*; both Bills opposed by the government (London: PRO, 1884).

127. An additional effect was the provocation of a rival discourse in *favor* of the tunnel. Despite the public animosity against the project and the enormity of the *Nineteenth Century* petition as an index of English society, many informed citizens of all classes remained unconvinced of its inherent threats. It should be noted, for example, that in April 1882, when the petition was having its greatest effect, the London Trades Council, with over 15,000 London-based members passed a resolution opposed to the aims of the petition. The council stated its belief "that the opposition to the Channel Tunnel is absurd," and it expressed "its astonishment at such opposition receiving the least countenance from anyone connected with the cause of labour. . . . It would be to the interests of this country if carried out, and tend to unite the sympathies and welfare of the peoples of England and France." Shipton's evidence to the Joint Select Committee, p. 127, cited in Wilson, *Channel Tunnel Visions*, 39–40.

128. MT 10/392, *Channel Tunnel Railway Company Bill*. See also RAIL 779/63, *The Channel Tunnel: A Few Notable Opinions in Support*, c. 1883 (London: PRO).

129. MT 10/392, *Channel Tunnel Railway Company Bill*.

130. Holliday, et al., *The Channel Tunnel*, 7.

131. Bonavia, *Channel Tunnel Story*, 36.

132. Clarke, *Voices Prophesying War*, 98.

133. Prestwich, French Businessmen and the Channel Tunnel, 712.

134. Gladstone, quoted in Wilson, *Channel Tunnel Visions*, 47–48 (emphasis added).

135. Prestwich, "French Businessmen and the Channel Tunnel," 703 (emphasis added).

136. Anon., *The Siege of London*, London, 1884 (emphasis added).

137. Bonavia, *Channel Tunnel Story*, 119.

138. Bonavia, *Channel Tunnel Story*, 122.

139. Bonavia, *Channel Tunnel Story*, 123.

140. Wilson, *Channel Tunnel Visions*, 48.

141. Holliday, et al., *The Channel Tunnel*, 8.

142. Hansard Parliamentary Records, vol. 537, col. 48, 12 November (London: HMSO, 1955).

143. See B. James, "Spectrum: The man with Chunnel vision—John Reeve," *Times*, 1 December 1987, M. Samuelson, "Visionaries' Challenge to History," The Channel Project, *Financial Times*, 16 December 1985.

144. *Financial Times*, 1 December 1990.

145. K. Morgan, *The Oxford History of Britain* (Oxford: Oxford University Press, 200), 658.

146. "12 Billion Pounds under the Sea," *Independent on Sunday*, 18 January 1998.

147. R. Weight, *Patriots: National Identity in Britain, 1940–2000* (London: Macmillan, 2002), 656.

148. P. Woodman, "Tunnel Outlives Historical Indecision," *The Press Association Ltd.*, October 25, 1990.

149. A. Sampson, *The New Europeans: A Guide to the Workings, Institutions and Character of Contemporary Western Europe* (London: Macmillan, 1968), 257.

150. P. Barker, "Eurostar to Paris—a Verdict on the *Grands Projets*," *New Statesman* (10 January 1997).

151. Barker, "Eurostar to Paris."

# 5

## The 1909 Navy Scare

### Englishness and National Security

> In the closing years of the nineteenth century British statesmen were
> forced to cope with . . . challenges to their "traditional supremacy." Their
> ability to understand and explain what was happening was constrained
> by the language available to them, a language devised to describe a situa-
> tion that was now passing swiftly and decisively away.
>
> —Aaron L. Friedberg[1]

As illustrated, IR theory tends to privilege systemic effects and to overlook
the particularist nuances that inform policy and affect state behavior.
Within the realist paradigm, states move in a pleasingly unified but ultimately monolithic manner, driven by the imperatives of rational power,
their foreign policy dictated by "the cold rules of statecraft."[2] All varieties
of realism can speak to the power buildup of the navy scare of 1909, can
comment on the ratio of British and German capital ships, incorporating
their varieties of strength in armor and gunnery range, rate of building
and total fleet tonnage.[3] However, materialist approaches can only identify that "the new standard . . . for British naval construction would be
*higher* than the earlier one" based purely on quantitative ratios of power
and generalized references to threats posed by Germany.[4] To ascertain the
broad spectrum of influences that the Royal Navy as a national "object"
brought to the decision-making forum of 1909, one must use a hypothesis whose starting point is *domestic* and whose endpoint is a clear analysis
of the unarticulated cultural and political power inherent in the formation and maintenance of *national identity* and the role of the Royal Navy
as part of that same identity.

While classical realist understandings of state motivation correctly include issues of national security, capabilities, and derivatives of power,
these are hardly exhaustive and rarely rational. Decision making that
puts these forces into play must also be analyzed for the domestic impulses that affect the perceptions of decision makers themselves. Based
on the "identity theme" of national security, this case study suggests that
the patterns of security formulation regarding the naval expenditure "of
both Britain and Germany [were] driven primarily by *internal factors*."[5]
The key internal factor is a discourse of Edwardian Englishness that was
informed by historic naval preeminence and which ultimately translated
into a policy fashioned to maintain that same identity. The Royal Navy
thus serves as a linchpin between the identity theme of national security
and the collective discourse of English national identity. Central to this
connection is the understanding that "the Briton's intuitive sense of the
relationship between sea power, prosperity, and national greatness"[6]
springs from a long-established belief that "the state which controlled the
seas controlled its own fate; [and] those which lacked naval mastery were
doomed to defeat or the second rank."[7]

From the perspective of security, the supremacy of the British navy represented "the most eloquent argument of diplomacy and the best guarantee
of national security," with trade, colonial possessions, and security from
immediate invasion dependent upon sea power.[8] From the perspective of
identity, "the British public was so sure of its navy that 'splendid isolation'
had become a way of life."[9]

## ENGLAND AND THE BRITISH NAVY

The institutional characteristics of the Royal Navy produced a readily
identifiable "navy type." As described by Admiral Colomb, the *British
sailor* exemplified *English attributes* that reflected England itself, as neither
England nor its navy possessed any "accurate limits. There was no greatness of soul that they might not ascend to."[10] Indeed, the largely English
officer class was required to be "absolutely fearless" with "boldness and
swiftness in decision . . . equalled by his readiness to take any and every
responsibility."[11] This in essence "was the kind of man the Navy wanted.
. . . Intolerant, insensitive, pig-headed, loud-mouthed and tyrannical as
many may have been, these were also necessary qualities" of individuality that featured within the ambit of national leadership.[12] Forms of
British authority were thus instilled in English, Scottish, Welsh, and Irish
sailors alike; qualities honed aboard a ship also functioned equally well
in the art of governance on land, at home, and abroad. As a result, navy
personnel of every rank "were uncompromising in their conception of

duty, whatever eccentric or occasionally certifiable forms it took."[13] More importantly was the "selfless belief that the good of the Service was the only thing that mattered."[14] As a result, ideals of duty and selflessness and even eccentricity were gradually recognized as English attributes of obligation, leadership, dedication, and tradition, manifested in the central British governing characteristic of unassailable self-confidence, underwritten, of course, by hefty material power. After two centuries a fully formed "nation-navy" dyad emerged, in which the Royal Navy represented in full the prominent traits of England itself. In protecting British trade and security, as well as eradicating piracy and "showing the flag," the navy represented the peculiarities of the English spirit that had carved out the British Empire.[15]

With this "apparently unassailable position . . . it was small wonder that naval officers, regardless of their own nationality, strode the world with the assurance of demi-gods, and a genuine belief not only that the Anglo-Saxon race was the most fit to bring law and civilization to the world," but also that "the British nation owned the world's supply of pluck."[16] Captain Cooper Key identified the overlap between English attributes and British power as experienced within the navy, writing that while one "cannot imagine the effect of a British man of war" in ensuring peace in various foreign ports, it was a form of respect earned principally by force:

> English influence still carries the day, and a word of advice from us will do anything. How glorious is the title of "Englishman"—and yet we are not loved. How is it? Is it our national conceit; or self-confident and supercilious bearing—the consciousness of superiority we show? Or is it jealousy? It is gratifying to think the latter, but I fear it cannot be that altogether."[17]

The English may have felt themselves superior to the rest of Europe and the wider world but it was a view from an increasingly insular vantage point. This insularity, however, was not without benefits, particularly regarding the navy. As David Duendeny points out "Britain's insular position and specialization in naval and merchant marine activities had enabled her to serve as the "balancer" of the European state system and [to] be the primary beneficiary of the European discovery and control over the world ocean."[18]

## Nineteenth-Century Sea Changes

By the end of the nineteenth century, changes were abroad. The "eternal interests" of Lord Palmerston had now become interdependent with various alliances, producing a trinity of Edwardian policies. First, "the maintenance of a stronger navy than that possessed by any likely combination of powers"; second, "the independence of the Low Countries" to assure the absence of threat from the Channel or the North Sea, and third (though largely undefined), "the maintenance of the balance of power in Europe."[19] Such policies indicated a shift from unchallenged supremacy to thresholds of uncertainty calculated chiefly by the number of new ships allocated in annual naval estimates. Significant among these challenges were the movements of Russia, France, and Germany, whose enhanced colonial attempts, aggressive nationalism, and rampant navalism "meant the end of Britain's low-cost piecemeal, largely inherited naval superiority."[20]

With the diminishment of naval predominance and the associated civilizational projects, the political culture of late nineteenth-century Britain incorporated a new, reactive national identity associated primarily with decline and one whose core sprang from codes of Englishness but was also subsumed within the political culture of Britain. From the perspective of the governing elites, the cultural certainty inherent in Englishness could possibly be regained via traditional naval superiority, strengthened in pursuit of national security. However, guaranteeing security required a steady increase in the annual naval estimates, which outlined the quantities of capital and secondary ships to be built. By 1889, the British Naval Defence Act, in which the "Two-Power Standard" of parity with the next two naval powers combined (France and Russia) "was pronounced very publicly as the cornerstone of policy, and a building programme was authorized for seventy new vessels costing £21.5 millions over five years."[21] By the early 1900s, both the national press and the wider public were characterized by a schizophrenic combination of "pride in their vast empire and anxiety lest their fleet was not strong enough to protect it."[22] The year 1897 marked the Diamond Jubilee, which attempted to dampen a variety of latent fears by consciously focusing upon themes of accomplishment, uniqueness, and preeminence. In this vein, the *Times* declared the Jubilee Naval Review as "truly a marvelous pageant and one which Britons may take pride in knowing to be such as could be exhibited by no other nation, nor indeed by all of them put together."[23]

British naval supremacy enjoyed real popularity through the Edwardian period. National identity entrenched in naval greatness reached its apogee as "the press and public [became] interested as never before in *their* Navy. . . . Music Halls echoed to popular pride of Navy and Empire; versifiers exhorted the people to reckon up their battleships. . . . Naval memoirs and naval history enjoyed a wider readership than ever before."[24] As this case illustrates, both public opinion and the press actively pushed the nation-navy discourse into the arena of policy making, which in 1909 saw the British politcal elite take a foreign policy decision that directly reflected the national identity inherent in this discourse.

## THE NAVY SCARE

The "scare" itself was based simply on the fear that by 1912, Germany would possess a greater number of new Dreadnought battleships than Britain.[25] Together with security fears, misperceptions of German intentions, and the consequences of a challenged English identity, such fears generated a discourse of alarm responsible for the hefty 1910 Naval Estimates Bill. The 1910 bill represented the largest shipbuilding program ever undertaken in modern Britain, and was designed to reassert British naval preeminence in the face of accelerated German shipbuilding. As will be seen, three issues lay at the heart of the navy scare: first, the swing of British foreign policy from a passive to a defensive status; second, the commissioning of the Dreadnought as the first "big-gun" battleship; third, the combination of press, public, and political opinion, which together generated a potent national discourse based upon rampant navalism and security fears.

### German Intentions

The perception of English sea power underwriting the greatness of the English, and eventually the British, state had long lain in the public consciousness. Even in the late nineteenth century, after the British state had been in formal existence for nearly two centuries, statesmen were still inclined to refer to their country as England, and its policies as English. Here, concepts of Englishness subsume British political identity, a trend reversed later in the twentieth century. The Foreign Office, for example, perceived "the general character of England's foreign policy" as "determined by the immutable conditions of her geographical situation . . . as an island State with vast overseas colonies and dependencies whose existence and survival as an independent community are inseparably bound up with the possession of preponderant sea power."[26]

The Admiralty, too, "saw in England the policeman of Europe, a moral force among the European nations" in which "the best guarantee for the peace of the world is a Supreme British fleet." [27] Concerns to retain the quintessential English qualities of this dogma significantly influenced policy making, particularly when that identity appeared to be challenged by a rival. Thus, while the Foreign Office was keen to retain English attitudes at the heart of British political culture by treating the newly ascendant Germany "with courtesy but with firmness on a *quid pro quo* basis," there existed a parallel understanding regarding the need for "a prompt and firm refusal to enter into any one-sided bargain or arrangements, and the most unending determination to uphold British rights and interests."[28] Indeed, the Foreign Office believed that precisely because in German diplomats "one never knows with whom one is dealing," there "will be no surer or quicker way to win the respect of the German Government and of the German nation" than a polite but firm approach.[29]

Despite such overtures, German policy during this period appeared from the English perspective to be "dominated by hostility towards England" and by a total "disregard for the elementary rules of straightforward and honourable dealing."[30] In various agreements between England and Germany "it was the abrupt and rough peremptoriness of the German action that gave [Foreign Secretary Grey] an unpleasant surprise . . . The method adopted by Germany . . . was not one of a friend. . . . It left a sense of discomfort and bad taste behind. . . . The noose had been roughly jerked by Germany."[31] Such roughness was in fact the result of a country experiencing rapid industrial, economic, and military growth.[32] As with Britain, expansion was not merely material in nature but "a matter of prestige and a measure of prosperity," in which surging domestic capacity denoted a deepening "sense of national destiny."[33] This destiny was articulated in the *Weltpolitik* of Kaiser Wilhelm II and Admiral Tirpitz, both of whom were dedicated to the goal of a superior German navy. It is interesting that Germany appears to have entangled concepts navy and nation as extensively as England.[34] German *Weltpolitik* represented not merely "*Eitelkeit,* a frivolous vanity or love of display," but illustrated that the country wanted a navy for the "general purposes of her greatness,"[35] and as a method of maintaining public consensus in a newly created state.[36] Here, the overlap of symbolic and instrumental factors at work in a seemingly material aspect of state defense is clear, and illustrates how foreign policy may be an emanation of the state constituted *by* and in defense *of* the articulated themes of the underlying national identity. As Paul Kennedy argues, "internal considerations applied in the formulation of German foreign policy" implied a method of policy formation in which "the sentiments of the nation could usually be united" around a thematic issue.[37]

Both Kaiser Wilhelm and Admiral Tirpitz were convinced "that once Britain saw and accepted the formidable nature of the German Fleet, Britain would respect . . . a friendship in which Germany would become the dominant partner."[38] Unfortunately, this "proved a catastrophic understanding of the psychology of Britons," to whom command of the sea remained a preeminent element of collective self-definition.[39] Only Ambassador Metternich had the foresight to prophesy that "nothing and no one will convince the English that a powerful fleet, increasing in strength and close to the English coasts, is not a danger—the greatest danger which an Englishman can imagine."[40] German national identity ultimately overrode material pragmatism. Despite vague platitudes from Berlin, the Kaiser had become convinced that naval programs "had become a point of national honor" for both countries.[41] In his view, "no discussion with a Foreign Government could be tolerated; such a proposal would be contrary to the national dignity, and would give rise to internal troubles if the Government were to accept it [preferring] war than accept such dictation."[42] Desirous of outstripping Britain as the "economic powerhouse of Europe,"[43] German ambition seemed centered upon a primordialist ideology of national predestination reinforced by material might, in which the future of the "German race" was increased by "army, navy, money and power . . . modern, gigantic instruments of power."[44] Stimulated by increasingly "aggressive nationalist attitudes," the resulting discourse was "an explosive psychological complex of power yearnings, overweening [cultural] ambitions, antagonisms, fears and neuroses that lay behind the disaster of an erratic, bullying *Weltpolitik*."[45]

## British Perceptions

For much of the 1880s and 1890s, Germany was regarded by Britain as prickly but manageable. The 1889 British Naval Defence Act establishing the Two-Power Standard provided numerical superiority over the combined French and Russians navies. The subsequent Second German Navy Law, however, augured "rapid, efficient expansion of the German battleship fleet," which by 1901 "seriously alarmed the British Admiralty."[46] Structural realism would regard such expansions as cause for a shift in British opinion, viewing the German navy not as benign but "designed for a possible conflict with the British fleet."[47] While the appearance of an increasingly material external threat provides some assistance in gauging unit motivation, it does not provide an accurate picture of the *perceptions* at work. Domestic forces, along with their myriad social and cultural undercurrents illuminate more richly the full range of Anglo-German naval issues. Paul Kennedy argues similarly, viewing German "*Weltpolitik* [as] driven . . . by *internal calculation*. . . . [It] not only eradicated any desire in Berlin for fixed treaty relations with Britain, it also caused an increasingly negative and hostile reaction in London and played a crucial part in the deterioration of the relations between the two nations."[48] British calculations functioned similarly; English political and cultural ascendancy embedded in naval preeminence produced the belief that "every *Englishman* would spend his last penny on maintaining *British* supremacy at sea."[49] This is precisely what occurred in 1910, when Parliament sanctioned a foreign policy manifestly influenced by that same uneasy national discourse.

German shipbuilding merely exacerbated older problems of national discontent, rooted in the challenge to English cultural life and British political culture. From the realist perspective, both 1909 and the outbreak of war in 1914 illustrated a curious ineffectuality that saw "British influence . . . [fall] far short of what British power in the international system warranted."[50] During this period, British foreign policy had gradually receded from its

Victorian policy of isolationism. Foreign Secretary Grey had stopped short of "a full-fledged alliance [of] effective control over French policy and an effective deterrent to German belligerence"; instead, he had pursued "a dangerous half-way adjustment . . . entail[ing] uncertain commitments and so a limitation of British freedom."[51] Two possible answers explain the inability of the Liberal government to rigorously restructure British policy; both emanate from within the particularist realm of English culture. The first entails the role of Englishness; the second entails nationalist responses as a result of threats to that identity.

With a highly articulated mode of unit self-reference, England possessed a particularist form of nationhood based on a "cultural and political bond, uniting in a single political community all who share an historical culture and homeland."[52] Within its political culture were competing ideas of what comprised the principles of Englishness, generally revealed as two sets of ideologies at constant and quiet odds with each other. The first ideology of nineteenth-century liberalism represented middle-class values of industrial entrepreneurial spirit, promoting individual merit ahead of historical patronage.[53] Against these liberal forces was the ancient stronghold of patrician and conservative tendencies, broadly representative of the heart of the English ethos in its rural, ecclesiastical, political, and wholly traditional values.[54] The concepts of industry, entrepreneurial commerce, and urbanism of the liberal ideology vied against the ancient patrician structure of England, including property, the House of Lords, and the Anglican Church. Conservative and liberal identities in the form of distinct political parties had emerged during the Georgian period and by the late Victorian era were sharply defined.[55]

Along with the dual ideologies at work in English political society lay the broad changes at work since the industrial boom of the Victorian era. As illustrated in the tunnel case study, in the minds of many, "urbanism and industrialism were symbols of all that was wrong with Edwardian society, representing its lost sense of purpose and its absence of [national] unity."[56] Economic liberalism and "laissez-faire capitalism [appeared to have] spawned a rootless, spiritually bankrupt society where once there had been a nation of organic rural communities"; as a result, the countryside became transformed into a paragon of Englishness, "a picturesque repository of [increasingly threatened] national values."[57]

Throughout the Victorian era, England was engaged in a potent domestic war against the loss of Englishness—the elision, erosion and vanquishing of a near-invincible nation.[58] Absent a specific external "other," this process instead represented a growing awareness that, despite the glories celebrated as recently as 1897 with the Jubilee, England had began to lose its particularist, missionary purpose and overall ascendancy. Instead of the totems of political stability and cultural particularism, the English identity increasingly reflected "an anxious nostalgic reaction to the speed and scope of social and cultural change" represented by growing class conflict, union and industrial unrest, rising unemployment, and the growth of the suffragette movement.[59] The identity had also become increasingly ambiguous with the rise of the British state, and associated ideas of Britishness as a political culture somehow separate from that of Englishness. Decline itself had also become entrenched as a national discourse, denoting fears of invasion, imperial disintegration, the weakening of the "English race" and the erosion of its civilizing mandate. Edwardian England had become a world of cultural anxiety and fragmentation where "decay, decline, fall and decadence were the language of the time."[60] Indeed, within England itself, national society was seen to have deteriorated, a term that had "negative moral connotations and implied comparisons to some form of preindustrial sturdiness, reflections of the "pathogenicity of the urban environment" and the deteriorating effect on the relative position of Britain in the international sphere."[61]

English politics were similarly convulsed by increasing strife among unions, classes, and industry.[62] The English Constitution and the workings of government were a leftover of Victorian Englishness, "based largely on tacit gentlemanly agreements—implicit rules of the game" that had become increasingly unviable.[63] The Liberals were unable to produce either a vision of *English society* to quell growing domestic anxiety or an image of a *British government* to provide a brake on imperial decline. This was compounded by weak Tory leadership that "encouraged an increasingly venomous political climate in which Conservative elements . . . became more and more irrationally opposed to all Liberal policies."[64] The Edwardian period was thus marked by a "profound tension between an older vision of the [English] national polity as a narrowly self-contained sphere occupied by the possessors of property, education, independence, and civic virtue, and a newer vision . . . as coterminous with all adult members of British society, regardless of economic standing, gender, character or class."[65]

By the time of the 1909 navy scare, two dominant behavioral patterns of identity had appeared. This first was an ethos of negotiation which had been gradually institutionalized as a result of reconciling working- and middle-class enfranchisement.[66] By the turn of the century, these traits had contributed to an English identity characterized as "private and individualistic with a love of eccentricity, fair play and tolerance towards others."[67] In the political realm, this ethos characterized Grey's policy of alliance and rapprochement, and indeed much of British foreign policy, which had until the navy scare remained moderate and broadly defensive.[68]

The second pattern of behavior represents a full-bodied reactive English identity, redefined in a vigorous reassertion of power and entitlement that affected political parties, the press, and the public throughout the Edwardian era and was directly influenced the 1909 navy scare. Ideas of British political decline and English cultural degeneration prompted an overall reclaiming of national greatness identified by "tariff reform, imperial unity, paternalistic welfarism, hostility to liberal parliamentarianism, a large standing army, and, not least, a bold foreign policy."[69]

Thus, the combination of decline and anxiety-based reassertion provided the constitutive content of a national discourse sharply focused around the predominant theme of physical security. The year 1909 represents the transference from discourse to discursive practices, first because it was *constituted* by the broad political and cultural sense of a challenged identity, and second because this took *causal* effect through the reactive decision of the Asquith Liberal government to build eight additional Dreadnought warships in a single year. This illustrates the neoclassical realist point that both external challenges in the form of Germany and internally driven processes in the form of reactive identity discourses are necessary to fully explain this policy decision.

## Dreadnought

At the turn of century, "the Royal Navy was still overwhelmingly larger and more splendid than any other, its history longer and prouder, its prestige higher."[70] As described by the *Times*, "The Navy is a very conservative service, tenacious of tradition, deeply and rightly imbued with the sentiment of its glorious past, and very suspicious of any innovations which seem to ignore that tradition."[71] While the peaceful routine of the Victorian era implied that Britain's role as "Mistress of the Seas" remained largely unchallenged, the navy had in fact become significantly outmoded, with scores of obsolete vessels languishing in the "bow and arrow epoch."[72] The combination of rivals, new technology, and advanced naval tactics created an "uncertain environment for British naval decision makers."[73] Admiral "Jacky" Fisher was well aware of this, and implemented the sweeping policies of reform that completely overturned the navy in the early 1900s. Fisher also cannily ensured that national anxieties over their "lost superiority were used to full effect" in both public and political support of his radical policies.[74] Vivacious and irascible, Fisher furthered naval greatness by eradicating many of the "hidebound" and "ridiculous tradition[s]" of the navy.[75] His most radical concept was an indestructible, all "big-gun" battleship, or Dreadnought, which was to have "the most dramatic effect on the naval balance of power and the prewar diplomatic history of Europe."[76]

The Dreadnought was both instrumental and symbolic. Materially, as outlined to the Committee on Designs in 1905, its "two governing conditions are guns and speed."[77] The ship would possess greater external armor, increased speed, and heavier guns with superior range than anything previously built.[78] The design committee accepted Fisher's proposals on 22 February

1905; the keel was laid in October, and by February 1906 the hull was complete. Symbolically, the Dreadnought encapsulated the core of English pride regarding centuries of naval preeminence. The very name Dreadnought was chosen because it bore historical significance, emphasizing that the ship itself "was of illustrious descent."[79] That battleships should enjoy a rather aristocratic pedigree is a particularly English concept, suggesting that the English did not merely build ships in defense of foes but also as cultural artifacts that reinforced their political culture. The Dreadnought was thus built and used with the purpose of wielding utter invincibility, a token of the fearlessness, resoluteness, and calmness of the British sailors whose task was to represent both their homeland and its core English civilizing project. Combining both material and ideological attributes, the Dreadnought embodied British security as a weapon of English identity, demonstrating that both ships and nations "are caught up in history and traditions."[80]

Christened in Portsmouth by King Edward VII, the first Dreadnought was launched upon the headlines of the world, beginning an enduring fascination by the press "with the greatest icon of power—the battleship."[81] A "breakthrough in speed, staying power, hitting distance and gunpower," English ingenuity and dedication had allowed Britain to regain its traditional naval preeminence, restoring national pride after the anxieties of the German Naval Bill.[82] Internationally, the Dreadnought "caused a tremendous sensation among the naval powers and paralyzed foreign admiralties for upwards of two years."[83] And, as Fisher had assumed, "when confirmation of the size, speed, and armaments of the Dreadnought reached Berlin, something close to panic ensued."[84] Successfully rendering the entire German navy obsolete, no shipbuilding of any kind was attempted "while German designers struggled to obtain and analyze details of the Dreadnought."[85] Ironically, with his decision to scrap 154 older vessels from the list of active ships, Fisher damned the efficacy of his own fleet. With mounting horror, it slowly dawned on both Parliament and the Admiralty that due to the Dreadnought's wholly unique design, Germany had been given the opportunity to compete anew for naval supremacy. In the view of the Conservative opposition led by Arthur Balfour, the Dreadnought actually placed Germany on level footing with Britain as a naval power, thereby obliterating the Two-Power Standard and any future guarantee of British naval supremacy.[86]

Within months of its euphoric launch, the Dreadnought was nationally lambasted. Fisher and the Admiralty became the chief targets in the "protests that poured into the Admiralty, rang in the House of Commons, [and] inundated the press."[87] Former First Sea Lord Richards argued that "the whole British Fleet was . . . morally scrapped and labelled obsolete at the moment when it was at the zenith of its efficiency and equal not to two but practically to all the other navies of the world combined."[88] Within the cabinet, Lloyd George condemned the Dreadnought as "a piece of wanton and profligate ostentation. . . . We said 'Let there be dreadnoughts.' What for? We did not require them. Nobody was building them."[89] Worse still, the Dreadnought was perceived as contradictory to British policy; as explained by the *Manchester Guardian*, the Dreadnought represented

> a departure from our traditional policy in construction, which as befitted a Power which had acquired so great a lead, was one of *conservatism*. It destroyed much of the *status quo* advantage that had been secured by past [Tory] expenditure, and enabled other nations to get on more even terms."[90]

Fisher defended himself and the policy decision to build the Dreadnought by articulating the quintessentially English virtue of duty, necessitated by the broader political need for security. Fisher argued that the Dreadnought's reinforced armor and speed were "only a continuation of long-established policy" of the Royal Navy, and constituted neither mere novelty, nor "a costly, majestic, but vulnerable basket . . ." for the nation's "naval eggs."[91] Gradually, Dreadnought came to be seen as the margin of superiority necessary to preserve the British state and its core English values, and this viewpoint slowly triumphed over the material concerns. By 1907, "seven dreadnoughts and battle cruisers . . . were built or building."[92]

## THE NAVY SCARE: THE POLITICAL DISCOURSE

The first two elements of the navy scare have been examined above: English domestic anxieties exacerbated by German ascendance, and the consecration of the Dreadnought as symbolic of both English identity and British security. The final element is the political and public discourses generated by a series of events: euphoria at Dreadnought's launch, anger at the subsequent erosion of the Two-Power Standard, and lastly anxiety at the German naval program, which swiftly emulated the Dreadnought and then appeared incontrovertibly to be accelerating past it.

### The Two-Power Standard

The Two-Power Standard had been a hallmark of the power of both the British state and English cultural ambition to extend its power and civilizing mandate globally.[93] It had however, been redefined according to differing contexts since 1901. During the Edwardian era, the Two-Power Standard represented not only British equality with the two next-largest fleets combined, but other various equations, from specific superiority over the French and Russian fleets to more general control of European waters; command of the seas; and ultimately, security of the British empire.[94] The crushing cost of maintaining naval supremacy had forced an uncomfortable reassessment of these options, which in turn had led to a new foreign policy stance. By relying on diplomatic understandings with peripheral states and European alliances, Britain gradually relinquished the goal of command of the seas and security of empire; this in turn prompted "a complete reevaluation of Britain's traditional diplomatic and colonial policies and its entire defensive posture."[95] There are two central points to be made here. First, as Aaron Friedberg argues, while Britain's international position of relative power and balancing abilities had been utterly transformed by its decision to restrict naval supremacy to European waters,

> British statesmen continued to talk as if nothing of any significance had really changed. . . . This was partly the result of habit and of the fact that the Royal Navy was still larger and more capable than any other in the world. But it was also the expression of conscious deception and, increasingly with the passage of time, of self-delusion.[96]

The ongoing refusal of British political identity—underwritten by an Englishness predisposed to cultural entitlement—to countenance such vast changes suggests not only the visibly central role that national identity plays in the ranking of national interests, but the ability of key security policies themselves to be understood culturally. Friedberg articulates this perfectly, arguing that the "reluctance to abandon old indexes reveals something of their symbolic power, and, in this case, it also shows how important it was for most Englishmen to believe that their country retained command of the seas."[97] Indeed, while "British public opinion was not much interested in the details of continental politics . . . on the question of naval supremacy there was no division of opinion."[98] The Dreadnought, while symbolizing one form of British security (and English ingenuity) had simultaneously undermined its own naval superiority by eroding Britain's naval edge. As illustrated, the Admiralty attempted to quash public hostility over the loss of the standard, arguing that the two Dreadnoughts "projected in the 1907–8 estimates would maintain Britain's relative battleship strength."[99] The country remained unconvinced. The erosion so soon after the zenith of the 1897 Jubilee celebrations, along with (rather than uniquely due to) the oblique motives of the German shipbuilding program presented a "serious challenge to British naval supremacy [that] would cause an outburst of feeling which no ministry could resist."[100]

Shipbuilding as a definition of both national greatness and the means to tackle an increasingly eroded domestic security due to the lost Two-Power Standard was thus the predominant national discourse from 1906 onward. Regardless of the information from the Kiel dockyards in Germany, Britain revealed itself to be singularly possessed of its shipbuilding identity. This was demonstrated in 1906, when the Liberals attempted to cut a single

Dreadnought from the 1907–1908 estimates and revealed for the first time the true extent of the nation-navy discourse. In Parliament, Tory opposition "interpreted every reduction of the navy as a cause for public anxiety and concern," while outside the House, "the Tory press poured scorn and obloquy both upon the government and its Admiralty advisers."[101] The *Daily Mail* exhorted that "the time has come to remind the Admiralty and the Government that the nation gave no mandate to weaken its Navy for the sole purpose of providing funds for doles to the Socialists."[102] Prime Minister Campbell-Bannerman attempted to outdo the Tories, admonishing them in tones ringing with personal identity. Tories, he contended, were "timid and shrinking persons naturally that went in for panics," and that there was "no more timid shrinking person than an Imperialist Jingo."[103]

## The 1909 Naval Estimates

By 1908, the "British nation was now resigned to an increase in naval expenditure; as a practical people, they would accept this necessity."[104] Equally, "it was taken for granted . . . that Germany would keep to her published time-table" of Dreadnought production.[105] The possibility of a settlement to allow each state a degree of respite was scrapped after a report by the Kaiser was made available to the Cabinet. In it, the Kaiser stated that if "the desire for a good relationship with England [was] the price of the development of the German Navy," it was "a boundless impertinence and a gross insult to the German people," and that Germany's Navy Law "will be carried out to the last detail; whether the British like it or not does not matter!"[106] The effect "was an almost unanimous demand in the [English] navalist press for more battleships."[107]

Despite this background, the Naval Estimates of 1909 (requested in December 1908 by First Sea Lord McKenna) still came as a shock. Rather than the expected four Dreadnoughts, the Admiralty was insisting upon six. Worse still, this request was based on alarming new information regarding an accelerated German naval program.[108] Three factors appeared to be in play. First, Germany's first Dreadnought was reputed to be far larger in size and more heavily armed than the British original. Second, Germany was supposedly introducing a supplementary program for twenty large cruisers to accompany its new Dreadnought. Third, evidence suggested that Germany was not merely reproducing the original Dreadnought design, but actually building it faster than British dockyards. The *appearance* of German acceleration, and its *perceived* implications based on the original sense of domestic loss that concretized the erosion of the Two-Power Standard (as a measurement of greatness) and the centrality of the nation-navy discourse (as the narrative of such greatness) are thus the twofold causes of the navy scare. Thus, as Massie puts it, "McKenna and the Sea Lords, led by Fisher, insisted that, unless six ships were authorized, they would not remain in office. The Navy Scare, which gripped Parliament, press, and country in the winter and spring of 1909, was under way."[109]

The news from Kiel was alarming for all concerned. The Admiralty and the Foreign Office had not only been caught off guard but had possibly ceded the ability to regain what was previously inviolable. The Dreadnought, as a symbol of Britain's insuperable Royal Navy and the values of an unchallenged English nation, now lay within degrees of overthrow, and by its own hand. The Cabinet's response was swift. On 3 January 1909, McKenna wrote to Prime Minister Asquith that while "anxious to avoid alarmist language . . . I cannot resist the following conclusions. . . . Germany is anticipating the shipbuilding program laid down by the law of 1907. . . . She is doing so secretly. . . . German capacity to build dreadnoughts is at this moment equal to ours."[110] By January 1909, the Cabinet had split over the issue. Radical members including Winston Churchill and Lloyd George led the "little navy" group and deemed four ships sufficient. Grey and Prime Minister Asquith represented not only the Liberal Imperialist identity (which viewed as impractical the Liberal idealism regarding armaments), but also the "big-navy" element of the Liberal party, and felt that six ships were required. Unsurprisingly, First Sea Lord McKenna, Admiral Fisher, and the Admiralty perceived the threat still more keenly and demanded eight, at a cost of £6,000,000.[111] The Radicals judged the Admiralty reaction as alarmist and unprepared; indeed Lloyd George was convinced of the "extraordinary neglect on the part of the Admiralty that all this should not have been found out before."[112]

McKenna spoke out on behalf of the "big-navy" party, which now reflected the majority of national opinion, and replied that the cabinet, particularly its pacifist "economaniac" members were similarly unprepared, having known "perfectly well that these facts were communicated to the Cabinet at the time we knew of them" and that the members of the cabinet had dismissed them as "contractor's gossip."[113] Anxious to keep the cabinet unified and to prevent the country from drifting into a deeper state of alarm, Prime Minister Asquith heeded Grey's earlier warning that "there is no half-way house . . . in naval affairs . . . between complete safety and absolute ruin," and supplied a solution.[114] Four Dreadnoughts would be requested in the 1909 Naval Estimates. Four additional Dreadnoughts would be laid down the following year "*if* careful monitoring of the German construction program proved them necessary."[115] Further, "the contingent four . . . would have no effect on the regular 1910 program, under which it was assumed that still another four dreadnoughts would be ordered."[116]

On 16 March 1909, the "four-plus-four" Naval Estimate was put before the House of Commons. McKenna spelled out the threat and the justification plainly: "No matter what the cost, the safety of the country must be assured. We do not know, as we thought we did, the rate at which German construction is taking place. . . . We now expect these ships to be completed, not in February 1911, but in the autumn of 1910. . . . We have to take stock of a new situation."[117] The estimates were voted in immediately, by a vote of 322–83.[118] Within a week however, the "four-plus-four" estimate, far from being thought too extravagant had been reviled as entirely too weak. The Admiralty feared that "the compromise is meant to throw dust in the eyes of the public by promising more than it is the intention of the Government to carry out."[119] Fisher, who had originally viewed the scare as overblown and inaccurate, had by March amended his opinion and exhorted both McKenna and Asquith that Germany "really might lay down 8 fresh ships, as 4 will be launched. *We have now only 12 in hand.*"[120] The policy provoked an enormous agitation in Parliament and the press. The Conservatives made clear to the public that even if all eight dreadnoughts were laid down instantly, Britain would still "have only a three-ship superiority over a one-power standard," the Two-Power Standard having been dismembered and increasingly unattainable.[121]

## Grey and the Motion of Censure

Worse was to follow in the Motion of Censure, which opposition leader Balfour attempted to pass upon the Liberal government: a form of public and political humiliation for imperiling English national might by diminishing British naval power. Asquith's response was to publicly deride the Conservatives as "[u]nscrupulous, unpatriotic, and manipulated by party agitation."[122] Following Asquith, Foreign Secretary Sir Edward Grey redressed both parliamentary and national balance by outlining the entirety of the security problem. On 29 March 1909, Grey denounced the Conservative's attempt at censure by getting straight to the point, namely "that Germany's expanding capacity, rather than her moderate intentions, might govern German naval construction."[123] Britain, Grey argued, as foremost among the great powers, and with a superior navy, stood alone in its ability to quell attempts at European hegemony and to ensure the freedom of commercial and colonial access, as well as in the prestige it enjoyed in underwriting the previous century of global peace. With missionary identity providing overt content to the security discourse, Grey argued that England could not sacrifice its great power status: "If we fall into a position of inferiority our self-respect is gone, and removes that enterprise which is essential . . . to the carrying out of great ideals. . . . We should cease to count for anything amongst the nations of Europe." The linchpin, as ever, was British naval strength—the metaphor for English greatness:

There is no comparison between the importance of the German Navy to Germany, and the importance of our Navy to us. . . . To have a strong navy would increase their prestige, their diplomatic influence . . . but . . . it is not a *matter of life and death to them as it is to us*. No superiority of the British Navy over the German Navy could ever put us in a position to affect the independence or integrity of Germany. . . . But if the German Navy were superior to ours, they, maintaining the Army which they do . . . our independence, our very existence would be at stake.[124]

Grey made his point effectively. The motion of censure was heavily defeated, and Asquith, Grey, McKenna, and Fisher were vindicated in the House. Winston Churchill described the outcome of the entire event with typical brevity: "In the end a curious and characteristic solution was reached. The Admiralty had demanded six ships; the economists offered four; and we finally compromised on eight."[125]

The political discourse of the navy scare was heightened by a public narrative of "excitement . . . verging upon panic" and strains of "hysterical jingoism.[126] The normally pragmatic foundations of English society and stolid British institutions of press and Parliament were badly shaken by a pervasive sense of anxiety regarding their physical security and challenged national role. In consequence, Parliament passed a reactive policy that reflected in its causal outcome the elements wholly constituted by the underlying national narrative of self-reference, based upon the nation-navy dyad. The "four-plus-four" motion became policy, and preparation to lay the first four keels began at once.[127] Quite simply, the anxiety about eroded material security and diminished identity was translated directly from a discourse embodying collective concerns over both national and naval supremacy into a foreign policy designed to meet those concerns.

## THE NAVY SCARE: THE PUBLIC AND CULTURAL DISCOURSE

A counterpart to political discourse, this section illustrates that the popularization by the press of the British navy in its qualitative essence and its quantitative weakness provided the context of public support required to maintain the extensive naval programs of Edwardian England. By 1908, the loss of the Two-Power Standard had resonated strongly with the public, while the national press began to take sides. The Conservative press established a connection between a diminished England and a rampant Germany. The Liberal press, however, while unhappy over the revised German program, did not find it alarming, viewing instead the election pledges regarding disarmament as greater in significance.

The rise of German competition, however, brought both sides together. By 1908, aware that Germany had laid down four ships to Britain's two, the country was growing uneasy. As accounts of German "stockpiling" began to circulate publicly, the "spectre of German acceleration had begun to materialize . . . culminat[ing] in the great Panic of 1909."[128] When publicized, McKenna's Naval Estimates request stunned the country; "accusations of incompetence and of abdicating naval supremacy [were] flung at the government, at the Admiralty, and at Fisher."[129] The *Daily Telegraph* denounced Asquith and his initial plan to build only four ships: "since Nero fiddled there has never been a spectacle more strange, more lamentable, than the imperiling of the whole priceless heritage of centuries to balance a party budget."[130] The Liberals stood accused of neglecting social welfare if all eight were built, and of jeopardizing national and imperial security if they were not. The Unionist Party and press, along with Conservatives in the House and the Lords converged on the "slogan coined by George Wyndham, MP: "We want eight and we won't wait!"[131] The phrase was sufficiently catchy to represent Edwardian *Zeitgeist*, and was repeated in the press, in music halls, on banners, flags, leaflets, and during numerous demonstrations outside Whitehall and Admiralty offices, until the nation rang with it. As Moll argues, "there was no question that public opinion and both Parties basically supported a policy of naval supremacy. . . . The Navy was 'one of the fixed points of the universe.'"[132] These fixed points of a distinctly English universe were reestablished within a British foreign policy that quantified national security identity instrumentally by constructing more Dreadnoughts and qualified it ideationally through the symbolism attached to the continuing ethos of naval predominance.

## The Culture of Invasion Literature

The English insecurities at work during the navy scare drew on a broader set of generic "invasion fears" prominent in the late nineteenth century. As first introduced in the previous chapter, blending fiction, opinion, and observation, the product of invasion literature "captured press headlines . . . and induced a state of near paranoia concerning the vulnerability of Britain's defensive preparations."[133] "Invasion literature" contributed significantly to the navy scare and the four-plus-four foreign policy outcome because it involved "chilling scenarios of impending national disaster, should the country fail to expand the fleet or fortify its coastline" as favorite subjects.[134] In particular, the literature "spawned a new apocalyptic vision entailing a Royal Navy failure . . . and a subsequent occupation of Britain by Prussian satyrs."[135]

Correspondent with political reality, the origins of fictional invasion had shifted from the Channel to across the North Sea. Two central pieces in particular provide a contextual discourse by which national anxieties contributed directly to the navy scare: *The Riddle of the Sands* by Erskine Childers

(1903) and *The Invasion of 1910* by William Le Queux (published in 1906, the year of the Dreadnought launch, and serialized in the *Daily Mail*).[136] *The Riddle of the Sands* is a spy story involving thousands of German secret agents who are covertly abroad in England in order to collect information on the British fleet as part of preparations for an imminent invasion. In *The Invasion of 1910*, England is subject to a lightning-like invasion by "Teuton forces" who, having encountered no naval resistance, pounce upon the unprepared nation. In both works, the Teuton foe is crudely drawn in its representation of German national identity. Le Queux, for example, portrays an "efficient, professional Teuton enemy. . . . The Germans are monsters who . . . slaughter the entire population of an English town. The Kaiser is . . . a bloodthirsty barbarian."[137] For its part, England is portrayed not merely as "a maritime nation" but a commander of the sea, "and if we lose command of it, we starve. We're unique in that way; just as our huge Empire, only linked by the sea, is unique."[138]

While the majority of invasion literature relies upon unsophisticated portrayals of each side's national identity and the fear accompanying diminished national security, the genre as a whole is an effective example of how prewar English popular culture formed a discourse that affected policy outcome. The warnings of English weakness in Childers, and German aggression in Le Queux, provoked strident, predictable responses along the fault lines of both political British identity and cultural English identity. Invasion literature thus stands alongside less sensationalist forms of Edwardian culture in demonstrating how the production of national policy was constituted from within and causally affected by the discursive forum of English national identity. Two particularly strong constitutive-causal connections may be analyzed in this regard, one pertaining to the army, and the other contributing directly to the 1909 navy scare.

## The Invasion of 1910

In 1906, the same year as the Dreadnought was launched, there was growing concern about the issue of a new standing army. While Admiral Fisher had successfully modernized the navy, Field Marshal Lord Roberts had argued repeatedly that "our armed forces, as a body, are absolutely unfitted and unprepared for war."[139] Unsuccessful in his jeremiads to Parliament, Roberts's "constant warnings that a weak and complacent England was open to invasion suggested a story," and the author Le Queux was subsequently hired to write it."[140] The purpose of *The Invasion of 1910* was quite deliberate, namely, to "illustrate our utter unpreparedness for war, to show how . . . England can be successfully invaded by Germany, and to present a picture of the ruin which must inevitably fall upon us."[141] The

book was serialized by the *Daily Mail* newspaper which "created a propi-
tious atmosphere through its serialization [of a] fictional account of a brutal
German invasion, replete with terrifying tales of Teutonic savagery and
arrogance."[142] Complete with "men in spiked helmets and Prussian blue
uniforms parading down Oxford Street," the story enjoyed tremendous
success; the *Daily Mail* sold out with each edition and the novel itself sold
more than a million copies.[143]

The *Daily Mail* series linked popular culture to foreign policy by focusing
upon the theme of invasion and national unpreparedness. Within days of
the *Daily* Mail publication, the War Office, the Admiralty, and MPs across
the country were immediately besieged with information regarding Teuton-
based plans to scuttle the Royal Fleet in preparation for invasion. Successfully generating a nationwide discourse of alarm, the theme worked its way
to the heart of government via MP Sir John Barlow, who requested that
War Secretary Haldane explain to the House of Commons his knowledge
of thousands of German Army reservists resident in London. In attempting to stem the tide, the government was well aware that, in response, it
"could decide on the policy matter of compulsory conscription."[144] Prime
Minister Campbell-Bannerman, however, publicly declared his faith in "the
good sense and good taste of the British people" and denied Lord Roberts's
appeal for expenditure on army materials.[145] Roberts denounced this decision in the Lords as unreflective of the needs and desires of the English
public, stating that a Continental foe required a mere ninety-four hours to
ferry 70,000 soldiers across the Channel. Opposition leader Arthur Balfour
supported Roberts's appeal by denouncing Campbell-Bannerman's weak
approach and strongly recommending that the Committee of Imperial Defense "reconsider England's vulnerability to invasion."[146] With the aid of the
*Daily Mail* and Le Queux, Roberts had successfully disturbed the government
into a response. Despite Haldane's argument that "Lord Roberts's repeated
statements that we are in danger of invasion . . . are doing a good deal of
mischief," a Subcommittee on Defense was soon formed to collect evidence
regarding issues of possible invasion and required army expansion.[147]

By April 1907, the discourse of anxiety, constituted by "a complexity of
fears about foreign invasion," produced a *specific policy outcome* within the
House of Commons, where the Territorial and Reserve Forces Bill of the
Liberal Government had reached its second reading.[148] The combination
of Le Queux's fiction and Roberts's alarmist statements (both forms of
discourse) testifies to the degree that invasion literature—based on underlying anxieties of security—now encompassed national views. The resulting
alarmist fears further illustrate the power of a discourse when based on
national themes that can obtain constitutively and causally within both
cultural forms and governmental outcomes.

## An Englishman's Home

The 1909 navy scare possessed its own cultural discourse. As the crisis heightened in February 1909, a play written by Guy du Maurier, entitled *An Englishman's Home*, opened at the Wyndham Theatre in London and played to a packed house each evening.[149] Including the irresistible features of English identity, British defeat, and the necessity for national preparedness, the drama concerns the fate of a middle-class family, captured in their home by a troop of "Nearland" soldiers.[150] Reminded by their leader, Prince Yoland that civilians cannot participate in war-making, the English father, Mr. Brown, denounces him: "Bah! What does that matter? I am an Englishman!"[151] This line in particular caused thunderous nightly applause and ovations; the more so when "brave Mr. Brown kills two Nearland soldiers and is then himself executed, transformed into both hero and victim of England's unpreparedness."[152]

Like Le Queux, du Maurier appears to have been aware that "compulsory military service could be raised only in direct connexion with the possibility of a [prior] defeat of the British navy [presumably] followed by a German invasion."[153] *An Englishman's Home* turns on the same causes as *The Invasion of 1910*, that is, a military defeat that presupposes a naval defeat, and a series of ongoing diminishments of English superiority, indefatigability, and inviolability. At the height of the scare, *An Englishman's Home* contributed to the popular alarm and anxiety already abroad in the nation. On stage were physical demonstrations of England unprepared, with the "sight . . . of foreign soldiers in spiked helmets trampling across an English lawn and bursting through French windows into the parlor of an English house."[154] The physicality of invasion was brutal, damaging, and deliberately warlike. Clearly, the English nation and its British state risked similar intrusions if government defense policy did not move swiftly. The play also echoed the vigorous reassertion of identity that girded Asquith's "four-plus-four" policy located in Grey's speech to rebuff censure and ensure the passage of the Dreadnought policy. As illustrated above, Grey spoke to the House of duty, obligation, supremacy, and inviolability, each of which feature as quintessentially English touchstones throughout du Maurier's play. This discursive overlap is particularly reinforced when Mr. Brown takes his own life in defense of English nationhood.

As a symbol of national culture and an index of public concern, the play not only prompted "renewed fascination in the subject" of naval defense but, parallel with many such questions in Parliament "performed the essential function of sowing doubt in the public [and political] mind concerning the ability of the Royal Navy to repel invading fleets."[155] Acting in such constitutive fashion, the play also produced a number of causal outcomes. Most directly, and due to the strength of the message of reassertion and preparedness in *An Englishman's Home*, "the army set up a special recruiting station in the lobby of the theatre so that fiery young men, erupting out of the stalls once the curtain had fallen, could volunteer on the spot for Haldane's new Territorial Army."[156]

To further articulate the heart of the identity-interest-policy dialectic outlined in chapter 3, *An Englishman's Home* may be understood as *constitutive* of (and by) the discourse generated during the time. The prevalent factor in this discourse was the highly articulated public and political furor that heightened the discourse of alarm and sharpened the collective focus upon the nation-navy dyad. As a widely popular thematic articulation regarding declinist themes, *An Englishman's Home* simultaneously contributed to the definition and generation of the overall discourse. The power of such purposive discourse was evident even in Germany; as commented by the *Berliner Tageblatt*, "the fairy tales . . . of the phantom ships . . . [while] a subject for merriment . . . overlooked that the state of public feeling which could lead to the circulation of such legends was in itself a subject for grave apprehensions, as in the case of a popular panic, even a peaceful Government might be driven into taking the most fatal steps."[157]

As a unified form of public and political self-reference, this discourse then produced a distinctly causal form of change.[158] Each outcome had first been constituted by the underlying cultural and social mores at work in defining national self-reference; when politicized as a form of national interest pertaining to security, they took on causal agency within the various decisions to split the Cabinet votes, to outline the Dreadnought policy, to censure the Asquith government, and most agential of all, to lay the keels of eight additional battleships. Du Maurier had arguably "exploited the dramatic value of the subject"; however, this merely added to the constitutive elements already at work in defining the ultimate reaction by the government to the prevalent themes of ill-preparedness via a policy that directly addressed those same fears.[159]

## CASE STUDY PREMISE: POLITICAL AND CULTURAL DISCOURSE AND POLICY MAKING

The linkages between the public, popular culture, the press, Parliament, and policy now appear concrete. Morgenthau's maxim that "the kinds of interests determining political action in a particular period of history depend upon the political and cultural context within which foreign policy is formulated" is both vindicated and visible in 1909.[160] From 15 October 1908 to the passage of the 1910 "four-plus-four" Naval Estimate, the narrative of identity worked to drive home the need for a policy of eight additional Dreadnoughts. The alarm in Parliament, combined with the hysteria in the press, and the centrality of cultural forms that reflected growing national unease over naval weakness constituted the national narrative. Coalesced within the unitary discourse of anxiety, these elements are also *causally* linked to the reactive policy response of Asquith, Grey, and McKenna.

By 1908, "only one ingredient was needed . . . to convert public uneasiness as well as uneasiness at Whitehall into a first-class scare" with tangible policy results.[161] Marder identifies that ingredient as "intelligence of German acceleration."[162] This, however, was a secondary process entirely contingent on a prior and permanent blow to English nation-navy identity: the dismemberment of the Two-Power Standard due to the introduction of the Dreadnought. English identity lies at the heart of all such alarms; what had been disturbed was the surety of its principal association between naval supremacy and national greatness. The loss of naval preeminence "inflamed the long-growing public uneasiness" and gave political voice to the public narrative, "strengthen[ing] their real opposition" into demanding "eight and we won't wait."[163]

To clarify, the surface hysteria of the navy scare is representative of the lack of national self-assuredness and its associated links with the German Other. The roots of the scare itself are however entirely focused upon the prior diminishment of the foundational naval identity at work within the English Self and the security concerns of the British state. A careful reading of the newspapers of the day makes this abundantly clear. In 1904, the *Times* had recorded that "[n]o phantom as to German aggression haunts us; but the consciousness we feel that it is our *duty* to watch the progress of German naval power, and to consider the possible purposes for which it might be used."[164] English identity, as examined in chapter 1, was at this point based upon perceptions of tacit, assumed superiority and an ability to exercise national duty by casting a watchful if isolationist eye from the sidelines. However, as illustrated, a change within the domestic identity rather than within systemic forces is equally capable of turning observations of equanimity regarding a rival into sentiments of alarm.

As examined in chapter 3, the greatest threat to identity formation is "a comprehensive alternative identity, an 'other' that can plausibly be understood as a replacement."[165] A threat such as that experienced by Edwardian England in the dramatic increase of the German navy represents a clear oppositional threat, an obvious juxtaposition of "self" and "other." However, one must question the validity of this easy opposition. Despite the material implications of a security dilemma and the need for a reaction on the part of the Admiralty and the country writ large, relations with Germany remained relatively civil during this episode. Indeed, during February and March 1909, when the Admiralty revelations were publicly coming to light, the German newspaper, the *Kölnische Zeitung* expressed the will of the German people "to live in peace and friendship with the People of Great Britain, whose sound good sense, tenacity of purpose, confident strength and eminent achievements in all spheres of life they heartily and honestly admire."[166] The German naval program could not effectively "oppose" the Royal Navy, as the objectives of the two fleets were largely incommensurate, rather than diametrically opposed. As argued by Grey, the clear objective of the Royal Navy, "was to maintain such complete command of the sea in our home waters that, even with the small Army we maintained, we should be safe from Invasion. If our objective was aggressive, foreign ships . . . would count for as much or more than those near us; but as our object was defence and not aggression ships at a distance did not count for so much."[167]

Far subtler is the internal or "relational" threat that emerges from domestic sources. The relational threat encountered during the 1909 panic diminished the internal sense of the English self, and its relation to its own modes of self-reference pertaining to its naval preeminence. In this way, otherness is not necessarily the uneasy "inclusion of foreigners in another state's identity, but rather . . . an outcome of a domestic cry for moral reform, motivated mainly by parochial considerations."[168] It may therefore be understood that the German building program represents a *consequent* and largely ideational threat to English nationhood rather than a direct or even oppositional material threat to the British unit.

The greater threat lay within a disturbed domestic identity, shifted from its foundational perceptions of tradition, naval preeminence, and the autonomy of a largely isolationist existence. In 1909 this discursive threat was embodied in the growing awareness of an *internally weakened* rather than externally challenged navy and a nation ill at ease with the relentless march of twentieth-century modernization. At the core of the navy scare was not German material acceleration but the possibility of English deceleration in both material *and* ideological terms—a disengaging from its former modes and sources of meaning and self-reference embodied in a gradual detaching of the national "self" from its normative, symbolic, and instrumental foundations. As Goschen of the Foreign Office astutely noted in May 1909, while "England's great grievance against Germany was that a German navy was in course of construction," the crucial point of the crisis was its endogenous roots: "It should, however, be borne in mind in England that her present naval embarrassments were entirely due to a fault of tactics on her own part as regards naval construction; by introducing the 'Dreadnought' type she had rendered former types obsolete and thus herself destroyed her former absolute predominance."[169]

The result was a situation in which the English national self perceived for the first time its *own* diminishment and even negation not only as a form of "otherness but—as a truly oppositional threat, all the more insidious for its endogenous roots. That the English self needed merely to glimpse its own negation as this form of *internal* otherness to produce the hysteria that consumed both public and parliamentary modes of self-reference denotes a broad pathology at work in forms of English national identity that arguably feature in the context of much of its subsequent national policy. Such a suggestion also explains the contradiction of a period characterized first by the fervent demands for new Dreadnoughts as a vital form of English national identity and second by the clearly "friendly tone towards Germany which . . . distinguished the speakers on both sides of the House of Commons and the delicacy which characterized the necessary allusions to the German naval policy [all which] met with full recognition in the German press."[170]

As Hopf elucidates, "it is not nominal difference that threatens but intersubjectively relevant difference."[171] A nominal German threat clearly held tangible, material consequences for the British state. However, a change in the intersubjective meanings of Englishness associated with naval supremacy and the resulting practices proved a far greater threat. As argued by Löwenheim, "the significance of prestige as an intrinsically valued good" commensurate with ideas of a superior self vested in policy explain the subtle, ideational motivations at work behind ostensibly material interests.[172] While the naval crisis care may be viewed by the realists as an obvious need to counter threats in a bid for unit preservation, the theory is wholly unequipped to explain how English prestige, underwritten by naval preeminence operates as the 'everyday currency' of international relations in the sense that it actually mirrors (materialist power) and thus can be a useful coercive or deterrent measure."[173]

In sum, the "four-plus-four" policy may be viewed as a practical extension of the underlying discourse denoting the qualities of the English state. Further, the policy attempted to maintain constancy with its historical naval-nation discourse through forms of agency entailed in building a twentieth-century Dreadnought. The disruption of that identity by realizations of endogenous declinism regarding obsolete vessels and the unit itself was subsequently exacerbated by external threats, and it caused the narrative to reconstruct itself once again through the agency at work in the accelerated shipbuilding program. Whether asserted dynamically or reconstructed defensively, English state policy remained "a direct enactment or reflection of [its] identity politics," a policy that perceived the building of twelve Dreadnoughts from an ideational rather than materialist sense of self-preservation.[174] As Markey argues, while evidenced in overtly material, even competitive forms, "the concrete ends of prestige motivated competition are *social and historically conditioned*, and the ends sought by one society might be incompatible, even incomprehensible, to another."[175]

## POST-PANIC RESULTS

Three results emerged from the navy scare. The first was an admission by Admiral Tirpitz that the while the contracts for two German Dreadnoughts from the 1910 program were begun in advance of the normal date, the ships themselves were not being constructed in an accelerated fashion. Tirpitz's admission however merely emphasized the prevalent air of uncertainty with an unconvincing explanation that omitted any real change of German intentions. Second, Britain's decision to complete the contingent four Dreadnoughts was affected not by further German plans but by the news that Austria and Italy had begun to construct Dreadnoughts of their own. "Naval fever" appeared to be spreading unchecked throughout Europe, and work on Britain's contingent Dreadnoughts began immediately. The relief greeting this decision not only contributed to the "restoration of calm and confidence" throughout the nation, but also by "three grand spectacles of naval strength, the fleet reviews at Spithead on 12 June for the Imperial Press delegates, on the Thames at Southend, 17 July, and, for the Tsar, at Cowes, 31 July."[176] From the perspective of the nation-navy dyad, English national identity thus moved from tacit cultural preeminence in its civilizing mandate to more a reactive and vocal form that incorporated the national interest of the British state.

Finally, the events of 1909 produced the necessary ships to ensure the slim margin of security that successfully contained the German Dreadnought fleet in their own harbors for much of the war. In the opinion of Marder, "The British dreadnoughts . . . met the test of battle at Jutland, their only major test in World War I."[177] The possibility exists therefore that the extent of the navy scare in Britain served as an adequate brake on German intentions to accelerate. As Foreign Office member Findlay reported to Grey in the spring of 1909, "It is obvious that the fear of British Naval Power must recently have had a considerable effect in restraining German combativeness within certain limits."[178]

## CONCLUSION

As with every discourse, there are oppositional elements. The year 1909 need not necessarily be viewed in the above terms; indeed, it runs counter to the grain of the general themes found in contemporary political theories. The majority of IR theories could view the crisis in realist, functionalist, or liberal perspectives. Structural realism could, for example, examine systemic constraints at work between the English and German units, as an arms race fuelled largely by security dilemma issues, or the various contending economic policies of the time. The navy scare may also be categorized as a security dilemma of sorts in that it invoked some clearly competitive practices; however, many of the statements emerging from the Admiralty and Foreign Office have a tendency to combine material and ideational statements, such as the observation by Grey that while "we positively must keep on the safe side, and allow for margins of error . . . the Navy was a matter of life and death to us in a sense which could never apply to Germany."[179] Traditional realism may be capable of capturing some of these nuances, but the variable of identity outflanks realism's ability to appreciate its deeply domestic roots, its use as a foreign policy resource, and the range of external forces that sparked that policy to begin with.

Neoclassical realism's use of an intermediary variable is methodologically sensible and yields a richer, more sophisticated analysis of the role of national culture and identity within foreign policy. It gets over the difficulty that structural realism encounters in explaining how a security entity like the Admiralty took its lead not from basic precepts of defense and offense but was driven in 1909 by post-Victorian morals in the service of the English sovereign state. Neoclassical realism emphasizes the endogenous, thereby revealing the ability of decision makers "to use cultural templates in complex patterns of reasoning and justification for solving dilemmas."[180] As Weber pointed out early on, while "material and ideal interests directly govern men's conduct . . . very frequently the world images that have been created by ideas have, like switchmen, determined the tracks along which action has been pushed by the dynamic of interests."[181] Culture, in other words, rather than materialist factors, provides the framework by which historical and social developments take root and produce forms of collective self-reference, which in turn produce distinct "patterns of behavior" that can be utilized to judge policy decisions.[182] As the navy scare has illustrated, English identity, based on nationalist ideologies of the cultured and politicized collective self; demonstrates the "constitutive role" of national identity in articulating its ontological frame of unit reference, its range of national goals in 1909 (physical security and naval power among them), and its clear instantiation of prevalent thematic images of nation within policies consciously designed to reinforce the ongoing generation of that collective self.

## NOTES

1. Aaron L. Friedberg, "Sea Power: The Surrender of Worldwide Supremacy," Chapter Four in *The Weary Titan, Britain and the Experience of Relative Decline, 1895–1905* (Princeton, NJ: Princeton University Press, 1988), 152.

2. M. Gordon, "Domestic Conflict and the Origins of the First World War: The British and the German Cases," *The Journal of Modern History* 46, no. 2 (June 1974): 191.

3. Friedberg, *The Weary Titan*, 148.

4. Stoll, R., "Steaming in the Dark? Rules, Rivals and the British Navy, 1860–1913," *The Journal of Conflict Resolution* 36, no. 2 (June 1992): 272.

5. N. Choucri and R. North, *Nations in Conflict: National Growth and International Violence*, (W.H. Freeman: San Francisco, 1975), 214–18 (emphasis added).

6. R. K. Massie, *Dreadnought: Britain, Germany, and the Coming of the Great War* (New York: Random House, 1991), xxi.

7. A. T. Mahan, *The Influence of Sea Power upon History, 1660–1783* (Boston: Brown, 1895), 10.

8. A. J. Marder, *From the Dreadnought to Scapa Flow: The Royal Navy in the Fisher Era, 1904–1919*, vol. 1, *The Road to War, 1904–1919* (London: Oxford University Press, 1961), 4. Marder's "Scapa Flow" collection comprises four volumes of observations and primary sources, including original correspondence from the cabinet, the Admiralty, various committee reports, and the observations of numerous central personages involved. The compendium by E. L. Woodward, *Great Britain and the German Navy* (New York: Oxford University Press, 1935) and the memoirs of S. McKenna, *Reginald McKenna, 1863–1943: A Memoir* (London: Eyre & Spottiswoode, 1948) contain similar firsthand material. Other primary sources include those from the Public Record Office (PRO), the Hansard Parliamentary series published by Her Majesty's Stationery Office (HMSO), Admiralty correspondence, and specific cabinet reports. PRO Crown Copyright material is reproduced by Her Majesty's Stationery Office Controller, London.

9. K. Moll, "Politics, Power, and Panic: Britain's 1909 Dreadnought 'Gap,'" *Military Affairs* 29, no. 3 (Autumn 1965): 133.

10. Admiral P.H. Colomb, *Navy and Army Illustrated*, (25 June 1897): 72.

11. Admiral Sir P. Scott, *Fifty Years in the Royal Navy*, (New York: George H. Doran, 1919), 23.

12. P. Padfield, *Rule Britannia: The Victorian and Edwardian Navy* (London: Pimlico, 2002), 59.

13. Padfield, *Rule Britannia*, 82.

14. Padfield, *Rule Britannia*, 82.

15. Stoll, "Steaming in the Dark," 269.

16. Padfield, *Rule Britannia*, 212. See also H. Keppel, *A Sailor's Life under Four Sovereigns*, vol. 1 (London: Macmillan, 1899).

17. P. H. Colomb, *Memoirs of Sir Astley Cooper Key* (London: Methuen, 1898), 164.

18. D. Duedeny, "Greater Britain or Greater Synthesis? Seeley, McKinder, and Wells on Britain in the Global Industrial Era," *Review of International Studies* 27, no. 2 (April 2001): 192.

19. Marder, *From the Dreadnought to Scapa Flow*, 5. See G. P. Gooch and H. Temperley, eds., *British Documents on the Origins of the War, 1898–1914*, 11 vols. (London: HMSO, 1926–1938), vol. 4, 111–12.

20. Padfield, *Rule Britannia*, 175.

21. J. A. S. Grenville, *Lord Salisbury and Foreign Policy: The Close of the Nineteenth Century* (London: Macmillan, 1964), 193.

22. A. Thompson, "The Language of Imperialism and the Meanings of Empire: Imperial Discourse in British Politics, 1895–1914," *Journal of British Studies* 35, no. 2, Twentieth Century British Studies (April 1997): 147–77, 149.

23. *Times*, 28 June, 1897.

24. Padfield, *Rule Britannia*, 196.

25. See P. Kennedy, *The Rise of the Anglo-German Antagonism: 1860–1940* (London: Fontana Press), 1976.

26. Gooch and Temperley, *British Documents on the Origins of the War, 1898–1914*, vol. 3, appendix A, Foreign Office Memorandum, E. Crowe, 403.

27. Z. Steiner, *The Foreign Office and Foreign Policy: 1898–1914*, (Cambridge: Cambridge University Press, 1969), 113.

28. Steiner, *The Foreign Office*, 114.

29. Gooch and Temperley, *British Documents on the Origins of the War*, vol. 3, appendix A, 419–20, and vol. 6, no. 150, "Sir Edward Grey to Sir Edward Goschen," 237.

30. Steiner, *The Foreign Office*, 113.

31. Viscount Grey of Fallodon, *Twenty-Five Years, 1892-1916*, vol. 1, (New York: Frederick A. Stokes, 1925), 10–11.

32. B. Waller, *Bismarck at the Crossroads: The Reorientation of German Foreign Policy After the Congress of Berlin, 1878-1880*, (London: Methuen, 1974).

33. Massie, *Dreadnought*, 135.

34. H. Koch, "The Anglo-German Alliance Negotiations: Missed Opportunity or Myth?" *History* 54, no. 182 (October 1969): 378–92.

35. E. L. Woodward, *Great Britain and the German Navy* (New York: Oxford University Press, 1935), 55.

36. W. O. Henderson, *The Rise of German Industrial Power, 1834–1914* (Berkeley: University of California Press, 1972), 200.

37. P. Kennedy, "German World Policy and the Alliance Negotiations with England," *The Journal of Modern History* 45, no. 4 (December 1973): 609.

38. Massie, *Dreadnought*, xxv.

39. Massie, *Dreadnought*, xxv.

40. Ambassador Metternicht, quoted in Woodward, *Great Britain and the German Navy*, 170.

41. Gooch and Temperley, *British Documents on the Origins of the War*, vol. 4, 184–90.

42. Gooch and Temperley, *British Documents on the Origins of the War*, vol. 4, 184–90.

43. Paul Kennedy, *The Rise and Fall of the Great Powers* (London: Fontana Press, 1989), 271.

44. F. Naumann, quoted in J. Steinberg, "The Copenhagen Complex," *Journal of Contemporary History* 1, no. 3 (1966): 26.

45. Gordon, "Domestic Conflict," 208-9.

46. Massie, *Dreadnought*, 184.

47. Landsdowne MSS, CAB (Cabinet), "Naval Policy," 7 Dec. 1903, "1902 Memorandum by Lord Selbourne" (London: HMSO).

48. Kennedy, "German World Policy and the Alliance Negotiations with England," 624.

49. Woodward, *Great Britain and the German Navy*, 171–72 (emphasis added).

50. H. Butterfield, "Sir Edward Grey in July 1914," *Historical Studies* 5 (1965): 20.

51. Gordon, "Domestic Conflict," 196. See A. J. P. Taylor, *The Struggle for Mastery in Europe, 1848–1918* (London: Oxford University Press, 1954).

52. A. Smith, *National Identity*, (London: Penguin Books, 1999), 14–15.

53. See G. M. Trevelyan, *English Social History: A Survey of Six Centuries, Chaucer to Queen Victoria* (London: Longmans, 1944), which remains the classic reference on this area.

54. D. Cannadine, *Class in Britain* (London: Yale University Press, 1998), in particular, chapter three, "The Nineteenth Century, a Viable Hierarchical Society."

55. The landed aristocracy under the Conservatives attempted to steer the nation through the first colonial upsets, in particular the Boer War, but lost national confidence and subsequently the 1906 election. The Liberals, under Campbell-Bannerman, swept in on a platform of liberal parliamentarianism emphasizing free trade, social welfare, and disarmament.

56. M. Hendley, "'Help Us to Secure a Strong, Healthy, Prosperous and Peaceful Britain': The Social Arguments of the Campaign for Compulsory Military Service in Britain, 1899–1914," *Canadian Journal of History* 30, no. 2 (August 1995): 280.

57. Hendley, "Help Us to Secure," 280.

58. Portrayed in a decidedly moral manner, rural areas themselves "seemed to be the antithesis of the crowded and politically questionable urban centres of Britain." Hedley, Help Us to Secure," p. 18.

59. S. Collini, *English Pasts: Essays in History and Culture* (Oxford: Oxford University Press, 1999), 93.

60. S. Hynes, *The Edwardian Turn of Mind* (Princeton, NJ: Princeton University Press, 1968), 45.

61. Hendley, "Help Us to Secure," 269.

62. J. Harris, *Private Lives, Public Spirit: Britain, 1870–1914* (London: Oxford University Press, 1993).

63. Gordon, "Domestic Conflict," 199.

64. Hendley, "Help Us to Secure," 275.

65. Harris, *Private Lives*, 180.

66. P. Thane (ed.), *Origins of British Social Policy* (London: Routledge, 1978).

67. R. Weight, *Patriots: National Identity in Britain, 1940–2000* (London: Macmillan, 2002), 9.

68. Z. Steiner, "Grey, Hardinge and the Foreign Office," *The Historical Journal* 10, no. 3 (1967): 415–39. As articulated by Hardinge of the Foreign Office, the view of the cabinet was that "in the view of a general conflagration, England should stand aside." A. Nicholson, *Diplomatic Narrative*, Hardinge to Nicholson, 12 April 1909, cited in Steiner, "Grey, Hardinge and the Foreign Office," 420.

69. K. Dewar, Vice Admiral, *The Navy from Within* (London: Brown, 1939), 25–26.

70. Padfield, *Rule Britannia*, 218

71. *Times*, 20 April, 1906.

72. Marder, *From the Dreadnought to Scapa Flow*, 8.

73. H. Strachan, "The British Way in Warfare Revisited," *The Historical Journal* 26, no. 2 (June 1983): 452.

74. J. Spears, "A Transition in Naval Efficacy," *World's Work* 5, (November 1902): 2772.

75. ADM 53/19807, *Dreadnought*, Nov. 20 1908–23 March 1909 (London: PRO).

76. Massie, *Dreadnought*, 461.

77. D. K. Brown, "The Design and Construction of the Battleship Dreadnought," *Warship IV* 43 (1905): 110.

78. The Dreadnought was 490 feet long and weighed 17,900 tons. Its "armament consisted of ten 12-inch guns, each capable of hurling an 850-pound projectile." O. Parkes, *British Battleships, 1860–1950: A History of Design, Construction and Armament* (London: Seely Service, 1966), 450. Containing the first turbine engine used in a British capital ship, the Dreadnought could reach a speed of twenty-one knots, two knots faster than any ship yet constructed. Dewar, *The Navy from Within*, 50.

79. Marder, *From the Dreadnought to Scapa Flow*, 44. Indeed, the first Dreadnought "was one of those gallant little vessels which had fought off the Invincible Armada in 1588." Marder, *From the Dreadnought to Scapa Flow*. See A. M. Hadfield, *Time to Finish the Game* (London: Phoenix House, 1964), 68, for a description of the first Dreadnought vessel.

80. B. Deer, "Disunited We Stand," *Times*, February 5, 1995.

81. R. Whalen, "The Commonwealth of Peoples to Which We Racially Belong: The National Press and the Manufacturing of an Arms Race," *Historian* (Winter, 2001): 6.

82. Moll, "Politics, Power, and Panic," 135. See ADM (Admiralty) 53/19809, *Dreadnought*, Mar. 9, 1910–Feb. 16, 1911 (London: PRO), and ADM 136/7, Ship: *H.M.S. DREADNOUGHT* Remarks: 1st Class Battleship (the first big gun ship), launched 10 February 1906, 1906–1921 (London: PRO).

83. Moll, "Politics, Power, and Panic," 135.

84. Massie, *Dreadnought*, 485.

85. Massie, *Dreadnought*, 486.

86. R. Bassett, *Battle Cruisers: A History, 1908–1948* (London: Macmillan, 1981), 50–51.

87. Massie, *Dreadnought*, 487.

88. Richards MSS, Richards to Beresford, 1909, quoted in Marder, *From the Dreadnought to Scapa Flow*, 56.

89. Lloyd George, quoted in Woodward, *Great Britain and the German Navy*, 105.

90. *Manchester Guardian*, 27 February 1910.

91. ADM 116, Admiralty Memorandum, "The Modern Battleship," October, 1906 (London: PRO). See also Admiralty MSS, "The Strategic Aspects of Our Building Program," 7 January 1907 (London: PRO).

92. Moll, "Politics, Power, and Panic," 135.

93. J. Gooch, *The Plans of War: The General Staff and British Military Strategy c. 1900–1916* (London: Routledge, 1974), and Friedberg, *The Weary Titan*, 168.

94. Friedberg, *The Weary Titan*, 168.

95. Friedberg, *The Weary Titan*, 168.

96. Friedberg, *The Weary Titan*, 169.

97. Friedberg, *The Weary Titan*, 189.

98. Woodward, *Great Britain and the German Navy*, 116–17.

99. Marder, *From the Dreadnought to Scapa Flow*, 129.

100. Woodward, *Great Britain and the German Navy*, 117.

101. A. J. A. Morris, "'The English Radicals' Campaign for Disarmament and the Hague Conference of 1907," *The Journal of Modern History* 43, no. 3 (September 1971): 381.

102. *Daily Mail*, 6 March, 1907.

103. Hansard, Parliamentary Debates, House of Commons, vol. 162, col. 100 (London: HMSO).

104. Woodward, *Great Britain and German Navy*, 203.

105. Woodward, *Great Britain and German Navy*, 203.

106. Kaiser Wilhelm, quoted in J. Lepsius, A. Mendelssohn-Bartholdy, F. Thimme, eds., *Die Grosse Politik der Europäischen Kabinette, 1871–1914*, vol. 24 (Berlin, 1922–1927), 104.

107. Marder, *From the Dreadnought to Scapa Flow*, 145.

108. CAB (Cabinet) 37/97, "A Note on Naval Estimates, 1909–10" [German Naval Armaments], 2 February (London: HMSO, 1909).

109. Massie, *Dreadnought*, 608.

110. McKenna, *A Memoir*, 72.

111. C. Hazlehurst, "Asquith as Prime Minister, 1908–1916," *The English Historical Review* 85, no. 336 (July 1970): 519.

112. McKenna MSS, Admiral Jellicoe's Memorandum to McKenna, 24 Jan. 1909, in McKenna, *A Memoir*, 80.

113. CAB 37/97, "A reply to Mr Churchill's note on Navy Estimates," 5 February, R. McKenna, nos. 24 and 25 (London: HMSO, 1909).

114. Grey, quoted in Woodward, *Great Britain and the German Navy*, 220.

115. Massie, *Dreadnought*, 615.

116. Massie, *Dreadnought*, 615.

117. McKenna, cited in the *Times*, 17 March 1909.

118. Moll, "Politics, Power, and Panic," 140.

119. Admiralty MSS, Hardinge to Knollys, 26 Feb. 1909 (London: PRO).

120. McKenna MSS, 4 March 1909, Memorandum to First Sea Lord McKenna and forwarded to Prime Minister Asquith, quoted in M. Brett, ed., *Journals and Letters of Reginald Viscount Esher*, vol. 2 (London: Nicholson & Watson, 1934), 249.

121. Marder, *From the Dreadnought to Scapa Flow*, 167.

122. *Daily Telegraph*, 24 March 1909.

123. Grey's speech is quoted in full in Woodward, *Great Britain and the German Navy*, 230–34.

124. Woodward, *Great Britain and the German Navy*, 230–34 (emphasis added).

125. W. Churchill, *The World Crisis, 1911–1918*, vol. 1 (New York: Scribner's, 1923–1929), 37.

126. Woodward, *Great Britain and the German Navy*, 227.

127. CAB (Cabinet) 37/98, [Navy Estimates, 1909–1910], 24 February (London: HMSO, 1909).

128. Moll, "Politics, Power, and Panic," 138.

129. Marder, *Anatomy of British Sea Power: A History of British Naval Policy in the Pre-Dreadnought Era, 1880–1905* (New York, Oxford University Press, 1940), 112–13.

130. *Daily Telegraph*, 24 March 1909.

131. Marder, *From the Dreadnought to Scapa Flow*, 167.

132. T. R. Threlfall, "Labour and the Navy," *The Nineteenth Century and After*, vol. LXXV, (March 1914): 688.

133. W. M. Ryan, "The Invasion Controversy of 1906–1908: Lieutenant-Colonel Charles à Court Repington and British Perceptions of the German Menace," *Military Affairs* 44, no. 1 (February 1980): 8.

134. Whalen, "The Commonwealth of Peoples," 5.

135. Ryan, "The Invasion Controversy," 8.

136. E. Childers, *The Riddle of the Sands* (New York: Dover, 1903), and W. Le Queux, *The Invasion of 1910* (London: Eveleigh Nash, 1906).

137. Le Queux, *The Invasion of 1910*, 34.

138. Childers, *The Riddle of the Sands*, 97.

139. Lord Roberts, quoted in Hynes, *The Edwardian Turn of Mind*, 40.

140. Massie, *Dreadnought* , 636.

141. Le Queux, *The Invasion of 1910*, i.

142. Ryan, "The Invasion Controversy," 9.

143. Massie, *Dreadnought* , 636.

144. Massie, *Dreadnought*, 637.

145. Campbell-Bannerman, quoted in Hynes, *The Edwardian Turn of Mind*, 42.

146. Balfour, quoted in Marder, *Anatomy of British Sea Power*, 378.

147. Major General Sir F. Maurice, *Haldane: 1856–1928*, vol. 2. (London: Faber and Faber, 1937–1939), 256.

148. N. Hiley, "The Failure of British Counter-Espionage against Germany, 1907–1914," *The Historical Journal* 28, no. 4 (December 1985): 836.

149. G. du Maurier, *An Englishman's Home* (London: Eveleigh Nash, 1908).

150. H. Weinroth, "Left-Wing Opposition to Naval Armaments in Britain before 1914," *Journal of Contemporary History* 6, no. 4, (1971), 113.

151. Hynes, *The Edwardian Turn of Mind*, 47.

152. Massie, *Dreadnought*, 639.

153. Woodward, *Great Britain and the German Navy*, 117.

154. Massie, *Dreadnought*, 639.

155. Ryan, "The Invasion Controversy," 9.

156. Massie, *Dreadnought*, 639.

157. Gooch and Temperley, *British Documents on the Origins of the War*, vol.6, no. 180, "Sir E. Goschen to Sir Edward Grey," May 20, 1909, 272.

158. G. King, R. Keohane, and S. Verba, *Designing Social Inquiry* (Princeton, NJ: Princeton University Press, 1994), 79.

159. Woodward, *Great Britain and the German Navy*, 117.

160. H. J. Morgenthau, *Politics among Nations: The Struggle for Power and Peace*, 3rd ed. (New York: Alfred A. Knopf, 1961), 9.

161. Marder, *From the Dreadnought to Scapa Flow*, 150.

162. Marder, *From the Dreadnought to Scapa Flow*, 150.

163. Moll, "Politics, Power, and Panic," 14, and Marder, *From the Dreadnought to Scapa Flow*, 167.

164. *Times*, 1 July 1904.

165. T. Hopf, *Social Construction of International Politics: Identities and Foreign Policies, Moscow, 1955 and 1999* (Ithaca, NY: Cornell University Press, 2002), 8.

166. Gooch and Temperley, *British Documents on the Origins of the War*, vol. 6, no. 146, "Note from Sir Edward Goschen to Sir Edward Grey," 232.

167. Gooch and Temperely, *British Documents on the Origins of the War*, vol. 5, no. 151, "Sir Edward Grey to Sir E. Goschen," January 4, 1909, 238.

168. O. Löwenheim, "'Do Ourselves Credit and Render a Lasting Service to Mankind': British Moral Prestige, Humanitarian Intervention, and the Barbary Pirates," *International Studies Quarterly* 47, no. 1 (March 2003): 26.

169. Gooch and Temperley, *British Documents on the Origins of the War*, vol. 6, no. 180, "Sir E. Goschen to Sir Edward Grey," May 20, 1909, 272–73.

170. Gooch and Temperley, *British Documents on the Origins of the War*, vol. 6, no. 157, "Sir E. Goschen to Sir Edward Grey," Berlin, March 19, 1909, 246.

171. Hopf, *Social Construction of International Politics*, 8.

172. Löwenheim, "British Moral Prestige," 27, citing R. Gilpin, *War and Change in World Politics* (New York: Cambridge University Press, 1981), 30–33.

173. Löwenheim, "British Moral Prestige," 27.

174. P. Katzenstein, ed., *The Culture of National Security: Norms and Identity in World Politics* (New York: Columbia University Press, 1996), 61.

175. D. Markey, "Prestige and the Origins of War: Returning to Realism's Roots," *Security Studies* 8 (1999): 161.

176. Marder, *From the Dreadnought to Scapa Flow*, 171.

177. Marder, *From the Dreadnought to Scapa Flow*, 70.

178. Gooch and Temperley, *British Documents on the Origins of the War*, vol. 6, no. 168, "Mr. Findlay to Sir Edward Grey," 259.

179. Gooch and Temperley, *British Documents on the Origins of the War*, vol. 6, no. 155, "Sir Edward Grey to Sir E. Goschen," March 17, 1909, 243.

180. F. Kratochwil, "Is the Ship of Culture at Sea or Returning?" in *The Return of Culture and Identity in IR Theory*, ed. Y. Lapid and F. Kratochwil (Boulder, CO: Lynne Rienner Publishers, 1996), 209.

181. M. Weber, quoted in H. Kissinger, *Diplomacy* (New York: Simon and Schuster, 1994).

182. C. Geertz, *The Interpretation of Cultures* (New York: Basic Books, 1973), 89.

# 6

## The 1982 Falklands Crisis

### Englishness, Britishness, and Ontological Security

As one moves from the nineteenth and early twentieth century to the postwar period, so the national identity under examination shifts from aspects of Englishness to that of Britishness. World War II, the fiasco of Suez, and the gradual disintegration of the British Empire had profound effects upon the strategic and symbolic status of Britain. During this period, England and Englishness recede as a major mode of self-reference, to be replaced by a defensively anxious Britishness, an identity preoccupied with retaining the trappings of international seniority while learning to operate in an increasingly interdependent environment. Even in the context of the Argentine invasion on British territory, Britain could not respond independently, but required comprehensive U.S. diplomatic support and economic assistance in the form of sanctions from the EC. Thus, while the Task Force was British alone, Britain received substantial assistance from a number of allies.

The architecture of Britain's response combined ideological, cultural, and strategic elements. The three key principles of sovereignty, law, and democracy comprised the basis of its ideological response; the concept of "islandness" constituted the cultural affiliation crafted between the British and the Falklanders, while the strategic element related to the conscious desire to rehabilitate Britain's postwar foreign policy status. Despite the association of sovereignty, law, and democracy with the historical development of English political culture, during the Falklands War these principles were not drawn upon as actionable touchstones of Englishness as in the previous case studies. They did however operate in three key ways. First, as state identifiers by which the majority of the British populace, the policy makers, and the Falklanders themselves could identify *with* Britain and British foreign policy. Second, these principles had something of a multiplier effect when used by Britain on behalf of the Falklanders (and in the absence of their use by Argentina) and as an example to the wider international realm, and they helped to reinforce the increasingly potent Self/Other categories between Britain and Argentina. Finally, these principles helped to address the slippage between an older era in which British political dominance was underwritten by English forms of self-reference and the postwar era in which British unity would draw more comprehensively upon a form of Britishness constituted largely by patriotism and reasserted ambition.

As will be seen, these ideological, cultural, and strategic forces also clarify the role that ontological security played in Britain's foreign policy response. Ontological security encompasses the measures taken by a state to ensure a measure of "predictability in relationships to the world, which creates a desire for stable social identities." This form of security is not merely material, but driven by ideational and cultural forces that require a state to augment its external sense of itself relative to others, usually by asserting its "moral prestige and credibility" both internally and within the wider state system.[1] An opportunity, in other words, needs to present itself in order for such assertions to take place and for new relationships and routines to be established. Foreign policy helps provide the framework for ordering Britain's relationship with Argentina and others, but national identity explains how the content of British foreign policy took on hyper-patriotic and postimperial rhetoric articulating a sense of the British political self.

## HISTORICAL BACKGROUND

The earliest records of the Falkland Islands are somewhat ambiguous. Spanish exploration and forays under Magellan date from 1522, followed by a Dutch landing in 1600 and a British naval expedition in 1690. England then claimed the islands, naming the sound between the eastern and western islands after Viscount Falkland, the Commissioner of the Royal Navy.[2] Responding in 1765 to the French settlement the previous year of East Falkland, by establishing a small garrison on the West Falkland Island, the British were followed by Spanish merchants, who then purchased the French settlement of Port Louis, which from their perspective entailed Spanish rights to the land.[3] In 1770, a Spanish flotilla requested the British inhabitants to leave the western islands. Only by threatening war with Spain did George III manage to retain the British West Falkland outpost, only to evacuate in 1774 for economic reasons. Spain swiftly asserted its rights over the ring of islands until 1811, when, faced with the upheaval of losing its American colonies, it turned its attention elsewhere.

After World War II, the gradual windup of the British Empire presented an opportunity in Argentine eyes to raise the issue of Falkland sovereignty, and the country made its first claim to the United Nations (UN) in 1945. Each of Britain's offers to have the dispute mediated at the International Court of Justice in The Hague (1947, 1948, and 1955) was declined by Argentina. The 1964 UN resolution called on both sides to reach a settlement "in the best interests of the population of the Falkland Islands."[4] There followed seventeen years of protracted diplomatic wrangling that produced some limited economic and transport cooperation but a stalemate over sovereignty. Some foreign policy pragmatism is evident in the British consideration to transfer sovereignty versus the benefit of solving the diplomatic impasse. Successive British governments however had little latitude due to the robust parliamentary Falklands lobby and the outspoken nature of the Islanders themselves, who were emphatic in their determination to remain British subjects. Britain consequently upheld the Islanders' right to self-determination, which Argentina in turn repeatedly rejected.

After failed talks in February 1982, the issue grew increasingly rancorous; the Argentine tone shifted considerably, suggesting that if the Islands were not returned, no further talks would be offered, and military action considered.[5] On 19 March 1982 the commander of the British Antarctic Survey base on South Georgia, an outlier of the Falklands, reported that an Argentine navy cargo ship had landed a dozen men at Leith harbor without permission, had begun removing scrap metal from a former whaling station, and had raised the Argentine flag. Confronted by Britain, Argentina responded that it had no knowledge of the excursion. After British requests to remove the men and the deploying of vessels by both sides, General Leopoldo Galtieri launched Operation Rosario, a force of 10,000 troops to the capital, Port Stanley on 31 March, under the command of the Admiral Jorge Anaya. Later that same day, Prime Minister Margaret Thatcher contacted U.S. President Ronald Reagan, requesting him to intervene directly with Galtieri before taking action. However, Galtieri spoke to Reagan only after the forces had been deployed.

In the early hours of 2 April 1982, Governor Reginald Hunt was joined in Port Stanley by Majors Noot and Norman.[6] After a vigorous but hopeless attempt by their sixty-eight men to repel the Argentine forces, the British officers surrendered. The news was received with jubilation in Buenos Aires; union riots the previous week were swiftly replaced by parades and shows of solidarity for Galtieri. When the news reached London later that day, a War Cabinet was established.[7] A day later, with the support of France's President Mitterrand and King Hussein of Jordan, the UN Security Council passed Resolution 502. Drafted by UK Ambassador Sir Anthony Parsons, it called first for an end to hostilities, followed by the immediate withdrawal of Argentine forces and the seeking of a diplomatic solution. With only Russia, Poland, China, and Spain abstaining, the main thrust of Britain's foreign policy had been set. On 5 April, the British Task Force set out from Portsmouth and other ports for the southern Atlantic; the force comprising forty-four ships: carriers, frigates, destroyers, submarines plus aircraft, and ten thousand troops, including the aircraft carriers HMS *Hermes* and HMS *Invincible*, left Portsmouth "at an eventual cost of £2,000 million."[8] On the same day, three government ministers, Lord Carrington, Humphrey Atkins, and Richard Luce resigned on the issue of British unpreparedness at the attack.

Between the departure of the force, its arrival, and the first attacks on 1 May, Britain found itself the subject of intense diplomatic activity by various international actors all keen to reach a nonmilitary solution. From 8 April, actively supported by President Reagan, the U.S. ambassador, Alexander Haig, undertook his fabled "shuttle diplomacy," traveling frequently between London, Washington, and Buenos Aires, brokering a deal for dual governance of the islands. On 10 April (despite some opposition from Spain and Italy), the EEC declared diplomatic support for Britain and imposed sanctions against Argentina. This was followed by similar support from the majority of Commonwealth countries trading with Argentina, as well as support from NATO. On 23 April, with Argentina having drafted more than 10,000 troops to the islands, Britain issued a warning to Argentina that any warship or military aircraft representing a threat to its Task Force would be dealt with accordingly. South Georgia was recaptured two days later, with Britain declaring a 200-nautical-mile maritime exclusive zone around the islands on 30 April, a day after Argentina rejected Haig's final attempt at a settlement.

Two days later, Peruvian president Belaundé outlined a new peace proposal. Galtieri appeared to have given his preliminary acceptance when the most disputed event of the entire conflict then occurred. The British submarine HMS *Conqueror* fired at the Argentine cruiser *General Belgrano*, supposing it to be inside the exclusive zone, sinking the ship along with 400 of its crew. The Argentine naval command immediately disputed the placement of the *Belgrano*, arguing that the cruiser was not only outside the zone but sailing away from the islands. On 4 May, Argentine reprisals took the form of air attacks using Exocet surface-to-air missiles, and sank the British destroyer HMS *Sheffield*. Another British Harrier was downed and the Argentine trawler *Narwal* was sunk in retaliation. Following the sinking of an Argentine supply ship and three Skyhawks, British Special Forces then conducted a night raid on Pebble Island, destroying eleven grounded Argentine aircraft.[9] On 18 May, the UN secretary general, Perez de Cuellar, presented a peace proposal, which was immediately rejected by Britain. Three days later, the British Second Battalion Parachute Regiment successfully landed on East Falkland, capturing the outposts of Darwin and Goose Green before marching on to Port Stanley.

The following week saw an overwhelming number of attacks. The British cruiser HMS *Ardent* was sunk, followed by the destruction of nine Argentine aircraft; the British cruiser HMS *Antelope* then sank after the detonation of an unexploded bomb, followed by the destruction of a further seventeen Argentine aircraft; the cruiser HMS *Coventry* was hit by three bombs dropped from Argentine Skyhawks while the *MV Atlantic Conveyor* was hit by another Exocet missile.[10] Throughout May 1982, Argentine positions were attacked by British warships and Harrier aircraft. On 31 May, British troops surrounded the capital Port Stanley, repeating its terms of cease-fire the following day while simultaneously vetoing the UN Security Council Panamanian-Spanish cease-fire resolution. One final British cruiser, the HMS *Glamorgan* was struck by an Exocet missile before the British Task Force overthrew the Argentine garrison in Port Stanley on 14 June, "much helped by American technical assistance," effectively bringing the conflict to an end.[11] After the Argentine commander Menendez had agreed to an unnegotiated cease-fire, Britain formally declared the cessation of hostilities and established a "Falkland Islands Protection Zone" of 150 miles to replace the 200-mile exclusion zone established around the islands during the war. In total, the Falklands conflict lasted seventy-two days, with nearly a thousand casualties, one-third of which were British.[12] The following year, the Islanders were granted full British citizenship and benefited from a wide range of British investments, as well as the liberalization of economic measures that had been stalled as a result of diplomatic tension with Argentina. A new constitution was enacted in 1985 that promoted a devolution-style form of self-government.

Similar to the 1909 naval scare, elements of national identity, public attitudes, and political misperceptions are strikingly evident in the outcomes of the Falklands conflict. At the mercy of enormous inflation and crippling national debt, the Galtieri junta, which had taken power in late 1981, appeared in need of an event to divert domestic attention from its radically imprudent fiscal policies and the regime's ongoing human rights violations.[13] A military solution was pushed by Admiral Jorge Anaya, who, along with Galtieri assumed that Britain would not respond militarily and that a successful invasion would prop up its receding legitimacy.

Due to the apparent "failure of British political intelligence to receive the warnings given by Argentina," Britain dismissed the very real seriousness of the Argentine threat of force emanating from the Argentinean press, "and largely misconstrued the nuances of the political discourse emanating from Buenos Aires and the New York negotiations."[14] In turn, Argentina underestimated the "willingness and ability [of Britain] to retake the islands by force," based on a miscalculation regarding the distance between Britain and the Falklands.[15] This was worsened by their dismissive attitude regarding British forces, the degree of personal charisma displayed by Prime Minister Thatcher, and the wide support for Britain generated domestically and internationally. Misperceptions, of course, contributed to the outbreak of hostilities; however, additional factors also require investigation.[16]

National identity is not a subtle force during this crisis. As an intervening variable, it requires attention in order to appreciate how it helped to contextualize the impact of ontological security on the making of foreign policy in the crisis. As above, ontological security refers broadly to the "security of the self" which is "achieved by routinizing relationships with significant others" with the result that states "become attached to those relationships."[17] While physical security is something that states cannot help but pursue, their choices regarding their ontological security are wider; their sense of self and their routines with others can be pursued firmly or flexibly. The choice between the two is by necessity an attempt to balance with the security demands of other states in the system, its past history of balancing (status quo or challenging), and the domestic dictates of its own political culture. The domestic element is vital here. Ontological security, like national identity—is "extrapolated from the individual level"; just as one feels the need to "experience oneself as a whole, continuous person in time—as being rather than constantly changing—in order to realize a sense of agency," national collectives too "need to feel secure in who they are, as *identities or selves*."[18] Uncertainty, threat, challenge, rivalry—all these undermine identity and security, rendering actors unable to "systematically relate ends to means."[19] The deeply unsettling climate of the late twentieth century represented a critical mass of uncertainty for an increasingly beleaguered English identity and an incoherent British self, dispossessed of its empire, humiliated at Suez, detached from historical entitlement but still retaining an attitude of entitlement regarding its engagement with other states. Thus, by 1982, the key factor in changing this situation was in large part motivated by Britain's (and Argentina's) dissatisfaction with their contemporary national identities and the subsequent requirement to shore up its ontological insecurity by rehabilitating its international status.[20]

## IDEOLOGICAL CONTENT: SOVEREIGNTY, LAW, AND DEMOCRACY

This section examines the role of sovereignty, democracy, legality and "islandness" as state signifiers. Substantively, these concepts provided the ideological template for British foreign policy; instrumentally, they operated by allowing the British public, the Falkland Islanders, and key international allies to identify *with* Britain as a result of its justificatory use of these principles in its foreign policy.

### Sovereignty

The Falkland conflict arose from a protracted diplomatic struggle regarding the claim of sovereignty of the islands. Argentina interpreted its own actions not as an invasion but as the legitimate reoccupation of its sovereign territory, the use of force being necessary for the "reassertion of the sovereign principle."[21] On the basis of having exercised *de facto* sovereignty over the Falklands since 1833, and *de jure* sovereignty since 1690, Britain characterized the Argentine action as an unprovoked invasion of a British dependent territory. In her statement to an extraordinary convening of the House of Commons on 3 April, Thatcher further clarified the principle of sovereignty and set the framework for the ensuing political discourse:

> The House meets this Saturday to respond to a situation of great gravity. We are here because, for the first time for many years, British sovereign territory has been invaded by a foreign power. . . . However, let us declare and resolve that our duty now is to repossess our possessions and to rescue our own people. Our right to the Falkland Islands is undoubted. Our sovereignty is unimpeachable. British interest in that part of the world, in my judgment, is substantial. . . . The British interest would be substantial even if we were discussing the affairs of just one fellow citizen. . . . Of course, we must explore every diplomatic and legal means to recover what is legitimately ours.[22]

Sovereignty is a key force in the development of European political history. As the cardinal attribute of the Westphalian state unit, the concept of sovereignty is first and foremost a feature of statehood. Its evolution in the British Isles generated a number of memorable incarnations, ranging from the power wielded by the Church to the monarchical sovereignty of the medieval and Tudor periods to the King-in-Parliament of the seventeenth century, the parliamentary sovereignty of the eighteenth century to the incremental democratization of the House of Commons in the late eighteenth and early nineteenth centuries. Colls suggests that England historically vested its "final wholeness, or sovereignty" not in a constitution nor in a monarch nor entirely in Parliament, but "in the national self" that served to knit all three together.[23] Indeed the combined "singularity and divisibility" exhibited by successive types of sovereign authority "was nothing less than the hallmark of English political genius."[24]

In addition to securing statehood, sovereignty assists the function of statecraft by establishing the contours of the national interest, specifically by underwriting external freedom of action. Gladstone's explanation of the political latitude inherent in sovereignty characterized British policy for decades: "England should keep entire in her own hands the means of estimating her own obligations upon the various states of facts as they arise; she should not foreclose and narrow her own liberty of choice by declarations made to other Powers, in their real or supposed interests, of which they would claim to be at least joint interpreters."[25] Contemporary interpretations continue to prioritize freedom of action as a vital application of the power of sovereignty, defined as the national interests pursued via statecraft.[26]

A further operation of state sovereignty involves its application within international law, in which it represents "not a legal authority over all other states, but rather legal authority which is not in law dependent on any other earthly authority. Sovereignty in the strict and narrowest sense of the term implies, therefore, independence all round, within and without the borders of the country."[27] In this way, the principle of sovereignty denoted the discursive principle of autonomy applicable for Britain and its colonial possessions including the Falkland Islands, and entailed the freedom of action to defend them. A breach of the autonomous realm of the Falkland Islands was therefore defined as a breach of British sovereignty itself. From the British perspective, Argentina had, by invading the islands, not merely abrogated the principle of state sovereignty but had attempted to reinterpret the particularly English principle of "liberty of choice" defined by Gladstone a century earlier. The declaration of the *Times* that "when British territory is invaded, it is not just an invasion of our land, but of our whole spirit" is an emotive reflection on the cardinal role played by sovereignty in defining English, and latterly British, statehood and its subsequent statecraft.[28]

Consequentially and as usually happens in such cases—those under duress are recast: the Falklanders were reincarnated as the "new British." Sovereignty functions as a state signifier in a number of ways. First, defined within the principle of sovereignty, the Islanders could be easily identified as British citizens, or in Thatcher's words, as "dear fellow citizens."[29] Second, after reconstituting the people, sovereign claims were reestablished. As argued by the *Times*: "the Falklanders are our people. They are British citizens. The Falkland Islands are British territory. We are all Falklanders now."[30] Third, as examined below, its application denoted the use of a domestic discourse of Britishness (underwritten with more than a trace of Englishness) rather than an imperial discourse in responding to the invasion. Bolstered by international support, Britain would not stand alone; it would, however, fight alone. This transformed the Falklands crisis into something of a "test-case for Britain's ability to defend her own boundaries . . . both [its] physical and ideological frontiers, to maintain . . . Britain's territorial and cultural sovereignty."[31]

## Democracy

Like sovereignty, democracy has undergone a number of permutations as modes of national self-reference *within* the broader British political unit. Colls again suggests that one can distinguish between English democracy as an "ideology of a separable and independent nation" and British state-hood.[32] This approach however does little to actually clarify modes of Englishness and earlier Britishness. More perceptive is Kissinger's observation that, "One cause of Great Britain's single-mindedness in times of crisis was the representative nature of its political institutions. . . . Because British foreign policy grew out of open debates, the British people displayed extraordinary unity in times of war."[33]

More importantly, the concept of democracy operated as an oppositional category to highlight the quintessential "otherness" of the Argentines. Britain and the Islanders were portrayed as *democratic* and free, both now and in the past. By contrast, the Argentine government embodied a tyrannical form of authority, whose people were utterly oppressed: "The people of Argentina are again today on their knees under the rifle butts of a military tyranny. . . ."[34] Contextualized against its last military victory, British democracy grew even more strident: "As in 1939, so today, the same principles apply to the Falklands. We have given our word and we must, where we can, prevent the expansionist policies of a dictatorship affecting our interests.[35] Generally, the Argentine government rather than the citizenry themselves was criticized: "We can hardly forget that thousands of innocent people fighting for their political rights in the Argentine, are in prison and have been tortured."[36] The national perspective was clear: democracy entailed the freedom of the collective will of the nation enshrined in a state to determine its government and interests in representative fashion. These principles had been removed from the Argentine people under Galtieri, and the invasion now physically imposed such "otherness" on the democratic society of the Falkland Islanders. Democracy was thus to be returned to the Falklanders, and the same lesson taught by extension to the Argentine government. As Thatcher argued, "We cannot allow the democratic rights of the islanders to be denied by the territorial ambitions of Argentina."[37] Opposition leader Michael Foot argued that the democratic principle at work also allowed Britain to uphold its claim "to be a defender of people's freedom throughout the world."[38] This had the effect of endowing Britain with a postwar national role as a defender of democracy, a major tool in its efforts to throw off ontological insecurity.

The democratic principle yielded much rhetorical juggling of British democracy against Argentine dictatorship, liberal versus military expansionism, and rule of law versus military rule. Clearly, Argentine rule was perceived as a transgression of both sovereign and democratic principles. The junta had amalgamated executive, legislative, and judicial powers, and oppressive practices had resulted. In Britain, "where these three powers were separated out . . . there was law, security of property and liberty."[39] Thus, much of the rhetoric emanating from the British state over the Falklands was a deliberate summoning up of a core national principle, traceable to a distinctly British and even English past. Evidence of this may be found within the concepts that designated 15 June 1982 as "Freedom's Day," and that declared the sovereign and democratic liberty of the Falklanders by drawing deliberate parallels with the anniversary of the Magna Carta and the Revolution of 1688, both watershed events in the national consciousness that inculcated the essence of the democratic ideal at work in the original English Parliament.[40]

The process of blending British sovereignty, democracy, and a hint of English liberties was lent moral credence by Robert Runcie, the Archbishop of Canterbury, who argued that, "We must stand by the Falkland islanders to ensure that they and other similar [*sic*] exposed groups of people in the world do not have to live in continual fear of aggression by more powerful neighbors."[41] In the emergency debate on 3 April, opposition leader Michael Foot had also married democratic ideals with moral necessity, juxtaposed against the immorality of dictators in a style reminiscent of Gladstone: "The rights and circumstances of the people in the Falkland Islands must be uppermost in our minds. . . . We have a moral duty, a political duty. . . . The people of the Falkland Islands . . . are faced with an act of naked, and unqualified aggression, carried out in the most shameful and disreputable circumstances."[42]

## Legality

In abrogating both sovereignty and the democratic principles of liberty and freedom, the Argentines were also portrayed as law breakers: "There is no basis in law for Argentina's claim to the Falklands. . . . At present we are operating under Article 51 of the UN Charter, which entitles us to take any action in the course of self-defence."[43] In addition to new-found international roles as upholders of contemporary sovereignty and defenders of democracy, Britain attempted to institute itself as guardians of law. As Thatcher argued, "the whole House will join me in condemning totally this unprovoked aggression. . . . It has not a shred of justification, and not a scrap of legality."[44] The role of law certainly evokes more genuine resonances of Englishness than either sovereignty or democracy. As Colls suggests,

> The case for the freeborn Englishman went deeper and wider than the case for the supremacy of Parliament [where] most people were not entitled to vote. Common-law doctrine, on the other hand, held that the law embodied nothing less than the historic *nature* of the English people . . . regarded as the most essential and the most intimate bond between the nation and their state. . . . *What was said of the law came to be said also of the nation.*[45]

The body of English common law represents an eminently *constructed* body of decisions that are arrived at by the application of reason on a case-by-case basis. As stated by Judge Mansfield, "The Common law of England . . . is only common reason or usage."[46] Rather than a mystic union in which sovereignty, democracy, law (and more) symbiotically represent the English nation, one need simply argue that England's legal corpus rested on "the original experience of a people" as a result of its usage, allowing the "law and nation [to] form and inform each other from the start."[47] From here, one can suggest that aspects of Englishness arise from a discourse of commonality, underwritten by common practice inherent in its legal framework, from which the principles of sovereignty and democracy *subsequently* arose as practices within the state unit.

Law provides an eminently discursive method of analyzing national identity, particularly when aspects of this law are drawn upon in practice. By defining the Argentine *junta* as a law-breaking society, Britishness was sharpened within the discourse of the law applied. In order for this identity to take effect, the English forms of law had to clearly inform British statehood and statecraft. In the case of the Falklands, this was possible due to a legal history in which English common law was perceived as

> not only a very just and excellent law in itself, but it is singularly accommodated to the Frame of the English Government, and to the Disposition of the English Nation, and such as by a long Experience and Use is as it were incorporated into their very *Temperament*, and in a Manner, become the Complection and *Constitution* of the English Commonwealth.[48]

The Falklands lay within the remit of this "frame of government" in terms of English and subsequently British statehood; but Argentina lay beyond it. What emerged was a dual discourse—the pitting of one identity against another: the sovereign, democratic, and legal principles embodied in British statehood versus a South American military state regarded as irrational, unjust, and tyrannical. This juxtaposition is nicely articulated by Hale:

> The British sought to characterize themselves as essentially *rational* and reasonable people. Thus in initial stages of the conflict we find pleas *against* jingoistic excesses . . . in favour of cool, restrained, political and public behavior. . . . This particular stress on rationality . . . was to set the dominant tone of the conflict, not jingoistic and patriot emotion. It was semiotically valorized as a rational, sensible, legal and professional conflict, undertaken in the defense of democracy, in which the means used were appropriate to the higher ends of the conflict.

What directs statehood also orients statecraft. Britain necessarily had to make these precepts work, not merely as state signifiers to gain domestic support, but to underwrite the ultimate correctness of its decision to resort to military power in its Falklands foreign policy. Sovereign foundations and rational (if not necessarily restrained) implementation were embodied in British military tactics, specifically through the doctrine of the "minimum use of force."[49]

## Cultural Content: The Role of "Islandness"

As well as the ideological roots of Britishness deployed in Falklands foreign policy, the cultural image of "islandness" also features prominently. Making reference to "this ancient country rising as one nation . . . [in which] the springs of pride in Britain flow again," Thatcher drew emphatically on the imagery of a broader British identity, now newly operationalized.[50] This proved effective for two reasons. First, the Task Force sent to liberate the islands represented the nationalities of the three British nations and symbolized an externalized form of a "renewed compact between the three nations of Britain."[51] Secondly, the Falklanders themselves, as islanders, hailed from a combined English, Welsh, and Scottish ancestry, re-creating in the South Atlantic a microcosm of British demography and territory. The "domestication" of the Falklanders, primarily by virtue of their islandness, is a key component of both the political discourse—Thatcher quickly picked up on both the strategic and cultural advantages inherent in the concept of islandness—and the public discourse, as evidenced in repeated statements by the press that "we are all Falklanders now."

This quality of islandness provided both a descriptive way of simultaneously identifying the Islanders with the Falklands and Britain, and a prescriptive way of subsequently identifying British foreign policy with their defense. In her statement to the House on 3 April, Thatcher makes both aspects clear. Descriptively, the Islanders are culturally "British in stock and tradition," and politically "still tremendously loyal" to Britain:

> The people of the Falkland Islands, like the people of the United Kingdom, are an island race. Their way of life is British; their allegiance is to the Crown. They are few in number, but they have the right to live in peace, to choose their own way of life and to determine their own allegiance. Their way of life is British; their allegiance is to the Crown.[52]

Since the "unequivocal wishes" of the Falkland Islanders was "to remain British in allegiance," the invasion left a very simple foreign policy prescription: "It is the wish of the British people and the duty of Her Majesty's Government to do everything that we can to uphold that right." Opposition leader M.P. Michael Foot took this further, arguing that "It is a question of people who wish to be associated with this country and who have built their whole lives on the basis of association with this country. We have a moral duty, a political duty and every other kind of duty to ensure that that is sustained." This is a good example not only of the inherent fusing of strategic and cultural dynamics in pursuance of a justifiable foreign policy, but of the sheer power inherent in authorship, in which actors who first define the issues can ascribe to it key characteristics that help to make it more palatable to both domestic and international audiences.

## THE DUAL POLITICAL DISCOURSE

Within Britain, "the decision to reconquer the Falkland Islands proved extremely popular, apparently uniting people of different backgrounds, class and political persuasion."[53] Indeed, the policy was so popular that it blurs to some extent the actual nuances of the domestic discourse. The inflammatory tone attributed to the public and media elements during the Falklands crisis tempts one to regard the foray as a last gasp at imperial glory. While there were latent elements of the former, the resurgent Britishness entailed in the process of rehabilitating British international status within the context of ontological security via a hard-line foreign policy on the Falklands is ultimately more representative. However, as elements of both contributed to the overall discourse, revealing that "the patriotism of 1982, like the national identity it expressed, was not seamless," both are briefly examined.[54]

### Imperialism Redux

The postimperial discourse of the crisis suggests the deliberate application of a liberal imperialist tone to the Falklands episode in order to create a pervasive sense of nostalgia for a period of past imperial greatness.[55] According to this view, one hears traces of neoimperialism in the words of Thatcher, who proclaimed:

> There were those who thought we could no longer do the great things we once did. Those who believed that our decline was irreversible . . . that Britain was no longer the nation that had built an Empire and ruled a quarter of the world. Well, they were wrong. The lesson of the Falklands is that Britain has not changed and that this nation still has those sterling qualities that shine through our history. This generation can match their fathers and grandfathers in ability, in courage and in resolution.[56]

Disseminated in newspapers, television, and radio, this discourse emphasized the allusions to history and empire, while ignoring the more interesting references to "sterling qualities." Suggesting that core elements of British society were unwilling to see the end of its past greatness, the discourse revolved around race-driven self/other dyads, including racist references to Argentine "bean-eaters [finally] . . . earn[ing] the fleet's respect," and classifying the Falklands as a former colonial area, which denoted a broad slippage to a form of unreconstructed imperial identity.[57] For E. P. Thompson, attuned to the subtler nuances of this discourse, the entire event "was about something other than the Falkland Islands. It was something more—a moment of imperial atavism drenched in the nostalgias of those now in their late middle-age; the officer class . . . it was as if the need for a pageant of this kind had long been working its way up to the surface of the collective unconscious and the Falklands crisis gave it the pretext to come out."[58]

Within the perimeters of this imperial discourse, the role of the Task Force was central: a military response to obliterate an inferior, tyrannical foe that had had the temerity to physically trespass on British political and cultural mores. From this perspective, Galtieri was regarded as a "fanatic, with complete disregard for [British] 'traditional' values, never mind international law."[59] Accordingly, such views wholly supported the war but used terms derived from an imperial rather than contemporary form of Britishness in its fervent support of the invasion.

Unsurprisingly, the imperial discourse featured primarily in the media. Thatcher referred to the unifying factor of boisterous national identity as the "Falkland Factor," which rendered the conflict as "the last of the old wars in so far as the public relied on the voices and dispatches of war correspondents and cohorts of armchair strategists."[60] As such, nationalist-oriented newspapers led by the *Sun* were keen to "indulge in emotions and language which had been denied to British newspapers for a generation. This was no shady [international] adventure like Suez, no messy, drawn-out conflict in Ulster," but rather an opportunity to "give those damn Argies a whole lot of bargy."[61] Arguably, Thatcher herself contributed to an element of the imperial tone in the popular discourse during the Falklands episode, and her "encouragement and exploitation of jingoism for her own political ends richly deserves to be criticized."[62] However, the militant imperial overtones "blinded many people to the central question at hand: the rule of international law," and a restoration of both principle and populace—Falklanders and British alike.[63]

National domestic identity is a potent force, especially within a country with a strong imperial past. However, domestic and imperial modes of self reference should not be confused when analyzing a given historic event. Arguably, twentieth-century Britain has struggled to exorcise "the spirit of Kipling and Cecil Rhodes" and not always successfully.[64] It is not altogether surprising, given such a perfect opportunity, that some forms of imperial sensationalism would arise. While the jingoist views in the popular newspapers and expressed by a minority in Parliament were certainly potent, they were not however pervasive enough to typify either the type of identity at work in the overall Falkland discourse or the justification behind the foreign policy decisions. As Porter argues:

There was no imperial *rationale* to it. Britain did not fight Argentines over the Falkland Islands for profit, or for the security of her sea-lanes, or for the material or spiritual good of anyone. She fought them for a principle (to resist aggression), to restore her amour propre, and possibly for electoral profit. . . . The jingoism released by the affair was, equally, not at all an imperial one; that is, one that revealed a particular imperial as against a merely national pride. . . . So far as the empire itself was concerned . . . few Britons cared at all for what remained. They were, most of them, proud of defending the Falklands; but none was particularly proud of *having* them to defend.[65]

Imperialism thus represents neither the symbolic and strategic factors "embodied in national self images" of late twentieth-century Britishness nor historic Englishness, and thus does not feature as a significant variable in the British response of its Falklands Task Force policy.[66] Indeed, "the jingoism of the Falklands petered out almost as soon as it began," returning the country "to the familiar domestic scene of strikes, economic decline, and social discontent."[67] It is thus neither accurate nor helpful to explain this foreign policy as an exemplar of imperial atavism.

### Resurgent Britishness

The second discourse suggests that the invasion of the Falkland Islands by Argentina sprang from the ongoing diminishment of Britain within the international state system. Similar to the 1909 naval crisis, the Falklands indicated "that the deep-seated concern at Britain's slow and apparently inexorable decline which had first manifested itself at least a century before was still an unavoidable component of the national psyche."[68] From this perspective, Britain, in the face of contemporary decline, required a conscious and emphatic reassertion based on references to modes of self-reference forged during an episode of British strength. Thus when MP Edward du Cann argued that "British interest in [the Falklands] . . . is substantial," he was arguing not that a former colonial area should be retaken in the manner befitting a former imperial power, but because "[o]ur sovereignty is unimpeachable."[69] The recasting of the domestic British self on an international plane meant that while the crisis itself was enormously popular, it did not encourage a revival of imperial grandeur, but rather confirmed "a rising tide of impatient insularity amongst the British people" over the issue of postwar decline.[70] As Thatcher demonstrated, British national identity in response to the crisis (embodied in the Task Force) provided both a constitutive discourse of resurgent contemporary Britishness and forms of causal agency by which to implement foreign policy. This policy, if not materially representative of national greatness, was *culturally tantamount* to it, both domestically and internationally. By the end of the crisis, and "in the face of international skepticism,"

Britain had achieved a good measure of its desired ontological security by "display[ing] great-power status, and demonstrating its military, naval, and technological superiority."[71] Domestically, the episode "seemed to mark the comeback of a . . . 'Little Englandism'" in which dreams of vanished supremacies based on prodigious forms of endogenous English values served as consolations for the collapse of British power" on the international stage.[72]

The combined strategic and cultural decline from 1945 onward certainly promoted a need for international recognition, understood as a national interest. With an invasion of its sovereign territory, Britain had an opportunity to define the situation in terms of Britishness, and construct a purposive discourse supportive of the Task Force policy of April 1982. Indeed, the relief and euphoria at the reconquest of the islands (as well as the hostility shown to critics of the venture) "indicated how fragile contemporary British self-esteem had become, and how badly it needed boosting."[73] Thatcher argued not merely for a "newfound confidence" in Britain, but asserted that "Britain had found herself again," implying a revival of key features of Britishness.[74] Thus, both materially and ideologically, the Falkland crisis was less about reconquering the Falkland Islands and more about recovering a contemporary international role and renewed national identity for those within the British Isles. Internationally, British actions were viewed favorably, the legitimacy of the Task Force and its success symbolic of a late twentieth-century resurgence that helped discredit the previous "international perception both of British deterrence failure and its overall military weakness."[75]

## THE MEDIA DISCOURSE

The discourse for the Falklands crisis emerged in a top-down fashion whereby parliamentary speeches emerged as the first sources making use of "the doctrine of nationalism . . . to *script* the Falklands War."[76] The various media sources, "as the main agent of mass communication, were the primary exponents of this narrative."[77] As numerous theorists on nationalism explore, values and beliefs regarding the social collective within the national unit are disseminated in both top-down and bottom-up fashion through a number of genres that inculcate societal norms and highlight core features of unit self-reference. There are a number of ways to view this process. One suggestion is an entirely instrumental and deliberate usage of modes of communication by sources of authority to generate forms of consensus, even reified forms of hegemony. Noam Chomsky, for example, views forms of media as "adjuncts of government."[78] Antonio Gramsci suggested that media activity has a similar mandate, namely, "to follow and monitor all the intellectual centres and movements" within a country, acting as both a "motive and formative force of cultural institutions of a mass associative type."[79] Gramsci observed that the ideological elements at work in media communication were by nature "philosophically 'transformable,' ductile, malleable, capable of transformation" and also "economic" in their function of sales and circulation.[80] The use of these "transformable" themes within the media suggests that the broad views held by a populace permit that same populace to "recognise [its own] mass nature in addition to [its] individual nature."[81] Narratives of recognizable unity are certainly the staple diet of today's mass media. As Adorno and Horhkeimer argue, "culture now impresses the same stamp on everything. Films, radio and magazines make up a system which is uniform in whole and in every part."[82]

The media was relatively uniform in its treatment of the Falklands War, perhaps because the media as a central forum of national discourse was broadly supportive of the patriotic stance of the government. Thus, one cannot suggest that "alternative opinions of the crisis were not in evidence, only that the 'official' version gained greater currency . . . within popular discourse."[83] The "reality" portrayed in the newspaper and film footage made use of national content to "construct a self-contained, internally consistent world [by] . . . imposing coherence and resolution"; in other words, media sources generated a public discourse that ran parallel with the central political narrative.[84] The media utilized both purposive and emotive mechanisms in detailing the national content of the crisis. The core of the emotive response was premised not only on the legitimacy of the actions of the Task Force emanating from core modes of national self-reference, including sovereignty, democracy, and legality, but on the Britishness of the identity extended to the Falklanders themselves. The purposive content acquired greater force when translated into forms of policy.

As outlined above, the instrumental identity of the islanders was made use of in the principle of citizenship. Their *symbolic* identity, however, relied upon "evidence of their Britishness . . . requir[ing] the utilisation of 'images' and ideals commonly construed as being part of a unique British culture and way of life."[85] Coverage of the territorial similarity between Britain and the Falklands produced a particularly emotive set of images: the Britishness of the island terrain was depicted by combining the rugged elements reminiscent of Scotland and the hills and valleys of Wales; the capital represented qualities of English landscape to argue that: "Port Stanley is rather like a waterside village in the West Country. . . . The island exists in a sense in a sort of timeless vacuum."[86] The inhabitants themselves represented forms of Britishness by virtue of the distinctiveness of their territoriality, whereby Britons and Falklanders were cataloged as members of the same "island race." This underscored not only their political allegiance within the remit of territorial sovereignty, but their cultural similarity arising from modes of territorial self-reference, which Thatcher herself outlined: "Like the people of the United Kingdom, [they] are an island race. . . . They are few in number, but they have the right to live in peace, to choose their own way of life and to determine their own allegiance. Their way of life is British: their allegiance to the Crown."[87]

The portrayal of the Argentine "other" is the second emotive element used in media narratives to highlight the "national" issue by drawing stark contrasts between Argentine and British national types. Arguably, the historic and endogenous rationale underlying the concepts of sovereignty, territoriality, and legality emanating from Parliament were largely lost within the media. The episode instead is characterized by crude tabloid treatment, rendering Argentine losses and British victories in terms of football goals lost and won: "Britain 6, Argentina 0," as the *News of the World* crowed gleefully.[88] In terms of identity, the Argentine "other" was vividly juxtaposed against the British "self"—both preformed identities before the fray erupted, and consolidated along these same lines during their subsequent interaction. Galtieri himself was variously illustrated as an embodiment of dictatorship and an emissary of the devil, and his army as napalm-smuggling barbarians.[89] Reports flooded in of Argentine soldiers keeping islanders "at gunpoint for 4 days . . . robb[ing] them of money, watches and jewellery."[90]

The image of Argentine otherness sharpened considerably when stocks of napalm were discovered at Goose Green. The comments of a British officer further entrenched the legality of the British position, the legitimacy of the overall operation, and the colorful typologies of otherness made use of during the conflict: "We had hoped the Argentines would stick to certain ground rules but this proved that they meant to burn our lads alive."[91] The Argentine militia was perceived as symbolic of the disregard for codes of conduct that was seen not only in the nature of the political regime in Argentina but in the invasion itself. All such images "provided a further illustration of the way in which 'images' of the two forces were utilized to provide an appropriate script of the war"[92] and supported the initial government opinion that "we are not dealing here with a democratic country . . . with which the matter could be thrashed out in a *civilised* way—but with a Fascist, corrupt and cruel regime."[93]

During the hostilities, a great deal of censorship and manipulation appears to have taken place, pitting the newspaper, radio, and television sources against the Ministry of Defence, with the British Broadcasting Corporation in particular being accused of "undue reverence" in its coverage of Argentine losses.[94] As Freedman observes, "The arguments between Whitehall and the media" included accusations "of the press giving aid and comfort to the enemy, and of the Ministry of Defence practicing the most sinister techniques of disinformation and manipulation."[95] The uproar was so great "that the House of Commons Defence Committee decided to investigate this issue as its first major postwar inquiry."[96] Paradoxically, the media had both erred in its nationalist excesses and strayed in its zealously unbiased approach: newspapers like the *Sun* and the *News of the World* stood accused of overzealous nationalism that bordered on racism, while the BBC "was attacked by the right for being even-handed" in its coverage of Argentine deaths.[97] The presence of dissident views "unable to gain a fair hearing" compounded the issue.[98] As Freedman observes,

> The Committee received evidence from most of the journalists who had been with the Task Force as well as from the major news agencies, papers, the BBC and ITV. All the frustrations of the previous months were poured out. The Ministry of Defence was then given a chance to answer all the criticisms. . . . However, overall it is clear just how much the handling of the media reflected *official instinct*, which is rarely loquacious, rather than any deliberate or considered policy.[99]

While media portrayals of the Britishness of the Falklanders and the "otherness" of the Argentines were frequently exaggerated, they were vital in adding to the overall discourse of the time, indicating how media scripts of the conflict intertwined with the official government position.

## Propaganda

Much of the media-generated discourse of the Falklands conflict was largely nationalistic in content and propagandist in intent. Propaganda is an eminently discursive convention "in which cultural understandings are imposed upon the masses by means of the systemic promulgation of ideologies by the state."[100] However, this is not an entirely accurate understanding of the role of media in this particular episode, examined in the previous case study.[101] Indeed, as with identity and the formation of its discursive rhetoric, propaganda "must originate in, and appeal to, the pre-existing discursive possibilities provided by the 'natural attitude' into which the codes are set."[102] Based on preexisting cultural meanings and given codes of identity, nationalist reportage "provides a rough guide to [extant] cultural codes" and allows one to place the events it politicizes in proper historical context. The nature of the episode has rather more in common with older forms of invasion literature in terms of its media treatment.

Apart from the forms of science fiction and Cold War espionage novels, the genre of invasion literature seems largely confined to the late nineteenth and early twentieth centuries. The British *press*, however, visibly drew upon the themes of identity and threat so successfully used in invasion literature to periodically convulse the nation around an aspect of the Falklands episode. During April and May 1982, the topics of national identity, sovereignty, territorial inviolability, and external threat were highlighted in the press, and the outcome was similar to that provoked by the onslaught of invasion literature at the turn of the nineteenth century. The *Sun*'s publications in 1982 had an almost identical effect upon the nation as did the publication of *The Invasion of 1910* by William Le Queux, examined in chapter 5; both successfully seized the nation with a gripping narrative and generating a public uproar that had both constitutive and causal impacts upon the resulting formation of foreign policy. Indeed, as I. F. Clarke argues, themes of identity are constantly highlighted by the "increasingly powerful forces of mass journalism"; with "the mass emotions of extreme nationalism" being marshaled as readily in 1982 as they were in 1906.[103]

While invasion literature had a proclivity for "novelty and sensation" British newspapers during this period remained "nationalistic to the point of hysteria," and occasionally "violent and vindictive both in matter and in manner."[104] The imaginative element regarding domestic invasion replaced instead by a public discourse that daily "imagines" and thus actively reconstituted the nation. During the Falklands war, the crucial "preexisting discursive" framework was a clear understanding of national modes of self-reference and a sense of their recent erosion to sharpen the need for an endogenous reassertion and an international relegitimation. The *Sun* newspaper, while jingoistic in many ways, successfully reflected the legitimacy of its underlying cultural modes of self-reference.

Certain modes of national self-reference and their subsequent reflection in popular culture clearly constitute a national discourse. This constitutive element of the discourse transforms into specific outcomes when a given theme is taken up within the arenas of the press, public, and Parliament, and subsequently informs the orientation of a given policy. The political rhetoric characterizing the Falklands episode was "founded upon cultural structures with a long [and distinctly English] tradition . . . provid[ing] strong evidence of a continuing trend of secularization, rationalization, and generalization" of domestic ideologies during a period of crisis.[105]

### Political and Cultural Discourses Combined: The Instrumental Use of National Identity in the Service of Ontological Security

To explain events, even those that rely upon identity content within the production of a national discourse, "necessarily involves neglects, suppressions, and exclusions because any process of concentration of identity in such a deliberate and systematic way involves the silencing of something else."[106] As such, there are numerous explanations regarding the deliberate usage of patriotic language and national values for political ends during the Falklands crisis. The first is an attempt to lessen the feelings of humiliation and inadequacy arising from the initial failure of British deterrence in the Falklands itself. Indeed, one of the first reactions to the crisis was a narrative of harsh criticism directed at the Conservative government. Several members argued that Britain "should prudently have taken precautions at an earlier date," and that the government had displayed "spectacular military and diplomatic humiliation with the public admission that Argentina had indeed captured Port Stanley, while the British Navy lay too far away to prevent it."[107]

Like the Liberal Party at the height of the 1909 naval scare, the Conservatives appeared both materially unprepared and culturally culpable of damaging domestic capacity. The response was to produce a discourse based not upon passive forms of negotiation but upon active forms of self-defense, girded by a core of national virtues. As such, the hyper-nationalist discourse emanating from Parliament in 1982 may be explained by the observation that "public needs . . . can be manipulated and used to provide symbolic, emotional substitutions for more concrete subsistence needs, which national leadership somehow perceives itself unable to deliver."[108]

The second reaction ensued from the first, namely, that reestablishing the damaged public perception of the Conservative Party by a successful and patriotic war over portions of Britishness would guarantee victory in the forthcoming general election. According to the Labour opposition, the Falklands conflict was focused entirely upon internal party machinations: "Mrs. Thatcher . . . is watching, not the interests of the islanders, but her own back-benchers and the Gallup Polls. Her administration has lost a bye-election in Glasgow and it needs to sink the Argentine navy in revenge."[109] According to this perspective, "the crisis was a heaven-sent gift to a government that was not merely deeply, perhaps fatally unpopular, but which also seemed to be presiding with some zest over the disintegration of the British economy and the breakdown of the nation's social structures."[110]

As Box and Jenkins have demonstrated empirically, "the war had a significant impact on Conservative popularity, net of any influences associated with inflation, unemployment and personal economic expectations."[111] The political dividends reaped by the Conservative Party were considerable; numerous studies testify that the election of 1983 was won by the Conservatives primarily due to the "Falklands factor." However, it seems equally likely that the war played an intermediary rather than directly causal role in the election outcome: "Thatcher's handling of the war seems to have dramatically altered public judgments about her competence as prime minister, and thereby prompted the development of more sanguine expectations about the future course of the nation's economy under her stewardship."[112]

The final suggestion entails the range of views generated within the international arena, linked primarily to the diminished role of Britain in the late twentieth century.[113] Salman Rushdie commented at the time that Thatcherist politics in general were "the politics of the Victorian nursery" and that the Falklands in particular were "fought to drown the noise of our own diplomatic chickens coming home to roost. It was a war to save Mrs. Thatcher's face."[114] In somewhat less dramatic terms, one might argue that Thatcher was well aware of Britain's diminished economic and political standing; a brief but victorious war could possibly provide the British actor unit with confidence in its own capabilities, maximized to full effect in full international view. Diplomatic respect and renewed interest in the full range of unit potential would follow if that potential corresponded with viable, continuing development rather than a momentary inflation of national pride.[115] Weight's testimony on the Falklands bears this out:

> The Falklands victory did restore national pride after a nadir in the 1970s. But . . . Britons were under no illusions that their country was economically healthy or that it was (or even should be) a political force in the world. The British had come to terms with their reduced situation. Post-Falklands patriotism therefore rested not on an inflated sense of national importance but on Britain's reputation abroad, an unstable foundation at the best of times.[116]

There are elements of all three suggestions at work in the British response. Overall, the approach attempted to reassert various British values at the end of a century that had seen a significant decline in the majority of British power; the particular discourse used and the policy-based "resort to aggression appeared to be a needed means to redress the pain that humiliation had brought upon Britain."[117] Political and media-based public discourse played a clear and significant role in promoting themes of British national unity and English national identity. The outcome was a "generic psychological result of internal and external mobilizations, stemming from a pride-enhancing script" which prioritized "a renewal of the sense of identity and dignity" within both the domestic and international forums of recognition.[118] In other words, "the emotional motivations underlying the British response to the Falklands crisis are clearly stated by British elites throughout the crisis. Humiliation stemming from a declining international image and an uncertain self-image" were compounded by the Argentine invasion.[119]

Arguably, "the patriotism generated by the Falklands during the 1980s rested to a large extent on Mrs. Thatcher's own reputation," and remained therefore a constructed event in the national British psyche, rather than resonating with historical events in the English national identity.[120] While fostering a singular conception of political unity by drawing upon a range of pertinent images and ideologies throughout the duration of the Falklands crisis, Thatcher was simultaneously redrawing the peripheries of twentieth-century Britishness. In the process, she was accused of destroying much of the foundational cultural identity of twentieth-century Britain during this period. It appears that "Mrs. Thatcher's legacy of a patriotic . . . Britain" had a great deal to do with her conception of an "industrious Britain."[121] Indeed, prior to the Falklands crisis, Thatcher had begun to establish a series of English ideals within a definitively British framework reminiscent of Victorian values, which emphasized "the acknowledgment of the Almighty, a sense of tolerance, an acknowledgment of moral absolutes and a positive view of work."[122] Including trenchant attacks on British higher education, the support of tabloid journalism, and the resurgence of a particularly aggressive and insular form of patriotism as a result of the Falklands crisis, this process entailed a "displacement of older traditions of veneration for high culture . . . in often crass disregard for older values of sophistication and refinement."[123] The re-creation of Britishness via "Victorian values" actually served to eradicate much of the quintessentially English elements of identity, and foreshadowed the passing of a "world in which the 'oldness' and 'ordinariness' of objects, landscapes and institutions had once been sources of reverence and love."[124]

The identity theme of ontological security established at the beginning of the case study provides the explanatory category for the series of image "slippages" that had undermined internal cohesiveness and external recognition in both Argentina and Britain.[125] Based on the premise that "[s]ocial actors are sensitive to suggestions that their conduct [or development] is inconsistent with their self-identity," ontological security denotes attempts to augment weakened corporate identities by injecting a measure of predictability into its endogenous and exogenous forms of national identity.[126] The "benign neglect" of Argentina by both Britain and the United States had weakened its original identity as a South American authority and fostered images of a despotic regime terrorizing its citizens.[127] As evidenced in the case study on the 1909 naval scare, national neuroses stemmed both from the irrelevance of its modes of English self-reference within a diminished sense of domestic Britishness and the finality of the passing of empire, marked painfully by the Suez crisis of 1956. Unable to summon a military response to the Egyptian attack in 1956, Britain had been forced to stand aside over a symbol of past imperial power, and a monument to its twentieth-century power status. Victory in the Falklands promised both states a form of "lost certitude . . . an ersatz consolation for national soul wounds" in the face of international neglect and domestic decline.[128] As W. H. Christie maintains, "After the terrible psychological shock of our defeat at Suez, the Falkland Islands recovery was an element of redemption."[129] The element of repossessed prestige at work in the British sense of self reflects how deeply identity marks the motivations of states as intrinsically social actors; as Löwenheim argues, the idea of internal slippage or external "reproofs can harm the self-esteem of an actor, damaging [its] moral prestige, wear out [its] legitimate authority, and through shame prevent the fulfillment of [its] identity."[130]

## CONCLUSION

To revisit the central argument of this study, symbolic and instrumental elements that define the origin of the nation-state, its identity, and the production of thematic "national self-images" are understood as "an essential tenet of every nation's foreign policy-making."[131] In linking identity with policy formation, a discursive translation of images needs to take place in which a given narrative is utilized for its portrayal of and solutions to a given policy problem. As argued, the political and media-generated narratives distilled various values and codes implicit in the identity of Britain, but which were traceable in their ancestry to self-referential forms of Englishness. While radical elements of imperialist reimaginings existed within the crisis, it is clear that the discourse of the Falklands episode is centrally "characterized by a tendency towards generalization from which an 'imagined community' of nation was, with partial success, to emerge."[132] As the *Times* observed, the breach of singularly English principles of sovereignty and democracy "somehow exposed all those deep feelings which had been suppressed in Britain and perhaps explains the vigor with which the nation responded to an invasion of its spirit. That spirit has been rediscovered as people have rediscovered something about themselves and their country."[133]

Both motivation and action operate in the translation of a wide body of meanings into a form of policy-enacted practice. The understandings of what the English nation and the wider British state unit represented permitted "the generation of [both] powerful semantic forces [producing a discourse] and human motivations" that produced a policy.[134] When symbols of national identity are transformed into "wider realms of meaning" that link identity to preference-based interest, they immediately become actionable. Defining the invasion not in materialist terms of a failed military deterrence, but in ideological terms of sovereignty allowed the invasion to be perceived as a breach of the nexus of "national" issues, an attempted abrogation of forms of British statehood founded on English values. The principal narrative emanating from Parliament and the media focused on notions of sovereignty, democracy, and legality by which to define the Islanders as British and thus ensure a vivid demarcation of the Argentine "other." This "ritual definition of events provided the motivational spark for action, a spark that was to make war a part of the 'rules of the game'—an acceptable response to an unacceptable invasion," an unacceptable denigration of core national values.[135]

As examined, the concepts of sovereignty, democracy, and legality represent conceptual aspects underlying a working domestic discourse. When these attributes and their emanating discursive rhetoric were fused into the political crisis engendered by the invasion of the Falklands, they produced a discourse that allowed the attributes themselves to be "typified" as part of the national character: representative of Englishness while simultaneously "linked to wider spheres of significance" representative of the British national interest.[136] To clarify, a form of discursive construction took place that knitted ideas of the English and British self to the actionable narrative of foreign policy. This policy had to "mobilize the maximum amount of national and international support."[137] This implied

> [that the] interpretation [of the crisis] was *created* and edited as it was *enacted*. In the process, the language and thus the character of the Falklands issue was transformed into a great symbolic drama composed of a wider variety of interweaving *national themes*, all of which focused on the future of the Islands and the outcome of the conflict. The Government's political will thus became closely identified with the validation of the country's values and symbol system.[138]

Clearly, the discourse of identity and the range of images and constructed realities directly affected the formation of the resultant discourse. In effect, "the policies chosen by the government were considered by the people to be consistent with commonsense understandings of what constituted reasonable action."[139] In other words, Conservative policies were seen to adequately reflect both the prevailing sense of self at work in the nation and the national interests of the state, and were therefore supported. A further demonstration that the category of identity actively informed domestic political outcomes was demonstrated in the landslide victory won by the Conservative government under Thatcher in the general election of June 1983. The Conservative Party had successfully made an asset not merely of the "Falklands factor" but the potent sense of the British self at work in its agency by which to reestablish endogenous solidity. Within the international system, the Falkland episode was also perceived as a reversal of postwar frailty by Britain and therefore represents an equally valid form of actionable discourse at work within systemic levels.

## NOTES

1. A. Wendt, "Identity and Structural Change in International Politics," in *The Return of Culture and Identity in IR Theory*, ed. Y. Lapid and J. Kratochwil (Boulder, CO: Lynne Rienner Publishers, 1996): 51; and O. Löwenheim, "British Moral Prestige, Humanitarian Intervention, and the Barbary Pirates," in Lapid and Kratochwil, *The Return of Culture and Identity in IR Theory*, 27.

2. D. Rock, *Argentina: 1516–1987* (New York: I.B. Tauris, 1987).

3. M. Middlebrook, *The Fight for the "Malvinas": The Argentine Forces in the Falklands War* (London: Viking, 1989).

4. Falkland Islands Information Portal. United Nations Resolution 2065, *Question of the Falkland Islands (Malvinas)* http://www.falklands.info/history/resolution2065.html

5. P. Calvert, *The Falklands Crisis: The Rights and the Wrongs* (London: Frances Pinter, 1982).

6. In 1982, Her Majesty's Stationery Office (hereafter HMSO) published a digest of the Commons debates entitled *The Falklands Campaign: A Digest of the Debates in the House of Commons 2 April to 15 June 1982* (London: HMSO, 1982). This provides a chronological history of each of the members' statements in the House and is utilized here as the chief source of primary information emanating from the government during the conflict. Also the "Franks Report" of the conflict: *Falkland Islands Review: Report of a Committee of Privy Counsellors*, Chairman The Rt. Hon. The Lord Franks, Cmnd 8787 (London: HMSO, 1983).

7. Calvert, *The Falklands Crisis*, 150.

8. R. Weight, *Patriots, National Identity in Britain, 1940–2000* (London: Macmillan, 2002), 611.

9. M. Honeywell and J. Pearce, *Falklands/Malvinas: Whose Crisis?* (London: Latin American Bureau, 1982).

10. J. Thompson, *No Picnic: The Story of 3 Commando Brigades in the Falklands War* (London: Leo Cooper for Secker & Warburg, 1985).

11. K. Morgan, *The Oxford History of Britain* (Oxford: Oxford University Press, 2001), 656.

12. DEFE (Ministry of Defence) 14: *Falkland Islands Campaign Instruments of Surrender* (London: PRO, 1982).

13. Rock makes clear the issue of Argentine economic difficulties in 1981: "inflation . . . over 600%, GDP is down 11.4%, manufacturing output is down 22.9%, and real wages by 19.2%," Rock, *Argentina: 1516–1987*, 375–78. Significant unrest had also been caused by the ongoing mass "disappearances" of citizens under the military junta.

14. K. Hipel, M. Wang, and N. Fraser, "Hypergame Analysis of the Falkland/Malvinas Conflict," *International Studies Quarterly* 32, no. 3 (September 1988): 344.

15. Hipel et al., "Hypergame Analysis," 344.

16. Lawrence Freedman, *Official History of the Falklands Campaign*, vol. 1 (London: Frank Cass, 2005), 15.

17. J. Mitzen, "Ontological Security in World Politics: State Identity and the Security Dilemma," *European Journal of International Relations* 12, no. 3 (2006): 341.

18. Mitzen, "Ontological Security in World Politics," 342 (emphasis added).

19. Mitzen, "Ontological Security in World Politics," 342.

20. N. Femenia, "Emotional Actor: Foreign Policy Decision-Making in the 1982 Falklands/Malvinas War," in *Social Conflicts and Collective Identities*, ed. P. Coy and L. Woehrle (Lanham, MD: Rowman & Littlefield, 2000).

21. N. Friedman, "The Falklands War: Lessons, Learned and Mislearned," *Orbis* 26 (1983): 927.

22. M. Thatcher, in *The Falklands Campaign*, Hansard Official Record of Members of Parliaments' Debates, 3 April 1982 (London: HMSO, 1982) (emphasis added).

23. R. Colls, *Identity of England* (Oxford: Oxford University Press, 2002), 50.

24. Colls, *Identity of England*, 21.

25. Gladstone letter to Queen Victoria, April 17, 1869, in H. Nicolson, *Diplomacy* (London: Oxford University Press, 1963), 137.

26. Henry Kissinger, *Diplomacy* (London: Simon and Schuster, 1994), 97.

27. R. Jennings and A. Watts, eds., *Oppenheim's International Law*, vol. 1, part 1, 9th ed. (Oxford: Oxford University Press, 1996), 122.

28. *Times*, 5 April 1982.

29. Thatcher, in *The Falklands Campaign*, 3 April 1982.

30. *Times*, 5 April, 1982.

31. M. Skye, "'Undue Reverence'—Questioning National Identity in the Media Coverage of the 1982 Falklands War," featured on the Falklands-Malvinas Discussion Forum: http://www.falklands-malvinas.com/engboard.mv (accessed January 3, 2003), 16.

32. Colls, *Identity of England*, 33.

33. Kissinger, *Diplomacy*, 100.

34. *Times*, editorial, 5 April 1982.

35. *Times*, editorial, 5 April 1982.

36. Opposition Leader M. Foot, Parliament, Debates, 4 April 1982, quoted in *Times*, 4 April 1982.

37. Prime Minister Thatcher, quoted in *Times*, 3 April 1982.

38. M. Foot, quoted in *Times*, 4 April 1982.

39. Colls, *Identity of England*, 21.

40. *Times*, 15 June 1982.

41. Archbishop of Canterbury Robert Runcie, quoted in *Times*, 8 May 1982.

42. M. Foot, quoted in A. Barnett, *Iron Britannia: Why Parliament Waged Its Falklands War* (London: Allison and Busby, 1982), 30–31.

43. *Times*, editorial, 5 April 1982.

44. M. Thatcher, in *The Falklands Campaign*, 3 April 1982.

45. Colls, *Identity of England*, 23 (emphasis added).

46. G. J. Postema, *Bentham and the Common Law Tradition* (Oxford: Oxford University Press, 1986), 9.

47. Colls, *Identity of England*, 24.

48. Sir M. Hale, *The History of the Common Law of England*, 1739, reprinted (Chicago: Chicago University Press, 1971), 30 (emphasis added).

49. P. Smith, "Codes and Conflict: Toward a Theory of War as Ritual," *Theory and Society* 20, no. 1, (February 1991): 117–20.

50. M. Thatcher, quoted in *Times*, 15 June 1892.

51. Weight, *Patriots*, 616.

52. Thatcher, in *The Falklands Campaign*, 3 April 1982.

53. D. Judd, *Empire: The British Imperial Experience from 1765 to the Present* (London: HarperCollins, 1996), 405.

54. Weight, *Patriots*, 618.

55. D. Monaghan, *The Falklands War: Myth and Countermyth* (London: Macmillan, 1998).

56. Barnett, *Iron Britannia*, 150-53.

57. *Times*, 7 May 1982; and *Sun*, 3 May 1982.

58. E. P. Thompson, *Times*, 20 April 1982.

59. Skye, "Undue Reverence," 21.

60. L. James, *Warrior Race: A History of the British at War from Roman Times to the Present* (London: Abacus, 2002), 756.

61. R. Harris, *Gotcha! The media, the Government and the Falklands Crisis* (London: Faber, 1983), 40.

62. Weight, *Patriots*, 619.

63. Weight, *Patriots*, 619.

64. Morgan, *The Oxford History of Britain*, 656.

65. B. Porter, *The Lion's Share: A Short History of British Imperialism: 1850–1995* (London: Macmillan, 1996), 365–66.

66. Femenia, "Emotional Actor," 3.

67. Morgan, *The Oxford History of Britain*, 656.

68. Judd, *Empire*, 405.

69. M. P. E. du Cann, in *The Falklands Campaign*, vol. 21, 3 April 1982.

70. Morgan, *The Oxford History of Britain*, 656.

71. Morgan, *The Oxford History of Britain*, 656.

72. R. Samuel, *Theatres of Memory, Past and Present in Contemporary Culture*, vol. 1 (London: Verso, 1994), 290.

73. Judd, *Empire*, 405.

74. M. Thatcher, cited in Barnett, *Iron Britannia*, 150–53.

75. Femenia, "Emotional Actor," 10.

76. Skye, "Undue Reverence," 1 (emphasis added).

77. Skye, "Undue Reverence," 1 (emphasis added).

78. N. Chomsky, *On Power and Ideology* (New York: South End Press, 1988), 75.

79. A. Gramsci, "Journalism: Intellectual Movements and Centres," "Types of Periodical: The Final Evolutionary Being," and "Journalism: Readers," in Antonio Gramsci, *Selections from Cultural Writings*, eds. D. Forgacs and G. Nowell-Smith, trans., W. Boelhower (London: Lawrence and Wishart, 1985), 402–5.

80. Gramsci, *Selections from Cultural Writings*, 402–5.

81. A. Smith, *Theories of Nationalism* (London: Duckworth, 1972), 195.

82. T. Adorno and M. Horkheimer, "The Culture Industry: Enlightenment as Mass Deception," in T. Adorno and M. Horkheimer, *Dialectic of Enlightenment* (New York: Verso Books, 1997), 120.

83. Skye, "Undue Reverence," 13.

84. J. Fiske, *Media Matters* (Minneapolis: University of Minnesota Press, 1994), 130.

85. Skye, "Undue Reverence," 12.

86. *Times*, 5 April 1982.

87. Thatcher, in *The Falklands Campaign*, vol. 21, col. 649, 3 April 1982. Indeed, the Falklands were seen to represent a country idyll, whose ethos "refer[red] back to a mythical Britain—characterised by social unity, class distinction and the predominance of the 'rural'—so beloved of conservative commentators." Skye, "Undue

Reverence," 17. Such timelessness evoked an ethos long lost within contemporary Britain. The abrogation of these values and the sacral quality attached to the territory of the Falkland Islands rendered the Argentine actions all the more barbaric in British eyes.

88. *News of the World*, 2 May 1982. The retaking of South Georgia, the downing of three warplanes and the destruction of two airstrips was translated by the paper as equivalent to six "goals." The "seventh" would take place the following day with the sinking of the Argentine cruiser, the *General Belgrano*, which prompted the infamous headline by the *Sun*: Gotcha!

89. *Sun*, 3 June 1982.

90. *Times*, 1 June 1982.

91. *Times*, 2 June 1982.

92. Skye, "Undue Reverence," 22.

93. MP B. Braine, in *The Falklands Campaign*, vol. 21, 3 April 1982 (emphasis added).

94. There are alternative viewpoints. As Pilger maintains, the BBC Weekly Review Board agreed that coverage of the hostilities "ought to be shaped to suit the emotional sensibilities of the public," while also promoting government policy. J. Pilger, "Here We Are Again," *New Statesman* (1 October 2001).

95. L. Freedman, "Bridgehead Revisited: The Literature of the Falklands," *International Affairs* 59, no. 3 (Summer 1983): 449.

96. Freedman, "Bridgehead Revisited," 449.

97. Weight, *Patriots*, 618.

98. Morgan, *The Oxford History of Britain*, 656.

99. Freedman, "Bridgehead Revisited," 449.

100. Skye, "Undue Reverence," 127.

101. Skye, "Undue Reverence," 128.

102. Skye, "Undue Reverence," 128.

103. I. F. Clarke, *Voices Prophesying War, 1763–3749* (Oxford: Oxford University Press, 1992), 57.

104. Clarke, *Voices Prophesying War*, 57.

105. Smith, "Codes and Conflict," 128.

106. Eley, "Culture, Britain, and Europe," in *Journal of British Studies* 31, no. 4, "Britishness and Europeanness: Who Are the British Anyway?" (October 1992): 413.

107. MP L. Callaghan and MP M. White, in *The Falklands Campaign*, 7 April and 3 April 1982, respectively.

108. Femenia, "Emotional Actor," 20.

109. E. P. Thompson, *Times*, 29 April 1982.

110. Judd, *Empire*, 402.

111. G. Box and G. Jenkins, *Time Series Analysis: Forecasting and Control* (San Francisco: Holden-Day, 1976), 110.

112. P. A. Clarke, *A Question of Leadership: From Gladstone to Blair* (London: Macmillan, 1999), 12.

113. FO (Foreign Office) 973/233, *International Reactions to the Argentine Invasion of the Falkland Islands* (London: P.R.O., April 1982).

114. C. Woolf and J. Moorcroft Wilson, eds. *Authors Take Sides on the Falklands* (London: Cecil Woolf, 1982), 170.

115. A. Orgill, *The Falklands War: Background, Conflict, Aftermath: An Annotated Bibliography* (London: Mansell, 1993).

116. Weight, *Patriots*, 626–27.

117. Femenia, "Emotional Actor," 19.

118. Femenia, "Emotional Actor," 13.

119. Femenia, "Emotional Actor," 13.

120. Weight, *Patriots*, 628.

121. P. F. della Torre, *Viva Britannia: Mrs. Thatcher's Britain* (London: HarperCollins, 1985), 90–91.

122. H. Young, *One of Us: A Biography of Margaret Thatcher* (London: Pan Macmillan, 1991), 244.

123. Eley, "Culture, Britain, and Europe," 402–3.

124. J. Stapleton, *Political Intellectuals and Public Identities in Britain since 1850* (Manchester: Manchester University Press, 2001), 160.

125. See J. Burton, ed., *Conflict: Human Needs Theory* (New York: St. Martin's Press, 1990).

126. O. Löwenheim, "British Moral Prestige," 28.

127. C. Waissman, *Reversal of Development in Argentina: Postwar Counterrevolutionary Policies and Their Structural Consequences* (Princeton, NJ: Princeton University Press, 1987).

128. R. N. Lebow, "Miscalculation in the South Atlantic: The Origins of the Falklands War," in *Psychology and Deterrence*, ed. Jervis, Lebow, and Stein (Baltimore: Johns Hopkins University Press), 340.

129. W. H. Christie, cited in M. Charlton, *The Little Platoon: Diplomacy and the Falklands Dispute* (London: Blackwell, 1989), 91.

130. Löwenheim, "British Moral Prestige," 28.

131. Femenia, "Emotional Actor," 1.

132. Smith, "Codes and Conflict." 114.

133. *Times*, 15 June 1982.

134. Smith, "Codes and Conflict," 118.

135. Smith, "Codes and Conflict," 118.

136. Smith, "Codes and Conflict," 118.

137. M. Dillon, "Thatcher and the Falklands," in *Belief Systems and International Relations*, eds. R. Little and S. Smith (London: Blackwell, 1988), 112.

138. Dillon, "Thatcher and the Falklands," 112.

139. Smith, "Codes and Conflict," 130.

# 7

## The 2003 Euro Debate

### Englishness, Britishness, and Sovereignty

The 1882 tunnel crisis examined in chapter 4 symbolized "the reluctance of British politicians, military leaders, and the general public to destroy an insularity that was widely held to be the foundation of the nation's greatness."[1] In the twenty-first century, membership in the European Union (EU) has complicated both British attitudes and English sensibilities about linking Britain's political and economic future with that of the continent. Structurally, British responses, both public and political, range from rabid Eurosceptic, to pragmatist, to reliably supportive.

Much like national identity, membership in the EU is not a static category. It waxes and wanes in both importance and impact. A key issue for Britain has been the "widening vs. deepening" debate. Britain has traditionally preferred a wider EU (in terms of expanding membership) over a deeper EU (in terms of heightened institutionalization, use of the supranational method of policy making, and increased competence transfer to EU institutions). Yet enlarging the EU from fifteen to twenty-seven states in 2004 and 2007 dramatically increased the size of the EU labor market permitted to travel within EU borders, raising the specter of uncontrolled immigration into Britain, and has subsequently impacted negatively on relations with the EU. A key symbol of deepening, the issue of joining the euro currency rarely results in outright public or political opprobrium; more usually, it sparks a heavily loaded, but by now well-worn, Self/Other reaction that illustrates both how much British attitudes have shifted since joining the EU in 1973 and how little English assumptions about their continental "other" have changed.

While the Falkland study illustrated that English national identity did not directly inform British foreign policy, elements of Englishness and

Britishness together and separately did inform British economic policy regarding the 2003 decision to refuse the euro. What must be borne in mind is that the EU itself is a moving target; it too has shifted and transformed beyond all recognition. Such changes have proved too demanding to core aspects of Englishness; others have contributed positively to a rehabilitated form of Britishness. Further, while Argentina represented a neatly delineated foe in ideological, cultural, and even moral terms, the EU is a far more ambiguous "other." Policy-specific otherness is a more oblique game, and Britishness is less than clear as to which aspects of the national self line up with EU goals and which aspects remain fundamentally opposed.

Nevertheless, this final study suggests that—on the basis of a more visible, but variable, English core, Britishness is a conglomerate state identity based on the explicit defense of strategic British interests abroad and British political culture at home, *and* a substantive cultural identity that derives some core values from a renewed sense of Englishness. While there is some evidence that key features of Englishness retain a collective belief in a destiny apart from Europe, contemporary Britishness manages its statecraft within the EU pragmatically rather than passionately. The 2003 refusal to join the euro certainly represents a pitting of the *uniqueness* of English symbols, history, and institutions against European political culture; equally, however, it revealed British interests to be derived from a collective identity based on a strategic-symbolic mix of separateness defined in relation *with*, rather than in stark opposition *to*, the EU.

## HISTORICAL BACKGROUND

The earliest postwar impetus for European integration was the European Coal and Steel Community (ECSC), whose 1951 preamble illustrates the objective of "peoples long divided by bloody conflicts . . . establishing a destiny henceforth shared."[2] Originally known as the Schuman Plan, the project was pushed forward by its first president, Jean Monnet, popularly acclaimed as the father of European integration. From this initiative, the 1957 Treaty of Rome formally established the European Economic Community (EEC), a process in which Britain declined to participate.[3] The Rome Treaty attempts to counterbalance political unity with economic integration. While the first commission president, Walter Hallstein, argued that "the Community is in politics, not business," Article 2 of the Treaty makes clear that economic unity was an early priority.[4] By the 1960s, Prime Minister Harold Macmillan and others came to believe that Britain had missed a significant opportunity and, under the guise of cooperative solidarity, announced to the House of Commons the need for Britain to request entry, or face the consequences of further international slippage. Grudgingly accepted domestically, the initiative was twice vetoed by French President de Gaulle, adding a significant element of anti-European rancor to British views of Europe.

In July 1971, the British populace answered a poll regarding the possible loss of national identity as a result of joining the Common Market; the majority confirmed that such fears did indeed concern them.[5] Prime Minister Heath, committed to pro-Europe policies, countered by publishing a pamphlet entitled *Europe and You*, arguing that "Britain will not lose its identity if we enter the Common Market. . . . The British way of life—based on our constitutional Monarchy—would continue unchanged. *National identities* are safeguarded by the way the Common Market operates."[6] Provided that the national character remained undamaged and the scope of British trade untrammeled in its growing association with Europe, so much the better. As illustrated by the *Times*, the Common Market was "a splendid adventure relating to trade. . . . It does not . . . touch the essential spirit of the individual and national character but it stimulates the best in it for the better deployment of national resources."[7] In 1975 the long-awaited referendum on the European Question resulted in 67 percent voting to stay in the EEC.

## THE POLITICAL DISCOURSE

### Thatcher, Major, and Europe

In 1979, Margaret Thatcher took the helm, and for the next decade, the British state practice fluctuated between commitment and rebellion regarding its "European vocation." Despite her imperious approach, Thatcher adhered to the "recovery of national distinctiveness, the resilience of the nation-state," and was quick to anticipate the eventual "inertia of national bureaucracy, even during the first flood of enthusiasts about European integration."[8] Initially, Thatcher merely dispensed with the idealism attached to integration, rather than disposing of the idea of Europe. Subsequent speeches bear this out, where sovereign autonomy plays a senior but not solitary role within the discourse of European cooperation.[9] In her infamous "College of Europe" speech in Bruges in 1988, Thatcher upheld the commercial principles of a free-trade region that extended her own belief in free-market capitalism, giving "one of the most powerful, emotive and passionate expressions of Britain's European destiny" since Winston Churchill pronounced on the need for a United States of Europe.[10] Her statement that

"Britain does not dream of some cosy, isolated existence on the fringes of the European Community [but] . . . in Europe, as part of the Community," should be borne in mind alongside subsequent defenses of a particularist British identity.[11] However, it was precisely these subsequent observances that chimed most strongly with the latent misgivings of the British public, in suggesting that

> Europe will be stronger precisely because it has France as France, Spain as Spain, Britain as Britain, each with its own customs, traditions and identity. It would be folly to try to fit them into some sort of identikit European personality. . . . Let Europe be a family of nations, understanding each other better, appreciating each other more, doing more together, but relishing our national identity no less than our common European endeavour.[12]

Under Thatcher, Britain may have been interested in long-term commercial possibilities, but it was unwilling to countenance the overall cost of political integration if it meant renouncing any aspect of political or economic sovereignty. Sovereignty, never an absolute category at the best of times, was fast becoming a relative concept as a result of the "deepening" goals of European agreements. Uncertain political terms and ambitious economic initiatives caused confusion regarding the sovereign means and federal ends.[13] Signing the Single European Act (SEA) should have moved Britain further within the discourse of European integration. However, the lack of a clear statement to the British public by the government regarding the actual implications of the SEA meant that few realized that the EC was heading steadily "towards monetary union, social solidarity, foreign policy and security cooperation" and possibly "towards a federal union . . . the prime political project for the present stage of the EC's development."[14] The result was confusion regarding the composition and objectives of the European project, and uncertainty as to the British role. Thatcher herself gradually moved from an emphasis on the nation-state to a preoccupation with the quantity of British sovereignty ceded to Brussels and the subsequent qualitative effect on British national identity.

John Major succeeded as prime minister, and although it split the Conservative party for a generation, he successfully kept Britain within the European orbit by getting the 1992 Treaty on European Union (TEU) through Parliament. Transforming the EC from a trade-focused marketplace into a European Union (EU) with a distinct political, legal, social, and foreign policy framework, the TEU deepened the level of integration among the twelve members, including plans for a common currency and an ambitious enlargement strategy. The expanded objectives of European integration slowly began to resonate with the British populace. The economist Samuel

Brittan wrote an illuminating article in the *Financial Times* regarding the connection between political and economic integration during this period:

> The British political and business classes have been victims of a self-imposed confidence trick. They have allowed themselves to believe that the European Community is mainly concerned with free trade and economic co-operation, and that political union has suddenly been sprung on them by other member countries. . . . The real enemy in the European Community negotiations was not federalism but centralisation. . . . The real threat to a liberal free market order comes not from Emu [economic and monetary union] —which is thoroughly sensible—but from economic and social moves which have been attempted in the political inter-governmental conference.[15]

Under Major, British policies regarding EU economic and monetary ambitions became increasingly fragmented, as the Conservatives slowly tore themselves to shreds between pro- and anti-euro camps. As a result, Britain lost the chance to participate in the first stage of European monetary union, leaving other EU states to establish a single currency, excluding itself from a framework in which it would still have to do the majority of its business. Major attempted to assuage the damage done by earlier Thatcherist perspectives, and the increasingly venomous Eurosceptic content emanating from the House of Commons during the early 1990s, through low-profile participation in discussions on the single currency where possible.

However, both the single currency and Conservative fortunes regarding the EU were felled in an instant on 16 September 1992, when "after intense pressure on sterling, Britain was forced to leave the European ERM [Exchange Rate Mechanism] and to devalue the Pound against all major currencies."[16] Tory economic management was utterly discredited, and with them all issues relating to the single currency. Conservative Party identity shifted emphatically from the placidly pro-European attitudes of Heath and Macmillan to one based on stark opposition to all things European via vocal support of all things British. Despite its ratification, "[the Treaty of] Maastricht, with its perceived challenge to the sovereignty of the Crown in parliament, with its pressure towards a European super-state and a 'Euro' currency which would wipe out the historic primacy of the Pound sterling, became the source of massive contention" in both the Commons and the Lords.[17]

An anti-Europe discourse formed around a set of core themes: the loss of sovereignty, national distinctiveness, national currency, the loss of British political separateness and English cultural uniqueness. In addition, "Europe" became a thoroughly party-political issue, symbolic of the tussle between Labour and Tory with the result that "the European issue was never decided on its [own] merits" but rather acted as a "totemic issue within the two parties because it pitted important parts of their traditions against each other."[18] In the waning years of Conservative rule, British Euroscepticism increased steadily. The event provoking unrestrained "Europhobia" occurred in 1996 with the outbreak of the bovine disease BSE in Britain, which immediately prompted the European Union (led redoubtably by Germany) to ban the export of British beef to Europe. As Mark Aspinwall points out, despite its authority to ban British beef, "the EU measure was successfully portrayed as a threat to British sovereignty, and the reaction by the government was to institute a policy of "non-cooperation."[19] In ascending order of farmers, rural constituents, Conservative MPs, and an increasingly Eurosceptic public, Britain turned both its perception of and policy on Europe markedly inward.[20]

## Blair and Europe

Labour leader Tony Blair swept to victory in the 1997 general election, winning a landslide total of 418 Labour MPs, producing a majority of 179. Blair's platform as leader of the Labour party since 1995 focused upon patriotic integration through a unitary *British* identity, thus providing a method by which to foster integration within Europe while permitting aspects of the Union to gain greater self-government. During the 1995 Party conference, Blair identified "New" Labour as "the *patriotic* party because it is the people's party."[21] R. Weight argues that "the equating of the nation with 'the people' was an attempt to co-opt the Continental rhetoric of popular, as opposed to Parliamentary, sovereignty which had dominated European political discourse."[22] Certainly an increased role in Europe was a primary goal of Labour; indeed "membership of the Euro club is central to [Blair's] understanding of Britain's place in Europe and of his own place in history."[23] However, Blair did not immediately instigate his plans for Europe.

Aware of the prevalent discourse regarding Europe, the Labour administration calculated "that after years of Euroscepticism, it would be unwise to hold a referendum on joining the UK's position in the EU" and thereby "take risks with its governing credibility."[24] Instead, Labour policy aimed to establish a strong domestic discourse that was capable of extension, alteration, even "spin," in accommodating a position between a "patriotic" British identity and the furtherance of pro-European strategies. The choice of popular patriotism rather than parliamentary nationalism as its own "identity theme" suggests a more even-handed approach to both national identity and the possibility of extension within Europe. Recent European studies regarding identity and euro acceptance are premised on categories that regard nationalism as a "jingoistic" appellation, while patriotism is merely a "positive emotional attachment to one's own country . . . [separated] from discrimination against others."[25]

Working from more tacit forms of national self-reference, Blair's "Third Way" also contained economic aims, moving to incorporate working- and middle-class demographics, the latter still uneasy after Tory vagaries. To produce such a discourse, New Labour shifted slowly from its recognized party identity, appealing not only to the traditional Labour quorum of working classes in the Midlands but more centrally to the gentrified representatives of "Middle England." The overall result "was a remarkably undoctrinaire Labour Party which rejected the State planning, the nationalization, the universalized welfare benefits, the income redistribution, and the links with the union which had characterised Attlee's party in 1945."[26] Blair in particular "spoke the language of British patriotism and brandished the Union flag"; utilizing such totems of nation, he then reintroduced the thorny issue of a British national identity as a "Third Way" between overt forms of heightened nationalism (either English or British) and whole-hearted European federalism.[27] As explained by Anthony Giddens,

The Third Way seeks to find a role for the nation in a cosmopolitan world. . . . Nations in the past were in some large part propelled to unity through antagonism to others. . . . Today national identities need to be sustained in a more open and discursive way, in cognizance not only of their own complexities but of the other loyalties with which they overlap. Implied is a more reflexive construction of national identity, a modernising project par excellence.[28]

Unlike the Edwardian English rurality evoked by John Major, Labour discourse was carefully a-historic, a-territorial. Its "undoctrinaire" and inclusive identity granted New Labour a trinity of tools. First, it worked to clarify the presently undefined British national identity; second, it legitimized the devolution as a policy working *within*, rather than *against* this inclusive British identity; and finally, it suggested further integration with Europe as an extension *of* rather than a superimposition *upon* this identity. Thus a policy of "[p]luralism at home and integration in Europe" comprised the Labour agenda, along with a transformation of "the roles of the law, parliament and Cabinet," which in the process "created a very different view of the British identity."[29]

Blair readjusted the thematic content of the national discourse of Britain, focusing upon themes of an inclusive form of patriotic identity rather than reviving its earlier isolationist image. Under Labour, British perceptions of self-reference had been encouraged to eschew former touchstones of Englishness and to adopt instead a broader discourse of "enlarged patriotism" and "common citizenship" originally outlined by Churchill. Blair's 1999 "Charlemagne" speech in Aachen, Germany, serves as an example of the active "constructing" of national attributes currently taking place in order to ensure the passage of a given policy. In it Blair articulated various British values:

> Britain must overcome its ambivalence about Europe. Then our creativity and our practical common sense can be accepted as the contribution of a partner, not an outsider. . . . The British, at their best, have two great characteristics: creativity and common sense. . . . We have never lacked boldness or courage. But our sense of adventure has always been tempered by practical realism. We are pragmatic visionaries, rather than utopians.[30]

British attributes of common sense and pragmatism, even courage may explain their enduring commitment to the precepts of the nation-state; Blair however suggested that the "creative" element of the national character somehow endows the British unit with a measure of flexibility capable of retaining core national qualities while undertaking further forms of integration:

> The practical part of the British character accepts we should be in Europe but worries about Europe's direction. . . . If we wish Europe to be guided by *our character*, we must also use our creative vision to see that only by participating can we shape and influence the Europe in which we live.[31]

Under the aegis of "Third Way" terminology, Blair articulated a solidly inclusive, cosmopolitan discourse demonstrative of a reflexive British national identity from which policies placing Britain within Europe could emerge. The next step was taken during the 1999 Labour Party conference where Blair unveiled his pro-Europe campaign, overt in images of patriotism but tacit in its objectives regarding the single currency. Nudging the discourse of a flexible British identity a step closer to Europe, Blair argued that "active British engagement in Europe [is] an act of patriotism—with local jobs, investment and industry linked to Europe's fortunes."[32] This however was the zenith of Blair's attempt to embed Britain within mainstream integrative EU policies. On virtually every other policy—including the euro—New Labour's EU policy was pragmatic at best and obstructive at worst.

At the beginning of its first term, the Labour government announced its firm intention to "wait and see" regarding British entry into the euro.[33] This was made clear with the establishment of the infamous "five tests," designed to benchmark the goodness of Britain's ability to fit within the Eurozone. The five tests include "sustainable convergence of the UK economy with those of the other EU states; sufficient flexibility for the UK to cope with future economic change; positive effect on business in the UK; favourable impact on our financial services industry and the business conducted by the City of London; finally that joining would be good for employment."[34]

At the beginning of Labour's second term, in June 2003, the Chancellor of the Exchequer, Gordon Brown, announced that after an intensive analysis, the five tests had not been met and that the Labour government would continue to wait and see. Despite Brown's own argument that "the Euro has been a successful currency," and that "commitment to and support for the principle of joining the Euro" had been previously outlined by the Labour party, the "clear and unambiguous case for British membership" in the euro was deemed to have not been met. Supporting the Chancellor was the entire Treasury establishment, which suggested that of the five tests, those of sustainable convergence and flexibility had most clearly not been met, and because the subsequent tests for investment and employment were contingent upon the first two, the British monetary framework could not fit the demands of euro conversions.[35]

Very little output on the euro followed during Labour's second term (June 2001–May 2005), despite another large majority in the House. The furor over the decision to ally with the United States in the 2003 invasion of Iraq, and the Labour party mutiny against Blair's leadership during Labour's second term (May 2005 onward) provided significant external and internal distractions. Those hoping that the succession of Chancellor Gordon Brown to the premiership in June 2007 would bring renewed interest in the currency issue have been disappointed.

Since the 2003 decision, only two recent documents of any note provide any real illumination of past motives and present intentions. The first is a report commissioned by the Royal Institute of International Affairs (Chatham House), entitled *A British Agenda for Europe*.[36] The language of the report is telling; with self-congratulatory headings like "Dynamic Britain versus Sclerotic Europe" the Euroscepticism is thinly veiled indeed; the overall implication being that Britain has done better to stay out of the Eurozone. Under the chancellorships of Kenneth Clarke (1993–1997) and Gordon Brown (1997–2007), the report argues that Britain has outperformed the majority of its EU counterparts in terms of GDP growth and foreign investment, and has undertaken more expansionary economic policies than others. The report however does make clear that the "euro has been a success in a number of senses."[37] Despite the need for EU member states to continue deeper economic reforms (a perennial British criticism of Brussels), the currency has

> helped usher in a period of historically low inflation and low interest rates across the European continent. It has been adopted smoothly by all of its member states, and further rounds of enlargement have not destabilized it. After an initial period of decline, the euro has strengthened dramatically against the dollar and other currencies. Euro-denominated corporate bonds now exceed the amount of dollar bonds and are traded in financial markets across the world. . . . The euro's role as a reserve currency is increasing steadily, accounting now for over 30% of official central bank reserves worldwide.[38]

Despite such praise, British criticism of the Eurozone itself is based on three problems: the visible divergences between the growth and inflationary pressures among all Eurozone members; the imperious behavior of France and Germany in repeatedly flouting the EMU's Growth and Stability Pact rules; and the failure of the Eurozone to act as a major stimulus for the European economy. It is clear to the authors of the report that, as of 2008, "the adoption of the euro has not coincided with a dramatic improvement in either absolute or relative growth figures" and that Britain, for its part "did not suffer directly from the government's decision to remain outside the single currency in 1999."[39]

While Labour's position on the euro "has become all but invisible," the central problem of uncertainty over the degree of divergence across Eurozone economies has not vanished. Joining the Eurozone before convergence between the British and EU monetary systems has been achieved could destabilize the pound and the British economy, undermining its fabled competitiveness, fueling inflation, and worsening its overall economic performance. The euro, while a qualified success for Europe, apparently has not proved itself for Britain. Consequently, membership would be considered from an economic perspective only if "over the next ten to twenty years, British economic performance deteriorated relative to that of the Eurozone for a sustained period of time."[40] The report makes two key recommendations. The first is a pithy restatement of Britain's traditional position relative to Europe on all policies, namely, to retain its political latitude and economic strength in a fashion separate from Europe, "We do not support the idea that Britain should give up the pound simply to avoid 'losing influence' in Europe."[41] As the report suggests, belief in the "sovereign national currency" of the pound underwrites the possibility that "British national economic performance will enable Britain to continue arguing for its economic vision for Europe from outside the Eurozone, whereas an under-performing Britain inside the Eurozone will gain minimal additional benefits for its economic future."[42] Europe, as a no-win economic prospect, thus holds no benefit for Britain.

The second recommendation makes clear that monetary policy is not solely an economic issue, but also a political one. Despite the economic turbulence of late 2008, the report suggests that a "narrow interpretation of the five economic tests" should include a political counterpart about "the net benefits" in which ministers "should be engaging the British public in a mature discussion of the risks and opportunities."[43] The political culture of Britain, in other words, and the forms of political, economic, and cultural self-reference by which the British define themselves largely in opposition to Europe should in fact continue to orient British policy. Only the most enormous global turmoil could induce a shift; and if so, the British can be relied on to refine themselves according to the contours of their identity, as quintessentially practical and sensible folk. As the report concludes, under such conditions, "Britain may need to reconsider its position and appeal to the pragmatic self-interest of the electorate over giving up the pound."[44] In other words, the state, in pursuance of its interests, would have to appeal to the nation on the basis of identity-driven interests.

The second document emerged from the European Union Committee of the House of Lords, reporting on issues between 2007–2008.[45] The report, entitled "The Euro," rather astonishingly fails to deal at all with the question of British membership. Their Lordships simply deem it inappropriate to "address the United Kingdom's position with respect to the currency," mainly because the euro is a "young currency," but also because, despite its decent start, it has yet to prove itself, and it "has not yet been fully tested."[46] Ten years of operation is evidently a "relatively short period in economic history."[47] Such a perspective could only emerge from a political unit that has enjoyed unrivalled trade and investment success pre- and post-empire, unblemished financial credibility, and apparently timeless economic stability with its own national currency. This has produced a national attitude that is disinclined culturally rather than economically to engage with a younger, somehow untried monetary structure.

These and the identity-based issues examined below all contribute to keeping the euro a backburner issue, despite some advances in Britain's ability to contribute to the expanding policy remit of the European Union. Within the government, in think tanks, and in academia as well as in some parts of British civil society, the majority of British society are still predisposed, like Churchill, to view themselves collectively as "with Europe but not of it . . . linked but not comprised . . . associated but **not** absorbed."[48]

## CURRENCY PERCEPTIONS

### The Euro as an Economic Instrument

The British debate regarding the euro is regarded by many "as a test . . . of whether it sees its destiny in the EU."[49] The Conservatives have generally demanded more of the process of economic integration, requiring "free market access and free market competition, without the additional restrictions of EMU or an industrial or social policy, but also without losing influence over EU decision-making by sitting on the sidelines."[50] Although less attached to this discourse, the Conservatives remain either Eurosceptics or "reluctant supporters of EMU as a necessary condition for preserving market access" and retaining decision-making power.[51] Labour has demonstrated more ambiguity. Encouragingly less attached to the ideal of sovereignty as an exclusive, unbending principle of state, Labour was unable to identify aspects of the EMU that make a legitimate case to the British people for further integration that could include civic connections with the continent, or economic forms of convergence as implied in the criteria for joining the euro.

Two clear arguments exist regarding currency conversion as a mechanism for greater integration. The first regards currency as simply an instrumental medium of exchange within the broader cycle of macroeconomics. The second regards currency as a symbolic extension of national identity—a tool representing economic sovereignty and aspects of national selfness. Both approaches are equally valid and continue to inform British disinclination to join the Eurozone. The first argument epitomizes the perspective of the government and has fostered numerous epistles whose primary focus is the macroeconomic consequences of EMU, economic growth, convergence, inflation, employment, and so on. Based largely upon the 1997 publication by Currie entitled *The Pros and Cons of EMU*,[52] H.M. Treasury outlined its approach in September, 2002:

> The determining factor underpinning any government decision is the *national economic interest* and whether the economic case is clear and unambiguous. . . .
> The five tests go to the heart of what is required for the long-term future of the UK economy: they are the means of judging the decision on Emu membership against the government's central objectives—full employment and high and sustainable rates of investment and growth.[53]

The five tests at work in governmental discourse not only work to "illuminate the implications of membership" but "ensure that economic, not political, considerations are still paramount."[54] This approach is distinctly at odds with the public and press discourse on the euro which has consistently, even dexterously prioritized *political* issues of euro acceptance over *economic* considerations. As a recent report makes clear, "Most people take the impetus behind the EMU to be political rather than economic, their evaluation being that the net economic benefits over costs would be small and uncertain."[55]

Two observations can be made. First, within the hugely detailed "five tests" exercise, many of the links between the national economy and its constitutive social and cultural framework were left completely unexamined.[56] Second, the answers to each of the five tests can in no way be expected to fulfill the Treasury requirements of a "clear and unambiguous" determination of convergence conditions, as the tests themselves present a wholly subjective understanding of the British economy. Lord Shore argues likewise:

> Commentators and critics have asserted that these tests are largely subjective and that the Chancellor could at any time declare they have been met. . . .
> The whole exercise is geared not so much to measuring convergence with the economy of the European Union as with measuring *the state of British public opinion* about joining the Euro as revealed in successive opinion polls. What is certainly true is that only some of the Chancellor's tests are capable of objective measurement. . . . Nobody could pretend that for example, the "flexibility" criterion is capable of anything other than opinion. . . . As aids

for helping to assist the wisdom of joining, his five tests are therefore virtually worthless.[57]

Despite the argument put forth by the *Financial Times* that "the Treasury is approaching these tests with what amounts to an intellectual dragnet," a slew of government reports, industry analysis, and specialist research has produced an unwieldy corps of contradictions rather than a representative, purposive, and ultimately actionable set of outcomes determining the subject of EMU.[58] The plethora of individual, group, industry, and lobby views attempting to assess the potential benefits and drawbacks of euro integration in no way represent a wholly objective analysis of a purely economic issue. Each group is guided by their own interests and perceptions; as such, there are equal amounts of sociological and psychological influences as there are economic analyses. The *Financial Times* prophesies as much: "It is a reasonable guess . . . that if the Treasury genuinely seeks a clear and unambiguous verdict it will, at this stage, be 'not proven.'[59] In other words, [an environment conducive to] convergence has increased substantially since 1997, but not by enough."[60] More broadly, the response to the euro by the fiscal systems of individual European states has not yet produced a reliable set of data by which to accurately gauge the efficacy of currency. It is clear that in examining "the economic preferences of individual countries, these [material] interests alone do not appear to explain the variation in [monetary or social] attitudes towards the Euro."[61]

Just as the Channel represents more than the differences between geography and political cultures, so the issue of a given *domestic economic culture* also generates an identity that is capable of goal setting and policy making. As Thomas Risse illustrates, the need for a broader methodology regarding euro convergence is clear; the need to include identity as a category of that analysis is fundamental:

> Explanations based on solely material conceptions of actors' interests—whether economic or geopolitical—are indeterminate with regard to explaining the variation in attitudes. The Euro is about European union rather than just lowering transaction costs. Institutionalist accounts about path-dependent processes . . . [only] offer significant insights if they are linked to the more *constructivist* reasoning . . . the visions about European order which give political meaning to EMU, need to be understood in the framework of *identity politics*. The controversies among the political elites . . . as well as the variation in attitudes can be explained by differences in the construction of national collective *identities* and their relationship to European order.[62]

## The Pound as a Cultural Instrument

Through "a torrent of analyses, guides, and commentaries," a substantial body of information has reached the British public on the economic impact of the euro; however, "the anticipated social, cultural and personal effects of monetary union . . . have received considerably less attention in public discussions of EMU."[63] To investigate this alternative discourse, it is necessary to see the national currency as constituting passively and functioning causally as a symbol of national identity, rather than merely a material token of economic exchange. Various sources support this argument.[64]

Based on the premise that the territory of a national unit operates as the physical configuration of the organizing principle of sovereignty (conveying an equal, if conceptual sense of bounded self), the currency of a national unit functions as an equally readily configured example of symbolic sovereignty, "boundedness," and national identity. As Risse argues, "Money has historically been closely linked to state- and nation-building. The Euro is no exception." The pound is perceived similarly.[65] In other words, "objects" such as national currency inscribe themselves upon the surface of the body politic, contributing to a discourse that signifies not only instrumental elements of "political affiliation" but to an exclusive "sense of nationness."[66] The pound operates within the national consciousness as both an instrumental and a symbolic totem of unity.

In 1997–1998, a broad study was undertaken by fifteen European researchers entitled *The Psychology of European Monetary Union: A Cross-National Study of Public Opinion towards the Euro*, based on the premise that the results of bi-annual eurobarometer studies regarding national attitudes to the euro "do not provide sufficient information about people's underlying hopes, fears, expectation and values."[67] Consequently, the team of Müller et al. made use of core conceptual domains including "involvement and knowledge concerning EMU and the euro," "satisfaction and values," and "national identity, national pride, and European identity." These categories represent an alternative methodology to the critically limited approach adopted by H.M. Treasury, successfully ameliorating the present neglect of popular consultation in determining the formation of public discourse. Müller et al. classify national identity as a sociocultural force that "evokes positive emotional attachment to one's own collective or group, with its specific symbols and values," encompassing elements such as the monarchy, aspects of history and culture, and the national currency.[68] As outlined in a parallel study by Meier-Pesti and Kirchler,

> National identity may be strengthened and represented by various national symbols. Among other symbols, the national currency stands for economic fitness and autonomy. . . . Currencies are symbols of (a) *the collective self-esteem of a nation*, (b) *national continuity*, (c) *differentiation* and (d) *efficacy*. A highly stable currency and national wealth strengthen collective self-esteem. Currencies are planned as "long term projects" and support the desire for national continuity.[69]

This argument highlights the ability of identity to sharpen the focus on the role played by the national currency. Here, identity functions as a category of reference encompassing currency by "designat[ing] the positive affective bond [with] specific national . . . symbols."[70] This perspective also suggests that currency—through the bounded principal of sovereignty—acts as an extension of the tangible physicality represented in the national territory. As Meier-Pesti and Kirchler argue, "Since currencies are restricted to a specific national geographic area, they also serve to differentiate. Moreover, currencies symbolise sovereign power in monetary policy and efficiency."[71] In other words, the symbolism inherent in national currency reflects the same concepts of identifying self-reference at work in national borders, both physical (territory) and conceptual (sovereignty), by reinforcing a sense of distinctive separateness that constitutes the group unto itself and emphasizes the currency area within which group boundaries persist.

As a national unit of currency, the pound has enjoyed a particularly lengthy history, visibly underwriting both British political sovereignty and English cultural identity. Having entrenched itself as the foremost tool of economic sovereignty in the national consciousness, the pound effectively represents the same form of island exclusivity as national territory. The euro however lacks precisely these symbolic forms of definition and appears instead as an instrumental economic mechanism rather than a self-referential point of collective identity. Undermined by its imprecise "national geographic area," the euro is unable to inform the various categories of national self-esteem, continuity, differentiation, and efficacy.[72] As Dyson argues, "The demographic profile of support for the Euro underlines the problem of social solidarity at the heart of the Euro-Zone project—namely, a core identity."[73] Thus,

> the Euro may well provide the citizen with a daily reminder of the European Union as a unit of belonging and a system of rule, but it is being introduced at a time when it seems increasingly difficult for any identity to make exhaustive and exclusive loyalty claims. The provision for different countries to put their own national symbols on coins is itself symbolic of an era of cacophonous identities.[74]

As Müller et al. have established, national currencies represent "a national symbol which [Europeans] did not want to lose."[75] British respondents in particular "express[ed] the fear that the loss of their national currency would threaten their identity."[76] From the British perspective, the dual issues of pound-versus-euro have become a question of national identity, most sharply articulated within the category of sovereignty.

The next step is to examine the role British identity in conjunction with the broad issue of European integration and the specific project of the euro.[77] The "collective perceptions and values" at work in British political culture suggest that a sense of *exclusivity* attached to both its identity and currency as forms of national "selfness" spring from a markedly realist understanding regarding the concept of sovereignty.[78] British state-centrism and its particularist perception of sovereignty are now briefly examined in reference to both the federal initiatives of Europe and the British unit itself before moving on to gauge the constitutive and causal nuances of its anti-Euro discourse and the wider implications for English national identity.

## CONTEXTUALIZING THE POLITICAL DISCOURSE: SOVEREIGNTY, STATE-CENTRISM, AND OPPOSITION TO EUROPE

### Sovereignty

As illustrated in the previous case study, the British sociopolitical ethos "stresses traditional conceptions of national interests and power" rather than espousing "supranational variants of neo-functionalist theory," and can be regarded as a "modified structural realist" unit.[79] A number of elements comprise the "realist" perspectives inherent in British attitudes: central is the principle of sovereignty, and its attachment to the Crown in Parliament. The Crown symbolizes a form of "external sovereignty" regarding independence from the continent since 1066 and a framework for subsequent imperial connections established by Britain, while Parliament symbolizes the "internal sovereignty" of a seven-century-old constitutional principle regarding the tradition of English government.[80] Parliament has emerged as the representation of popular democratic consensus, but also as the embodiment of law. The Magna Carta of 1215 and the Bill of Rights of 1688 both embody "the doctrine of parliamentary sovereignty" endowing Parliament with "a status [of supremacy] exceeding that of statutory law."[81] As such, "the extent to which Parliament has concerned itself with other sources or potential sources of elected political authority illustrates not only the supremacy of Parliament, but also its determination that such supremacy should not be successfully challenged."[82]

More so than any other European state, the English mechanism of the Crown in Parliament symbolizes a sovereign principle, a practice of governance, and the identity of the nation. In a process of "remarkable continuity," this symbolic trinity is regularly invoked as a discourse of the uniqueness of English political culture against supranational initiatives that extend not merely to current EU projects, but—as the three previous case studies have demonstrated—to *any force* attempting to undermine components of English autonomy within the British state.[83] Within Britain, sovereignty remains a distinct "legal concept, a status [that] cannot be surrendered unless the units which form the political community, whether individuals or groups, abdicate their political rights."[84] Correspondingly, supranational initiatives are seen to embody a clearly illegitimate attempt to undermine sovereign political autonomy by renouncing the "associative" elements of sovereignty, including territorial integrity and monetary exclusivity.

Sovereignty is thus a key legal principle and a central political practice; if a curtailing of its instrumental or symbolic role is entailed, a reaction will ensue. As Thatcher argued, there are "powerful, non-economic reasons for the retention of sovereignty and, as far as possible, of power, by nation-states. Not only [are] such nations functioning democracies, but they are also . . . intractable political realities which it would be folly to . . . suppress in favour of a wider but as yet theoretical European nationhood."[85] British perceptions of the euro are currently contextualized by the above views; its reluctance, even truculence regarding both federalism and the euro is based on "the primacy of the nation" as an idée fixe, "whose painful [de-]establishment might require one's lasting withdrawal from the pressing and exalting daily contest."[86] Despite "profound policy changes . . . the fundamental [British] orientations toward the European Community have remained essentially the same since the end of World War II."[87] In a point originally made by Churchill, Britain remains "with" Europe in an adjacent sense, but not "of" Europe in a political and still less a cultural sense.[88]

Current Conservative attitudes emphasize the "partnership of nations" as discrete units, with Britain as an autonomous unit "in Europe but not run by Europe."[89] Current Labour party ethos has maintained this same perspective by arguing that its "vision of Europe is of an alliance of *independent nations* choosing to cooperate" and clear in its "opposition to a European federal superstate."[90] Two points can be made from this observation. First, based on its traditional perception of sovereignty as a zero-sum entity, it is clear that Britain wishes to retain its state-centric ideology, which has in the past few decades generated an irreconcilable divergence between the nation-state paradigm and the supranational paradigm. Second, from the British perspective, Europe's "longstanding tradition of social and cultural pluralism" and recent federal initiatives ultimately render both it and the euro project inadequate as a framework upon which to build national values.[91] The discourse generated, within both political and public spheres, is therefore institutionally and culturally opposed to the euro.

## State-Centrism

The process of European integration is a challenge to realist philosophy on a number of levels. The process of integration clashes with three centuries of history, as European political reality from the Treaty of Westphalia in 1648 until 1945 was based upon a consummate, even obstinate dedication to the concept of discrete nation-states and a relatively inflexible appreciation of sovereignty. Only after the impact of two world wars was the idea of institutionalized intergovernmental cooperation proposed as a mitigating remedy to warlike imperatives. Rather than an environment of maximizing states at work in an anarchic environment, "Euro-Zone states are assumed to be rational actors, motivated by the prudent pursuit of economic self-interests rather than [the] moral argument" of the Kantian paradigm.[92] Politically, the goal of EU member states is to transcend "the extant system of nation states and reallocat[e] their existing sovereignties within international organisations concerned with maximising harmony and minimising conflict."[93] This presents the EU with the following challenge:

> European policy regimes are shaped neither by a deterministic dynamic of integration nor by a static bargain between state interests, but as a series of compromises that intertwine the realisation of national preferences with an enlarged role for supranational actors, while substantially changing the domestic character of participating states and societies.[94]

Theorists espouse the need to regard integrationist projects as a *complementary* rather than a displacing initiative. As Wallace argues, "the Community is neither supra- nor international but 'extra-national'; neither above nor below the nation-state, but 'alongside.'"[95] However, the assorted neoliberal and functionalist theories of the EU integration projects embody only one perspective. Bulmer, for example, argues that "too much literature has concentrated on the upper tier—the formal institutional framework of the Communities—without examining the *domestic sources* of national negotiating positions. . . . The term 'domestic politics' also underlines the fact that the lower decisional tier of the EC is rooted in *policy environments* which differ between member states."[96] Moravcsik concurs, arguing that European integration is a form of supranational transcendence occurring via "a series of pragmatic bargains among national governments based on concrete national interests, relative power, and carefully calculated transfers of sovereignty."[97]

The terminology of "reallocation" of competence and "transfers" of policy entails clear forms of agency at work within the EU structure. However, as examined previously, interactive agency at the systemic level is generated by specific interests endogenous to nation-state units themselves; as such, "each national polity has a different set of social and economic conditions that shapes its national interests and policy content. Each state has different *ideological cleavages* which determine the extent of consensus."[98] This coincides with the views of Morgenthau, in which "the national interest . . . is determined by the political traditions and the total cultural context within which a nation formulates its foreign policy."[99] In other words, the ideological and cultural context of a national society determines its social consensus, which in turn produces a political environment that constitutes national interests and works causally to affect policy content.

Despite its supranational powers, the EU continues to be characterized by "the persistence of *national* power and the centrality of *domestic* political calculations."[100] This is an outcome of a shared continental history; as Bellier and Wilson observe, "while states were defining boundaries, governance and sovereignty, they also developed a shared resistance to Europe being united under the hegemony of a single state or political master."[101] One cannot therefore be content with explanations that community paralysis "between sovereignty and integration" is the result of "domestic preoccupations of the member governments . . . [or] their lack of spare resources, political or financial, to invest in the European dimension."[102] Individual EU states represent innately endogenous sources of *statecraft*, which at times perceive integration to impinge on the nuances of their *state practice*.

The British national state is a clear example of a state-centrist perspective continuing to vie against supranational imperatives. The underlying English ethos (which informs the values of the British state) clearly views supranationalism not as a complementary tool to traditional intergovernmentalism but incommensurate with its domestic *practices* of governance and its understanding of the *principle* of national sovereignty. British attempts to retain a measure of autonomy in the face of increasing federal forces are thus accurately analyzed via "the realist doctrine [that] lies at the heart of [its] sceptical account of the European project."[103]

## Opposition to Europe

While attempts by Tony Blair to inculcate pro-Europe policies into current national perspectives may appear anomalous, perceptions identifying the benefits of integration, even federalism, have existed in parallel with the prevalent anti-Europe discourse. Early British spokesmen for this perspective include Lord Lothian, J. B. Priestley, and H. N. Brailsford. Brailsford regarded federalism as an ideational broadening of fraternal ideals and in 1939 invoked such concepts in tones echoing the decidedly English quality of civility:

> If we can realise anything resembling this project of Federation . . . we shall abolish internecine war in Europe. . . . We shall rescue the priceless values

of this civilisation itself. . . . If we abandon the old concept of the Sovereign State, it will not be because we have changed our views about a legal theory. It will be because we have reached an ideal of human fraternity that embraces our neighbours, who in other languages think the same civilised thoughts.[104]

England, as the nation of civilizing values, would as the wider British state rescue Europe from the perils of further uncivilized and warlike behavior. Lord Lothian believed in realist fashion that anarchy was both the cause and effect of war in Europe: "The real cause of our troubles is that the nations are living in anarchy. . . . Anarchy cannot be ended by any system of co-operation between sovereign nations but only by the application of the principle of federal union."[105] In 1940, J. B. Priestley attempted to contemplate the merits of federalism in tandem with English local particularism:

> I cannot see the slightest reason why the delegation of national sovereignty to a federal authority should blot out all regional influences, depending as they do, not on political organization but on local climate, landscape, social tradition and the like. . . . We substitute for the nation a greater federation of peoples, with whom we co-operate instead of competing. . . . We can [then] attend to what is in all truth our own bit of the world, our own hills and dales and woodlands, our own wind and rain, our own folk whom we know by name.[106]

Priestley evokes an exquisite world of untouched English rurality in which the discourse of federalism will support a more refined sense of the distinctively English national self. A further benefit in "prefer[ing] a functional to a constitutional approach" was not only the Kantian paradigm of inhibiting war by providing a commercial environment conducive to peace, but a reconciling of Hobbesian and Lockeian images.[107] Outlined by David Mitrany, such "international collaboration" would attempt to overcome the practical difficulties of renouncing sovereignty by "offer[ing] a practical line of action that might overcome the deep-seated division between the needs of material unity and stubborn national loyalties. . . . The task is essentially one of practical statesmanship."[108]

From this perspective, state-centrist concepts obscure methods by which federal integration may be perceived as beneficial; within Britain, widespread ignorance regarding functionalist initiatives appears to have compounded their obscurity and thus feasibility. As Michael Burgess argues, "The European idea to this extent is impoverished. A wholly intergovernmental perspective of the European Community while firmly grounded in the constituent state reality . . . devalues an important rival conception of Europe."[109] The "European idea," however, currently lacks a consonant political and cultural unity, which consequently shifts attention back to its discrete nation-states. Unsurprisingly, the "oppositional" discourse is marked by its minority status. The majority adopt a moderately pragmatic approach, and still identify with the emotive aspects of Englishness that continue to inform their views on both Europe and the euro. Julia Stapleton articulates these perceptions as "an aversion to the uniformity and compulsion (and profligacy) of the [federal] 'slave state' [marked by] a love of the ingrained spontaneity and diversity of the English character reflected in a culture and matched by a landscape marked by contrasts."[110] As examined below, identity is a helpful tool in assessing British attitudes regarding the euro; the true discourse of opposition is in fact the majority of the British populace who, guided by the values of their English core, work "avidly to keep alive the notion of an English *patria* in the collective consciousness of postwar Britain" by maintaining a steadfast opposition to the euro.[111]

From this brief history, the ethos of Englishness underwrites British perceptions of Europe in an eminently conservative vein: "Britain has always seen itself as a *status quo* power: the knee-jerk reaction of British Governments has been to believe that change will inexorably harm British national interests."[112] Consequently, British statecraft is defined by "the ongoing belief that British interventions would be counterproductive."[113] Transforming these perceptions into a national discourse, and further into policies of "patriotic inclusiveness" and "pro-Europe" attitudes implies considerable agency. Despite alleging that Britain would be mad "to shut the door on the option of joining the single currency in future . . . if it was in our clear interests to do so,"[114] the *Financial Times* recorded that "the prime minister has been adroit in making Britain's case in Europe but he has yet to make Europe's case in Britain."[115]

Agency relies upon broader requirements of a contextualizing ethos. This ethos is currently an exclusivist one: "The British are different—or at the very least determined to see themselves as such. . . . Two-thirds of voters say that they do not want to join the single currency."[116] Ultimately, both ethos and agency rely wholly upon motivating perceptions; in other words, while "winning a referendum on Euro entry is not impossible—(exceptionalism must always be weighed against pragmatism) . . . the British are a long way from discovering what comes instinctively to a Frenchman or a German: that Europe is an extension of rather than a substitute for nationhood."[117] British beliefs and self-perceptions lie at the heart of the following analysis, which illustrates that Britain continues to be guided by a nexus of self-referential, particularist values and images—explicitly English in ilk—from which ideas of self-perception, interest, and policy formation are constitutively formed and causally influenced.

## THE CULTURAL DISCOURSE

The endogenous focus of this study supports the view by Simon Bulmer that "the national polity is the basic unit in the European Community. It is the level at which governments, interest groups, parliamentary bodies and political parties derive their legitimacy, their power," and modes of self reference.[118] Perceptions emanating from the British domestic unit regarding the euro have been illustrated as incommensurate with the instrumental and symbolic concepts of sovereignty and realist principles. However, these perceptions form part of a broader discourse arising from concerns over contemporary European identity. Current British wariness "cannot simply be blamed on an ignorant, xenophobic population. Skepticism sprang just as much from the failure of Europhiles to define and promote a European identity which had some relevance to the lives of ordinary Britons."[119] Dyson articulates the core fear behind British reticence regarding Europe:

> Given [its] historical context of different embedded national identities, and the historical and cultural complexity of the EU as a political community, the Euro-Zone can aspire to no more than a broadly shared and "thin conception of European identity . . . a cosmopolitan idea of an open *civic* society whose members are dedicated to critical comparison and moral justification and who are held together by shared rights of citizenship. . . . European identity does not take the form of a "thick" identity, grounded in ethnicity and *cultural* history, ancient symbols, myths and legends, and generating a sense of *cultural unity*. It is a cosmopolitan form of civic identity more appropriate to a multicultural society.[120]

As Bellier and Wilson argue, "The EU as an object and a project has no modern historical antecedent, and no cultural template or political form."[121] Lacking a collective foundation myth, the EU therefore must rely on its constructed institutional and economic linkages and corps of shared civic principles. As such, EU initiatives continue to represent "that deepest and most intractable of all political cleavages, a cleavage between the people and the political class."[122] M. Elliott notes that the "large and difficult issues facing Europe [include] weak political leadership, [and] an unresolved tussle between national identity and supranational power."[123] Thus, "whilst the EU has a formal (legal) legitimacy, it may lack social (empirical) legitimacy," particularly "the lack of a sense of homogeneity."[124] Two results have occurred. First, with regard to identity, "EU-level socialization plays a relatively small role in the determination of elite attitudes by comparison with national-level socialization"; the nation-state still commands the primary modes of self reference.[125] Second, with regard to the euro, the European Union has begun the process of "fiscal centralization" "in the near absence of a set of beliefs and values which are specifically European or of a European party system."[126] Together, these two outcomes pertain to facets of "public acceptance of the EU," both of which have been delayed in Britain because of the overriding instrumental appearance of much EU policy, entrenching "the popular perception that the EU operates under different rules from those operating within more generally understood left/right party lines."[127] The nature of the British perspective is *both* inherently state-centric and innately symbolic; its predilection for historical, primordial qualities of collective self-reference balanced by modernist, pragmatic efforts to remain different from Europe by design and by default.

A cosmopolitan entity founded purely on instrumental elements remains an unapproachable concept for the British perspective primarily because of its English self-referential core.[128] Current British perspectives emphasize that the national state and its associated sovereign concepts of territorial and economic exclusivity remain a discursive prerogative that overrides current supranational policies. While Burgess argues that "there is a basic continuity of federal ideas in the European Community's political development,"[129] the failure to convert a portion of European economic initiatives into modes of cultural self-reference suggests that British attitudes regarding European unity, identity, and goals will remain "beset by confusion and contradiction," where "'Brussels' is . . . a homogenizing force that chooses corporatism over enterprise, bloated welfare systems and egalitarianism over individual responsibility and foists regulation on a nation that prefers its markets free."[130]

While the ultimate endpoint of multipolicy integration remains at odds with contemporary British interests, Europe itself still provides a cultural home for Britain and its English core. Thatcher herself emphasized the importance of a cultural legacy for both Britain and Europe: the "British are as much heirs to the legacy of European *culture* as any other nation," with English churches, literature, and language "all bear[ing] witness to the cultural riches which we have drawn from Europe."[131] The richness of its civic culture illustrates "the European legacy of political ideas," which in sum, emphasize that the "European Community is *one* manifestation of that European identity," which if it is to belong "to *all* its members . . . must reflect the traditions and aspirations of *all* its members."[132] The true dilemma is a paradigmatic irreconcilability between the view of a federal Europe and the present incarnation of the English national identity foundational to state-centrist British attitudes. As a result, the political and public discourses generated in Britain clearly prioritize the national "belief in the overriding importance of existing national identities," particularly the merits of Englishness, and the specific forms of history and culture they preserve.[133] References incorporating the English core of the

British unit present its inhabitants with a deeply entrenched sense of the "island" self at work in identity categories that include physical and ontological security, territoriality, and sovereignty, all with more than a thousand years of rich social, cultural, and political tradition. English modes of self-reference are "as old as Shakespeare, matured through the experience of the English Civil War and the struggles against the threat of Catholic absolutism . . . [engendering perceptions of] a free England defying an unfree continent."[134] English identity contains equal elements of primordial symbolism and state-centric realist pragmatism to embody a form of "Anglo-Saxon exceptionalism" in which Europe is perceived as the 'other.'"[135] It differs radically from the constructed European identity of the past few decades, which, as Frognier explains, is an "evaluative kind of identity [when] compared to the more affective ancient national identities."[136] Because of this foundational insecurity, British attitudes perceive Europe and its initiatives as less stable than those garnered through "patriotic sentiments," because of their dependence upon "rational calculation [varying] with economic cycles."[137]

Two points can be made to conclude this section. First, political and monetary integration entails a process whereby "political actors in several distinct national settings are persuaded to shift their loyalties, expectations, and political activities toward a new center, whose institutions possess or demand jurisdiction over the pre-existing national states."[138] Using the present example of Britain, discourses constituted by expectations and made causal by such activities originate from groups "forward[ing] interdependent sets of values—ideologies—in their struggle . . . for political prominence."[139] Second, because identity informs state-based ideologies of national self-reference, "the decision to join in or to abstain from the proposed steps of integration is [now largely] defended in terms of national *values*" rather than explicit *interests*.[140] While the Treasury has attempted to articulate an instrumental discourse regarding the congruence between currency convergence and the national economic interest, the ongoing anti-euro discourse emanating from public and political forums is wholly premised upon the value of national sovereignty and the retention of a particularist state-based identity. The constitutive nature of this discourse appears to have had a causal impact on the policy environment regarding the latest decision to delay the procedures of euro introduction.

## POLITICAL AND CULTURAL DISCOURSES IN POLICY MAKING

Risse correctly argues that the ongoing reluctance demonstrated by political parties and the general public regarding the euro is "grounded in particular collective understandings of Englishness and English identity."[141] Clearly, there are qualities of Englishness currently invested in the pound and lacking in the euro that informs anti-euro attitudes with effects upon policy making. Chief among such qualities of Englishness is a characteristic displaying an overt reluctance to "embrace change, particularly if such a change is perceived to pose a threat to national identity."[142] The pound clearly symbolizes British unity and English values within a singular discourse capable of generating statements such as "Losing the Pound is like losing the Royal Family."[143] The national currency is therefore best analyzed from the perspective of identity. As demonstrated, identity is an eminently flexible and viable category, comprising both a "sentimental attachment reflecting cultural [historical and national] symbols and an "instrumental [or civic] attachment associated with the benefits of citizenship," entailing concepts of legitimacy and judgments regarding "the quality of various social goods and mechanisms."[144] The pound also represents an "economic-political dimension." It is "part of the national culture and is as integral to cultural-historical pride as language or history."[145] However, for the majority of the British public, schooled broadly in modes of English self-reference, "the *tradition* factor, which focuses upon the more symbolic and cultural aspects of identification with Britain is the more potent in evaluations of what Britain may lose in joining the single currency."[146]

As argued above, territorial integrity and the exclusive domain of national currency possess the same role: both signify the uniqueness of the English state by demarcating it within a bounded sense of the sovereign national self. Within the precept of sovereignty, as the principle and practice of power and control within a clearly demarcated geographic area, the categories of territorial and monetary exclusivity find a conceptual context of an exclusive ilk. If suggestions to "abandon" the pound are currently regarded as equivalent to the "abrogation" of territorial integrity implicit in national sovereignty, it appears that both concepts of territorial and monetary sovereignty represent foundational components of the broader state-based, realist tradition that continues to inform English modes of political and cultural self-representation. As such, the "replacement of the national currency by the Euro is certain to result in the loss of an essential symbol of national demarcation."[147] Within Britain, this is "viewed negatively [because] . . . it is precisely this superior demarcation from other countries which is basic to high levels of nationalistic values.[148] Lord Shore articulates a strongly pro-British perspective by which the national economic unit represents the principle of sovereignty:

[There is] a need to demonstrate and persuade the British people that there are not lined and adverse political constitutional consequences of joining the Single Currency: that there is not a non-economic price in terms of loss of our democracy, our self-government and *our sovereignty* that most British people will never consent to pay.[149]

Current British reactions against the Euro represent a defense not merely of the autonomy of their "policy environment" through the maintenance of this sovereign principle, but also a defense against the more intangible nuances of its endogenous environment, that is, the English, social, cultural, and political modes of meaning from which British policy decisions take form and are informed of their content.[150] Despite the efforts of convergence to "cosmopolitanize" the idea of currency by extending the application of sovereignty, the British state remains entrenched in its realist, state-centric perspective in which the pound continues to be informed by a decidedly communitarian perspective of exclusivist uniqueness. It appears that "the more national self-definition is threatened by introduction of the Euro, the more negatively the Euro will be judged."[151]

The "communitarian" aspect characterizing units of currency is a particularly apt approach by which to explain the recent era of British anti-euro discourse, as it hinges upon concepts of exclusivity that can be extended to sovereignty, territoriality, and currency. The methodology used by Meier-Pesti and Kirchler utilizes "in-groups" and "out-groups" to judge the impact of currency symbolism upon national identity. Because both instrumental and emotive elements contribute to its identity, Britain (and its English heartland) is a vivid example of "in-group"—or communitarian unit psychology. British identity concepts clash with concepts of European integration and the euro project because "the identity of a high-status group will be threatened when they are combined with a group of lower status [because] aggregation challenges positive distinctiveness."[152] Within British identity, the highest degree of distinctiveness is found within the body of Englishness as a core of considerable agential power; correspondingly, understandings of exclusive English values possess the greatest opposition to the euro.

The connection between Englishness and anti-euro discourse emanates from a history of self-reference that prioritizes emotive over instrumental elements. As outlined earlier, currencies testify not only to the economic, instrumental strength of a nation but also denote the concept of sovereign autonomy emotively by highlighting categories of "collective self-esteem, national continuity, differentiation and efficacy."[153] These four categories accurately represent the current identity crisis at work in Britain and the English core. To elaborate, British, and more accurately, English, national self-esteem is based upon its historical continuity, founded upon geographical, and thus cultural, differentiation, all of which complete the efficacy of national self-identification within a given role or identity according to various goals or interests. Undermining the meaning-based content of these four categories shakes collective self-esteem to the point where it turns inward in the search for points of self-reference that have not yet been altered or devalued. However, various qualities in the armament of Englishness have been steadily eroded by the assorted forces of declinism and modernity visited upon Britain and its English core in the past century.

Apart from its "disastrous flirtation with the Exchange Rate Mechanism [which] has left a lasting Eurosceptic legacy," the British disease is not confined to the material realm of economics, business cycles, and unemployment, but is most perceptible when entwined with forms of self-representation.[154] Chief among such forms is identity, coalesced into the categories of national sovereignty, territoriality, a particularist sociopolitical ethos, a unique national culture, and in this case, the currency unit of the pound, all of which have suffered from elements of decline. The result is that "British attitudes toward the European project reflect collectively held beliefs about British, particularly English identity."[155]

British participants in the Müller study examined above confirm that the pound-euro debate operates as a catalyst in revealing deeper issues of decline at work in British and English identities. As witnessed by one interviewee: "My idea of the British nation as a state is that of a declining post-empire, a post-colonial force. I have somehow injected that into my image of what the Pound is: a limping old thing."[156] Declinism entails an acute awareness of the past, and a reluctance to disengage with it; thus, the British populace "feel[s] torn between being bound to the tradition of their currency and the problematic economic reality of the Pound."[157] With a tradition steeped in history rather than contemporary challenges, "recollections seem emotionally more real than the possible forthcoming change."[158] Not only are such attitudes difficult "to admit to, since money is seen as a serious, rather rational topic, rather than an emotional one," the British in particular have an identity that applies a pragmatic view to even the most emotive of national elements.[159]

Despite this element of decline, the anti-euro discourse also constitutes an assertion of national identity—a core characteristic of English self-reference. Thus, "theme[s] of national decline . . . [are] secondary to that of expounding and celebrating the contours of England's substantial former glory, in the hope that it would stir in others . . . new depths of patriotism and the revival of a cultural inheritance rooted squarely in tradition."[160] This identity, steeped in tradition, is overtly cultural and thus largely unconnected with material projects. The anti-euro discourse is thus premised on:

> a glimmer of hope that the English [in the wake of Common Market acceptance] would renounce their newly acquired tendency for material prosperity

to outweigh all other values, and revert to a national type . . . characterised by energy to the point of bawdiness, but which was also resoundingly upright, Christian and patriotic . . . a retreat from the postwar obsession with wages and welfare, a bureaucracy-driven state and contentment with diminutive world status, and the resump[tion], under new forms, [of its] ancient precedence of "teaching the nations how to live," becoming once more a source of strength and stability.[161]

This in essence, is the crux between lived reality and past imaginings; between the current Labour ethos of British patriotism and a vision of an older, immemorial England so unrepentantly unrepresentative that it acts as its own form of invasion literature. From the perspective of this case study, the protagonist remains the nation-state; the antagonist, rather than an external "other" is the creeping force of change, of which federalism and the euro are merely extensions.[162] Even English nationhood appears to differ in its concept of "self" from current British forms of inclusiveness, as the former "link[s] the values and beliefs of ordinary people to a tradition of patriotic expression that has now been "increasingly abjured" by political parties attempting to foist British national interests over the English national identity.[163] Britain continues "to celebrate English distinctiveness as opposed to Europeanness" which has resulted in Europe's failing to become "a political community of fate" for British political discourse, and increased the "symbolic quality" of the pound as a measure of national identity.[164]

The disjuncture between ideologies of English separateness and British integration, past and present, preeminence and collective equality, Britishness and Englishness, and ultimately British-Englishness and Europe can only be analyzed endogenously via identity, after which principles of sovereignty, territoriality, and currency gain both context and focus. As Cottam argues, national identity "carries with it a package of values producing clear predispositions in terms of identification of threats and opportunities to the nation and responses to those threats and opportunities."[165] Britain and its English core are both predisposed to viewing the past as an inviolable area and the recent present as a period of decline and change symbolized by the euro (itself representative of a threat rather than an opportunity). The English core of the British unit is dedicated to retaining forms of cultural primacy by which to identify with and retain sovereignty over their political unit; as a result, "no country apart from the UK has consistently seen the EU as a threat to its national identity."[166]

British pragmatism regarding convergence criteria does not extend solely to the mechanisms of governance in which "the rigor of the assessment [of convergence criteria] is a sign of whether we take the issues seriously"; more accurately, it is a cultural shorthand for its own identity: a series of national characteristics in which are embedded its continuing dedication to the state-centric and monetarist merits of the realist paradigm.[167] The quintessence of the newer British and older English response to all things European is contextualized through its perennial reverence for the sacral nature of the nation-unit, denoted by the exclusive nature of its territory, its currency, and the inviolability of its sovereignty by which all national concepts continue to be informed. Because the national space is sharply defined by its vivid island borders, the unit itself is thus especially sensitive to the symbolism of its sovereignty.

As illustrated, national identity is the operationalization of public consciousness, which takes agential form when "the positive affective bond to specific national achievements and symbols" such as currency become consciously and publicly articulated in the construction of a discourse that either challenges or supports the status quo.[168] Two discursive elements have arisen regarding the current euro debate: a constituted discourse and a causally affected policy. The former encompasses the view that "the British are different from the rest of Europe"; while the exclusivist themes of this discourse makes this readily apparent, the empirical evidence of Müller-Peters et al. supports the view "that an anti-European nationalistic attitude in Great Britain can by no means be reconciled with the acceptance of the Euro."[169] This understanding supports the hypothesis in which a constitutive discourse affects a policy outcome in a distinctly causal way. This proves a most provable hypothesis in the present instance when taking into account the announcement by the chancellor of the exchequer in June 2003 that "irrespective of achieving convergence and flexibility . . . membership of the European single currency" would not necessarily be "automatically countenanced."[170]

Leonard argues that "at a time when the political stakes in the European debate have never been higher . . . [Britain] is at a clear junction in the painful debate about its identity."[171] Leonard however is incorrect to conclude that "Euroscepticism is a cause" of current perceptual entanglements regarding the euro. While it may be said that such skepticism indeed "incites real passions and galvanizes people into action," it is more correctly a *result*. Englishness and the "painful debate" over its composition and prospects is the cause; this concept acts causally, first, to constitute a context of identity and interest, and then to draw from that context images and themes that produce a policy environment reflective of those same themes, which are themselves understood to possess causal efficacy as a result.[172] The observation by Weight neatly encapsulates the discursive response to the euro while articulating an ongoing argument of this study, namely, that "the extent to which *culture* ha[s] become a substitute for world power and how much British patriotism still depended on a sentimental, conservative vision of that culture."[173] Identity clearly continues to operate as a pervasive force of material cohesion and ideational self-reference; the British are perhaps one of its most potent examples. There are, for example, various studies that reveal unambiguously that "citizens in all the EU states have a significantly stronger identity with national . . . units than with the supranational EU."[174] As such, the elements of "national consciousness, established linguistic, geographic, economic and other ties built up over long periods [are] essential prerequisites for the nationalizing process" of which identity is a central category.[175]

## CONCLUSION

As illustrated, British parliamentary debates about the euro contain fascinating references to British and English identity.[176] These references drive debates and catalytically influence policy making. Identifying such causality however involved requires a robust conceptual framework like neoclassical realism. Without the tripartite balance of external factors (EU), and internal factors including the British interests and English identity, the dependent variable of British economic policy remains an unexplored decision. One cannot simply take the Müller-Peters study at face value, and accept that "the introduction of a single European currency cannot be reconciled with the British self-image"; the findings of the study need to be connected to the cultural bedrock of national identity and the particular version of Englishness at work in 2003 to understand clearly why "anti-European nationalism is even more relevant for explaining the attitude toward the Euro in the UK than elsewhere."[177] For the purpose of the present case studies, national identity appears an invaluable, pervasive, and surprisingly constant variable by which to deconstruct British policy preferences in various eras.

Arguably, other explanations for the euro debate may be identified, from materialist, instrumental theories to the more recent realist-revisionism adopted throughout this study. Simply put, materialist theories revolve around power and interest with foreign policy acting to ensure the maximum retention of both.[178] Indeed, according to central realist precepts, political and economic integration with Europe impinges on the discretionary capabilities of the British political unit, ultimately undermining the "autonomy of its independent decision-making."[179] From a monetarist standpoint, the euro unit is simply economically unfeasible until conditions prove themselves more conducive. Various realists could advance similar theories that would deviate no less from these two suggestions. Hoffman suggests that the ingenuity and initiative required to carry out projects of the magnitude of integration and the euro is itself an exercise of power: "In international relations, the possession of power is to be sought not only for the sake of prestige or domination but also because only the mighty create."[180]

However, without the assistance of a cultural framework or a set of categories by which to deal with the essence of unit endogeneity, realist analyses can do no more than make a few rough judgments regarding Britain and the euro. Broader analyses have been undertaken by Pisani-Ferry et al., who argue first, that "British attitudes are always influenced by the desire to adapt *endogenous* market solutions, rather than impose some externally designed blueprint from outside."[181] Their second observation is that "by tradition, British debates follow the 'rules' of parliamentary democracy—that is, direct representation of popular views 'from the bottom up' [where] decisions, once taken, are then administered in a rather centralised way."[182] While pertinent to the discursive attributes of the above euro debate, these two observations also highlight failings in traditional realist analyses, which apart from vague assertions regarding the composition of the domestic economy and methods of governance would not necessarily register the nuances of such "attitudes," "traditions," and "rules." The conclusion touches one final time upon the benefits provided by this school of thought, as well providing an overview of the triad of identity, interests, and foreign policy investigated in these four case studies.

The 2009 ratification of the Lisbon Treaty presented Britain with a rather surprising opportunity to once again find itself at the heart of Europe by placing Baroness Catherine Ashton in the newly created position of High Representative of the Union for Foreign Affairs and Security Policy of the European Union (EU). The opportunity for a traditionally Eurosceptic country to make a significant representative contribution regarding the most challenging aspect of the EU—its foreign and security policy—is both highly ironic and possibly oddly appropriate.

## NOTES

1. P. E. Prestwich, "French Businessmen and the Channel Tunnel Project of 1913," *French Historical Studies* 9, no. 4 (Autumn 1976): 690.

2. Treaty Establishing The European Coal and Steel Community (1951), http://Europa.eu.int/abc/obj/treaties/en/entoc29.htm (accessed 30 August 2002).

3. The Treaty of Rome, together with the ECSC and the formation of Euratom (the European Atomic Energy Community), established the European Community (EC) in July 1967—the central portion of the European Union (EU).

4. *Financial Times*, 21 November 1992.

5. Common Market Conservative Party Poll, conducted by Gallup, July 1971, London, Conservative Party Literature, Bodleian Library, Oxford.

6. Conservative Pamphlets, *Europe and You, Sovereignty in the Common Market*, London, 1971, Conservative Party Literature, Bodleian Library, Oxford (emphasis added).

7. Lord Goodman, *Times*, January 2 1973.

8. W. Wallace, "Europe as a Confederation: The Community and the Nation-State," *Journal of Common Market Studies* 20 (1982): 65.

9. As Leonard observes, having played a central role in the 1975 "Yes to Europe" campaign, "it was not until she lost the premiership that Margaret Thatcher became viscerally opposed to the EU. D. Leonard and M. Leonard, eds., *The Pro-European Reader* (London: Palgrave/Foreign Policy Centre, 2002), 4.

10. Leonard, *The Pro-European Reader*, 4.

11. M. Thatcher, "Our Destiny Is in Europe," Speech to the College of Europe, Bruges, Belgium, September 1988, Conservative Party Literature, Bodleian Library, Oxford.

12. M. Thatcher, *The Downing Street Years, 1979–1990* (New York: HarperCollins, 1993), 745.

13. Pinder explains the difference, though few in Britain seem to have grasped the nuances: A federation comprises "federal institutions with powers over trade, money, the environment . . . armed forces and external relations." Armed with the institutions of a legislature, an executive, and a federal court, a federation includes "member states [that] hold their powers by right under the constitution." Thus, "a federation is a state whereas a federal union . . . falls short of that." J. Pinder, "Why the Single Market Is a Step towards Federal Union," in *The European Community and the Challenge of the Future*, ed. J. Lodge (London: Palgrave MacMillan, 1993), 61-2.

14. Lodge, *The European Community*, 63.

15. S. Brittan, "Let Fools Contest about the Forms," *Financial Times*, 21 November 1991.

16. K. Morgan, *The Oxford History of Britain* (Oxford: Oxford University Press, 2001), 664.

17. Morgan, *The Oxford History of Britain*, 666.

18. Leonard, *The Pro-European Reader* 4.

19. M. Aspinwall, "Odd Man Out: Rethinking British Policy on European Monetary Integration," *Review of International Studies* 29, no. 3 (July 2003): 347.

20. K. Dyson, *The Politics of the Euro-Zone: Stability or Breakdown?* (Oxford: Oxford University Press, 2000): 235.

21. P. Clarke, *A Question of Leadership: From Gladstone to Blair* (Macmillan: London, 1999), 344 (emphasis added).

22. R. Weight, *Patriots: National Identity in Britain, 1940–2000* (London: Macmillan, 2002), 672.

23. *Financial Times*, "Britain and Europe," Part I, 4 November 2002.

24. M. Levitt and C. Lord, *The Political Economy of Monetary Union* (London: MacMillan Press Ltd., 2000), 76.

25. A. Müller-Peters, et al., "Explaining Attitudes towards the Euro: Design of a Cross-National Study," *Journal of Economic Psychology* 19 (1998): 704. See also R. Kosterman and S. Feshbach, "Towards a measure of patriotic and nationalistic attitudes," *Political Psychology* 10 (1989): 260.

26. Morgan, *The Oxford History of Britain*, 671.

27. Morgan, *The Oxford History of Britain*, 671.

28. A. Giddens, "The Third Way," *New Statesman*, 1 May 1998

29. Morgan, *The Oxford History of Britain*, 674.

30. T. Blair, "The New Challenge for Europe," acceptance speech for the Charlemagne Prize, Aachen, Germany, 29 September 1999, Labour Party Literature, Labour Party Archives, Manchester.

31. Blair, "The New Challenge for Europe" (emphasis added).

32. "EMU: Blair's Pro-Europe Campaign Inches towards Single Currency," *European Report*, 16 Oct. 1999.

33. "Cook rules out early EMU entry for Britain," *Telegraph*, 9 June 1997.

34. Lord Shore, "No to the Euro," in R. Beetham (ed.), *The Euro Debate: Persuading the People* (London: The Federal Trust for Education and Research, London, 2001), 65.

35. G. Brown, Hansard Parliamentary Records, House of Commons, col. 414 and 415, 9 June 2003 (London: HMSO).

36. Chatham House Commission Report, *A British Agenda for Europe: Designing Our Own Future* (London: Royal Institute of International Affairs, 2008).

37. Chatham House Commission Report, *A British Agenda for Europe*, 40–43.

38. Chatham House Commission Report, *A British Agenda for Europe*, 43.

39. Chatham House Commission Report, *A British Agenda for Europe*, 44, 48.

40. Chatham House Commission Report, *A British Agenda for Europe*, 49.

41. Chatham House Commission Report, *A British Agenda for Europe*, 50.

42. Chatham House Commission Report, *A British Agenda for Europe*, 49, 50.

43. Chatham House Commission Report, *A British Agenda for Europe*, 50.

44. Chatham House Commission Report, *A British Agenda for Europe*, 50.

45. House of Lords, European Union Committee, 13th Report of Session 2007–2008, *The Euro*, HL Paper 90 (London: The Stationery Office Limited, May 2008).

46. House of Lords, *The Euro*, foreword, i.

47. House of Lords, *The Euro*, foreword, i.

48. W. Churchill, cited by D. Weigall in Peter M. R. Stirk and David Willis, eds. *Shaping Post-War Europe: European Unity and Disunity, 1945–1957* (New York: St. Martin's Press, 1991), 97.

49. *Financial Times*, "Britain and Europe," Part IV, 7 November 2002.

50. A. Hughes Hallett, "The UK Position on Economic and Monetary Union," in *The Political Economy of EMU: France, Germany and the UK*, ed. J. Pisani-Ferry et al. (Brussels: Centre for European Policy Studies, 1997), 74.

51. Hughes Hallett, "The UK Position on Economic and Monetary Union," 74.

52. D. Currie, *The Pros and Cons of EMU* (London: The Economist Intelligence Unit, 1997).

53. *H.M. Treasury Submission to the House of Commons Treasury Committee*, 6 September 2002 (London: HMSO) (emphasis added).

54. *Financial Times*, "Britain and Europe," Part II, 5 November 2002.

55. A. Hughes Hallett, "The UK Position on Economic and Monetary Union."

56. The magnitude of the project is immense. As the *Financial Times* illustrated, in three hundred years of policy making: "Never can the British government have made a comparably detailed analysis of any policy decision. It certainly did not do so before joining the European Community." The *Financial Times*, "Britain and Europe," Part II, 5 November 2002.

57. Lord P. Shore, in R. Beetham, ed. *The Euro Debate, Persuading the People,* 65–66 (emphasis added).

58. *Financial Times,* "Britain and Europe," Part II, 5 November 2002.

59. *Financial Times,* "Britain and Europe," Part II, 5 November 2002.

60. *Financial Times,* "Britain and Europe," Part II, 5 November 2002.

61. T. Risse, "To Euro or Not to Euro? The EMU and Identity Politics in the European Union," ARENA Working Papers, European University Institute, (1998), 3.

62. Risse, "To Euro or Not to Euro?" 1 (emphasis added).

63. Müller-Peters, A. et al., "Explaining Attitudes towards the Euro: Design of a Cross-National study," *Journal of Economic Psychology* 19 (1998): 665–66.

64. See in this regard E. Helleiner, "National Currencies and National Identities," *American Behavioral Scientist* 41 (1998); G. M. Breakwell, *Coping with Threatened Identities* (London: Methuen, 1986); B. Cohen, *The Geography of Money* (Ithaca, NY: Cornell University Press, 1998); J. Driffill, and M. Beber, eds., "A Currency for Europe" (London: Lothian Foundation Press, 1995).

65. Risse, "To Euro or Not to Euro?" 1.

66. H. Bhabha, ed. *Nation and Narration* (London: Routledge, 1990), 2.

67. Müller-Peters et al., "Explaining Attitudes towards the Euro," 670. The original findings of the cross-national study now comprise a full text: A. Müller-Peters, R. Pepermans, G. Kiell, and M. Farhangmehr, eds., *The Psychology of European Monetary Union: A Cross-National Study of Public Opinion towards the Euro* (Santiago de Compostela, Spain: Compostela Group of Universities, 2001).

68. Müller-Peters et al. "Explaining Attitudes towards the Euro," 672.

69. K. Meier-Pesti and E. Kirchler, "Attitudes towards the Euro by National Identity and Relative National Status," *Journal of Economic Psychology* 24 (2003): 2 (emphasis added).

70. A. Müller-Peters, "The Significance of National Pride and National Identity to the Attitude toward the Single European Currency: A Europe-wide Comparison," *Journal of Economic Psychology* 19 (1998): 702.

71. Müller-Peters, "The Significance of National Pride," 702 (emphasis added).

72. Meier-Pesti and Kirchler, "Attitudes towards the Euro by National Identity and Relative National Status," 2.

73. Dyson, *The Politics of the Euro-Zone,* 236.

74. Levitt and Lord, *The Political Economy of Monetary Union,* 243.

75. Müller-Peters et al., "Explaining Attitudes towards the Euro," 671.

76. Müller-Peters et al., "Explaining Attitudes towards the Euro," 671.

77. A. Smith, "National Identities and the Idea of European Unity," *International Affairs* 68 (1992): 57.

78. A. Smith, "National Identities and the Idea of European Unity," 57.

79. A. Moravcsik, "Negotiating the Single European Act: National Interests and Conventional Statecraft in the European Community, *International Organization* 45 (1991): 21.

80. "English sovereignty" extends from the composition of the English parliamentary system, with its houses of Lord and Commons derived from the Norman *Curia Regis* and Edward II's "Commonality," respectively. M. Mather, *The European Union and British Democracy: Towards Convergence* (Houndmills: Macmillan, 2000).

81. Mather, *The European Union and British Democracy,* 36.

82. Mather, *The European Union and British Democracy*, 59–60.

83. T. Risse, "The Euro and Identity Politics in Europe," unpublished paper presented at "The Year of the Euro" Conference, Nanovic Institute for European Studies, University of Notre Dame, 2002, 17.

84. Mather, *The European Union and British Democracy*, 60.

85. Thatcher, *The Downing Street Years*, 745.

86. S. Hoffman, "Obstinate or Obsolete? The Fate of the Nation-State and the Case of Western Europe," *Daedelus* 95 (1966): 901.

87. Risse, *The Euro and Identity Politics in Europe*, 16,

88. W. Churchill, House of Commons Speech, Hansard Parliamentary Records, vol. 513, col. 895, 11 May 1953 (London: HMSO).

89. Conservative Manifesto, *"Our Vision for Britain"*: http://www.conservative-party.org.uk/manifesto/ defe3.html (accessed 1 February 2001).

90. Labour Manifesto, "Britain Will Be Better with New Labour," http://www.labourwin97.org.uk/ manifesto/index/ html (accessed 1 February 2001).

91. V. Orchard, "Culture as Opposed to What? Cultural Belonging in the Context of National and European Identity," *European Journal of Social Theory* 5, no. 4 (2002): 425.

92. Dyson, *The Politics of the Euro-Zone*, 109.

93. M. O'Neill, *The Politics of European Integration* (London: Routledge, 1996): 22.

94. Levitt and Lord, *The Political Economy of Monetary Union*, 245.

95. Wallace, "Europe as a Confederation," 66

96. S. Bulmer, "Domestic Politics and European Community Policy Making," *Journal of Common Market Studies* 21 (1983): 353 (emphases added).

97. A. Moravcsik, *The Choice for Europe* (London: UCL Press, 1999), 472.

98. Bulmer, "Domestic Politics and European Community Policy Making," 354 (emphasis added).

99. H. Morgenthau, "Another "Great Debate": The National Interest of the United States," *The American Political Science Review* 46, no. 4 (December 1952): 972.

100. Dyson, *The Politics of the Euro-Zone*, 110 (emphases added).

101. I. Bellier and T. Wilson, "Building, Imagining and Experiencing Europe: Institutions and Identities in the European Union," in *An Anthropology of the European Union*, ed. I. Bellier and T. Wilson (Oxford: Berg, 2000), 13.

102. O'Neill, *The Politics of European Integration*, 68.

103. O'Neill, *The Politics of European Integration*, 63.

104. H. N. Brailsford, "The Federal Idea" (1939), in *Federal Union: The Pioneers*, ed. R. Mayne, J. Pinder, and J. C. Roberts (Basingstoke: Palgrave Macmillan 1991), 81.

105. Lord Lothian, "The Ending of Armageddon" (1939), in Mayne, Pinder and Roberts, *Federal Union: The Pioneers*, 35.

106. J. B. Priestley, "Federalism and Culture" (1940), in Mayne, Pinder, and Roberts, *Federal Union: The Pioneers*, 37. For a more recent perspective, see also L. Fawcett and A. Hurrell, eds., *Regionalism in World Politics: Regional Organization and International Order* (Oxford: Oxford University Press, 1995).

107. D. Mitrany, "A Working Peace System," in *The Functional Theory of Politics*, ed. P. Taylor and A. J. R. Groom (London: Oxford University Press, 1975), 126.

108. Mitrany, "A Working Peace System," 126

109. M. Burgess, *Federalism and European Union* (London: Oxford University Press, 1989), 2. *Federalism and European Union*, 1.

110. J. Stapleton, *Political Intellectuals and Public Identities in Britain since 1850* (Manchester: Manchester University Press, 2001), 157.

111. Stapleton, *Political Intellectuals*, 157.

112. Leonard, *The Pro-European Reader*, 7.

113. Leonard, *The Pro-European Reader*, 7.

114. "EMU: Blair's Pro-Europe Campaign Inches towards Single Currency."

115. *Financial Times*, "Britain and Europe," Part I, 4 November 2002.

116. *Financial Times*, "Britain and Europe," Part I, 4 November 2002.

117. *Financial Times*, "Britain and Europe," Part I, 4 November 2002.

118. Bulmer, "Domestic Politics and European Community Policy Making," 354.

119. Weight, *Patriots*, 515.

120. Dyson, *The Politics of the Euro-Zone*, 233 (emphasis added).

121. Bellier and Wilson, "Building, Imagining and Experiencing Europe," 5.

122. V. Bogdanor, "The European Union, the Political Class, and the People," in J. Hayward, *Élitism, Populism, and European Politics* (Oxford: Clarendon Press, 1996), 105.

123. M. Elliott, "Europe Then and Now," *Time*, 10 August 2003, A.9–12.

124. Mather, *The European Union and British Democracy*, 64. See also D. Beetham and C. Lord, *Legitimacy and the European Union* (London: Addison Wesley Longman, 1998).

125. M. Pollack, "International Relations Theory and European Integration," *Journal of Common Market Studies*, incorporating *The European Union Annual Review* 39, no. 2 (June 2001): 236.

126. D. Mackay, "The Political Sustainability of European Monetary Union," *British Journal of Political Science* 29 (1999): 476.

127. J. H. Weiler, "After Maastricht: Community Legitimacy in Post-1992 Europe," in *Singular Europe: Economy and Polity of the European Community after 1992*, ed. W. Adams (Ann Arbor: University of Michigan Press, 1992), 31–32.

128. As the *Financial Times* observes: "The British, or more properly the English, will never love the European Union. The relationship is one of realism rather than emotional attachment." *Financial Times*, "Britain and Europe," Part I, 4 November 2002.

129. Burgess, *Federalism and European Union*, 6.

130. *Financial Times*, "Britain and Europe," Part V, 8 November 2002.

131. M. Thatcher, "Our Destiny Is in Europe," Speech to the College of Europe, Bruges, Belgium, September 1988, Conservative Party Literature, Bodleian Library, Oxford.

132. Thatcher, "Our Destiny Is in Europe."

133. Smith, "National Identities and the Idea of European Unity," 64.

134. Wallace, "Europe as a Confederation," 625, cited in M. Marcussen et al., "Constructing Europe? The Evolution of French, British and German Nation State Identities," special issue, *Journal of European Public Policy* 6, no. 4 (1999): 625.

135. Wallace, "Europe as a Confederation," 625.

136. M. Frognier, "Les identités territoriales: Concepts, constitution et diffusion," in "National v. European Identities? French and Germans in the European Multi-Level System," ed. J. Schild, *Journal of Common Market Studies* 39, no. 2 (June 200): 343.

137. Frognier, "Les identités territoriales," 343.

138. Ernest B. Haas, *The Uniting of Europe: Political, Social and Economic Forces: 1950–1957* (Stanford, CA: Stanford University Press, 1968), 16-17.

139. Haas, *The Uniting of Europe*, 16–17.

140. Haas, *The Uniting of Europe*, 16–17.

141. Risse, "To Euro or Not to Euro?," 11.

142. Risse, "To Euro or Not to Euro?," 743–44.

143. Risse, "To Euro or Not to Euro?," 52.

144. Müller-Peters et al., *The Psychology of European Monetary Union*, 743.

145. Müller-Peters, "The Significance of National Pride," 710.

146. Müller-Peters et al., *The Psychology of European Monetary Union*, 433. See also L. Dowds and K. Young, "National Identity," in *British Social Attitudes: The 13th Report*, ed. R. Jowell et al. (Aldershot: Ashgate, 1996).

147. Müller-Peters et al., *The Psychology of European Monetary Union*, 433.

148. Müller-Peters, "The Significance of National Pride," 705.

149. Lord Shore, "No to the Euro," 70 (emphasis added).

150. Bulmer, "Domestic Politics and European Community Policy Making," 353.

151. Müller-Peters, "The Significance of National Pride," 706.

152. Meier-Pesti and Kirchler, "Attitudes towards the Euro by National Identity," 3. See also N. Ellemers et al., "Status Protection in High Status Minority Groups," *European Journal of Social Psychology* (1992): 123–240, and S. L. Gaertner et al., "The Common Ingroup Identity Model: Recategorization and the Reduction of Intergroup Bias," *European Review of Social Psychology* 4 (1993): 24.

153. Meier-Pesti and Kirchler, "Attitudes towards the Euro by National Identity," 2.

154. *Financial Times*, "Euro Map: Who's In and Who's Out," 11 July 2001.

155. Risse, "The Euro and Identity Politics in Europe," 16.

156. Müller-Peters et al., *The Psychology of European Monetary Union*, 52.

157. Müller-Peters et al., *The Psychology of European Monetary Union*, 53.

158. Müller-Peters et al., *The Psychology of European Monetary Union*, 53.

159. Müller-Peters et al., *The Psychology of European Monetary Union*, 53.

160. Stapleton, *Political Intellectuals*, 150.

161. Stapleton, *Political Intellectuals*, 150.

162. Stapleton, *Political Intellectuals*, 156.

163. Stapleton, *Political Intellectuals*, 156.

164. Risse, "The Euro and Identity Politics," 17–18.

165. M. Cottam and R. Cottam, *Nationalism and Politics: The Political Behaviour of Nation States*, (Boulder, CO: Lynne Rienner Publishers, 2001): 123.

166. Leonard, *The Pro-European Reader*, 6.

167. G. Brown, Hansard Parliamentary Records, House of Commons col. 426, 9 June 2003.

168. Müller-Peters, "The Significance of National Pride," 702.

169. Müller-Peters, "The Significance of National Pride," 711.

170. Brown, Hansard Parliamentary Records, House of Commons col. 434, 9 June 2003.

171. Leonard, *The Pro-European Reader*, 1.

172. Leonard, *The Pro-European Reader*, 1.

173. Weight, *Patriots*, 585.

174. Mackay, "The Political Sustainability of European Monetary Union," 474–76.

175. Mackay, "The Political Sustainability of European Monetary Union," 474–76.

176. Risse, "To Euro or Not to Euro," 18.

177. Müller-Peters, "The Significance of National Pride," 713 (emphasis added).

178. J. Mearsheimer, "The False Promise of International Institutions," *International Security* 19, no. 3 (1994/95): 110.

179. K. Waltz, *Man, the State and War* (New York: Columbia University Press, 1959), 150.

180. S. Hoffman, "Europe's Identity Crisis: Between the Past and America," *Daedelus* 93 (1964): 1294.

181. Pisani-Ferry et al., *The Political Economy of EMU*, 79–80.

182. Pisani-Ferry et al., *The Political Economy of EMU*, 79–80.

# 8

---

# Conclusion

The strength of a national discourse when filled with pervasive ideas about national self-identification has been revealed in each of the preceding case studies. Each case study demonstrates how late-Victorian conceptions of the English self, its virtues and values, were sustained well into the twentieth and twenty-first centuries to lend cultural credence and political legitimacy to the wider British unit. Thus the "moral and political ideas" that inform current British discourse are utilized and retained precisely because "they [are] believed to be the lived ideals of a supremely practical English nation"; they epitomize the "best national self underlying all the activities of the English people."[1] The national self in this case contributes to a clearer sense of how national identity is catalytic in the motivational perceptions, decision making, and execution of British foreign policy.

## BOOSTING THE USE OF NEOCLASSICAL REALISM

As suggested, a domestic perspective is a vital requirement in examining the contextual nature of the national unit and the manner in which various ideational forces explain the motivations behind its policy formulation. Including detailed narratives gained from well-researched historical episodes is a crucial first step in appreciating the nation-state as a nexus of both cultural and political forces that actively construct both the identity of its *statehood* and the practices of its *statecraft*. One can examine the history of a given nation state. In so doing, one will inevitably come across the historic role of national identity in constructing intersecting social, national, and political groupings. Neoclassical realism uses intervening variables to include both external challenges and internal proclivities facing states, thereby generating a more sophisticated explanation of both the problems and the prospects to be navigated on the high seas of foreign policy. The case studies illustrate that national interests and foreign policy choices arise from precisely such cultural particularisms, and they underscore the need for theorists to "recognise the role of ideas embedded in military doctrine as an influence on national foreign policy," now manifestly more possible with the advent of neoclassical realism.[2]

This study suggests that there is very little theoretic distance between the unitary concept of statehood and diverse forms of state practice; between realist concepts of sovereignty, security, and territoriality as inherent attributes of the state, and neoclassical perspectives that use them as examples of national separateness, political distinctiveness, and cultural uniqueness. Here, the "neo" element of neoclassical realism entails a multidisciplinary approach that makes central the role of national identity as a political and cultural mechanism that obtains in foreign policy at moments of crisis.

Those interested in making use of neoclassical realism must approach their own projects with a measure of flexibility, ready to affirm that the primary source of meaning or agency for a given policy decision is as much affected by sources endogenous to the nation as it is by forces exogenous to the state. As illustrated, unit preferences are frequently guided by cultural attitudes as well as political expediency. Morgenthau was prophetic indeed in this, arguing that national interests contain generic requirements for the state's survival, including security and prosperity, as well as "all the cross currents of personalities, public opinion, sectional interests, partisan politics, and political and moral folkways" that connect the national self to the state unit.[3]

The ability of neoclassical realism to bring the nation back in rests largely on rereadings of the current canon, as well as a renewed appreciation for culturalist and historicist approaches that have gained traction in political science of late. For instance, Valerie Hudson's inclusion of culture in the assessment of national foreign policy has contributed new viability to middle-range theorizing in foreign policy analysis. Paul Schroeder's overhaul of neorealism presents an even firmer validation for the neoclassical realist approach, suggesting that theorists should commit to seeking the various "strategies alternative to balance, or the different functions and roles of various actors within the system."[4] From these observations, it is a small step to accepting that while anarchy remains the permissive cause of security-seeking behavior in the international system, this behavior is itself constituted by the interests that emerge from national political cultures of individual states and conditioned by their own discrete historical circumstances.

Theorists must seize history, grasp culture, and confront the motivational, transformative role of ideas. Chief among these ideas is the dominating power of the ideology of nationalism, capable of generating ideas of a national self that obtain as political strategy. This occurs both generically and uniquely, and the combination yields a particular texture that can only be grasped with an appreciation of the role of history, and the use of historical case studies. O'Neill is particularly instructive in this:

> The nation state is more in this paradigm than the historically conditioned contrivance performing temporally specific tasks. . . . They represent natural and timeless, rather than merely conditional human needs; in essence, they are *communities of belonging and identity* as much as they are organisations for coercion or governance. They embody the human need—both functional and spiritual—to belong somewhere; the need to locate a communal, ethnic or linguistic identity within distinct political bounds. As such, they are a more culturally rooted, organic and clearly conservative force, than is envisaged by the political engineers or textbook constitutionalists of either the federalist or functionalist paradigms who missed entirely th[e] enduring political dynamics of competing national interests . . . the abiding sense of cultural and political differences, and the enduring impact of particularistic historical identities. Certainly, states have to pursue their interests in a rapidly changing world order . . . but they continue to do so by steering by ancient lights.[5]

The case studies in this book have illustrated that the perceptions at work within the roles of identity for the English self and determination of national interest for the wider British unit explain the policy choices behind the breakneck construction of eight Dreadnoughts in 1909, the outrage at attempts to construct a Channel tunnel, the ideational and material impetus behind the Task Force sent to the Falkland Islands, and the ongoing reluctance to engage with the euro currency. All four policy decisions are political reflections of innately cultural and specifically English values. They are also strongly suggestive of the dialectical link between national identity and policy formulation.

> Excavating national identities should throw light on national attitudes, the choice of strategic and symbolic forces embedded in the national interest, and the modes of agency that allow a state to move between choice and constraint in dealing with its neighbors. The case studies have demonstrated that the source of British state interests lies not solely with structural theories, but also in domestic politics, where myriad competing forces demand greater investigation. British decision makers in government were found time and again to unite their identity-based interests with identity-based foreign policy. The result was frequently uneasy, contingent, and fractious. As Prizel's own explorations of British foreign policy revealed, "Great Britain's island-based national identity, forged over a millennium of quasi-detachment from the continent, has greatly hindered the pursuit of seemingly pragmatic foreign policy and still requires considerable psychological adjustments on the part of the British public."[6]

This study has unearthed further tensions in Britain's seemingly pragmatic foreign policy between tacit senses of cultural entitlement vested in
civilizational projects and reactive political nationalism with the subsequent slippage of these projects. It has revealed that Victorian, Edwardian,
and contemporary British security environments are material, institutional,
and cultural.[7] Its use of neoclassical realism has highlighted the role of invasion literature, public opinion, English literature, and English history, and
illustrated how these—in tandem with material capabilities—provide the
British state with an identity that is both primordial and constructed; national interests that are optional, rather than deterministic; and a national
identity torn between the diversity of the Isles, the integration with Europe,
and the fragmentation between a bygone ethos of Englishness and contemporary Britishness. Identity itself has been revealed as a most dynamic,
multidimensional category, expanding the series of national interests and
policy options, rather than remaining a one-dimensional, generic attribute,
and the state a static object.[8]

The power of harnessing identity as an explanatory theory of state and
policy formulation lies in its ability to widen its topics to explore shifts,
overlaps, constructions, and reconstructions in a dynamic rather than
static epistemology. While IR has been criticized above for its proclivity to continue as a largely reified and inflexible approach to state-based
concepts of motivation and perception, it should be noted that identity
theory itself previously fell within a "dominant ontology and epistemology of stability and continuity that have hitherto informed depictions
of individual and collective identity."[9] Twentieth-century discourse has
successfully challenged the a priori nature of identities, just as IR itself
is beginning to reorient itself toward nonessentialist categories. Indeed,
the tension "between the notion that identity is essential, fundamental,
unitary, and unchanging, and the notion that identities are constructed
and reconstructed through historical action" mirrors the move "away
from categorical, essentialist, and unitary understandings" that IR itself
must undertake in making viable use of these categories.[10] I suggest that
Schroeder's point about the use of history works just as well for the use
of culture, namely, that theorists and foreign policy analysts alike must
renounce their "unconscious disdain" of culture as a key variable, their
"disregard of its complexity and subtleties and the problems of doing it
well or using it wisely." Doing so would prevent cultural insights from
appearing to "lie on the surface for anyone to pick up," tempting us to
shortcuts "like a looter at an archeological site, [remaining] indifferent
to context and deeper meaning, concerned only with taking what can be
immediately used or sold."[11]

More broadly, foreign policy itself becomes clearer when we realize that
it is not merely an "external orientation of pre-established states with secure

identities" but, reworked within the contours of national identity, operates as "one of the boundary-producing practices central to the production and reproduction of identity in whose name it operates."[12] The difference between these two definitions provides the broad difference of perspectives currently at work in IR regarding definitions of the nation-state. As a purely political unit embedded in a wider structure of materialist means and ego-ist intentions, foreign policy is quite naturally "a modern cultural artefact implicated in the intensification of power in the state."[13] However, as per neoclassical realism, if the state is conceived of as a social nexus of political and cultural objectives articulated in policies that clearly reflect endogenous norms, values, and attributes to produce correspondingly unique practices, then it is social and ideational rather than material forms of power that both instantiates the state and articulates the preferences of its policy. In other words, the overlap of social, cultural, and political perceptions produces motivations that link forms of unifying self-reference to the manner in which policy environments are created.

To revisit an earlier point, within all policy making "the interpretation [of the event] was created and edited *as it was enacted*."[14] As demonstrated by the case studies, national themes overlap with policy both constitutively and causally because in all matters pertaining to the nation-state, "the Government's political will . . . be[comes] closely identified with the validation of the country's values and symbol system."[15] Cooper's argument captures this nicely:

> The point is that foreign policy is the external reflection of domestic politics; what a government's domestic priorities are, what issues arouse strong popular feeling, what makes it succeed or fail. In times of war, foreign policy is of supreme importance; but that is because the threat faced—invasion, occupation and all its consequences, including loss of property, violence and loss of autonomy—would be catastrophic domestic events.

There is, of course, opposition entailed in any theory put forward, and the understanding of identity at work in providing an enhanced theory of state motivation and policy formulation is no different. The central oppositional argument is that identity, as a multifarious and overly broad method of asserting frequently contradictory concepts of the content, objectives, and policies of the national self, in no way provides additional assistance in clarifying exogenous behavior or endogenous perceptions and, further, can in no way affect interests or policy formulation.

While detractors may be tempted to consign this and similar studies to the works of "fringe" theorists, one merely needs to note that such views were put forth with great insight more than fifty years ago by the doyen of modern realism, Morgenthau. Morgenthau argued not only that the national character was an "incontestable" part of policy formation but that "the survival of a political unit, such as a nation, in its *identity* is the irreducible minimum, the necessary element of its interests vis-à-vis other units. Taken in isolation, the determination of its content in a concrete situation is relatively simple; for it encompasses the integrity of the nation's territory, of its political institutions, and of its *culture*."[16]

Clearly, identity is not a new concept, either in isolation or as a method of gauging state motivation vis-à-vis policy. Neoclassical realism is an equally well-founded approach, whose most recent incarnation allows identity a new toehold in foreign policy analysis, permitting analysis to discover, in Hoffman's words, that the "international system owes its inner logic and its unfolding to the diversity of domestic determinants [and] geo-historical situations."[17] This text aims to join a number of others in the growing canon of neoclassical realism, whose strength lies in its ability to blend a range of disciplinary foci judiciously and viably, permitting an especially significant fusion between cultural studies, diplomatic history, and foreign policy analysis. As Zakaria suggests, it is high time to connect international behavior and domestic forces by "constructing a domestic politics model that . . . stays within the realist tradition." The challenge is to pay close attention to the role of the intermediary variable; this requires simultaneous acknowledgment of the "powerful effects of the international system on state behaviour" and "domestic explanations that take full account of systemic pressures" to prevent theorists from merely rehashing the *Innenpolitik* approach.[18] It also requires a commitment to mid-range theorizing in which particularist forces endogenous to the nation-state unit are capable of being examined collectively to the point where one can tolerably make generalizations that stand up as foreign policy analysis. The challenge can undoubtedly be met, and this text is a small contribution to that challenge.

## NOTES

1. J. Stapleton, *Political Intellectuals and Public Identities in Britain since 1850* (Manchester, Manchester University Press: 2001), 147.

2. Richard Rosecrance and Arthur Stein, "Beyond Realism: The Study of Grand Strategy," in *The Domestic Bases of Grand Strategy*, ed. Richard Rosecrance and Arthur A. Stein (Ithaca, NY: Cornell University Press, 1993), 14.

3. Hans J. Morgenthau "Another 'Great Debate': The National Interest of the United States," *American Political Science Review* 46, no. 4 (1952): 973.

4. Paul Schroeder, "Historical Reality vs. Neo-realist Theory," in *The Perils of Anarchy: Contemporary Realism and International Security*, ed. Michael E. Brown, Sean M. Lynn-Jones, and Steven E. Miller (Cambridge, MA: MIT Press, 1995), 461.

5. M. O'Neill, *The Politics of European Integration* (London: Routledge, 1996), 67.

6. I. Prizel, *National Identity and Foreign Policy: Nationalism and Leadership in Poland, Russia and Ukraine* (Cambridge: Cambridge University Press: 1998), 6.

7. P. Katzenstein, "Introduction: Alternative Perspectives on National Security," in *The Culture of National Security: Norms and Identity in World Politics*, ed. P. Katzenstein (New York: Columbia University Press, 1996), 33.

8. Y. Lapid, "Culture's Ship: Returns and Departures in International Relations Theory," in *The Return of Culture and Identity in IR Theory*, ed. Y. Lapid and F. Kratochwil (Boulder, CO: Lynne Rienner Publishers, 1996), 7.

9. Y. Lapid, "Culture's Ship," 7.

10. R. Handler, "Is 'Identity' a Useful Cross-Cultural Concept?" in *Commemorations*, ed. J. Gillis (Princeton, NJ: Princeton University Press, 1994), 29.

11. Schroeder, "Historical Reality vs. Neo-realist Theory," 461.

12. D. Campbell, *Writing Security: United States Foreign Policy and the Politics of Identity* (Minneapolis: University of Minnesota Press, 1992), 75.

13. Campbell, *Writing Security*: 75.

14. M. Dillon, "Thatcher and the Falklands," in *Belief Systems and International Relations*, ed. R. Little and S. Smith (London: Blackwell, 1988), 112 (emphasis added).

15. Dillon, "Thatcher and the Falklands," 112.

16. H. Morgenthau, "Another 'Great Debate,'" 973 (emphasis added).

17. S. Hoffman, "Obstinate or Obsolete? The Fate of the Nation-State and the Case of Western Europe," *Daedelus* 95 (1966): 864.

18. F. Zakaria, "Realism and Domestic Politics: A Review Essay," in *The Perils of Anarchy: Contemporary Realism and International Security*, ed. Michael E. Brown, Sean M. Lynn-Jones, and Steven E. Miller (Cambridge, MA: MIT Press, 1995), 463.

# Bibliography

## PRIMARY SOURCES

### Texts

A.F. *The Seizure of the Channel Tunnel.* London, 1882.

Anon. *The Battle of Boulogne; or, How Calais Became English Again.* London, 1882.

Anon. *"India in 1983,* Calcutta, Ulidia (pseud.) *The Battle of Newry.* London, 1883.

Anon. *"A German Opinion on the Projected Channel Tunnel."* Trans. from the Militär-Wochenblaff," no. 30, 1882.

Anon. *A History of Wonderful Inventions.* London, 1862.

Anon. *How Glasgow Ceased to Flourish.* Glasgow, 1883.

Anon. *Submarina: Green Eyes and Blue Glasses: An Amusing Spectacle of Short Sight.* London: Yates Alexander and Shepheard, 1882.

Anon. *The Battle of Moy; or, How Ireland Gained Her Independence in 1892–1894.* London, 1883.

Anon. *The Battle of Port Said.* London, 1883.

Anon. *The Siege of London.* London, 1884.

Anon. *The Story of the Channel Tunnel.* London, 1882.

Arnold, M. *Culture and Anarchy: An Essay in Political and Social Criticism.* Cambridge: Cambridge University Press [1869], 1961.

Beresford, Lord C. *Memoirs.* Vol. 1. Boston: Little, Brown, 1915.

Bradlaugh, C., MP. *The Channel Tunnel: Ought the Democracy to Oppose or Support It?* London: A. Bonner, 1887.

Brett, M., ed. *Journals and Letters of Reginald Viscount Esher.* Vol. 2. London: Nicholson & Watson, 1934.

Burnley, J. *The Romance of Invention.* London, 1886.

Butler, Sir W. *The Invasion of England.* London, 1882.

Carr, E. H. *The Twenty Years' Crises 1919–1939: An Introduction to the Study of International Relations*. London: Macmillan, 1946.

Chesney, Sir G. *The Battle of Dorking*. London, 1871.

Childers, E. *The Riddle of the Sands*. New York: Dover, 1903.

Colomb, Admiral P. H. *Memoirs of Sir Astley Cooper Key*. London: Methuen, 1898.

du Maurier, G. *An Englishman's Home*. London: Eveleigh Nash, 1908.

Durkheim, E. *The Rules of Sociological Method*. New York: Free Press, 1964.

Fisher, Admiral J. *Fear God and Dread Nought: Correspondence of Admiral of the Fleet Lord Fisher*, ed. A. J. Marder, Vol. 2. London: Jonathan Cape, 1952–1959.

Forbes, H. C. G. *Shall We Have a Tunnel?* Aberdeen: A. Brown & Co; Edinburgh: John Menzies & Co; London: Simpkin, Marshall, & Co, 1883.

Gooch, G. P., and H. Temperley, eds. *British Documents on the Origins of the War, 1898–1914*. 11 volumes. London: Foreign Office, 1926–1938.

Green, J. R. *A Short History of the English People*. London: Brown, 1874.

Grey of Fallodon, Viscount. *Twenty-Five Years, 1892–1916*. Vol. 1. New York: Frederick A. Stokes, 1925.

Grip. *How John Bull Lost London: The Capture of the Channel Tunnel*. London: Sampson Low, Marston, Searle, and Rivington, 1882.

Guthrie, T. A. *The Seizure of the Channel Tunnel*. London, 1882.

Hale, Sir M. *The History of the Common Law of England* [1739]. Chicago: University of Chicago Press, 1971.

Hobbes, T. *Leviathan*. ed., Macpherson, C. B. Harmondsworth: Penguin, [1651], 1968.

Hume, D. *A Treatise of Human Nature*, ed., Selby-Bigge, L. A. Oxford: Clarendon Press, [1888], 1990.

Keppel, H. *A Sailor's Life under Four Sovereigns*. Vol. I. London: Macmillan, 1899.

Lawrence, D. H. *England, My England*. Harmondsworth: Secker, 1924.

Le Queux, W. *The Invasion of 1910*. London: Eveleigh Nash, 1906.

Lepsius, J., A. Mendelssohn-Bartholdy, and F. Thimme, eds. *Die Grosse Politik der Europäischen Kabinette, 1871–1914*. 40 Volumes. Berlin, 1922–1927.

Macaulay, Lord. *Literary Essays*. Oxford: Oxford University Press, 1932.

Machiavelli, N. *The Prince*. ed. Skinner, Q. Cambridge: Cambridge University Press, 1988.

Mahan, A. T. *The Influence of Sea Power upon History, 1660–1783*. Boston: Brown, 1895.

Marder, A. J. *From the Dreadnought to Scapa Flow: The Royal Navy in the Fisher Era, 1904–1919*. Vol. I, *The Road to War, 1904–1919*. London: Oxford University Press, 1961.

———. *The Anatomy of British Sea Power: A History of British Naval Policy in the Pre-Dreadnought Era, 1880–1905*. New York: Oxford University Press, 1940.

Matthews, H. C. G., ed. *The Gladstone Diaries*. 10 volumes. London, 1982.

Maurice, Major General, Sir F. *Haldane: 1856–1928*. Vol. 2. London: Faber and Faber, 1937–1939.

McKenna, S. *Reginald McKenna, 1863–1943: A Memoir*. London: Eyre & Spottiswoode, 1948.

Meinecke, F. *Cosmopolitanism and the Nation State*. Princeton, NJ: Princeton University Press, [1907], 1970.

Milton, J. *Angli. Pro Populo Anglicano Defensio*. In F. A. Patterson, *The Works of John Milton*, Vol. 7. New York: Columbia University Press, [1651], 1932.

Morgenthau, H. J. *Politics among Nations: The Struggle for Power and Peace*. New York: Knopf [1948], 1955.

Penrose, B. "An Account of the Last Expedition to Port Egmont in the Falkland Islands." *Universal Magazine*, London, April 1775.

Rousseau, J.-J. *The Government of Poland*. W. Kendall, trans. New York: Bobbs-Merrill, 1972.

Routledge, R. *Discoveries and Inventions of the Nineteenth Century*. London: Oxford University Press, 1876.

Ruskin, J. *The Crown of Wild Olive: Four Lectures on Industry and War*. London, 1859.

Scott, Admiral Sir P. *Fifty Years in the Royal Navy*. New York: George H. Doran, 1919.

Shakespeare, W. *The Tragedy of Richard II*. In E. Dowden, ed., *The Histories and Poems of William Shakespeare*. London: Oxford University Press, 1912.

Smiles, Sir S. *Lives of the Engineers*. Vol. 1. London: Marshall, 1874.

Spears, J. "A Transition in Naval Efficacy." *World's Work*, Vol. 5. London, 1902.

Spender, J. A. *The Life of the Right Hon. Sir Henry Campbell-Bannerman*. Vol. 2. London: Hodder and Stoughton, London, 1923.

"The Building Programme of the British Navy." *Naval Necessities*, Vol. 3. London, 1906.

"The Channel Tunnel and Public Opinion." *Nineteenth Century*, London, April 1882.

Threlfall, T. R. "Labour and the Navy." *The Nineteenth Century and After* 75. London, March 1914.

Turner Perkins, W., ed. *The Channel Tunnel*. London: Marshall and Co., 1913.

Valbert, G. "*L'agitation Anglaise contre le tunnel de la Manche*." *Revue des Deux Mondes* 51, Paris, 1882.

von Bülow, B. *Denkwürdigkeiten*. Vol. 1. Berlin, 1930.

*Warship IV* 43 (1905).

Wolseley, Field Marshal Viscount. *The Story of Soldier's Life*. London, 1903.

Woodward, E. L. *Great Britain and the German Navy*. New York: Oxford University Press, 1935.

## Official Documents

ADM (Admiralty) 116 940B, NID (Naval Intelligence Department). *Notes on a Visit to Kiel and Wilhelmshaven*, 1902. London: PRO.

ADM (Admiralty) 116. Memorandum. *The Modern Battleship*, October, 1906. London: PRO.

ADM (Admiralty) 136/7. Ship: H.M.S. *DREADNOUGHT Remarks: 1st Class Battleship (the first big gun ship), launched 10 February 1906*, 1906–1921. London: PRO.

Admiralty MSS. "Comparative Strength in Battleships and Armoured Cruisers of Great Britain, France, United States, and Germany," June 1907. London: PRO.

Admiralty MSS. "Asquith Memorandum to Fisher," June 1908. London: PRO.

Admiralty MSS. "Goschen Memorandum to Grey," 25 August 1909. London: PRO.

Admiralty MSS. "Hardinge to Knollys," 26 February, 1909. London: PRO.

Admiralty MSS. "J. Fisher Memorandum." *Admiralty Policy: Replies to Criticisms*, October 1906. London: PRO.

Admiralty MSS. *The Strategic Aspects of Our Building Program*, 7 January 1907. London: PRO.

Asquith MSS. "McKenna to Asquith," 3 January 1909. London: PRO.

Asquith MSS. "Lloyd George to Asquith," 2 February 1909. London: PRO.

Blair, T. "The New Challenge for Europe," Acceptance Speech for the Charlemagne Prize, Aachen, Germany, 29 September 1999. Manchester: Labour Party Literature, Labour Party Archives.

Braine, B., MP. *The Falklands Campaign*. Hansard Official Record of Members of Parliaments' Debates. Vol. 21, 3 April 1982. London: HMSO.

Bourne, K., and D. C. Watt, eds. *British Documents on Foreign Affairs: Reports and Papers from the Foreign Office*. Confidential Print, Part I, Series F, Vol. 10, Doc. 47. Bethesda. MD: University Publications of America, 1989.

Brown, G., MP. G. Brown, *Hansard Parliamentary Records*, House of Commons col. 426, and col. 434, 9 June 2003. London: HMSO.

CAB (Cabinet) 16/3A. *Report and Proceedings of a Sub-Committee of Imperial Defence, Appointed by the Prime Minister to Reconsider the Question of Overseas Attack*, 22 October 1908. London: HMSO.

CAB (Cabinet) 16/8. *Terms of Reference*, 25 March 1909. London: HMSO.

CAB (Cabinet) 37/100. *Battleship Building Programmes of Great Britain, Germany, France, United States, Italy and Austria*, 14 July 1909. London: HMSO.

CAB (Cabinet) 37/100. *Imperial Conference on Defence: Admiralty Memorandum*, 20 July 1909. London: HMSO.

CAB (Cabinet) 37/100. *Naval Programme*, 20 July 1909. London: HMSO.

CAB (Cabinet) 37/97. *A Note on Naval Estimates, 1909–10* [German Naval Armaments], 2 February 1909. London: HMSO.

CAB (Cabinet) 37/97. *A Reply to Mr. Churchill's Note on Navy Estimates*, 5 February 1909, R. McKenna, nos. 24 and 25. London: HMSO.

CAB (Cabinet) 37/97. *Great Britain and Germany in April, 1909* [A Comparison of naval strengths], 8 February, 1909. London: HMSO.

CAB (Cabinet) 37/98. [*Navy Estimates, 1909–1910*], 24 February 1909. London: HMSO.

CAB (Cabinet) 37/98. *Anglo-German Naval Affairs* (originally a Foreign Office memorandum), 22 March 1909. London: HMSO.

CAB (Cabinet) 37/98. *Conversations with the German Ambassador on German Naval Expenditure* (originally a Foreign Office memorandum), 18 March 1909. London: HMSO.

CAB (Cabinet) 38/25. no. 36, reprint of 16 June 1882 Memorandum. London: HMSO.

CAB (Cabinet). "Naval Policy," 7 December 1903, "1902 Memorandum by Lord Selbourne." London: HMSO.

Cabinet Papers CAB 38/26. "Economic Aspects of the Channel Tunnel Scheme" and CAB 38/27, no. 26. London: PRO.

*Channel Tunnel Parliamentary Blue Book*. Including the Precis, the Anglo-French Joint Commission, Scientific Committee Findings, Farrer Departmental Committee evidence, Board of Trade Memorandum, Observations by H.R.H. Duke of Cambridge, Memorandum 10 December 1881, Second Memorandum, Letter to Lord Northbrook, Lord Derby Memorandum, and The British Channel Tunnel Company (limited) Act. London: War Office, HMSO, 1882.

Churchill, W. S. House of Commons Speech, Hansard Official Record of Members of Parliaments' Debates, vol. 513, col. 895, 11 May 1953. London: HMSO.

Conservative Pamphlets. *Europe and You, Sovereignty in the Common Market.* London: Conservative Party Literature Bodleian Library, Oxford, 1971.

du Cann, E., MP. *The Falklands Campaign,* Hansard Official Record of Members of Parliaments' Debates, vol. 21, 3 April 1982. London: HMSO.

*Falkland Islands Review: Report of a Committee of Privy Counsellors.* Chairman The Rt. Hon. The Lord Franks, Cmnd 8787. London: HMSO, 1983.

First Report from the Defence Committee. *The Handling of Press and Public Information during the Falklands Conflict.* 2 vols. Session 1982–1983, 1982. London: HMSO.

H.M. Treasury. Submission to the House of Commons Treasury Committee, 6 September, 2002. London: HMSO.

Hansard Official Record of Members of Parliaments' Debates. House of Commons: 1882, 1906, 1908, 1909, 1982, and 2003. London: HMSO.

Hansard Parliamentary Debates. House of Commons. *Territorial and Reserve Forces Bill,* April 1907. London: HMSO.

L. Callaghan, MP, and MP M. White. *The Falklands Campaign.* Hansard Official Record of Members of Parliaments' Debates. 7 April and 3 April 1982, respectively. London: HMSO.

Mates, M., MP. *The Falklands Campaign.* Hansard Official Record of Members of Parliaments' Debates, 7 April, 1982. London: HMSO.

Report From the Joint Committee of the House of Lords and the House of Commons on The Channel Tunnel. *Papers by Command,* 1883. London: HMSO.

Straw, J., MP. J. Straw, *Hansard Parliamentary Records,* House of Commons, col. 398, 18 June, 2003. London: HMSO.

Thatcher, M. "Our Destiny Is in Europe," Speech to the College of Europe, Bruges, Belgium, September 1988. London: Conservative Party Literature, Bodleian Library, Oxford.

Thatcher, M. *The Falklands Campaign,* Hansard Official Record of Members of Parliaments' Debates, vol. 21, 3 April, 4 April, 29 April, 1982. London: HMSO.

*The Falklands Campaign.* Hansard Official Record of Members of Parliaments' Debates, 14 June 1982. London: HMSO.

*The Falklands Campaign: A Digest of the Debates in the House of Commons 2 April to 15 June 1982.* London: HMSO, 1982.

The Secretary of State for Defence, *The Falklands Campaign: The Lessons,* Cmnd. 8758. London: HMSO, 1982.

WO 32/6269. War Office Memorandum to the Treasury, mid-April 1875. London: PRO.

WO 33/39. War Office Memorandum, 12 May 1882. London: PRO.

## Newspapers and Dailies

*Annual Register*
*Daily Mail*
*Daily News*
*Financial Times*
*Globe*

*Guardian*
*Independent*
*Le Bulletin*
*London Gazette*
*Manchester Guardian*
*National Review*
*Naval Necessities*
*Navy and Army Illustrated*
*News of the World*
*Nineteenth Century*
*Observer*
*Railway News*
*Railway Times*
*Standard*
*Sun*
*Sunday Times*
*Times*
*Warship*
*Weekly News*

## SECONDARY DOCUMENTS

### Articles

Adamson, F., and M. Demetriou. "Remapping the Boundaries of the 'State' and 'National Identity': Incorporating Diasporas into IR Theorizing." *European Journal of International Relations* 13 no. 4 (2007): 489–526

Adler, E. "Seizing the Middle Ground: Constructivism in World Politics." *European Journal of International Relations* 3 (1997): 319–63.

Alexander and Smith. "The Discourse of American Civil Society: A New Proposal for Cultural Studies." *Theory and Society* 22 (1993): 151–207.

Andrews, B. "Social Rules and the State as a Social Actor." *World Politics* 27, no. 4 (July 1975): 521–40.

Ashley, R. K. "Political Realism and Human Interests." *International Studies Quarterly* 25, no. 2 (1981): 204–36.

———. "The Geopolitics of Geopolitical Space: Toward a Critical Social Theory of International Politics." *Alternatives* 12 (1987).

———. "Untying the Sovereign State: A Double Reading of the Anarchy Problematique." *Millennium: Journal of International Studies* 17 (1988).

Aspinwall, M. "Odd Man Out: Rethinking British Policy on European Monetary Integration." *Review of International Studies* 29, no. 3 (July 2003): 341–65.

Axelrod, R. "The Emergence of Cooperation Among Egoists." *American Political Science Review* 75 (1981): 306–18.

Ayoob, M. "Inequality and Theorizing in International Relations: The Case for Subaltern Realism." *International Studies Review* 4, no. 3 (Fall 2002): 27–48.

Bacevich, A. J. "Morality and High Technology." *The National Interest* (Fall 1996).

Barker, P. "Eurostar to Paris—a Verdict on the *Grands Projets*." *New Statesman* (January 10, 1997).

Barkin, S., and B. Cronin. "The State and the Nation: Changing Norms and the Rules of Sovereignty in the International Relations." *International Organization* 48, no. 1 (Winter 1994): 107–30.

Barnett, M. "Culture, Strategy and Foreign Policy Change: Israel's Road to Oslo." *European Journal of International Relations* 5, no. 1 (1999): 5–36.

———. "Radical Chic? Subaltern Realism: A Rejoinder." *International Studies Review* 4, no. 3 (Fall 2002): 50–62.

———. "Regional Security after the Gulf War." *Political Science Quarterly* 111, no. 4 (Winter 1996–97): 597–618.

Bassin, M. "Studying Ourselves: History and the Philosophy of Geography." *Progress in Human Geography* 24, no. 3 (2000): 475–87.

Baumant, Z. "On the Origins of Civilization: A Historical Note." *Theory, Culture and Society* 2, no. 3 (1985): 7–14.

Beck, P. J. "Britain's Antarctic Dimension." *International Affairs* 59 (1983): 429–44.

Bennett, A. "Causal Inference in Case Studies: From Mill's Methods to Causal Mechanisms." Paper presented at the American Political Science Association Conference, Atlanta: Georgia, 1999, cited in University of Kent at Canterbury amalgamated text entitled *Workshop of Research Design*, 2002.

Berger, P. "Identity as a Problem in the Sociology of Knowledge." *European Journal of Sociology* 7, no. 1 (1966): 32–40.

Biersteker, T. "Eroding Boundaries, Contested Terrain." *International Studies Review*, no. 1 (1999).

Bishop, G. "1992 and Beyond: Visits to Eculand—Reflections upon Its Financial System." Salomon Brothers, Economic and Market Analysis. London, September 1991, 18 S.

Booth, K. "Security Emancipation." *Review of International Studies* 17, no. 4 (1991): 313–26.

Brace, C. "Looking Back: The Cotswolds and English National Identity, c. 1890–1950." *Journal of Historical Geography* 25, no. 4 (1999): 502–16.

Brooks, S. "Dueling Realisms." *International Organization* 51 (1997).

Brown, R. "Social Identity Theory: Past Achievements, Current Problems and Future Challenges." *European Journal of Social Psychology* 30 (2000): 745–78.

Bueno de Mesquita, B. "Domestic Politics and International Relations." *International Studies Quarterly* 46, no. 1 (March 2002): 1–9.

Bulmer, S. "Domestic Politics and European Community Policy Making." *Journal of Common Market Studies* 21 (1983): 353–55.

Butterfield, H. "Sir Edward Grey in July 1914." *Historical Studies* 5 (1965).

Campbell, J. "Institutional Analysis and the Role of Ideas in Political Economy." *Theory and Society* 27 (1998): 377–409.

Carlsnaes, W. "The Agency-Structure Problem in Foreign Policy Analysis." *International Studies Quarterly* 36 (September 1991): 245–70.

Checkel, J. "International Norms and Domestic Politics: Bridging the Rationalist-Constructivist Divide." *European Journal of International Relations* 3, no. 4 (1997): 473-95.

———. "Norms, Institutions, and National Identity in Contemporary Europe." *International Studies Quarterly* 43, no. 1 (1999): 83-114.

———. "The Constuctivist Turn in International Relations Theory." *World Politics* 50, no. 2 (1998): 324-48.

Christiansen, T., et al. "The Social Cconstruction of Europe." *Journal of European Public Policy* 6, no. 4, special issue (1999): 528-44.

Citrin, J., E. B. Haas, and C. Muste. "Is American Nationalism Changing? Implications for Foreign Policy." *International Studies Quarterly* 38 (1994): 1-31.

Clarke, I. F. "Forecasts of Warfare in Fiction, 1803-1914." *Comparative Studies in Society and History* 10, no. 1 (October 1967): 1-12.

Cohen, R. "Threat Perception in International Crisis." *Political Science Quarterly* 93, no. 1 (Spring 1978): 93-107.

S. Collier, "The First Falklands War? Argentina Attitudes." *International Affairs* 59 (1983): 459-64.

Commission of the European Communities. "One Market, One Money: An Evaluation of the Potential Benefits and Costs of Forming an Economic and Monetary Union." *European Economy*, no. 44 (October 1990).

Connor, W. "A Nation Is a Nation, Is a State, Is an Ethnic Group, Is a . . ." *Ethnic and Racial Studies* 4, no. 1 (1978): 379-88.

Cottam, M. "The Carter Administration's Policy toward Nicaragua: Images, Goals and Tactics." *Political Science Quarterly* 107, no. 1 (Spring 1992).

Cox, R. W. "Gramsci, Hegemony and International Relations: An Essay on Method." *Millennium* 12, no. 2 (1983).

———. "Multilateralism and World Order." *Review of International Studies* 18 (1992).

———. "Social Forces, States and World Orders: Beyond International Relations Theory." *Millennium* 10, no. 2 (1981).

Dawes, R. M., J. McTavish, and H. Shaklee. "Behaviour, Communication, and Assumptions About Other People's Behavior in Common Dilemma Situations." *Journal of Personality and Social Psychology* 35 (1977).

Dawisha, A. "Nation and Nationalism: Historical Antecedents to Contemporary Debates." *International Studies Review* 4, no. 1 (Spring 2002): 3-22.

Der Derian, J. "Philosophical Traditions in International Relations." *Millennium* 12, no. 2 (1988).

Desch, M. "Culture Clash: Assessing the Importance of Ideas in Security Studies." *International Security* 23, no. 1 (1998): 141-200.

Dessler, D. "What's at Stake in the Agent-Structure Debate?" *International Organization* 43 (Summer 1989): 441-73.

Doty, R. L. "Foreign Policy as Social Construction: A Post-Positivist Analysis of U.S. Counterinsurgency Policy in the Philippines." *International Studies Quarterly* 37 (1993): 297-320.

Deudeny, D. "Greater Britain or Greater Synthesis? Seeley, McKinder, and Wells on Britain in the Global Industrial Era." *Review of International Studies* 27, no. 2 (April 2001): 187-208.

Duffield, J. "Political Culture and States Behavior." *International Organization* 54, no. 4 (2000): 850–77.

Eckstein, H. "A Culturalist Theory of Political Change." *American Political Science Review* 82 (1988): 789–804.

Eley, G. "Culture, Britain and Europe." *Journal of British Studies* 31, no. 4, special issue, "Britishness and Europeanness: Who Are the British Anyway?" (October 1992): 390–414.

Elkins, D., and R. Sibeon. "A Cause in Search of Its Effect, or What Does Political Culture Explain." *Comparative Politics* 11, no. 2 (1979): 129–37.

Ellemers, N., et al. "Status Protection in High-Status Minority Groups." *European Journal of Social Psychology* 22 (1992): 123–240.

Elliott, M. "Europe Then and Now." *Time*, Amsterdam, (August 2003): A.9–12.

Emery, F. E., and E. L. Trist. "The Causal Texture of Organizational Environments." *Human Relations* 18 (1965): 21–32.

Euben, R. "Contingent Borders, Syncretic Perspectives: Globalization, Political Theory, and Islamizing Knowledge." *International Studies Review* 4, no. 1 (Spring 2002): 23–48.

European Central Bank Monthly Bulletin. *The Euro Area at the Start of Stage Three.* Frankfurt (January 1998).

European Commission. "Economic Policy in EMU, Part B." *Economic Papers*, no. 125 (1997), Brussels.

European Opinion Research Group, Directorate General Press and Communication, European Commission. "The Euro: Support from the Danes, Swedish Reticence, British Resistance." *Eurobarometer* 59, Brussels (Spring 2003).

Farrell, T. "Culture and Military Power." *Review of International Studies* 24, no. 3 (1998): 407–16.

——. "Constructivist Security Studies: Portrait of a Research Program." *International Studies Review* 4, no. 1 (Spring 2002): 49–72.

Feaver, P. D., et. al. "Correspondence: Brother Can You Spare a Paradigm? (or Was Anybody Ever a Realist?)." *International Security* 25, no. 1 (2000): 165–93.

Finnemore, M., and K. Sikkink. "International Norm Dynamics and Political Change." *International Organization* 52, no. 4 (Autumn 1998): 887–917.

Freedman, L. "Bridgehead Revisited: The Literature of the Falklands." *International Affairs* 59, no. 3 (Summer 1983): 445–52.

Friedman, N. "The Falklands War: Lessons, Learned and Mislearned." *Orbis* 26 (1983): 907–40.

Frognier, M. "Les identités territoriales. Concepts, constitution et diffusion." In J. Schild, "National v. European Identities? French and Germans in the European Multi-Level System." *Journal of Common Market Studies* 39, no. 2 (June 2001): 331–51.

Gaertner, S. L., et al. "The Common Ingroup Identity Model: Recategorization and the Reduction of Intergroup Bias." *European Review of Social Psychology* 4 (1993): 1–26.

Giddens, A. "The Third Way." *New Statesman*, 1 May 1998.

Gibbs, D. "Taking the State Back Out: Reflections on a Tautology." *Contention* 3, no. 3 (1994): 115–38,

Good, R. "The National Interest and Political Realism: Niehbuhr's 'Debate' with Morgenthau and Kennan." *The Journal of Politics* 22 (1960): 597–619.

Gordon, M. "Domestic Conflict and the Origins of the First World War: The British and the German Cases." *The Journal of Modern History* 46, no. 2 (June 1974): 191–226.

Gray, C. S. "Strategic Culture as Context: The First Generation of Theory Strikes Back." *Review of International Studies* 25, no. 1 (1999).

Guillaume, X. "Foreign Policy and Politics of Alterity: A Dialogical Understanding of International Relations." *Millennium* 31, no. 1 (2002): 1–26.

Haas, E. "Nationalism: An Instrumental Social Construction." *Millennium* 22, no. 3.

Habermas, J. "Citizenship and National Identity: Some Reflections on the Future of Europe." *Praxis International* 12, no. 1 (1992): 1–99.

Hajdu, J. G. "Japanese Capital on Australia's Gold Coast as a Catalyst of a Localist-Globalist Conflict on National Identity." *Global Society: Journal of Interdisciplinary International Relations* 13, no. 3 (July 1999): 327–48.

Hall, R. B. "The Discursive Demolition of the Asian Development Model." *International Studies Quarterly* 47, no. 1 (March 2003): 71–99.

Hanson, D. W. "Thomas Hobbes's 'Highway to Peace.'" *International Organization* 38 (1984): 329–31.

Hazlehurst, C. "Asquith as Prime Minister, 1908–1916." *The English Historical Review* 85, no. 336 (July 1970): 502–31.

Helleiner, E. "National Currencies and National Identities." *American Behavioral Scientist* 41 (1998): 1409–36.

Hendley, M. "Help Us to Secure a Strong, Healthy, Prosperous and Peaceful Britain": The Social Arguments of the Campaign for Compulsory Military Service in Britain, 1899–1914." *Canadian Journal of History* 30, no. 2 (August 1995): 261–88.

Hendrickson, K. Review: "Sir John Fisher's Naval Revolution." *Historian*, Winter 2001.

Herz, J. H. "Idealist Internationalism and the Security Dilemma." *World Politics* 2, no. 2 (1950).

——. "The Rise and Demise of the Territorial State." *World Politics* 9, no. 4 (July 1957): 473–93.

Hiley, N. "The Failure of British Counter-Espionage against Germany, 1907–1914." *The Historical Journal* 28, no. 4 (December 1985): 835–62.

Hinkson, J. "Post-Lyotard: A Critique of the Information Society." *Arena* 80 (1987): 123–55.

Hipel, K., M. Wang, and N. Fraser. "Hypergame Analysis of the Falkland/Malvinas Conflict." *International Studies Quarterly* 32, no. 3 (September 1988): 335–58.

Hoffman, S. "Obstinate or Obsolete? The Fate of the Nation-State and the Case of Western Europe." *Daedelus* 95 (1966): 863–911.

Hoffmann, M. "Critical Theory and the Inter-Paradigm Debate." *Millennium* 16, no. 2 (1987): 321–49

Hollis, M., and S. Smith. "Beware of Gurus: Structure and Action in International Relations." *Review of International Studies* 17 (October 1991): 393–410.

——. "Structure and Action: Further Comment." *Review of International Studies* 18 (April 1992): 187–88.

Holsti, K. "National Role Conceptions in the Study of Foreign Policy." *International Studies Quarterly* 14, no. 3 (September 1970).

Hopf, T. "Constructivism All the Way Down." *International Politics* 37, no. 3 (2000): 369–78.

——. "Identity, Legitimacy, and the Use of Military Force: Russia's Great Power Identities and Military Intervention in Abkhazia." *Review of International Studies* 31 (2005): 225–43.

——. "The Promise of Constructivism in International Relations Theory." *International Security* 23, no. 1 (1998): 141–200.

Hudson, V. M. "Culture and Foreign Policy: Developing a Research Agenda." Paper presented at the 36th annual International Studies Association, Chicago (February 1995).

Hurwitz, J., and M. Peffley. "How are Foreign Policy Attitudes Structured? A Hierarchical Model." *American Political Science Review* 81 (December 1987): 1099–1120.

Ikenberry, G. J., and C. Kapuchan. "Socialization and Hegemonic Power." *International Organization* 44, no. 3 (1990): 283–315.

Jabri, V., and S. Chan. "The Ontologist Always Rings Twice: Two More Stories about Structure and Agency in Reply to Hollis and Smith." *Review of International Studies* 22 (January 1996): 107–10.

Jachtenfuchs, M. "The Governance Approach to European Integration." *Journal of Common Market Studies, The European Union Annual Review* 39, no. 2 (June 2001).

Jackson, P., and D. Nexon. "Relations before States: Substance, Process, and the Study of World Politics." *European Journal of International Relations* 5, no. 3 (1999): 291–332.

Jones, F. L., and P. Smith. "Individual and Societal Bases of National Identity: A Comparative Multi-Level Analysis." *European Sociological Review* 17, no. 2 (2001): 103–18.

Kahl, C. "Constructing a Separate Peace: Constructivism, Collective Liberal Identity, and Democratic Peace." *Security Studies* 8, nos. 2–3 (1998–1999): 94–144.

Kandiyoti, D. "Identity and Its Discontents: Women and the Nation." *Millennium* 20, no. 3 (1991).

Kastner, S., and C. Rector. "International Regimes, Domestic Veto-Players, and Capital Controls Policy Stability." *International Studies Quarterly* 47, no. 1 (2000): 1–22.

Kaufmann, C., and R. Pape. "Explaining Costly International Moral Action: Britain's Sixty-Year Campaign Against the Atlantic Slave Trade." *International Organization* 53 (1999): 631–68.

Kennan, G. "The GOP Won the Cold War? Ridiculous." *New York Times*, 28 October 1992.

Kennedy, P. "German World Policy and the Alliance Negotiations with England." *The Journal of Modern History* 45, no. 4 (December 1973): 605–25.

Koch, H. "The Anglo-German Alliance Negotiations: Missed Opportunity or Myth?" *History* 54, no. 182 (October 1969): 378–92.

Kosterman, R., and S. Feshbach. "Towards a Measure of Patriotic and Nationalistic Attitudes." *Political Psychology* 10 (1989): 257–74.

Kowert, P. "Nation Identity: Inside and Out." *Security Studies* 8, nos. 2–3 (1998/1999).

Krasner, S. "Approaches to the State: Alternative Conceptions and Historical Dynamics." *Comparative Politics* 16, no. 2 (January 1984): 223–46.

Kratochwil, F. "History, Action and Identity: Revisiting the 'Second' Great Debate and Assessing its Importance for Social Theory." *European Journal of International Relations* 12, no. 1 (2006): 5–29.

Kymlicka, W., and W. Norman. "The Return of the Citizen: A Survey of Recent Work on Citizenship Theory." *Ethics* 104 (1994): 352–81.

Lantis, J. S. "Strategic Culture and National Security Policy." *International Studies Review* 4, no. 3 (Fall 2002): 87–113.

Lepgeld, J., and A. Lambornm. "Locating Bridges: Connecting Research Agendas on Cognition and Strategic Choice." *International Studies Review* 3, no. 3 (Fall 2001): 3–30.

Legro, J., and A. Moravcsik. "Is Anybody Still a Realist?" *International Security* 24, no. 2 (1999): 5–55.

Legro, J. "Which Norms Matter? Revisiting the Failure of Internationalism." *International Organization* 51, no. 1 (1997): 31–63.

Linklater, A. "The Question of the Next Stage in International Relations Theory: A Critical-Theoretical Point of View." *Millennium* 21 (1992): 77–98.

———. "Dialogue, Dialectic and Emancipation in International Relations at the End of the Post-War Age." *Millennium* 23 (1994): 119–131.

Lobell, S. "Britain's Paradox: Cooperation or Punishment Prior to World War I." *Review of International Studies* 27 (2001): 169–86.

Loiperdinger, M. "The Beginnings of German File Propaganda: The Navy League as Traveling Exhibitor, 1901–1907." *Historical Journal of Film, Radio and Television* (August 2002).

Lords, House of. European Union Committee, 13th Report of Session 2007–8, *The Euro*, HL Paper 90, London: The Stationery Office Limited, May 2008.

Löwenheim, O. "'Do Ourselves Credit and Render a Lasting Service to Mankind': British Moral Prestige, Humanitarian Intervention, and the Barbary Pirates." *International Studies Quarterly* 47, no. 1 (March 2003): 23–48.

Mackay, D. "The Political Sustainability of European Monetary Union." *British Journal of Political Science* 29 (1999): 463–85.

MacLaughlin, J. "Reflections on Nations as 'Imagined Communities.'" *Journal of Multilingual and Multicultural Development* 9, no. 5 (1988): 449–57.

Maddrell, A. "Empire, Emigration and School Geography: Changing Discourses of Imperial Citizenship, 1880–1925." *Journal of Historical Geography* 22, no. 4 (1996): 373–87.

March, J. G., and J. P. Olsen. "The Institutional Dynamics of International Politics Orders." *International Organization* 52, no. 4, Autumn (1998): 943–69.

———. "The New Institutionalism: Organizational Factors in Political Life." *American Political Science Review* 78, no. 3, 734–49.

Marcussen, M., et al. "Constructing Europe? The Evolution of French, British and German Nation State Identities." *Journal of European Public Policy* 6, no. 4, special issue (1999): 614–33.

Markey, D. "Prestige and the Origins of War: Returning to Realism's Roots." *Security Studies* 8 (1999): 126–73.

Marks, G., L., Hooghe, L., and K. Blank. "European Integration from the 1980s: State-Centric vs Multi-Level Governance." *Journal of Common Market Studies* 34, no. 3 (1996): 341–78.

McLennan, G. "Critical or Positive Theory? A Comment on the Status of Anthony Giddens' Social Theory." *Theory, Culture and Society* 2, no. 2 (1984): 123–29.

Mearsheimer, J. "Back to the Future." *International Security* 15, no. 1 (1990): 5–56.

———. "The False Promise of International Institutions." *International Security* 19, no. 3 (1994/95).

Meier-Pesti, K., and E. Kirchler. "Attitudes towards the Euro by National Identity and Relative National Status." *Journal of Economic Psychology* 24 (2003).

Mercer, J. "Reputation and Rational Deterrence Theory." *Security Studies* 7 (1999): 100–13.

Merlingen, M. "Identity, Politics and Germany's Post-TEU Policy on EMU." *Journal of Common Market Studies* 39, no. 3 (September 2001): 463–83.

Mitzen, J. "Ontological Security in World Politics: State Identity and the Security Dilemma." *European Journal of International Relations* 12, no. 3 (2006): 341–70.

Moll, K. "Politics, Power, and Panic: Britain's 1909 Dreadnought 'Gap.'" *Military Affairs* 29, no. 3, Autumn (1965): 133–44.

Moravcsik, A. "Is Something Rotten in the State of Denmark? Constructivism and European Integration." *Journal of European Public Policy* 6, no. 4, special issue (1999): 669–81.

———. "Negotiating the Single European Act: National Interests and Conventional Statecraft in the European Community, *International Organization* 45 (1991): 19–54.

Morgan D., and M. Schwalbe. "Mind and Self in Society: Linking Social Structure and Social Cognition." *Social Psychology Quarterly* 53 (June 1990): 148–64.

Morgenthau, H. J. "Another 'Great Debate': The National Interest of the United States." *The American Political Science Review* 46, no. 4 (December 1952): 961–88.

———. "The Mainsprings of American Foreign Policy: The National Interest vs. Moral Abstractions." *The American Political Science Review* 44, no. 4 (December 1950): 833–54.

Morris, A. J. A. "The English Radicals' Campaign for Disarmament and the Hague Conference of 1907." *The Journal of Modern History* 43, no. 3 (September 1971): 367–93.

Muir Wood, A., J. Bird, J. Thompson, K. Wickenden, H. Grimon, and M. Bonavia. "The Channel Tunnel." *The Geographical Journal* 139, Part 2 (June 1973).

Müller-Peters, A. "The Significance of National Pride and National Identity to the Attitude toward the Single European Currency: A Europe-wide Comparison." *Journal of Economic Psychology* 19 (1998): 701–19.

Müller-Peters, A., et al. "Explaining Attitudes towards the Euro: Design of a Cross-National Study." *Journal of Economic Psychology* 19 (1998): 663–80.

Nairn, T. "The Left against Europe?" *New Left Review* 75 (1972): 5–20.

Norpoth, H. "Guns and Butter and Government Popularity in Britain." *American Political Science Review* 81 (1987): 949–59.

Nye, J. Jr. "Neorealism and Neoliberalism." *World Politics* 40 (January 1988): 235–51.

Onuf, N. "The New Culture of Security Studies." *Mershon International Studies Review* 42 (1998): 132–34.

Orchard, V. "Culture as Opposed to What? Cultural Belonging in the Context of National and European Identity." *European Journal of Social Theory* 5, no. 4 (2002): 419–33.

Parsons, Sir A. "The Falklands Crisis in the United Nations, 31 March–14 June 1982." *International Affairs* 59, no. 2 (1983): 169–78.

Pilger, J. "Here We Are Again." *New Statesman,* 1 October 2001.

Pollack, M. "International Relations Theory and European Integration." *Journal of Common Market Studies,* incorporating *The European Union Annual Review* 39, no. 2 (June 2001): 221–44.

Prestwich, P. E. "French Businessmen and the Channel Tunnel Project of 1913." *French Historical Studies,* Vol. 9, no. 4 (Autumn 1976): 690–715.

Price, R., and C. Reus-Smit. "Dangerous Liaisons? Critical International Theory and Constructivism." *European Journal of International Relations* 4, no. 3 (1998): 259–61.

Putnam, R. "Diplomacy and Domestic Politics: The Logic of Two Level Games." *International Organization* 42 (1988): 427–60.

Pye, L. "Political Culture Revisited." *Political Psychology* 12, no. 3 (September 1991): 487–508.

Raymond, G. A. "Problems and Prospects in the Study of International Norms." *Mershon International Studies Review* 41 (1997): 205–246.

Risse, T., et al. "To Euro or Not to Euro? The EMU and Identity Politics in the European Union." *European Journal of International Relations* 5, no. 2 (1999): 147–87.

———. "The Euro and Identity Politics in Europe." Unpublished paper presented at The Year of the Euro Conference, Nanovic Institute for European Studies, University of Notre Dame (2002).

———. "To Euro or Not to Euro? The EMU and Identity Politics in the European Union." *ARENA Working Papers,* European University Institute, 1998.

Risse-Kappen, T. "Democratic Peace—Warlike Democracies? A Social Constructivist Interpretation of the Liberal Argument." *European Journal of International Relations* 1, no. 4 (1995): 491–517.

Rose, G. "Neoclassical Realism and Theories of Foreign Policy." *World Politics* 51, no. 1 (October 1998): 144–72.

Roth, A. I. "A Bold Move Forward for Neoclassical Realism." *International Studies Review* 8, no. 3 (September 2006): 486–88.

Ruggie, J. G. "Continuity and Transformation in the World Polity." *World Politics* 35 (January 1983): 261–85.

———. "International Regimes, Transactions and Change: Embedded Liberalism in the Post-War Economic Order." *International Organisation* 36, no. 2 (1982).

———. "What Makes the World Hang Together? Neo-Utilitarianism and the Social Constructivist Challenge." *International Organization* 52, no. 4 (Autumn 1998): 855–85.

Rushdie, S. *New Statesman,* 10 April 1983.

Ryan, W. M. "The Invasion Controversy of 1906–1908: Lieutenant-Colonel Charles à Court Repington and British Perceptions of the German Menace." *Military Affairs* 44, no. 1 (February 1980): 8–12.

Salomon Brothers. *Economic and Market Analysis*. London (1991).

Sandel, M. J. "America's Search for a New Public Philosophy." *Atlantic Monthly* 277, no. 3 (1996): 57–78.

Sanders, D., H. Ward, and D. Marsh. "Government Popularity and the Falklands War." *British Journal of Political Science* 17 (1987): 281–313.

Sassatelli, M. "Imagined Europe: The Shaping of a European Cultural Identity through EU Cultural Policy." *European Journal of Social Theory* 5, no. 4 (2002): 435–51.

Schweller, R. "Tripolarity and the Second World War." *International Studies Quarterly* 37, no. 1 (March 1993): 73–103.

Smith, A. "Ethnocentrism, Nationalism and Social Change." *International Journal of Comparative Sociology* 13 (1972): 1–20.

———. "National Identities and the Idea of European Unity." *International Affairs* 68 (1992): 57–76.

———. "Nationalism and Classical Social Theory." *The British Journal of Sociology* 34, no. 1 (1983): 19–38.

———. "Will and Sacrifice: Images of National Identity." *Millennium* 30, no. 3 (2001): 571–82.

Smith, P. "Codes and Conflict: Toward a Theory of War as Ritual." *Theory and Society* 20, no. 1 (February 1991): 103–38.

Smith, S. "The United States and the Discipline of International Relations: 'Hegemonic Country, Hegemonic Discipline.'" *International Studies Review* 4, no. 2 (Summer 2002): 67–85.

Snyder, R. "Farewell to 'Old Thinking': A Reply to Gibbs." *International Studies Perspectives* 2 (2001): 427–37.

Sobel, A. "Domestic Policy Choices, Political Institutional Change, and Financial Globalization." *International Interactions* 24, no. 4 (1998): 345–77.

Solingen, E. "Mapping Internationalization: Domestic and Regional Impacts." *International Studies Quarterly* 45, no. 4 (December 2001): 517–55.

Somers, M. "The Narrative Constitution of Identity: A Relational and Network Approach." *Theory and Society* 23 (1992): 605–49.

Steinberg, J. "The Copenhagen Complex." *Journal of Contemporary History* 1, Part 3 (1966).

Steiner, Z. "Grey, Hardinge and the Foreign Office." *The Historical Journal* 10, no. 3 (1967): 415–39.

Stewart, M., and G. Zuk. "Politics, Economics and Party Popularity in Britain, 1979–1983." *Electoral Studies* 6 (1987): 3–16.

Stoll, R. "Steaming in the Dark? Rules, Rivals and the British Navy, 1860–1913." *The Journal of Conflict Resolution* 36, no. 2 (June 1992): 263–83.

Strachan, H. "The British Way in Warfare Revisited." *The Historical Journal* 26, no. 2 (June 1983): 447–61.

Swidler, A. "Culture in Action: Symbols and Strategies." *American Sociological Review* 51, no. 2 (1986).

Thompson, A. "The Language of Imperialism and the Meanings of Empire: Imperial Discourse in British Politics, 1895–1914." *Journal of British Studies* 35, no. 2 (April 1997): 147–77.

Thompson, W. R. "Identifying Rivals and Rivalries in World Politics." *International Studies Quarterly* 45, no. 4 (December 2001): 557–86.

Wagner, H. "The Theory of Games and the Problem of International Cooperation." *American Political Science Review* 77 (1983): 330–41.

Walker, R. B. J. "International/Inequality." *International Studies Review* 4, no. 2 (Summer 2002): 7–24.

Wallace, W. "Europe as a Confederation: The Community and the Nation-state." *Journal of Common Market Studies* 20 (1982): 57–68.

Weinroth, H. "Left-Wing Opposition to Naval Armaments in Britain before 1914." *Journal of Contemporary History* 6, no. 4 (1971): 93–120.

Welch, D. "Why IR Theorists Should Stop Reading Thucydides." *Review of International Studies* 29, no. 3 (July 2003): 301–19.

Weldes, J., and D. Saco. "Making State Action Possible: The United States and the Discursive Construction of 'The Cuban Problem,' 1960–1994." *Millennium* 25 (1996): 361–395.

Wendt, A. "Anarchy Is What States Make of It: The Social Construction of Power Politics." *International Organization* 46 (Spring 1992): 391–425.

———. "Bridging the Meta-Theory Gap in International Relations." *Review of International Studies* 17 (October 1991): 383–92.

Wendt, A. "Collective Identity Formation and the International State." *The American Political Science Review* 88, no. 2 (June 1994): 384–96.

———. "Constructing International Politics." *International Security* 20 (1995): 71–81.

———. Constructing International Politics, *International Security* 24, special issue (1998): 101–17.

———. "Levels of Analysis vs. Agents and Structures, Part 3." *Review of International Studies* 18 (April 1992): 181–85.

———. "On Constitution and Causation in International Relations." *Review of International Studies* (1998): 101–17.

———. "The Agent-Structure Problem in International Relations Theory." *International Organization* 41 (Summer 1987): 335–70.

———. "The State as Person in International Theory." *Review of International Studies* 30 (2004): 289–316.

Whalen, R. "The Commonwealth of Peoples to Which We Racially Belong: The National Press and the Manufacturing of an Arms Race." *Historian* (Winter 2001).

White, T. "Confronting Bias in International Relations: Lessons from the Cold War Experience" in ISP Forum: "Confronting Bias in International Relations: Responses to the ISP Forum (2:4) Articles by David Gibbs and Robert Snyder." *International Studies Perspectives* 3, no. 4 (November 2002): 438–51.

Woodman, P. "Tunnel Outlives Historical Indecision" (October 25 1990) and "The Climax of Two Centuries of Dreams" (April 29, 1994): *The Press Association Ltd.*

Zeldin, T. "Europe: The Bulldog Barrier." *Guardian*, November 2, 1990.

## Texts

Abrams, M. H., ed. *Norton Anthology of English Literature*. 5th ed. New York: W.W. Norton and Co. 1987.

Ackroyd, R. *Albion: The Origins of the English Imagination*. London: Chatto & Windus, 2002.

Adorno, T., and M. Horkheimer. "The Culture Industry: Enlightenment as Mass Deception." In *Dialectic of Enlightenment*, ed. T. Adorno and M. Horkheimer. New York: Verso Books, 1997.

Albert, M., and L. Brock. In *Identities, Borders, Orders. Rethinking International Relations Theory*, ed. M. Albert, et al. Minneapolis: University of Minnesota Press, 2001.

Albert, M., et al. *Identities, Borders, Orders: Rethinking International Relations Theory*, Minneapolis, University of Minnesota Press, 2001.

Alexander, J., ed. *Durkheimian Sociology: Cultural Studies*. Cambridge: Cambridge University Press, 1988.

Allot, P. *The Health of Nations: Society and Law beyond the State*. Cambridge: Cambridge University Press, 2002.

Almond, G. A., and S. Verba. *The Civic Culture: Political Attitudes and Democracy in Five Nations*. Princeton, NJ: Princeton: University Press, 1963.

Anderson, B. *Imagined Communities: Reflections on the Origin and Spread of Nationalism*. London: Verso, 1991.

Anderson, D. *The Falklands War, 1982*. London: Osprey, 2002.

Anderson, P. R. *The Background of Anti-English Feeling in Germany, 1890–1902*. Washington DC: Georgetown Press, 1939.

Arblaster, A. *The Falklands: Thatcher's War: Labour's Guilt*. London: Socialist Society, 1982.

Arendt, H. *The Human Condition*. Chicago: University of Chicago Press, 1958.

Ashley, R. K. In *International/Intertextual Relations: Postmodern Readings of World Politics*, ed. J. Der Derian and M. Shapiro. Lexington, MA: Lexington, 1989.

Axelrod R., and R. Keohane. In *Neorealism and Neoliberalism: The Contemporary Debate*, ed. D. Baldwin. New York: Columbia University Press, 1993.

Axelrod, R. *The Evolution of Cooperation*. London: Penguin, 1990.

Bach, J. *Between Sovereignty and Integration*. New York: St. Martin's Press, 1999.

Baldwin, D., ed. *Neorealism and Neoliberalism: The Contemporary Debate*. New York: Columbia University Press, 1993.

Barnett, A. *Iron Britannia: Why Parliament Waged Its Falklands War*. London: Allison and Busby, 1982.

Barry, B. *The Liberal Theory of Justice*. Oxford: Clarendon Press, 1973.

Bartelson, J. *A Genealogy of Sovereignty*. Cambridge: Cambridge University Press, 1995.

Bassett, R. *Battle Cruisers: A History, 1908–1948*. London: Macmillan, 1981.

Baycroft, T. *Nationalism in Europe, 1789–1945*. Cambridge: Cambridge University Press, 1998.

Baylis, J., and S. Smith. *The Globalization of World Politics*, 2nd ed. Oxford: Oxford University Press, 2001.

Becker, L., and C. Becker. *Encyclopedia of Ethics*. 2nd ed. Vol. 2. New York: Routledge 1998.

Beetham, D., and C. Lord. *Legitimacy and the European Union*. London: Addison Wesley Longman, 1998.

Beetham, D. *The Legitimation of Power*. Basingstoke: Macmillan, 1991.

Bellier, I., and T. Wilson, eds. *An Anthropology of the European Union*. Oxford: Berg, 2000.

Benedict, R. *The Chrysanthemum and the Sword*. Boston: Houghton Mifflin, 1946.

Benjamin, W. *The Arcades Project*. Cambridge, MA: Harvard University Press, 1999.

Berger, P., and T. Luckmann. *The Social Construction of Reality*. New York: Anchor Books, 1966.

Berlin, I. *Vico and Herder: Two Studies in the History of Ideas*. London, 1976.

Bernstein, R. *The Restructuring of Social and Political Theory*. London: Macmillan, 1976.

Best, G. *Mid-Victorian Britain, 1851–1875*. London: Macmillan, 1979.

Bhabha, H., ed. *Nation and Narration*. London: Routledge, 1990.

———. *The Location of Culture*. London: Routledge, 1994.

Blake, J., and K. Davis. "Norms, Values and Sanctions." In *Handbook of Modern Sociology*, ed. R. Harris, Chicago: Rand McNally, 1964.

Blumer, H. *Symbolic Interactionism: Perspective and Method*. Englewood Cliffs, NJ: Prentice-Hall, 1969.

Bogdanor, V. in J. Hayward, *Élitism, Populism, and European Politics*. Oxford: Clarendon Press, 1996.

Bonavia, M. R. *The Channel Tunnel Story*. Newton Abbot: David and Charles, 1987.

Booth, K., and R. Trood, eds. *Strategic Cultures in the Asia-Pacific Region*. New York: St. Martin's Press, 1998.

Bordieu, P. "Identity and Representation: Elements for a Critical Reflection on the Idea of Region." In *Language and Symbolic Power*. Cambridge, MA: Harvard University Press, 1991.

Box, G., and G. Jenkins. *Time Series Analysis: Forecasting and Control*. San Francisco: Holden-Day, 1976.

Brass, P. *Ethnicity and Nationalism: Theory and Comparison*. London: Sage Publications, 1991.

Brailsford, H. N. "The Federal Idea." In *Federal Union: The Pioneers*, ed. R. Mayne, J. Pinder, and J. C. Roberts. Basingstoke: Palgrave Macmillan, 1991.

Breakwell, G. M. *Coping with Threatened Identities*. London: Methuen, 1986.

Breuilly, J. *Nationalism and the State*. Manchester: Manchester University Press, 1993.

Brown, C. In *Identities, Borders, Orders. Rethinking International Relations Theory*, ed. M. Albert, et al. Minneapolis: University of Minnesota Press, 2001.

———. *International Relations Theory: New Normative Approaches*. Hemel Hempstead: Harvester Wheatsheaf, 1992.

———. *Understanding International Relations*. London: Macmillan, 1997.

Brubaker, R. *Citizenship and Nationhood and France and Germany*. Cambridge, MA: Harvard University Press, 1992.

———. *Ethnicity without Groups*. Cambridge, MA: Harvard University Press, 2004.

Brown, M. E., Sean M. Lynn-Jones, and Steven E. Miller, eds. *The Perils of Anarchy: Contemporary Realism and International Security*. Cambridge, MA, MIT Press: 1995.

Bull, H. *The Anarchical Society: A Study of Order in World Politics*. London: Macmillan, 1977.

Burchill, S., and A. Linklater, eds. *Theories of International Relations*. New York: St. Martin's Press, 1996.

Burgess, M. *Federalism and European Union*. London: Oxford University Press, 1989.

Burrow, J. W. *A Liberal Descent: Victorian Historians and the English Past.* Cambridge: Cambridge University Press, 1981.

Burton, J., ed. *Conflict: Human Needs Theory.* New York: St. Martin's Press, 1990.

Buti, M., and A. Sapir, eds. *EMU and Economic Policy in Europe: The Challenge of the Early Years.* Brussels: The Commission of the European Communities, 2002.

Butler, J. *Gender Trouble: Feminism and the Subversion of Identity.* New York: Routledge, 1990.

Byers, M. *Custom, Power and the Power of Rules: International Relations and Customary International Law.* Cambridge: Cambridge University Press, 1999.

Calhoun, C. *Nationalism.* Minneapolis: University of Minnesota Press, 1997.

Calvert, P. *The Falklands Crisis: The Rights and the Wrongs.* London: Frances Pinter, 1982.

Cameron, K., ed. *National Identity.* Exeter: Intellect European Studies Series, 1999.

Campbell, D. *Writing Security: United States Foreign Policy and the Politics of Identity.* Minneapolis: University of Minnesota Press, 1992.

Cannadine, D. *Class in Britain.* London: Yale University Press, 1998.

Carens, J. "Migration and Morality: A Liberal Egalitarian Perspective." In *Free Movement,* ed. B. Barry and R. Goodin. Hemel Hempstead: Harvester Wheatsheaf, 1992.

Carr, E. H. *Nationalism and After,* Harmondsworth: Penguin, 1945.

———. *The New Society.* Harmondsworth: Penguin, 1951.

———. *The Twenty Years' Crisis.* London: Macmillan, 1939.

———. *What Is History?* Harmondsworth: Penguin, 1961.

———. *The Russian Revolution from Lenin to Stalin 1917–1929.* London: Palgrave Macmillan (reprinted) 2003.

Castle, B. *Castle's Diaries 1964–70.* London: Orion Publishing Co., 1984.

Carter, R., and P. Simpson, eds. *Language, Discourse and Literature: An Introductory Reader in Discourse Stylistics.* London: Unwin Hyman, 1989.

Charlton, M. *The Little Platoon: Diplomacy and the Falklands Dispute.* London: Blackwell, 1989.

Charmley, J. *Splendid Isolation? Britain and the Balance of Power, 1874–1914.* London: Hodder and Stoughton, 1999.

Chatham House Commission. *A British Agenda for Europe: Designing Our Own Future.* London: Royal Institute of International Affairs, 2008.

Chomsky, N. *On Power and Ideology.* New York: South End Press, 1988.

Choucri, N., and R. North. *Nations in Conflict: National Growth and International Violence.* San Francisco: W.H. Freeman, 1975.

Christensen, T. J. *Useful Adversaries: Grand Strategy, Domestic Mobilization, and Sino-American Conflict, 1947–1958.* Princeton, NJ: Princeton University Press, 1996.

Coulthard, M. *An Introduction to Discourse Analysis.* London: Longman, 1977.

Churchill, W. S. *A History of the English-Speaking Peoples.* Vol. 4, *The Great Democracies.* London: Cassell and Co. Ltd., 1958.

———. *The World Crisis, 1911–1918.* Vol. 1. New York: Scribner's, 1923–1929.

Clarke, I. F. *Voices Prophesying War, 1763–3749.* Oxford: Oxford University Press, 1992.

Clarke, P. *A Question of Leadership: From Gladstone to Blair.* London: Macmillan, 1999.

Claude, I., Jr. *National Minorities: An International Problem*. Cambridge MA: Harvard University Press, 1955.

———. *Swords into Plowshares*. New York: Random House, 1984.

Cohen, A. P. *Symbolic Construction of Community*. New York: Tavistock, 1985.

Cohen, B. *The Geography of Money*, Ithaca, NY: Cornell University Press, 1998.

Colley, L. *Britons: Forging the Nation, 1707–1837*. New Haven, CT: Yale University Press, 2009.

Coll, A., and A. Arendt. *The Falklands War: Lessons for Strategy, Diplomacy and International Law*. Boston: Allen & Unwin, 1985.

Collini, S. *English Pasts, Essays in History and Culture*. Oxford: Oxford University Press, 1999.

Colls, R. *Identity of England*. Oxford: Oxford University Press, 2002.

Cottam, M., and R. Cottam. *Nationalism and Politics: The Political Behaviour of Nation States*. Boulder, CO: Lynne Rienner Publishers, 2001.

Cox, M., G. J. Ikenberry, and T. Inoguchi, eds. *American Democracy Promotion: Impulses, Strategies and Impacts*. Oxford: Oxford University Press, 2000.

Cox, R. W. In *Neorealism and its Critics*, ed. R. Keohane. New York: Columbia University Press, 1986.

Cox, R. W. In *Theories of International Relations*, ed. S. Burchill and A. Linklater. New York: St. Martin's Press, 1996.

Crawford, M. *One Money for Europe? The Economics and Politics of Maastricht*. London: The Macmillan Press, 1993.

Crewe, I. In *Britain at the Polls: 1983*, ed. A. Ranney. Durham, NC: Duke University Press, 1985.

Currie, D. *The Pros and Cons of EMU*. London: The Economist Intelligence Unit, 1997.

Dabhour, O., and M. R. Ishay, eds. *The Nationalism Reader*. Atlantic Highlands, NJ: Humanities Press, 1995.

Dahbour, O. In *Cultural Identity and the Nation-State*, ed. C. Gould and P. Pasquino. Lanham, MD: Rowman & Littlefield Publishers, Inc., 2001.

Dallymr, F. *Alternative Visions: Paths in the Global Village*. New York: Rowman & Littlefield, 1998.

Dallmyr, F., and J. Rosales, eds. *Beyond Nationalism? Sovereignty and Citizenship*. Lanham: Lexington Books, 2001.

Davies, N. *The Isles: A History*. Oxford: Oxford University Press, 1999.

De Grauwe, P. *The Economics of Monetary Integration*. Oxford: Oxford University Press, 1991.

della Torre, P. F. *Viva Britannia: Mrs Thatcher's Britain*. London: HarperCollins, 1985.

Der Derian, J., and M. J. Shapiro, eds. *International/Intertextual Relations: Post-modern Readings of World Politics*, Lexington, MA: Lexington, 1989.

Derrida, J. *Dissemination*. Chicago: University of Chicago Press, 1981.

———. *Limited Inc*. Evanston, IL: Northwestern University Press, 1988.

———. *Writing and Difference*, Chicago: University of Chicago Press, 1978.

Deutsch, K. *Nationalism and Social Communication*. Cambridge, MA: MIT Press, 1966.

———. *Political Community at the International Level*, Garden City, NY: Doubleday and Company, 1954.

Devetak, R. In *Theories of International Relations*, ed. S. Burchill and A. Linklater. New York: St. Martin's Press, 1996.

Dewar, K. Vice Admiral. *The Navy from Within*. London: Brown, 1939.

Dillon, M. In *Belief Systems and International Relations*, ed. R. Little and S. Smith. London: Blackwell, 1988.

Dowds, L., and K. Young. "National Identity." In *British Social Attitudes: The 13th Report*, ed. R. Jowell, et al. Aldershot: Ashgate, 1996.

Doyle M., and G. J. Ikenberry, eds. *New Thinking in International Relations Theory*. New York: Westview Press, 1997.

Dreyfus, H., and P. Rabinow. *Michel Foucault: Beyond Structuralism and Hermeneutics*, Brighton: Harvester, 1982.

Driffill, J., and M. Beber, eds. *A Currency for Europe*. London: Lothian Foundation Press, 1995.

Duffield, J. *World Power Forsaken: Political Culture, International Institutions, and German Security Policy after Unification*. Stanford, CA: Stanford University Press, 1998.

Dunne T., and B. Schmidt. In *The Globalization of World Politics*, ed. J. Baylis and S. Smith, 2nd ed. Oxford: Oxford University Press, 2001.

Dunne, T. *Inventing International Society*. London: Macmillan, 1998.

Dyson, K., and K. Featherstone. *The Road to Maastricht: Negotiating Economic and Monetary Union*. Oxford: Oxford University Press, 1999.

Dyson, K. *The Politics of the Euro-Zone: Stability or Breakdown?* Oxford: Oxford University Press, 2000.

———. *The State Tradition in Western Europe*. Oxford: Martin Robertson, 1980.

Ebbinghause, B., and A. Hassel. In *International Finance*. Princeton, NJ: Princeton University Press, 1996.

Eden, L. *Constructing Deconstruction: Organizations, Knowledge, and U.S. Nuclear Weapons Effects*. Ithaca, NY: Cornell University Press, 2003.

Elstrom, G., ed. *International Ethics*. Santa Barbara, CA: ABC-CLIO, 1998.

Etzioni, A. In *Decision Making: Alternatives to Rational Choice Models*, ed. M. Zei. New York: Sage, 1992.

Evans, P., D. Rueschemeyer, and T. Skocpol, eds. *Bringing the State Back In*. Cambridge: Cambridge University Press, 1985.

———. *Embedded Autonomy: States and Industrial Transformation*. Princeton, NJ: Princeton University Press, 1995.

Falk, R. In *The Future of the International Legal Order*, eds. C. Black and R. Falk, vol. 1. Princeton, NJ: Princeton University Press, 1969.

Fawcett, L., and A. Hurrell, eds. *Regionalism in World Politics: Regional Organization and International Order*. Oxford: Oxford University Press, 1995.

Femenia, N. In *Social Conflicts and Collective Identities*, eds. P. Coy and L. Woehrle. Lanham, MD: Rowman & Littlefield, 2000.

———. *National Identity in Times of Crises: The Scripts of the Falklands-Malvinas War*. New York: Nova Science Publishers, 1996.

Ferguson, Y., and R. Mansbach. In *The Return of Culture and Identity in IR Theory*, ed. Y. Lapid and F. Kratochwil. Boulder, CO: Lynne Rienner Publishers, 1996.

Ferguson, Y., and R. Mansbach. *Polities: Authorities, Identities, and Change*. Columbia: University of South Carolina Press, 1996.

Feyerabend, P. *Against Method*. London: Verso, 1978.

Finnemore, M. *National Interests in International Society*, Ithaca, NY: Cornell University, 1996.

Fischer, F., and J. Forester, eds. *The Argumentative Turn in Policy Analysis and Planning*. London: University College of London Press, 1993.

Fiske, J. *Media Matters*. Minneapolis: University of Minnesota Press, 1994.

Foucault, M. *Discipline and Punish: The Birth of the Prison*. New York: Vintage/Random House, 1979.

——. *Language, Counter-memory, Practice: Selected Essays and Interviews*. Ed. D. F. Bouchard. Trans. D. F. Bouchard and S. Sherry. Blackwell: Oxford, 1977.

——. *Nietzsche, Genealogy, History*. New York: Pantheon Books, 1990.

——. *Politics, Philosophy and Culture: Interviews and Other Writings*. Ed. L. Kritzman. Trans. A. Sheridan. New York: Routledge, 1988,

——. *The Archaeology of Knowledge*. Trans. A. Sheridan Smith. New York: Pantheon Books, 1972.

——. *The History of Sexuality: An Introduction*. Middlesex: Penguin, 1978.

Franck, T., and W. Weisband. *Word Politics: Verbal Strategy among the Superpowers*. New York: Oxford University Press, 1972.

Frankel, B, ed. *Realism: Restatements and Renewals*. London: Frank Cass, 1996.

Fraser, M., ed. *Britain in Europe*, Strategems Publishing: London, 1997.

Freedman, L. *Official History of the Falklands Campaign, Vol 1*. London: Frank Cass, 2005.

Friedberg, A. *The Weary Titan: Britain and the Experience of Relative Decline, 1895–1905*, Princeton, NJ: Princeton University Press, 1988.

Gaddis, J. L. *Strategies of Containment: A Critical Appraisal of Postwar American National Security Policy*. New York: Oxford University Press, 1982.

Gamble, A. *Between Europe and America: The Future of British Politics*, Hampshire: Palgrave Macmillan, 2003.

Garfinkel, H. *Studies in Ethnomethodology*. Englewood Cliffs, NJ: Prentice-Hall, 1967.

Garrett, R. *Cross Channel*. London: Methuen, 1972.

Geertz, C. *The Interpretation of Cultures*. New York: Basic Books, 1973.

——. "The World in Pieces: Culture and Politics at the End of the Century." In *Available Light: Anthropological Reflections on Philosophical Topics*. Princeton, NJ: Princeton University Press, 2000.

Gellner, E. *Thought and Change*. Englewood Cliffs, NJ: Prentice-Hall, 1967.

——. *Nations and Nationalism*. London: Basil Blackwell, 1983.

——. *Spectacles and Predicaments: Essays in Social Theory*. Cambridge: Cambridge University Press, 1979.

——. *Contemporary Thought and Politics*. London: Routledge and Kegan Paul, 1974.

——. *Culture, Identity and Politics*. Cambridge: Cambridge University Press, 1987.

——. *Encounters with Nationalism*. Oxford: Blackwell, 1994.

Gerth, H. H., and C. Wright-Mills, ed. and tr. From *Max Weber: Essays in Sociology*. London: Routledge and Kegan Paul, 1948.

Giddens, A. *A Contemporary Critique of Historical Materialism*. Vol. 1: *Power, Property and State*. London: Macmillan, 1981.

——. *A Contemporary Critique of Historical Materialism.* Vol. 2: *The Nation-State and Violence.* Cambridge: Polity Press, 1985.

——. *Central Problems in Social Theory.* Berkeley: University of California Press, 1979.

——. *The Constitution of Society: Outline of the Theory of Structuration.* Berkeley: University of California Press, 1984.

——. *The Philosophy of Social Science: An Introduction.* Cambridge. Cambridge University Press: 1994.

Giles, J., and T. Middleton, eds. *Writing Englishness, 1900–1950: An Introductory Sourcebook on National Identity.* London: Routledge, 1995.

Gill, S. ed. *Gramsci, Historical Materialism and International Relations.* Cambridge: Cambridge University Press, 1993.

Gilmour, R. *The Victorian Period: The Intellectual and Cultural Context of English Literature, 1830–1890.* Harlow: Longman, 1993.

Gilpin, R. *The Political Economy of International Relations.* Princeton, NJ: Princeton University Press, 1987.

——. In *Economic Issues and National Security,* ed. K. Knorr and F. Tager. Lawrence: University Press of Kansas, 1977.

——. In *Neorealism and its Critics,* ed. R. Keohane. New York: Columbia University Press, 1986.

——. *War and Change in World Politics.* New York: Cambridge University Press, 1981.

Goffman, E. *The Presentation of Self in Everyday Life.* Edinburgh: University of Edinburgh, Social Sciences Research Centre, 1958.

Goldblat, J., and V. Millan, *The Falklands/Malvinas Conflict: A Spur to Arms Build-ups.* Stockholm: International Peace Research Institute, 1983.

Goldstein, J., and R. Keohane, eds. *Ideas and Foreign Policy: Beliefs, Institutions, and Political Change.* Ithaca NY: Cornell University Press, 1993.

Gooch, J. *The Plans of War: The General Staff and British Military Strategy c. 1900–1916.* London: Routledge, 1974.

Gorer, G. *The American People.* New York: W.W. Norton, 1948.

Gould, H. R. In *International Relations in a Constructed World,* ed. V. Kubálková, N. Onuf, and P. Kowert. Armonk, NY: M.E. Sharpe, 1998.

Gramsci, A. *Antonio Gramsci, Selections from Cultural Writings.* Ed. D. Forgacs, and G. Nowell-Smith. Trans. W. Boelhower. London: Lawrence and Wisehart, 1985.

——. *Selections from the Prison Notebook.* Ed. and trans. Q. Hoare, and G. Nowel-Smith. London: Lawrence and Wisehart, 1971.

Gray, C. *Nuclear Strategy and National Style.* Lanham, MD: Hamilton Press, 1986.

Gray, J. *Enlightenment's Wake: Politics and Culture at the Close of the Modern Age.* London: Routledge, 1995.

Green, E. H. H. *The Crisis of Conservatism: The Politics, Economics and Ideology of the British Conservative Party, 1880–1914.* London: Routledge, 1995.

Greenfeld, L. *Nationalism: Five Roads to Modernity.* Cambridge MA: Harvard University Press, 1992.

Grenville, J. A. S. *Lord Salisbury and Foreign Policy: The Close of the Nineteenth Century.* London, Macmillan, 1964.

Griffin, E. *A First Look at Communication Theory.* New York: The McGraw-Hill Companies, 1997.

Guibernau, M. *Nations without States: Political Communities in a Global Age.* Cambridge: Polity Press, 2000.

Haas, E., and P. Haas. "How We Learned to Escape Physics Envy and to Love Pluralism and Complexity." In *Mainstream Paradigms in International Studies: Institutionalism,* ed. M. Brecher and F. Harvey. Ann Arbor: University of Michigan Press, 2002.

Haas, Ernest B. *The Uniting of Europe: Political, Social and Economic Forces: 1950–1957.* Stanford, CA: Stanford University Press, 1968.

Habermas, J. *Communication and the Evolution of Society.* Trans. T. McCarthy. Boston: Beacon Press, 1979.

———. *Legitimation Crisis.* London: Heinemann, 1976.

Hadfield C., and A. M. Hadfield, eds. *The Cotswolds: A New Study.* Newton Abbot: David and Charles, 1981.

Hadfield, A. M. *Time to Finish the Game.* London: Phoenix House, 1964.

Hadfield, C. *British Canals: An Illustrated History.* Newton Abbot: David and Charles, 1993.

Haig, A. *Caveat: Realism, Reagan and Foreign Policy.* London: Weifendel & Nicolson, 1984.

Hall, J. A., ed. *The State of the Nation: Ernest Gellner and the Theory of Nationalism.* Cambridge: Cambridge University Press, 1998.

———. "Ernest Gellner." In *Diagnoses of Our Time: Six Views on Our Social Condition.* London: Heinemann, 1981.

Hall, R. B. *National Collective Identity: Social Constructs and International Systems.* New York: Columbia University Press, 1999.

Halliday, F. "The Future of International Relations: Fears and Hopes." In *International Theory: Positivism and Beyond,* ed. S. Smith, K. Booth, and M. Zalewski. Cambridge: Cambridge University Press, 1996.

Handler, R. In *Commemorations,* ed. J. Gillis, Princeton, NJ: Princeton University Press, 1994.

Harris, J. *Private Lives, Public Spirit: Britain, 1870–1914.* London: Oxford University Press, 1993.

Harris, R. *Gotcha! The Media, the Government and the Falklands Crisis.* London: Faber, 1983.

Hastings M., and S. Jenkins. *The Battle for the Falklands.* London: Macmillan, 1983.

Held, D. *Democracy and the Global Order: From the Modern State to Global Governance.* Stanford, CA: Standford University Press, 1995.

Herb, G., and D. Kaplan, eds. *Nested Identities: Nationalism, Territory, and Scale.* Lanham, MD: Rowman & Littlefield Publishers, Inc., 1999.

Henderson, W. O. *The Rise of German Industrial Power, 1834–1914.* Berkeley: University of California Press, 1972.

Hermann C., and G. Peacock. In *New Directions in the Study of Foreign Policy,* ed. Hermann, Kegley, and Rosenau. New York: Routledge, 1987.

Hertz, F. *Nationality in History and Politics: A Study of the Psychology and Sociology of National Sentiment and Character.* New York: Oxford University Press, 1944.

Herz, J. H., *International Politics in the Atomic Age.* New York: Columbia University Press, 1959.

Hewitt, J. P. *Self and Society: A Symbolic Interactionist Social Psychology.* Amherst: University of Massachusetts, Allyn & Bacon, 2003.

Hill. C. *The Changing Politics of Foreign Policy.* London: Palgrave, 2003.

Himmelfarb, G. *The Demoralisation of Society: From Victorian Virtues to Modern Values.* London: Macmillan, 1995.

Hindess, B. *Choice, Rationality and Social Theory.* London: Unwin Human, 1988.

Hobsbawm E., and T. Ranger. *The Invention of Tradition.* Cambridge: Cambridge University Press, 1983.

Hobsbawm, E. In *Nationalism,* ed. J. Hutchinson, and A. Smith. Oxford: Oxford University Press, 1994.

——. In *Imagination and Precision in the Social Sciences: Essays in Memory of Peter Nettl,* ed. T. Nossiter, A. Hanson, and S. Rokkan. London: Faber and Faber, 1972.

——. *Nations and Nationalism since 1780: Programme, Myth and Reality.* Cambridge: Cambridge University Press, 1990.

Hobson, J. H. *The State and International Relations.* Cambridge: Cambridge University Press, 2000.

Holliday, I., G. Marcou, and R. Vickerman. *The Channel Tunnel: Public Policy, Regional Development and European Integration.* London: Belhaven Press, 1991.

Hollis, M., and S. Smith. *Explaining and Understanding International Relations.* Oxford: Oxford University Press, 1990.

Honeywell, M., and J. Pearce. *Falklands/Malvinas: Whose Crisis?* London: Latin American Bureau, 1982.

Hooper, A. *The Military and the Media.* Aldershot: Gower, 1982.

Hopf, T. *Social Construction of International Politics: Identities and Foreign Policies, Moscow, 1955 and 1999.* Ithaca, NY: Cornell University Press, 2002.

Hoppe, R. In *The Argumentative Turn in Policy Analysis and Planning,* ed. F. Fischer and J. Forester. London: University College of London Press, 1993.

Horne, D. *God Is an Englishman.* Sydney: Angus and Robertson, 1969.

Hosking G., and G. Schöpflin, eds. *Myths and Nationhood.* London: Hurst & Company, 1997.

Houghton, W. E. *The Victorian Frame of Mind, 1830–1870.* New Haven, CT: Yale University Press, 1957.

Howard, M. *The Lessons of History.* New Haven, CT: Yale University Press, 1991.

Hudson, V. M., ed. *Culture and Foreign Policy.* Boulder, CO: Lynne Rienner, 1997.

Hughes-Hallett, A. In *The Political Economy of EMU: France, Germany and the UK,* ed. J. Pisani-Ferry, et al. Brussels: Centre for European Policy Studies, 1997.

Hughes, J. R. T. In *1859: Entering an Age of Crisis,* ed. P. Appleman, W. Madden, and W. Wolf. Bloomington: University of Indiana Press, 1959.

Hutchinson, J., and A. Smith, eds. *Nationalism.* Oxford: Oxford University Press, 1994.

Hynes, S. *The Edwardian Turn of Mind.* Princeton, NJ: Princeton University Press, 1968.

Inayatullah, N., and D. Blaney. In *The Return of Culture and Identity in IR Theory,* ed. Y. Lapid and F. Kratochwil. Boulder, CO: Lynne Rienner Publishers, 1996.

James, L. *Warrior Race: A History of the British at War: From Roman Times to the Present.* London: Abacus, 2002.

James, P. *Nation Formation: Towards a Theory of Abstract Community.* London: Sage Publications, 1996.

Jameson, Rear Admiral W. *The Fleet That Jack Built: Nine Men Who Made a Modern Navy.* New York: Harcourt Brace, 1962.

Jenkyns, R. *The Victorians and Ancient Greece.* Oxford: Oxford University Press, 1981.

Jennings, Sir R., and Sir A. Watts, eds. *Oppenheim's International Law.* Volume I, Part I, 9th ed. Oxford: Oxford University Press, 1996.

Jepperson, R., A. Wendt, and P. Katzenstein. In *The Culture of National Security: Norms and Identity in World Politics,* ed. Katzenstein. New York: Columbia University Press, 1996.

Johnston, A. I. *Cultural Realism: Strategic Culture and Grand Strategy in Ming China.* Princeton, NJ: Princeton University Press, 1995.

Johnston, W. *England as It Is: Political, Social and Industrial in the Middle of the Nineteenth Century.* Vol. 1. Dublin: Irish University Press, 1971.

Jones, G. S. In *Citizenship and Nationhood in France and Germany,* ed. R. Brubaker. Cambridge, MA: Harvard University Press, 1992.

Jones, R. W. *Security, Strategy and Critical Theory.* Boulder, CO: Lynne Rienner, 1999.

Judd, D. *Empire: The British Imperial Experience from 1765 to the Present.* London: HarperCollins, 1996.

Kamanka, E. ed. *Community as a Social Ideal.* London, Edward Arnold, 1982.

Kant, I. *Kant's Political Writings.* Cambridge: Cambridge University Press, 1970.

Kaplan, M., and N. de B. Katzenbach. *The Political Foundation of International Law.* New York: Wiley, 1969.

Katzenstein, P., ed. *The Culture of National Security: Norms and Identity in World Politics.* New York: Columbia University Press, 1996.

Kaufman, A. *Welfare in the Kantian State.* Oxford: Oxford University Press, 1999.

Kedourie, E. *Nationalism.* London: Hutchinson, 1960.

Kennedy, P. *The Rise and Fall of British Naval Mastery.* London: Oxford University Press, 1976.

———. *The Rise and Fall of the Great Powers.* Fontana Press: London, 1989.

———. *The Rise of the Anglo-German Antagonism: 1860–1940.* London: Fontana Press, 1976.

Keohane R., and J. Nye. *Power and Interdependence: World Politics in Transition.* Boston: Little and Brown, 1977.

———. *Transnational Relations and World Politics.* Cambridge, MA: Harvard University Press, 1971.

Keohane, R. In *Neorealism and Neoliberalism: The Contemporary Debate,* ed. D. Baldwin. New York: Columbia University Press, 1993.

Kershen, A. *A Question of Identity.* Aldershot: Ashgate, 1998.

Kier, E. *Imagining War: French and British Military Doctrine between the Wars.* Princeton, NJ: Princeton University Press, 1997.

———. In *The Culture of National Security: Norms and Identity in World Politics,* ed. P. Katzenstein. New York: Columbia University Press, 1996.

King, G., R. Keohane, and S. Verba. *Designing Social Inquiry.* Princeton, NJ: Princeton University Press, 1994.

Kissinger, H. *Diplomacy.* London: Simon and Schuster, 1994.

Keal, P. *Unspoken Rules and Superpower Dominance.* London: Macmillan, 1984.

Klosko, G. *Democratic Procedures and Liberal Consensus*. Oxford: Oxford University Press, 1999.

Kohn, H. *Nationalism: Its Meaning and History*. New York: Van Nostrand Reinhold, 1965.

——. *The Ideal of Nationalism: A Study in Its Origins and Background*. New York: Collier Books, 1944.

Koselleck, R. *Critique and Crisis: Enlightenment and the Pathogenesis of Modern Society*. Cambridge, MA: Harvard University Press, 1988.

Kowert P., and J. Legro. In *The Culture of National Security: Norms and Identity in World Politics*, ed. P. Katzenstein. New York: Columbia University Press, 1996.

Krasner, S. *Structural Conflict: The Third World against Global Liberalism*. Berkeley: University of California Press, 1985.

——. *Defending the National Interest*. Princeton, NJ: Princeton University Press, 1987.

——. *International Regimes*. Ithaca, NY: Cornell University Press, 1983.

Kratochwil, F. "How Do Norms Matter?" In *The Role of Law in International Politics: Essays in International Relations and International Law*, ed. M. Byers. Oxford: Oxford University Press, 2000.

——. In *The Return of Culture and Identity in IR Theory*, ed. Y. Lapid, and F. Kratochwil. Boulder, CO: Lynne Rienner Publishers, 1996.

——. *Rules, Norms, and Decisions: On the Conditions of Practical and Legal Reasoning in International Relations and Domestic Affairs*. Cambridge: Cambridge University Press, 1989.

Kubálková, V., N. Onuf, and P. Kowert, eds. *International Relations in a Constructed World*. Armonk, NY: M.E. Sharpe, 1998.

Kumar, K. *The Making of English National Identity*. Cambridge: Cambridge University Press, 2003.

Laclau E., and C. Mouffe. *Hegemony and Socialist Strategy: Towards a Radical Domestic Politics*. Trans. W. Moore and P. Cammack. London: Verso, 1985.

Lakatos, I., and A. Musgrave, eds. *Criticism and the Growth of Knowledge*. Cambridge: Cambridge University Press, 1970.

Lambert, N. *Sir John Fisher's Naval Revolution*. Columbia: University of South Carolina Press, 1999.

Lambi, I. N. *The Navy and German Power Politics, 1862–1914*. London: Macmillan, 1984.

Lapid, Y., and F. Kratochwil, eds. *The Return of Culture and Identity in IR Theory*. Boulder, CO: Lynne Rienner Publishers, 1996.

Lapid, Y. In *Identities, Borders, Orders: Rethinking International Relations Theory*, ed. M. Albert, et al. Minneapolis: University of Minnesota Press, 2001.

Laudan, L. *Progress and Its Problems*. Berkeley: University of California, 1978.

Lebow, R. N. In *Psychology and Deterrence*, ed. Jervis, Lebow, and Stein. Baltimore: Johns Hopkins University Press, 1990.

Leffler, M. *A Preponderance of Power: National Security, Truman Administration and the Cold War*. Stanford, CA: Stanford University Press, 1993.

Legro, J. *Cooperation under Fire: Anglo-German Restraint during World War II*. Ithaca, NY: Cornell University Press, 1995.

Lee, L. *Cider with Rosie*. Harmondsworth: Secker, 1959.

Leonard, D., and M. Leonard, eds. *The Pro-European Reader*. London: Palgrave/Foreign Policy Centre, 2002.

Levitt, M., and C. Lord. *The Political Economy of Monetary Union*. Macmillan Press Ltd.: London, 2000.

Linklater, A. *Transformation of Political Community*. Oxford: Blackwell Publishers Polity Press, 1998.

Lipset, S. M. *Political Man*. London: Heineman, 1960.

Lipson, C. In *Neorealism and Neoliberalism: The Contemporary Debate*, ed. D. Baldwin. New York: Columbia University Press, 1993.

Lobban, M. *The Common Law and English Jurisprudence, 1760–1850*. Oxford: Oxford University Press: 1991.

Lobell, S. E., N. M. Ripsman, and J. W. Taliaferro. *Neoclassical Realism, the State and Foreign Policy*. Cambridge: Cambridge University Press, 2009.

Lothian, Lord. "The Ending of Armageddon." In *Federal Union: The Pioneers*, ed. R. Mayne, J. Pinder, and J. C. Roberts. Basingstoke: Palgrave Macmillan, 1991.

Lyotard, J. P. *The Postmodern Condition: A Report on Knowledge*. Manchester: Manchester University Press, 1984.

Manguel, A. *The City of Words*. Toronto: Anansi Press, 2007.

Mann, M. *The Sources of Social Power*. Cambridge: Cambridge University Press, 1988.

March, J. G., and J. P. Olsen. *Rediscovering Institutions: The Organizational Basis of Politics*. New York: Free Press, 1989.

March, J. G. In *Perspectives on Organization Design and Behaviour*, ed. A. Van De Ven and W. F. Joyce. New York: Wiley, 1981.

Marquand, D. In *Thatcherism*, ed. R. Sidelsky. London: Chatto and Windus, 1988.

Massie, R. K. *Dreadnought: Britain, Germany, and the Coming of the Great War*. New York: Random House, 1991.

Mather, R. *The European Union and British Democracy: Towards Convergence*. Houndmills: Macmillan Press Ltd, 2000.

Mathias, P. *The First Industrial Nation: An Economic History of Britain, 1700–1914*. London: Macmillan, 1969.

Matless, D. *Landscape and Englishness*. London: Reaktion, 1998.

Mayall, J., and S. O. Vandersluis. In *The State and Identity Construction in International Relations*, ed. S. O. Vandersluis. London: London School of Economics Millennium Series, Macmillan Press, Ltd., 2000.

Mayer, A. J. In *The Responsibility of Power: Historical Essays in Honor of Hajo Hoborn*, ed. L. Krieger and F. Stern. New York: Doubleday, 1967.

Mayne, R., J. Pinder, and J. C. Roberts. *Federal Union: The Pioneers*. Basingstoke: Palgrave Macmillan, 1991.

McAdam, D., J. McCarthy, and M. Zald, eds. *Comparative Perspective on Social Movements: Political Opportunities, Mobilizing Structures, and Cultural Framing*. New York: Cambridge University Press, 1996.

McSweeney, B. *Security, Identity and Interests: A Sociology of International Relations*. Cambridge: Cambridge University Press, 1999.

Mead, G. H. *Mind, Self and Society*. Chicago: University of Chicago Press, 1934.

Meehan, E. *Citizenship and the European Community*. London: Sage, 1993.

Meinecke, F. *Weltbürgertum und Nationalstaat: Studien zur Genesis des Deutschen Nationalstaates*. Munich: R. Oldenbourg [1907] 1919.

Mény, Y. *Government and Politics in Western Europe.* London: Oxford University Press, 1993.

Merton, R. *Social Theory and Social Structure.* New York: Free Press, 1968.

Middlebrook, M. *The Fight for the "Malvinas": The Argentine Forces in the Falklands War.* London: Viking, 1989.

Milne, A. *DG: The Memoirs of a British Broadcaster.* London: Faber, 1988.

Milner, H. In *Neorealism and Neoliberalism: The Contemporary Debate,* ed. D. Baldwin. New York: Columbia University Press, 1993.

———. *Interests, Institutions, and Information,* Princeton, NJ: Princeton University Press, 1997.

Mitrany, D. In *The Functional Theory of Politics,* ed. P. Taylor and A. J. R. Groom. London: Oxford University Press, 1975.

———. *The Progress of International Government.* London: Elliots Books, 1934.

Monaghan, D. *The Falklands War: Myth and Countermyth.* London: Macmillan, 1998.

Monger, G. *The End of Isolation: British Foreign Policy 1900–1907.* London: Macmillan, 1963.

Moravcsik, A. *The Choice for Europe.* London: UCL Press, 1999.

Morgan, K. *The Oxford History of Britain.* Oxford: Oxford University Press, 2001.

Morgenthau, H. J. *Politics among Nations: The Struggle for Power and Peace.* 3rd ed. New York: Alfred A. Knopf, 1961.

———. *Scientific Man vs. Power Politics.* Chicago: University of Chicago Press, 1946.

Morris, A., and C. Mueller, eds. *Frontiers in Social Movement Theory.* New Haven, CT: Yale University Press, 1992.

Müller-Peters, A., R. Pepermans, G. Kiell, and M. Farhangmehr, eds. *The Psychology of European Monetary Union: A Cross-National Study of Public Opinion towards the Euro.* Santiago de Compostela, Spain: Compostela Group of Universities, 2001.

Nairn, T. *The Break-up of Britain: Crisis and Neo-Nationalism.* London: New Left Books, 1977.

Neumann, I., and O. Wæver, eds. *The Future of International Relations.* New York: Routledge, 1997.

Newman, D. In *Identities, Borders, Orders: Rethinking International Relations Theory,* ed. M. Albert, D. Jacobson, and Y. Lapid. Minneapolis: University of Minnesota Press, 2001.

Newsome, D. *The Victorian World Picture.* London: John Murray, 1997.

Nicolson, H. *Diplomacy.* London: Oxford University Press, 1963.

Noakes, L. *War and the British: Gender and National Identity, 1939–1991.* London: Oxford University Press, 1998.

Nye, J. S., Jr. *Bound to Lead: The Changing Nature of American Power.* New York: Basic Books, 1990.

O'Neill, M. *The Politics of European Integration.* London: Routledge, 1996.

Oakes, P. J., S. A. Aslam, and J. C. Turner. *Stereotyping and Social Reality.* Oxford: Oxford University Press, 1994.

Oakshott, M. *On Human Conduct.* Oxford: Oxford University Press, 1975.

Oberweis, T., and M. Musheno. *Knowing Rights, State Actors' Stories of Power, Identity and Morality.* Aldershot: Ashgate, 2001.

Oldman, E., and E. Rhodes, eds. *The Politics of Strategic Adjustment: Ideas, Institutions, and Interests.* New York: Columbia University Press, 1999.

Olson, M. *The Logic of Collective Action*. New York: Schocken, 1969.

——. *The Rise and Decline of Nations, Economic Growth, Stagflation and Social Rigidities*. New Haven, CT: Yale University Press, 1982.

Onuf, N. "A Constructivist Manifesto." In *Constituting International Political Economy*, ed. K. Burch and R. Denemark. Boulder, CO: Lynne Rienner, 1997.

——. "Constructivism: A User's Manual." In *International Relations in a Constructed World*, ed. V. Kubálková, N. Onuf, and P. Kowert. Armonk, NY: M.E. Sharpe, 1998.

——. "Rules, Agents, Institutions: A Constructivist Account." *Working Papers on International Society and Institutions*, 96–92. Irvine: Global Peace and Conflict Studies, University of California, 1996.

——. *World of Our Making: Rules and Rule in Social Theory and International Relations*. Columbia: University of South Carolina Press, 1989.

Orgill, A. *The Falklands War: Background, Conflict, Aftermath: An Annotated Bibliography*. London: Mansell, 1993.

Padfield, P. *Rule Britannia: The Victorian and Edwardian Navy*. London: Pimlico, 2002.

Parkes, O. *British Battleships, 1860–1950: A History of Design, Construction and Armament*. London: Seely Service, 1966.

Parsons, T. *The Social System*, Glencoe, IL: Free Press, 1951.

Pasic, S. C. "Culturing International Relations." In *The Return of Culture and Identity in IR Theory*, ed. Y. Lapid and J. Kratochwil. Boulder, CO: Lynne Rienner Publishers, 1996.

Paterson, T. G. *Meeting the Communist Threat: Truman to Reagan*. New York: Oxford University Press, 1988.

Paul, T. V., and J. A. Hall. *International Order and the Future of World Politics*. Cambridge: Cambridge University Press, 1999.

Paxman, J. *The English: A Portrait of a People*. London: Michael Joseph, 1998.

——. *The English: A Portrait of a People*. London: Penguin Books, 1998.

Pearson, R. *European Nationalism, 1789–1920*. London: Longman, 1994.

Perkin, H. *The Origins of Modern English Society, 1780–1880*. London, 1969.

Pfaff, W. *The Wrath of Nations: Civilization and the Furies of Nationalism*. New York: Simon and Schuster, 1993.

Pinder, J. "Why the Single Market Is a Step towards Federal Union." In *The European Community and the Challenge of the Future*, ed. J. Lodge. London: Palgrave Macmillan, 1993.

Potter, E. B., ed. *Sea Power: A Naval History*, Annapolis: University of Maryland, 1981.

Popper, K. *Conjectures and Refutations: The Growth of Scientific Knowledge*. London: Routledge and Kegan Paul, 1963.

——. *Realism and the Aim of Science: Postscript*. London: Hutchinson, 1983.

——. *The Logic of Scientific Discovery*. London: Hutchinson, 1934.

Porter, B. *The Lion's Share: A Short History of British Imperialism: 1850–1995*. London: Macmillan, 1996.

Postema, G. J. *Bentham and the Common Law Tradition*. Oxford: Oxford University Press, 1986.

Priestley, J. B. "Federalism and Culture." In *Federal Union: The Pioneers*, ed. R. J. Mayne, R. J. Pinder, and J. C. Roberts. Basingstoke: Palgrave Macmillan, 1991.

Prizel, I. *National Identity and Foreign Policy: Nationalism and Leadership in Poland, Russia and Ukraine*. Cambridge: Cambridge University Press, 1998.

Ramm, A., ed. *The Political Correspondence of Mr. Gladstone and Lord Granville, 1868–1876*. London: Camden, 1952.

Rawls, J. *A Theory of Justice*. Oxford: Oxford University Press, 1971.

Renan, E. *"Qu'est qu'une nation?"* Trans. Ida Mae Snyder. Paris, 1882.

Richardson, J., ed. *European Union: Power and Policy-Making*. London: Routledge, 1996.

Ringmar, E. *Identity, Interest and Action*. Cambridge: Cambridge University Press, 1996.

Risse-Kappen, T. "Collective Identity in a Democratic Community: The Case of NATO." In *The Culture of National Security: Norms and Identity in World Politics*, ed. P. Katzenstein. New York: Columbia University Press, 1996.

Ritter, G. *The Sword and the Sceptre: The Problem of Militarism in Germany*. 4 vols. Miami: University of Miami Press, 1970.

Rizopoulos, N., ed. *Sea-Changes: American Foreign Policy in a World Transformed*. New York: Council on Foreign Relations, 1990.

Rock, D. *Argentina: 1516–1987*. New York: I.B. Tauris, 1987.

Röhl, J. C. *Germany without Bismarck*. London: Methuen, 1976.

Roper, M., and J. Tosh, eds. *Manful Assertions: Masculinities in Britain since 1800*. London: Routledge, 1991.

Rosecrance, R., and A. A. Stein. *The Domestic Bases of Grand Strategy*, Ithaca, NY: Cornell University Press, 1993.

Rosenau, J. "Nascent Norms: Legitimacy, Patriotism, and Sovereignty." In *Turbulence in World Politics: A Theory of Change and Continuity*, ed. J. Rosenau. Princeton, NJ: Princeton University Press, 1990.

Rotberg, R. I., and T. K. Rabb, eds. *The Origin and Prevention of Major Wars*. Cambridge: Cambridge University Press, 1989.

Rustow, D. *A World of Nations*, Washington, DC: Brookings Institution, 1967.

Sack, R. *Place, Modernity and the Consumer's World: A Relational Framework of Geographical Analysis*. Baltimore: Johns Hopkins University Press, 1992.

Sampson, A. *The New Europeans: A Guide to the Workings, Institutions and Character of Contemporary Western Europe*. London: Macmillan, 1968.

Samuel, R. *Island Stories, Unravelling Britain*, Vol. 2. London: Verso, 1998.

———. *Theatres of Memory, Past and Present in Contemporary Culture*, Vol. 1. London: Verso, 1994.

Sandel, M. *Liberalism and the Limits of Justice*. Cambridge: Cambridge University Press, 1982.

Schelling, T. C. *Arms and Influence*, New Haven, CT: Yale University Press, 1966.

———. *The Strategy of Conflict*. Oxford: Oxford University Press, 1960.

Schweder, R., and R. LeVine, eds. *Culture Theory*. Cambridge: Cambridge University Press, 1984.

Seton-Watson, H. *Nations and States: An Inquiry into the Origins of Nations and the Politics of Nationalism*. Boulder, CO: Westview Press, 1977.

Schweller, R. L. *Deadly Imbalances: Tripolarity and Hitler's Strategy of World Conquest.* New York: Columbia University Press, 1998.

———. *Unanswered Threats: Political Constraints on the Balance of Power.* Princeton, NJ: Princeton University Press, 2006.

Scott, J. S. "Inculcation of Nationalism in French Schools after 1870." In *The Dynamics of Nationalism,* ed. L. Snyder. Princeton, NJ: Van Nostrand, 1964.

Scruton, R. *England: An Elegy.* London: Pimlico, 2001.

Searle, J. R. *The Construction of Social Reality.* Penguin Books: London, 1995.

Shapiro, M. *Reading the Postmodern Polity: Political Theory as Textual Practice.* Minneapolis: University of Minnesota Press, 1992.

———. *Reading the Postmodern Polity: Political Theory as Textual Practice.* Minneapolis: University of Minnesota Press, 1992.

———. *The Politics of Representation,* Madison: University of Wisconsin Press, 1988.

Shearman, P. "Nationalism, the State, and the Collapse of Communism." In *The State and Identity Construction in International Relations,* ed. S. O. Vandersluis. London: London School of Economics Millennium Series, Macmillan Press, Ltd., 2000.

Shirely, M., and T. Larson, eds. *Splendidly Victorian: Essays in Nineteenth- and Twentieth-Century British History in Honour of Walter L. Arnstein.* Aldershot: Ashgate, 1998.

Shore, Lord. "No to the Euro." In *The Euro Debate: Persuading the People,* ed. R. Beetham. London: The Federal Trust for Education and Research, 2001.

Sibeon, R. *Contemporary Sociology and Policy Analysis: The New Sociology of Public Policy.* Liverpool: University of Liverpool, Tudor Business Publishing Ltd., 1988.

Slater H., and C. Barnett. *The Channel Tunnel.* London: Oxford University Press, 1957.

Smith, A. *National Identity.* London: Penguin Books, 1991.

———. *The Ethnic Revival.* Cambridge: Cambridge University Press, 1981.

———. *Theories of Nationalism,* 1st ed. London: Duckworth, 1971.

———. *The Ethnic Origins of Nations.* Oxford: Basil Blackwell, 1986.

Smith, M. J. *Pressure, Power and Policy: State Autonomy and Policy Networks in Britain and the United States.* London: Harvester Wheatsheaf, 1993.

Smith, M. *Realist Thought from Weber to Kissinger.* Baton Rouge: Louisiana State University Press, 1986.

Smith, S., A. Hadfield, and T. Dunne, eds. *Foreign Policy: Theories, Actors, Cases.* Oxford: Oxford University Press: 2008.

Snyder, J. *The Soviet Strategic Culture: Implications for Nuclear Options,* R–2154-AF. Santa Monica, CA: RAND Corporation, 1977.

Sobhan, S. "National Identity, Fundamentalism and the Women's Movement in Bangladesh." In *Gender and National Identity: Women and Politics in Muslim Societies,* ed. V. Moghadam. London: Zed Books, 1994.

Stapleton, J. *Political Intellectuals and Public Identities in Britain since 1850.* Manchester: Manchester University Press, 2001.

Stavridis, S., and C. Hill, eds. *Domestic Sources of Foreign Policy: Western European Reactions to the Falklands Conflict.* Oxford: Berg, 1996.

Stein, A. "Coordination and Collaboration: Regimes in an Anarchic World." In *Neorealism and Neoliberalism: The Contemporary Debate,* ed. D. Baldwin. New York: Columbia University Press, 1993.

Steinberg, J. *Yesterday's Deterrent: Tirpitz and the Birth of the German Battle Fleet.* New York: Macmillan, 1965.

Steiner, H. *Essay on Rights.* Oxford: Blackwell, 1994.

Steiner, Z. *The Foreign Office and Foreign Policy: 1898–1914.* Cambridge: Cambridge University Press, 1969.

Stirk, P. M. R., and D. Willis, eds. *Shaping Post-War Europe: European Unity and Disunity, 1945–1957.* New York: St. Martin's Press, 1991.

Stephanson, A. *Kennan and the Art of Foreign Policy.* Cambridge MA: Harvard University Press, 1989.

Strange, S. *States and Markets: An Introduction to International Political Economy.* London: Pinter, 1988.

Suganami, H. *The Domestic Analogy and World Order Proposals.* Cambridge: Cambridge University Press, 1986.

Taylor, A. J. P. *The Struggle for Mastery in Europe, 1848–1918.* Oxford: Oxford University Press, 1954.

Thane, P., ed. *Origins of British Social Policy.* London: Routledge, 1978.

Thatcher, M. *The Downing Street Years, 1979–1990.* New York: HarperCollins, 1993.

Thompson, J. *No Picnic: The Story of 3 Commando Brigade in the Falklands War.* London: Leo Cooper for Secker & Warburg, 1985.

Trevelyan, G. M. *English Social History: A Survey of Six Centuries, Chaucer to Queen Victoria.* London: Longmans, 1944.

Twining, W. *Globalisation and Legal Theory.* London: Butterworths, 2000.

Van Evera, S. *Guide to Methods for Students of Political Science.* Ithaca, NY: Cornell University Press, 1999.

Vandersluis, S. O., ed. *The State and Identity Construction in International Relations.* London: London School of Economics Millennium Series, Macmillan Press, Ltd., 2000.

Vasquez, J. *The Power of Power Politics: From Classical Realism to Neotraditionalism.* Cambridge: Cambridge University Press, 1998.

———. *The War Puzzle.* Cambridge: Cambridge, University Press, 1993.

Vasquez, J. A., and C. Elman, eds. *Realism and the Balancing of Power: A New Debate.* Englewood Cliffs, NJ: Prentice Hall, 2003.

Waissman, C. *Reversal of Development in Argentina: Postwar Counterrevolutionary Policies and Their Structural Consequences.* Princeton, NJ: Princeton University Press, 1987.

Walker, R. B. J. "History and Structure in the Theory of International Relations." In *International Theory: Critical Investigations,* ed. J. Der Derian. New York: New York University Press, 1995.

Waller, B. *Bismarck at the Crossroads: The Reorientation of German Foreign Policy after the Congress of Berlin, 1878–1880.* London: Methuen, 1974.

Walt, S. *Revolution and War.* Ithaca, NY: Cornell University Press, 1996.

———. *The Origins of Alliances.* Ithaca, NY: Cornell University Press, 1987.

Waltz, K. "The Origins of War in Neorealist Theory." In *The Origins and Prevention of Major Wars,* ed. R. Rotberg and T. Rabb. Cambridge. Cambridge University Press, 1989

———. *Man, the State and War.* New York: Columbia University Press, 1959.

——. *Theory of International Politics*, Reading, MA: Addison-Wesley, 1979.

Walzer, M. *Spheres of Justice*. New York: Basic Books, 1983.

Weber, M., and T. Parsons, eds. *The Theory of Social and Economic Organization*. New York: Free Press, 1945.

——. *Economy and Society*, ed. Roth and Wittich. Berkeley: University of California Press, 1978.

——. *From Max Weber: Essays in Sociology*. New York: Oxford University Press, 1956.

Weight, R. *Patriots: National Identity in Britain, 1940–2000*. London: Macmillan, 2002.

Weiler, J. H. "After Maastricht: Community Legitimacy in Post-1992 Europe." In *Singular Europe: Economy and Polity of the European Community after 1992*, ed. W. Adams. Ann Arbor: University of Michigan Press, 1992.

Weiler, J. *The Constitution of Europe*. Cambridge: Cambridge University Press, 1999.

Weinroth, M. *Reclaiming William Morris: Englishness, Sublimity, and the Rhetoric of Dissent*. Montreal: McGill-Queen's University Press, 1996.

Wendt, A. "Identity and Structural Change in International Politics." In *The Return of Culture and Identity in IR Theory*, ed. Y. Lapid and J. Kratochwil. Boulder, CO: Lynne Rienner Publishers, 1996.

——. *Social Theory of International Politics*. Cambridge: Cambridge University Press, 1999.

Wheeler, N. J. *Saving Strangers: Humanitarian Intervention in International Society*. Oxford: Oxford University Press, 2000.

Whiteside, T. *The Tunnel under the Channel*. London: Macmillan, 1962.

Wiebe, R. *Who We Are: A History of Popular Nationalism*, Princeton, NJ: Princeton University Press, 2002.

Wiener, M. *English Culture and the Decline of the Industrial Spirit, 1850–1980*. Cambridge: Cambridge University Press, 1981.

Williams, L. "National Identity and the Nation State: Construction, Reconstruction and Contradiction." In *National Identity*, ed. K. Cameron. European Studies Series. Exeter: Intellect, 1999.

Williamson, S., Jr. *The Politics of Grand Strategy: Britain and France Prepare for War, 1900–1914*. Cambridge MA: Harvard University Press, 1969.

Williamson, S. *The Politics of Grand Strategy*. Cambridge MA: Harvard University Press, 1969.

Wilson, K. *Channel Tunnel Visions, 1850–1945: Dreams and Nightmares*. London: The Hambledon Press, 1994.

Wilson, T., and H. Donnan. "Nation, State and Identity at International Borders." In *Border Identities: Nation and State at International Frontiers*, ed. T. Wilson and H. Donnan. Cambridge: Cambridge University Press, 1998.

Wohlforth, W. C. *The Elusive Balance: Power and Perceptions During the Cold War*. Ithaca, NY: Cornell University Press, 1993.

Wolfers, A. *Discord and Collaboration*. Baltimore: Johns Hopkins University Press, 1962.

Woolf, C., and J. Moorcroft Wilson, eds. *Authors Take Sides on the Falklands*. London: Cecil Woolf, 1982.

Young, H. *One of Us: A Biography of Margaret Thatcher*. London: Pan Macmillan, 1991.

Zakaria, F. "Realism and Domestic Politics: A Review Essay." In *The Perils of Anarchy: Contemporary Realism and International Security*, ed. Michael E. Brown, Sean M. Lynn-Jones, and Steven E. Miller. Cambridge, MA: MIT Press, 1995.

Zangwill, I. "The Principle of Nationalities." In H. Kohn, *The Idea of Nationalism: A Study in Its Origins and Background*. New York: Macmillan, 1944.

Žižek, S. *For They Know Not What They Do: Enjoyment as a Political Factor*. London: Verso, 1991.

Zakaria, F. *From Wealth to Power: The Unusual Origins of America's World Role*. Princeton, NJ: Princeton University Press, 1998.

## WEBSITES

British Broadcasting Corporation News Website. Subsection: UK Politics: http://news.bbc.co.uk (accessed 30 November 2002).

"Channel Tunnel Facts." Geology Shop: http://www.geologyshop.co.uk/chtunfacts.htm (accessed 11 February 2003).

Falklands-Malvinas Discussion Forum: http://www.falklands-malvinas.com/engboard.mv (accessed 3 January 2003).

Herbert Blumer's Symbolic Interactionism. University of Colorado at Boulder, Spring 1998: http://www.colorado.edu/communication/meta-discourses/Papers/App_Papers/Nelson.htm (accessed 1 February 2003).

Jackson, P., and D. Nexon. "Whence Causal Mechanisms? A Response to Jeffrey W. Legro, 'Whence American Internationalism'": *International Organization—Dialogue*, 2000, available at http://www.Mitpress.mit.edu/io (accessed June 2002).

Single European Act (1987): http://europa.eu.int/abc/obj/treaties/en/htm (accessed March 2002).

Symbolic Interactionism as Defined by Herbert Blumer. The Society for More Creative Speech, 1996: http://www.thepoint.net/-usul/text/blumer.html (accessed 1 February 2003).

Symbolic Interactionism Website. Hosted by Grinnell College, Department of Sociology: http://www.grinnell.edu/courses/soc/s00/soc111-01/IntroTheories/Symbolic.html (accessed 30 December 2002).

Treaty of Rome (1957): http://europa.eu.int/abc/obj/treaties/en/htm (accessed 25 July 2002).

Treaty Establishing the European Coal and Steel Community (1951): http://europa.eu.int/abc/obj/treaties/en/entoc29.htm (accessed 30 August 2002).

UK Conservative Party Website: http://www.conservative-party.org.uk/manifesto/defe3.html (accessed 1 February 2001).

UK Labour Party Website: http://www.labourwin97.org.uk/ manifesto/index/html (accessed 1 February 2001).

U.S. State Department, National Archive: http://www.firstgov.gov/fgsearch/index.html (accessed 5 April 2003).

# Index

*Note:* Page numbers in *italics* designate tables.